Graves:

A. E. Housman

Alfred Housman *c.* 1910

# A. E. Housman

## The Scholar-Poet

## Richard Perceval Graves

Routledge & Kegan Paul

LONDON AND HENLEY

First published in 1979
by Routledge & Kegan Paul Ltd
39 Store Street, London WC1E 7DD and
Broadway House, Newtown Road,
Henley-on-Thames, Oxon RG9 1EN

Photoset in Linoterm Palatino by
Oxprint Ltd Oxford, and printed
in Great Britain by
Lowe & Brydone Ltd

British Library Cataloguing in Publication Data
Graves, Richard Perceval
A. E. Housman.
1. Housman, Alfred Edward – Biography
2. Poets, English – 19th century – Biography
3. Poets, English – 20th century – Biography
821'.9'12    PR4809.H15

ISBN 0 7100 0340 4

To my dear parents
John Tiarks Ranke Graves and Mary Graves
and to all members of the Society
of St John's College, Oxford
this book is affectionately and respectfully dedicated

Possess, as I possessed a season,
The countries I resign,
Where over elmy plains the highway
Would mount the hills and shine,
And full of shade the pillared forest
Would murmur and be mine.

A. E. Housman, *Last Poems*, 40

I do not mind how many biographies of him are brought out,
so that they are accurate and kindly.

*Katharine E. Symons, sister to A. E. Housman from a letter
to Cyril Clemens, 29 October 1936, now among the Housman collection
in the Library of Columbia University, New York*

# Contents

# Plates

# Acknowledgments

The author and publishers would like to thank the following for permission to reproduce copyright material: a letter by A. V. B. Stamfordham is reproduced by gracious permission of Her Majesty the Queen; Mrs Ernestine Carter for extracts from a letter by the late Mr John Carter; Oxford University Press for an extract from an unpublished letter by Robert Bridges and for extracts from Grant Richards, *Housman 1897–1936*; the Estate of A. E. Housman for extracts © 1979 from his unpublished and published writings including those in The Letters of A. F Housman, The Manuscript Poems of A. E. Housman, Percy Withers, *A. E. Housman: A Divided Life*; The Society of Authors as the Literary Representative of the Estate of A. E. Housman, and Jonathan Cape Ltd, London, and Holt Rinehart, New York, as publishers for extracts from A. E. Housman, *Collected Poems*; Paul Roche for an extract from an unpublished translation of Sappho; Contemporary Books Inc., Chicago, for extracts from Maude Hawkins, *A. E. Housman: Man behind a Mask* (1958); Jonathan Cape Ltd for extracts from Percy Withers, *A Buried Life*; Jonathan Cape Ltd and The Seven Pillars Trust for an extract from T. E. Lawrence, *The Seven Pillars of Wisdom*; Jonathan Cape Ltd and the executors of the R. W. Chambers Estate for extracts from R. W. Chambers *Man's Unconquerable Mind*; Jonathan Cape Ltd and the executors of the Laurence Housman Estate for extracts from unpublished letters by Laurence Housman, a quote from the preface by Laurence Housman to A. E. Housman, *A Shropshire Lad*, quoted from an article in *Encounter*, extracts from letters from Laurence Housman to Katharine Symons and short quotes from *A Modern Antaeus* (all the unpublished material listed is © 1979 Jonathan Cape Ltd); Jonathan Cape Ltd and the executors of the Laurence Housman Estate for extracts from Laurence Housman, *The Unexpected Years*, and from his *My Brother A. E. Housman*; Doubleday & Co., New York, for an extract from T. E. Lawrence, *The Seven Pillars of Wisdom*; The Bromsgrove Library and Jonathan Cape Ltd for extracts from the Laurence Housman Letters given by Gilbert Turner; Charles Scribners & Sons, New York, for extracts from Laurence Housman, *My Brother A. E. Housman*; Robert E. Symons and Granada Publishing Ltd for extracts from Henry Maas (ed.), *The Letters of A. E. Housman*; Cambridge University Press for extracts from: A. S. F. Gow, *A. E. Housman: A Sketch*, G. H. Hardy, *Bertrand Russell and Trinity*, Sir Sydney Roberts, *Adventures with Authors*, A. E. Housman, *The Confines of Criticism*, J. Diggle and S. D. R. Goodyear (eds), *The Classical Papers of A. E. Housman*, A. E. Housman *Selected Prose*, ed. John Carter (including extracts for the introductory Lecture (1892) and 'The Name and Nature of Poetry' (1933)); Professor Otto Skutsch for passages from his lecture on A. E. Housman (1959); A. P. Watt Ltd for lines from two poems by Rudyard Kipling and six lines from two poems by W. B. Yeats; Bell & Hyman Ltd for extracts from J. J. Thomson, *Recollections and Reflections* (1936); Turner & Devereux of London for extracts from the *Housman Society Journal*, vols 1 and 2; Robert E. Symons and The Tregara Press for extracts from Alan Bell (ed.), *Fifteen Letters to Walter Ashburner*; J. D. S. Hedley and The Committee of the Society of Bromsgrove School for extracts from H. E. M. Icely, *Bromsgrove School through Four Centuries* and from the *Bromsgrovian*; Kathleen Tillotson for extracts from an article by Geoffrey Tillotson; Joseph W. Scott for extracts from the Catalogue of the Housman Centenary Exhibition, 1959; Saundra Taylor and The Lilly Library, Indiana University, for material from their Housman Collection; Mrs J. Percival and The Library, University College London, for extracts from a number of unpublished documents; A. Tattersall and University College London for a quotation from the Council Minutes, and for extracts from writings by Professor R. W. Chambers; Kenneth A. Lohf and Colombia University, New York, for extracts from unpublished letters by, and relating to, A. E. Housman in their possession; the President and Fellows of St John's College, Oxford, for extracts from papers, books and records in their possession; the Master and Fellows of Trinity College, Cambridge, for unpublished documents in their possession (and Dr P. Gaskell for his friendly co-operation); the Trustees of Street Library, Somerset, for quotations from unpublished documents in their possession; Lloyds Bank Ltd for extracts from unpublished letters of Hugh Last; N. V. H. Symons for extracts from unpublished letters and other writings of Mrs Katharine Symons and for Plates 2, 3, 7, 8, 10, 13, 17, 30; The Board of the British Library for extracts from the Diaries of A. E. Housman; C. A. Brodie for an unpublished extract from papers of T. H. Warren; M. Higham Esq. for unpublished extracts from documents and books in his possession; the Executors of A. S. F. Gow for extracts from his unpublished letters; Ethel Manin for extracts from published and unpublished writings by Clemence Housman; Mrs C. Gleadowe for an extract from an unpublished letter written by her late husband, R. M. Y. Gleadowe; Col. M. C. P. Stevenson, OBE, MC, for an extract from an unpublished letter by R. Laffan; Major-General T. A. Richardson and Rooks, Ryder & Co. (Sols) for the beneficiaries of Professor A. W. Pollard dec'd and Mrs J. K. Roberts dec'd for extracts from unpublished material by Professor A. W. Pollard.

The author and publishers would also like to acknowledge the use of material from *The Cleveland Street Scandal* by H. Montgomery Hyde (W. H. Allen, 1976); *Oscar Wilde* by H. Montgomery Hyde (Eyre Methuen, 1976); 'A. E. Housman at Oxford', an article by A. S. F. Gow in the *Oxford Magazine*, 11 November 1937; an article by John Quinlan in the *Musical Times* (March 1959); *A History of Woodchester* by Rev. W. N. R. Black (Spring, 1972); *A Traveller at Forty* by Theodore Dreiser (Grant Richards, 1914); *Max* by David Cecil (Constable, 1964); *E. M. Forster: The Personal Voice* by John Colmer (Routledge & Kegan Paul); *A Room with a View* by E. M. Forster (Penguin, 1961); *A. E. Housman: Scholar and Poet* by Norman Marlow (Routledge & Kegan Paul, 1958); *Romanticism and Revolt* by J. L. Talmon (Thames & Hudson, 1957); *Cambridge Doctor* by Rex Salisbury Woods (Robert Hale Ltd., 1962); *A Number of People* by Edward Marsh; *E. M. Forster: A Life*, vol, 1: *The Growth of a Novelist 1879–1914* by P. N. Furbank (Secker & Warburg, 1977); *Swinburne Letters*, ed. Cecil Y. Lang, vol. 6 (Yale University Press, 1962); *Caviare* by Grant Richards (London, 1912); *Stories and Episodes* by Thomas Mann (Dent, 1940); *Treatise on the Steppenwolf* by Herman Hesse (Penguin); *The Once and Future King* by T. H. White (Fontana Books); *Oxford* by James Morris (Faber & Faber, 1965); Petronius, *Tremalchio's Banquet* with an Introduction by M. J. Ryan (The Walter Scott Publishing Co.); a letter to *The Times* by A. E. Housman (23 September 1924); an extract from the memorial number of the *Mark Twain Quarterly* (Winter, 1936); articles on A. E. Housman by Edmund Wilson, John Wain and J. P. Sullivan, as reproduced in Christopher Ricks (ed.), *A. E. Housman; A Collection of Critical Essays* (Spectrum Book (1968)); an article by E. M. Forster in the *Listener* (11 November 1936); extracts from the A. E. Housman Memorial Number of the *Mark Twain Quarterly* (Winter, 1936); *A. E. Housman: A Divided Life* by George L. Watson (Rupert Hart Davis, 1957); extracts from copies of documents held by John Pugh; an extract from 'An evening with A. E. Housman', by Cyril Clemens.

The author and publishers would also like to acknowledge the use of the following material for which, despite strenuous efforts, the copyright holders could not be traced: extracts from unpublished letters of Ellinor M. Allen, L. P. Brown, M. H. Eyre, Ralph Griffin, F. W. Hodges, Canon Nance, Arthur Platt, Sir Arthur Quiller-Couch, Grant Richards, E. L. Robins, W. Fothergill Robinson, W. Snow, George Addison Turner, E. W. Watson, Oscar Wilde.

# Introduction

'But when the hundred-and-thirty-eighth night had come
SHE SAID
Time reaps all and does not remember; therefore let him
who would know the fate which will befall his name in time to
come, guard the fame of those who have passed before him
into the room of death.'
*The Thousand Nights and One Night, Mardrus and Mathers*

My chief aim has been to write a balanced and sympathetic account of a
remarkable but troubled life. A secondary aim has been to introduce a
new generation to the neglected beauties of A. E. Housman's poetry.

A. E. Housman was a great classical scholar, a distinguished poet and a
vintage academic character. There has so far been no general biography.
A. S. F. Gow's *Sketch* (1936) was only intended as an outline of
Housman's life, for the benefit of those who were primarily concerned
with Housman as a classical scholar. Other volumes of recollections by
Laurence Housman, Percy Withers, Grant Richards and others illu-
minated different aspects of A. E. Housman's life, without attempting
a general view. George L. Watson in *A. E. Housman: A Divided Life* (1957)
did not have access to a great number of important letters and papers; and
so, there were many gaps which he could only fill with speculation.
Maude M. Hawkins's *A. E. Housman: Man Behind a Mask* (1958), the most
recent biography, is not thought to be dependable.

The publication in *Encounter* (October 1967) of an article by Laurence
Housman gave an important insight into his brother Alfred's personal
life; and then in 1971 the appearance of *The Letters of A. E. Housman*
provided – as their editor, Henry Maas, had hoped – some solid material
for the study of Housman's life and character. By the mid-1970s, in
addition to these and other printed sources, a great number of
unpublished papers had also become accessible to any would-be
biographer. These included documents in public institutions, such as the
Housman collection in the Lilly Library, Indiana; and documents in

private hands, such as those generously shown to the present author by M. Higham. It was now possible, for the first time, to try to see the full pattern of Housman's life.

Any account of Housman's life must of course describe Housman's achievements as a classical scholar. Here I thank two of Housman's successors to the Latin Chair at University College London: O. Skutsch; and also – and in particular – Professor G. P. Goold, the modern translator of Manilius.

Others who have given me the benefit of their expert knowledge, or who have contributed to the readability of my book, include H. M. Colvin of St John's College, Oxford; Dr R. Robson of Trinity College, Cambridge; Mrs J. Percival, Archivist of University College London; N. V. H. Symons; John Pugh; H. E. M. Icely; J. T. R. Graves; Timothy O'Sullivan; Frank Sutterby; Alan Harding; and my wife Anne Graves.

I also thank the following for supplying me with original material or for corresponding with me on some aspect of my book: the Hon. Sir Steven Runciman, Dr R. Salisbury Woods, H. Montgomery Hyde, the Rev. Geoffrey T. Carlisle, R. M. Simkins, G. Robertson, A. G. McL. Pearce Higgins, E. G. Bothroyd, J. Hunt, and E. Dalby. I have also had useful conversations with, among others, the late A. S. F. Gow, the late Professor A. V. Hill, Mrs Phyllis Symons, Professor Sandbach, A. Prior, Dr E. P. Cadbury, Mrs David Ollier, and the Rev. A. Butler.

I owe a considerable debt of gratitude to librarians and other owners or custodians of manuscript documents who have allowed me to study material from their collections; to the owners of copyright, and the rights and permissions managers of publishers who have given me the permissions which I asked for; and to others who have smoothed my path. In particular I thank Miss Anne Munro-Ker and Miss Doris Beer of the Society of Authors for their help. Finally, I should make it clear how much I owe to the cooperation of the Housman Society, and of Housman's literary executor Robert E. Symons.

# CHAPTER 1

# Background and Early Years

'In this world of contention and hostility, what inspires the humble Christian, in his journey through it, with more confidence, tranquillity and joy, than the consoling thought, that the Lord God omnipotent reigneth?'

Rev. John Williams DD of Stroud,
Grandfather to A. E. Housman[1]

'She that hath borne seven languisheth: she hath given up the ghost; her sun has gone down while it was yet day:'

Jer. 15:9

When Alfred Housman was an old man in his seventies, he lived for much of the time in the seclusion of a neo-Gothic tower in a remote corner of Trinity College, Cambridge. For many years he had been a famous and popular poet, and recognised as one of the great classical scholars of his day. But he was a shy man, who relished his privacy. His more perceptive friends guessed at mysteries in his personal life which he would not reveal; and beyond their circle and that of his acquaintances, men found it hard to understand how the austere classical scholar could have written the beautiful, romantic lyrics of *A Shropshire Lad* or *Last Poems*.

Much of his poetry is nostalgic; and as Professor Housman sat after lunch in his rooms, surrounded by books, a pair of boots warming beside the fire in preparation for his afternoon walk, his emotions stirred, perhaps, by a glass or two of his Burgundy, he had only to look around him, or to pull open a drawer or two, to be reminded vividly of the past. There was the silver loving-cup presented by his students at University College, London; on his desk, a Wedgwood medallion presented when he left the Patent Office; on the wall above the fireplace, a picture of Moses Jackson, his friend from Oxford days;[2] in a drawer, a photograph of the church in Woodchester where his parents were married, and other documents, including a family tree which traced his ancestry back to his great-grandfather, Robert Housman, 'the Evangelist of Lancaster'.

1

Robert, with his great and enduring reputation as a preacher, was the most famous of Alfred's ancestors. By nature he was a reserved and formal man, so shy that, like his great-grandson, Alfred, he hated being in the company of strangers, and was usually incapable of making first advances. But when he felt that duty demanded it, or that he was in the right, 'nothing could daunt him'.[3] Like Alfred, he also set himself high standards, and was proud of them. His wife inherited a considerable fortune from a distant relative, and in time much of this was passed on to their sons, William, and Thomas, who was to be Alfred's grandfather. William became a solicitor at Bromsgrove in Worcestershire, but his wealth robbed him of the motivation to work and eventually he ran away to America with an actress, abandoning his wife and seven children. Thomas, a more stable character, followed his father into the church, and chose for his wife Anne Brettell, a woman whose private fortune compensated for her lack of intellect.

Fourteen years after his marriage, Alfred's grandfather left his vicarage in Kinver, Staffordshire, and moved to Bromsgrove, to be near his elderly parents-in-law. A new church was specially built for him in the neighbouring village of Catshill; and when his mother-in-law died, he and his family moved into nearby Fockbury House, to join Joseph and his unmarried daughter, Mary. When Joseph himself died in 1847, at the age of eighty-eight, half his fortune went to Mary, and the other to Thomas Housman's wife Anne. Joseph had also left a sum of £1,000 to be divided among Thomas and Anne's seven surviving children, the eldest of whom, Thomas, was the black sheep of the family having been caught in his youth leaving the nanny's bedroom; later he became the focus for romantic stories about 'Uncle Tom'.

Edward, the second son – but effectively the eldest after his brother's disgrace – spent much of his childhood at Fockbury House, which he came to regard as the family seat. He and his younger brothers became good shots and good anglers, and 'lived an active county life', behaving more like young squires than parson's sons. Edward himself was not a man of great intellect or strong character – though he had enough intelligence to recognise others' strength – but he enjoyed the life in which he had been brought up, and was a determined Tory, later delighting in telling his children that he had been born in the year of England's greatest disaster: the First Reform Bill of 1832. His great-uncle, John Adams of Perry Hall, was glad to assist Edward, later Alfred's father, to become a solicitor. On Adams's death arrangements were made whereby Edward acquired Perry Hall as a life tenant.

It was under the friendly auspices of his cousin Lucy that Edward was introduced to her best friend, the daughter of the Rector of Woodchester. Sarah Jane Williams had no money to speak of, and, at twenty-nine, she was nearly three years older than Edward, but she was witty and attractive, with the intellectual strength of Edward's father, and the physical warmth of his mother. Edward found this combination irresistible; and Sarah in her turn was won over by his easy charm and polished manners, finding him more sympathetic and accomplished than the young men who had previously taken an interest in her. They were soon engaged to be married; and, after the postponement of the ceremony for some months in order to mourn her father's death, the wedding took place in the lovely old church of Woodchester on 17 June 1858, with Lucy Housman acting as Sarah Jane's bridesmaid.[4]

Apart from being a classical scholar, her father was something of a poet and Sarah Jane had inherited her father's talent for composing verses, writing 'skits in verse on the people she wanted to ridicule',[5] a harmless practice which sometimes had amusing consequences. Once she composed a mild verse lampoon on village doings which was circulated anonymously among her friends, and created quite a stir in the little village. Eventually, news of it reached the ears of a young curate, who, hoping to impress her, whispered to Sarah Jane at supper one day that he was the author, and that he trusted her to tell no-one![6]

If Sarah Jane's sense of humour was sometimes rather sharp, the tragedies of her family life may have had something to do with it. She was one of twelve children, but few of her brothers and sisters lived into their twenties. Yet she was not the sort of woman to let her mind dwell in an unhealthy way on her family misfortunes, and she had found some consolation in the ceremonies and prayers of the Church of England. However, among its nine hundred inhabitants, Woodchester contained a sizeable and influential Roman Catholic enclave;[7] and in moments of real unhappiness Sarah Jane had sometimes cast a longing eye at the comforting rituals of the Roman Catholic Church. Certainly, she did not at all incline towards anything that was low-church; and she was far from puritanical, or even prim.

When Edward and Sarah Jane Housman returned from their honeymoon – with Sarah Jane already pregnant – they moved into the Valley House, in the hamlet of Fockbury, owned by the Rev. Thomas Housman, and only a few hundred yards away from the Clock House where Edward's parents lived. The Valley House was a picturesque red-brick Georgian farm-house, faced from across the small country road by a fine cedar tree, whose branches almost touched its windows.

Towards the end of March 1859, as the time for their first child to be born drew near, there were some complications which the local doctor did not feel able to deal with, and at Sarah Jane's request, Edward summoned her old family doctor all the way from Woodchester. The doctor duly arrived; and, twenty-four hours later, on 26 March 1859,

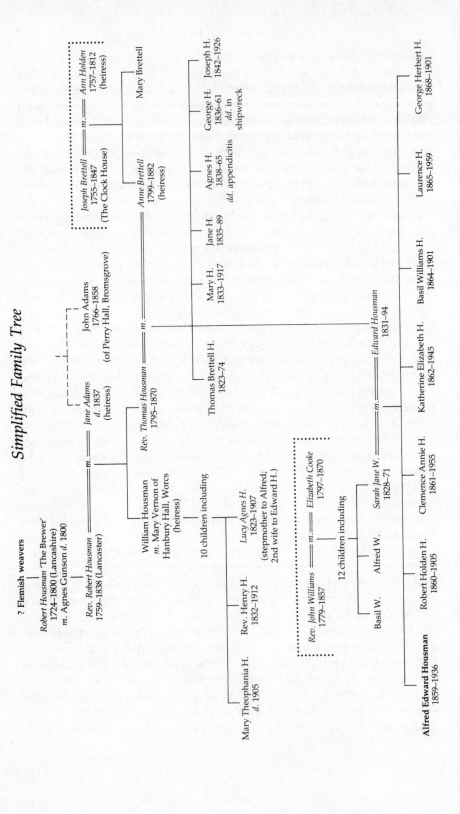

*Simplified Family Tree*

? Flemish weavers

Robert Housman 'The Brewer'
1724–1800 (Lancashire)
*m.* Agnes Gunson *d.* 1800

Rev. Robert Housman
1759–1838 (Lancaster)

Joseph Brettell ════ *m.:* ════ Ann Holden
1755–1847                         1757–1812
(The Clock House)                 (heiress)

Mary Brettell

Jane Adams ════ *m.* ════ John Adams
*d.* 1837                        1766–1858
(heiress)                        (of Perry Hall, Bromsgrove)

William Housman                 Rev. Thomas Housman ════ *m.* ════ Anne Brettell
*m.* Mary Vernon of              1795–1870                        1799–1882
Hanbury Hall, Worcs                                               (heiress)
(heiress)

10 children including

Thomas Brettell H.    Mary H.    Jane H.    Agnes H.    George H.    Joseph H.
1823–74               1833–1917  1835–89    1838–65     1836–61      1842–1926
                                            *dd.* appendicitis  *dd.* in shipwreck

Mary Theophania H.
*d.* 1905

Rev. Henry H.
1832–1912

Lucy Agnes H.
1823–1907
(stepmother to Alfred;
2nd wife to Edward H.)

Rev. John Williams ════ *m.:* ════ Elizabeth Cooke
1779–1857                          1797–1870

12 children including

Basil W.    Alfred W.    Sarah Jane W. ════ *m.* ════ Edward Housman
                         1828–71                      1831–94

Robert Holden H.    Clemence Annie H.    Katherine Elizabeth H.    Basil Williams H.    Laurence H.    George Herbert H.
1860–1905           1861–1955            1862–1945                 1864–1901            1865–1959      1868–1901

**Alfred Edward Housman**
1859–1936

Sarah Jane gave birth to a healthy boy. On Easter Sunday, the baby was christened Alfred Edward by his grandfather, the Rev. Thomas Housman, in the red-stone church at Catshill. Sarah Jane's mother and brother may have been present; certainly many of her Woodchester friends were there, including John Woolwright, who became one of Alfred's godfathers; and Mrs Wise, the wife of a Woodchester mill-owner, and a special friend of Sarah Jane's, who became Alfred's godmother.[8] On the Housman side, quite apart from more distant relations, at least five of Alfred's uncles and aunts attended the ceremony.

When the christening celebrations were over, and the various guests had departed, Edward and Sarah Jane settled down with their baby son into the peace and seclusion of the Valley House. But Edward had become life tenant of Perry Hall in the year of his wedding, and when Alfred was only a few months old the family moved there.

The fine house had been built by John Adams in about 1821 in the grounds of a much earlier building, on the western outskirts of Bromsgrove; but, with its neo-Gothic windows, and a thick coat of ivy over its walls, it looked older than it really was. Inside the front door, on the east side of the house, there was a stone-flagged hall, from which opened a number of large rooms, pleasantly furnished with some of the imposing Tudor and Queen Anne furniture which had come from Dr Williams's Rectory at Woodchester. There was a huge double kitchen, with two cellars, two coppers, a bread-oven, two or three grinding mills, and a closed-up plate-warmer of vast dimensions; and out in the yard, a beer-cooler left over from the days of home brewing. Edward's small range of offices ran out from the north side of the house towards the Kidderminster Road, where the entrance to the property lay, and beyond which climbed the way to the church: a sloping path, with wide flights of steps, which has been built by John Adams and was therefore known as Adams' Hill.[9]

The next few years were happy, contented ones for the Housmans of Perry Hall. As a baby and a small child, Alfred lived at the heart of a well-organised community of family and servants, with a devoted and stimulating mother, and an amiable, kindly, easy-going father. Before he was one-and-a-half years old, Alfred had a baby brother, Robert, so close to him in age that it was not long before they were good company for each other. Alfred later claimed to remember Robert's christening, and through that experience to have an indirect memory of his own baptism, because during the ceremony the thought struck him: 'But this is something I've seen before; only then they were doing it to me!' Alfred's father planted two chestnut trees in the gardens at Perry Hall, one for each of his sons; and by the end of 1862, when Alfred was still only three-and-a-half years old, there were two more chestnut trees: one for Clemence, the other for Katherine.

While Sarah Jane was busily occupied with her young and rapidly expanding family, Edward, often at his father's side, was making a name for himself in Bromsgrove public life, and both were active in local government.

Sarah Jane's mother visited the Housmans at Perry Hall from time to time; but in 1862, Sarah Jane's brother Basil died. She visited him on his deathbed, and knowing how grief had previously made her think of leaving the Church of England, Basil made Sarah Jane promise him never to become a Roman Catholic.

Edward and Sarah Jane still visited Woodchester from time to time. Mrs Williams no longer lived there, and Edward's Housman cousins had left the village – but their place in Woodchester House had been taken by the Wises, a family with whom they were equally friendly. Edward Wise, now in his fifties, had been running a local cloth mill for the last ten years, and his wife was Alfred's godmother. Wise had been a churchwarden in Dr Williams's old church; when this was pulled down and part of the material incorporated in a new church a quarter of a mile away, Sarah Jane took great interest in the work. Her involvement in the new church was not always to the satisfaction of other parishioners. Her memorial window to Dr Williams and his children caused mounting irritation among those who considered that its theme, 'The Communion of Saints', had been depicted in an overtly Roman Catholic manner. In October 1863, Edward Wise wrote to Sarah Jane asking for some explanation which he could pass on to the objectors; and Sarah Jane replied in a letter which gives us a very rare glimpse of the mind and personality which were so important to her son Alfred, still at this time a small boy not four years old.

Sarah Jane began very bitingly that she and her mother regretted having to give explanations, but that:

> silence might seem to imply that the late Dr. Williams was as deficient in common sense and common honesty as those who raise the objections which you have mentioned appear to be. For instance, concerning the inscription, in which we describe him as 'Sometime Priest of this Parish'. . . . A perusal of the Office for the ordering of Priests, in the Book of Common Prayer, will show what is the 'high dignity' of a 'Priest in the Church of God'. . . . 'Priest' *ought not* to be a Popish term.

Her letter ended by stating that she and her mother could not afford to be judged unjustly in Woodchester; for, although it was no longer their home, 'the place and the people will be ever remembered by us with the greatest interest and affection'; and, to ensure that her message did not go unheeded, she had Edward Wise's letter and her own reply printed and bound together into a small pamphlet for general distribution to the people of the village.

Sarah Jane did not visit Woodchester herself at this time, as she was already six months pregnant with her fifth child, who was born in January 1864 and named Basil in memory of her dead brother. Her sixth child, Laurence, was born in July of the following year; and it was probably in the summer of 1866, when Alfred was seven years old, that Sarah Jane took him with her on a visit to her old home.

Woodchester is a charming village of grey stone houses set along the side of Selsley Hill, just at the edge of the Cotswolds, in beautiful unspoilt countryside; and this happy visit first imprinted on Alfred's mind the close association between Woodchester, his mother, and the Wise family, which was always to be such an important part of his mental landscape, and which was later to draw him back to Woodchester year after year. This visit was a happy one – but there was an alarming moment for Sarah Jane when Alfred, unknown to her, decided to invent a sort of parachute. She discovered him just in time at the top of a steep ladder, with an umbrella in his hand which he had planned to use to float down to the ground fifteen or twenty feet below![10]

Most of Alfred's childhood games and adventures took place in the large gardens of Perry Hall. It was a delightful place for children, made more interesting because it contained parts of the old house which John Adams, Alfred's great-great-uncle, had knocked down when he built Perry Hall. Near the house, there was an ornamental garden, with lawn and flower-beds and a flowering cherry tree; beyond that, a well-screened fruit and vegetable garden; and, to one side, and most important of all to the children, was the 'rubbish garden', with its apples and damsons, and its seclusion from the world of the grown-ups. Certainly, their father encouraged them to share his interests; he was pleased to be in the Bromsgrove Volunteer Rifle Corps, and in the autumn of 1866, when Alfred was seven and Robert was six years old, Edward took a photograph of them standing together just outside Perry Hall, carrying the toy rifles which he had given them (see Plate 7). But it was in the rubbish garden that their real battles took place, over and around a clay hill where the babies of the family made mud pies, and the older children fought 'in the most militaristic spirit imaginable'.[11] Over the next four or five years, Alfred 'used to try to make a boomerang work',[12] and also invented a number of new instruments of war: the Bath Bridge, which was a drainpipe to swallow and send out lighted candles — 'We got some candle ends', his brother Laurence later recalled, 'and tried the experiment; but only a melting mess and no fire came of it'; – the Martin Luther – 'a species of gatling gun which never gatled'; – and the Flying

Torpedo – 'a stump of wood which he threw. But', wrote Laurence, 'if they failed to do much execution, the names made us happy; for Alfred was always able to make us believe that his word-inventions had a meaning, and that the meaning was good.'

Alfred's delight in words was hardly surprising. With the Evangelist of Lancaster on one side of his family tree, and Dr Williams on the other, he had inherited an aptitude for writing, no doubt stimulated and encouraged by his mother, with her 'amusing choice of phrase'. Certainly, Alfred was already writing verse 'at eight or earlier', which already suggests that he was gifted. He received his first formal education from a governess, before going with his brother Robert to a small 'dame-school' in Bromsgrove High Street. Miss Johnson kept order with the help of a slipper, which she may have used rather often, because one day Alfred, showing a good deal of spirit, managed to get hold of it and threw it up on to the school roof, hoping that this would put an end to her punishments. But it is hard to believe that Alfred was ever a really difficult child. He enjoyed learning, and one of his earliest interests, 'almost as early as I can remember', was in astronomy. He found 'a little book we had in the house', and devoured it greedily. [13]

Alfred also enjoyed passing on what he had learned to others, for which he had a gift even as a small child. Laurence later remembered how Alfred one day took him and Basil out on to the lawn:

> I was the sun, my brother Basil the earth, Alfred the moon. My part in the game was to stay where I was and rotate on my axis; Basil's was to go round me in a wide circle rotating as he went; Alfred, performing the movements of the moon, skipped round him without rotation. And that is how I have learned, and have ever since remembered, the primary relations, of the sun, the earth, and the moon.

The children were clever, and naturally competitive. In the garden, each had his or her special climbing tree; and one of their family quarrels took place because they each wanted what was best for themselves. It was early one morning, and they were looking out of the night nursery window at clouds beautifully coloured with the light of a winter dawn, and arguing fiercely over which cloud belonged to whom. Sarah Jane came into the room while they were still arguing, and told them never again to take things belonging so much to heaven as their own.

Their mother was a deeply religious woman, and her children were brought up to be good Christians; but, as things turned out, this influence was not always beneficial. In *A Modern Antaeus*, a semi-autobiographical novel, Laurence described with keen symbolism how 'his late home . . . had lain too low, draining an old graveyard';[14] and, indeed, Perry Hall and its gardens lay at the very foot of the hill which supported the massive physical and spiritual weight of Bromsgrove Church. From the front lawn, Alfred and his brothers and sisters looked up over yew, laurel, birch and laburnum to the church tower and its tall spire; and their life was dominated and timed by the sound of the church bells.

Inside the house, there were family prayers in the dining-room before breakfast every day. The cook was excused from this ritual; but the maids were summoned from the kitchen, and stood in a row in front of the sideboard, while the rest of the household, including governess and nurse, assembled by their chairs. When Mr Housman began with the words: 'In the name of the Father, the Son, and the Holy Ghost', the family pulled out their chairs and knelt against the seats; while the maids whisked round and knelt with their backs to the family. Then Edward Housman led them all in prayer. Any child who was late had to do without his share of the bacon which the cook had been preparing, and have only porridge and dry bread. At night, too, the children said their prayers before going to sleep. On Sundays, there were church services to be attended, morning and evening. Then the church bells rang for a full half hour, while the children got into their newest boots, brushed their hair, washed their hands, put on their gloves, and were assembled by their governess. When their parents joined them, they all walked down the drive, over the road, up Adams' Hill, and into the church where, in Laurence's words, they 'enjoyed church as much as was reasonable for young things'.

As head of the household, it was Edward Housman's duty to take family prayers, and to see that his children went to church; but he was much more kindly and good-natured towards his children – who worshipped him[15] – than many a Victorian father. He would not punish them at all until they were seven or eight, and then only lightly. If he heard an outcry in the nursery at tea, instead of finding out what the fuss was about, and punishing whoever he thought was in the wrong, 'he would come and without inquiry put sugar on our bread and butter'. If they were ever upstairs and heard him going down, the children would rush from their rooms, and put their legs through the banisters to have their toes pulled as he passed below; and, in the garden, they all knew that the cry of 'Grubs, grubs, grubs!' meant that their father was waiting for them with some of the fruit which he had just picked for the house.

Sometimes, in those happy days, there would be 'a delicious hour before bed-time; dim gas-lights burned on the landing, and turned low in the bedrooms, curtained to a fire-light glow'. This was the time, between six and seven o'clock, when their parents were dining, and the maids were doing the downstairs rooms for the night. John Adams had fitted Perry Hall with elaborate precautions against burglary, including swing-bells on the passage doors, and an alarm in the roof; and every evening the house was filled with the rumbling of shutters, which rose up from the ground and had to be locked into place with cross-bars and screws. At this hour, the children had the run of the upstairs rooms, and played hide-and-seek or other games; and then, tired and almost ready for bed, they would be allowed to go down to the dining-room to join the grown-ups for dessert. Here they would find Edward and Sarah Jane – perhaps wearing her brown muslin dress, dotted with silken disks – sitting with the governess at the table; and they would be given a biscuit or a piece of fruit, and a sip of wine, before bidding their parents goodnight.

The Housmans of Perry Hall were a happy family, and might have expected to be prosperous – though not because of Edward Housman's work as a solicitor. His practice brought in some useful income, but he had been brought up as a country gentleman, and unfortunately he took his many hobbies rather more seriously than his work. In fact, none of the Housmans had earned much money since the previous century. Nor had Edward added to the inherited wealth when he married Sarah Jane; but he must have expected that, in time, he would acquire a considerable sum from his parents. Indeed, in 1867, when Alfred was a boy of eight, still more unearned wealth poured into the family coffers, when Alfred's great-aunt, Mary Brettell, died.

Thomas Housman was now seventy-two, but he conducted Mary's funeral service at Catshill Church, although he had retired as vicar three years before. He had then been presented with a signed memorial, thanking him for his 'unbounded liberality to poorer neighbours of all denominations', and adding:[16]

> To the female members of your family, we are also greatly indebted, for their untiring, willing, and efficient services in all matters tending to promote the interest, comfort, and well-being of the residents in this district; and it is our ardent hope that your official separation from us will not be the means of our losing their valuable and much needed charitable assistance.

This had encouraged him to remain in the area; and he had continued to be active in Bromsgrove public life. But now that Mary Brettell was dead, and his son Edward had been well established in the town, Thomas began to think about giving up his local commitments, and moving south to enjoy some years of a more complete retirement.

While he was preparing for this move, he found that he needed to raise a sum of money to settle a debt, and for other expenses. Seeing no reason why he should not now benefit directly from his share of John Adams's bequest, Perry Hall, which he had allowed his son Edward to occupy as life tenant, he came to an arrangement by which a mortgage of £1,100 was raised on the property, in Edward's name, and the capital sum was paid to Thomas. This left Edward with the responsibility of paying the interest on the mortgage, as a sort of rent.[17] Later in the year, Alfred's grandparents, with their daughters, let Fockbury House, and moved to a cottage at Lyme Regis on the Dorset coast.

In the summer of 1868, Sarah Jane's last child, George Herbert, was born; and a seventh chestnut tree was planted in the gardens of Perry Hall. Alfred was now nine years old, and so far he had enjoyed a wonderfully happy childhood; but already the days of his greatest happiness were drawing to a close; in the autumn of 1869 Sarah Jane was found to have cancer in both breasts, and as the months went by she gradually became an invalid.[18]

At the beginning of 1870, the Rev. Thomas Housman also fell ill, and realised that he ought to settle his affairs. The mortgage on Perry Hall was in Edward's name; and Edward had recently spent a considerable sum of his father's money on enlarging and improving the house. Thomas did not wish to favour Edward more than his other children, and now had a legal document drawn up which made it clear that Perry Hall really belonged to Thomas, though it was agreed that Edward and his heirs should be allowed to hold Perry Hall in trust for Thomas's heirs.[19] Then Thomas made his will. Twelve days after signing it, he died, and his family went into mourning. Alfred, then ten, attended the funeral service and watched as his grandfather was committed to the ground, 'in sure and certain hope of the Resurrection to eternal life'.

Edward Housman, who had always depended on the strength of those around him, had suffered a great loss when his father left for Lyme Regis; but at least his forceful wife, Sarah Jane, had been in good health. Now his father was not just remote, but dead; and his wife's health was slowly deteriorating; Edward simply did not have the strength to cope. Instead of trying to make the children's lives as normal as possible, in his anxiety he became forgetful and withdrawn, and began drinking.

Unprotected by their father, a great burden of worry descended on the children: Alfred, aged eleven; Robert, ten; Clem, eight; Kate, seven; Basil, six; Laurence, four; and Herbert, two. The younger children, living from day to day, probably did not feel their mother's gradual decline so strongly, but for the older ones, and especially for Alfred, Robert, and Clem, it was a dreadful period in their lives. Robert had a weak chest, and in the worry about his mother his asthma became so bad that in the autumn of 1870 he was sent away to spend three years at a school in Bath, where it was hoped that the climate would be good for him. Laurence's health also gave cause for alarm: he had a long illness which left his legs very weak.

In this worrying year, there was the problem of deciding what to do about Alfred's education. Edward Housman had great expectations, but not much ready cash; and with the expense of interest repayments on the mortgage of Perry Hall, and the additional burden of paying for Robert's fees at a boarding school, he might have found it difficult to send Alfred as a fee-paying pupil to the local school which he himself had once attended: King Edward's School, Bromsgrove.

There had always been a place at the school for twelve free scholars, 'Blue Boys', so called because they had to wear a coarse, blue coat reaching to the knees, blue breeches and stockings, and a mushroom-like cap with a big cloth button on the top, but by 1869 the endowment to support them had dwindled to a pittance. However, in 1868, a reforming headmaster, the Rev. George John Blore, a brilliant classicist and a dedicated schoolmaster, took over the school. Within a year he had formally abolished the Blue Coat School. Instead, there were to be twelve foundation scholars, day-boys who were to be admitted on complete educational equality with the boarders.[20] In this way the door was opened almost at the last minute to Alfred Housman, who was elected as one of the new scholars in July 1870, and entered the school as a day-boy in September that year.

Bromsgrove School – which Alfred attended, like all the other pupils, wearing a black mortar-board – was only a few hundred yards from Perry Hall. After going down through the southern end of the town, over a bridge crossing the stream which had powered John Adams's Indigo Mill, Alfred would walk a few yards along the Worcester Road. Here, at the head of a short slope, facing back westwards towards Bromsgrove Church, stood Cookes building, a dominating pile of brickwork which dated back to the seventeenth century, and housed a classroom, a dining hall, and a library. Behind what was now an architectural monstrosity, a pleasantly built Regency wing containing the headmaster's house ran eastwards. From here, the headmaster could look across a lawn to the chapel – his view unimpeded by passing boys, for whom a tunnel had been built from Cookes building to just beside the chapel – and he could also see a further range of buildings. Beyond these again, there was a large walled playground, with plenty of room in it for the sixty or seventy boys who made up the school.[21]

Alfred settled down quickly, and enjoyed his work at school; but he missed the companionship of his brother Robert, and of Edwin Grey, a carpenter's son who lived close to Perry Hall, and who had been a friend of his until he went to Bromsgrove School.[22] Besides this, his mother was very ill; so it is not surprising that, when he first arrived at his new school, he was so solemn and quiet that 'he was nicknamed "Mouse"', and the other boys, knowing nothing about his mother's illness, would according to Katherine Symons, sometimes 'tread on him, pretending they had not seen him'.

During the winter months Alfred and Clemence – whose ninth birthday was in November – began to spend more and more time with their mother, Alfred often writing letters for her, and Clem helping the nurse to care for her.[23] As she grew physically weaker, and finally bed-ridden, Sarah Jane's love for all her children grew more fierce and more possessive. Particularly, she clung to the company of her eldest son, almost as if she was trying to pour some of herself into him before she died. Her mind centred to an unhealthy extent on memories, and on prayer; Alfred and Clem, who were so close to her during this period, suffered a deeply disturbing emotional experience, from whose effects neither of them ever fully recovered.

Sometimes, talking to Alfred as though he were a grown-up, his mother ranged nostalgically through her memories of days at Woodchester, telling him many stories about her life there as a girl.[24] At other times – despite the fact that she had already written a letter to her friend Mrs Wise, telling her it was certain that she would not live to see her children grow up, she would pray with Alfred for her recovery, thus fixing in his impressionable mind the idea that she could be saved, that, if there was a God, He *would* save her. And as she turned to religion for comfort, her old doubts and uncertainties about the Church of England returned. Her own mother had died not many months ago, and there was now no member of the Williams family left alive to reproach her for thinking about becoming a Roman Catholic. She told Edward what was in her mind, but he refused to let her see a Roman Catholic priest, only allowing her to talk to a certain high church Anglican. How much Sarah Jane said to Alfred about all this is unknown; but, in later life, Alfred used to assert that high-church Anglicanism was the best religion ever invented.

By March 1871, it was clear that Sarah Jane had not long to live, and one day, admitting this to Clemence, she asked her to 'Take care of little Laurence. His legs are weak, and he will need you.' For some time, Sarah Jane's responsibilities in the household had been taken over by Edward's cousin Mary Housman, an elder sister of the Lucy Housman who had been his wife's bridesmaid. More recently, Sarah Jane's bed had been moved downstairs into a room which led off from the dining-room, so that she could join in family prayers. The strain on Alfred of watching his mother get worse and worse, in spite of his prayers, became almost unbearable; and on 19 March his family at last had the sense to send him away to his godmother, Mrs Wise, and her family in Woodchester.

From the station building, a short road ran up westwards over a bridge, from which Alfred could look down at the stream which flowed along the valley, powering the local cloth mills. At the top of the road, a lane ran north and south to the two scattered halves of the village; and to the north, only twenty-five yards away, were two stone pillars which marked the entrance to the Wise's property. Through this gateway, a drive ran round in a long slow curve to the left, with fields on either side of it; then past a carriage house and stable block, and up through trees to where the Wise family lived, in a delightful eighteenth-century family home, solidly built in grey stone to a formal but unpretentious design. From the front of the house, one looked south across unspoilt countryside; at the back, there was a small lawn, and a rise in the ground hid North Woodchester from view, so that only distant slopes were visible beyond the shrubs and trees of the garden. It was a peaceful, secluded, and happy place. This was the Woodchester to which Alfred was later to return so often and whose occupants were to afford him so much solace.

A feature of the house was the impressive hallway which ran the length of the building, with four main rooms, including the kitchen, leading off from it. On the next floor were the family bedrooms and, above them, the servants' quarters. The master of the household, Edward Wise, was now in his sixties, and the decline of the woollen industry in Gloucestershire had recently forced him to close his two mills; but he appeared to have other interests, and to remain comfortably off.[25] Mrs Wise, a sympathetic and practical woman of almost the same age as Alfred's mother, had already promised Sarah Jane that she would keep a special eye on Alfred, and she did her best to make him feel at home. Her own children were rather older than Alfred: Edward Tuppen, or 'Ted' Wise, was already nineteen, but her two daughters, Edith and Wilhelmina, or 'Minnie', were, at sixteen and thirteen, not too old to enjoy Alfred's company. The girls were both taught by Sophie Becker, a warm-hearted German governess then in her early thirties. Alfred's sister Kate, who met Miss Becker a few times, described her as: 'small and dark and sallow, not exactly ugly, but not good-looking. She was a shrewd, cheerful, capable person, much valued in the Wise family.'[26] She was also witty and amusing, and she drew Alfred into their games and conversations, and their rambles through the surrounding countryside, and so began what was to become a life-long relationship of mutual admiration and sympathy.

The area was full of happy associations for Alfred. His mother's stories about her childhood were still fresh in his mind, and he could also remember his last visit to Woodchester with her, when she was in good health. From the drive, a footpath ran northwards down a slope, and then up again to the new church, where Alfred could see the memorial windows to his grandfather and uncle Basil. Beyond the church, and across the main street, he could examine the Elizabethan rectory where his mother had lived; or he could walk down the lane which led to the remains of the church where his parents had been married, and to the churchyard where a previous rector of Woodchester had discovered a remarkable Roman mosaic pavement.

With Edith and Minnie and Miss Becker, he sometimes climbed the steep main street, which ran up westward to the oddly shaped slopes and hollows of Selsley Common. From these heights, bare of trees, he could look back down to the village, or further westward across miles of farmland towards the River Severn and the distant Welsh hills.

Then, on Sunday 26 March, he celebrated his twelfth birthday among his friends. Soon afterwards a letter arrived from his father to tell him of his mother's death: by a cruel coincidence which haunted Alfred for the rest of his life, she had died on his birthday.

# CHAPTER 2

# *Schooldays*

And the stately ships go on
    to their haven under the hill;
but oh for the touch of a vanished hand,
    and the sound of a voice that is still.
Break, break, break
    at the foot of the crags, o Sea;
but the tender grace of a day that is dead
    will never come back to me.

Lines from 'Break, break, break' by Alfred Lord Tennyson
as quoted in *Sabrinae Corolla*

On the morning of 26 March 1871, the Housman children still at Perry Hall – Kate, aged eleven, Clem aged nine, Basil aged eight, Laurence aged five, and Herbert aged two – had been taken to church as usual. The first sign that something was wrong came when the mid-day meal was transferred from the dining- to the drawing-room. 'I asked why', Laurence recalled, 'and was told . . . that it was because I was late in getting ready for church that morning.' A few minutes after the meal had ended, Clem and Kate were on the front lawn with Herbert, while Laurence was walking with his nurse along the drive. Then Laurence saw their house-keeper cousin, Mary, come out of the front door: 'She said something I could not hear. I saw my two sisters burst into tears, and throw themselves into her arms.' Then all the children were taken into the darkened room where their mother had died. Sarah Jane's body was still lying in bed, her face pale, her eyelids smoothed down; at the foot of the bed lighted candles burned on either side of a crucifix in a wooden shrine. It was a solemn, haunting, and strangely beautiful sight, which explained, more than any words could have done, that their mother was finally dead; and, for those of the children who understood and believed in Christianity, the cross and the candles were a reminder that she had already begun a new life in heaven.

16

For the moment Alfred was simply overwhelmed. Indeed, Sarah Jane had told her husband that she was afraid that Alfred would lose his faith when she died, and Edward unfortunately implanted this idea in Alfred's mind by mentioning it to him in the letter giving news of her death that he sent to Woodchester. Alfred's prayers for his mother's recovery had, as it seemed to him, been callously ignored.[1] Not that there was an immediate rejection of God. But the depth of his feeling is shown by the fact that, for the rest of his life, he carefully preserved every scrap of writing that he had ever received from or about her; and it is from this time that Alfred began to suffer from 'that most distinctly Romantic feeling — infinite, never appeased longing'[2] which was always to weigh heavily upon him.

Wishing to spare his son unnecessary suffering, Edward suggested that Alfred should stay on at Woodchester until after the funeral, a separation of father and son at the very time when shared grief might have brought them closer together; and he was also apart from his brothers and sisters at one of the most important emotional turning-points of all their lives. Instead, Alfred turned for comfort to Miss Becker, and for companionship to Edith Wise. Edith became a very close friend, closer to him than any of his brothers or sisters; and when the sympathetic Miss Becker consoled him, he transferred to her some of the love which he had felt for his mother.[3] She was less attractive than his mother had been; but she was witty, and clever, and made much of him, as his mother had done. The understanding which developed between them became, for Alfred, one of the most important relationships in his life; when as an old man he heard of her death, he admitted that he had loved and revered her from youth, 'his voice faltered, and a look of unutterable sadness suffused his face'.[4]

By the time that Alfred had returned home to Perry Hall, the moment for shared feelings and confidences with his immediate family had gone. As the eldest son, he felt responsible for putting a brave face on things; and, largely because of his influence, the children never discussed their loss among themselves. Alfred might have talked to Robert, but he was still an exile in Bath, suffering from his asthma. Grief was kept for the secrecy of the bedroom, where Laurence, for one, cried in bed at night for his mother to come back to him, half believing that if he prayed faithfully enough she would. Hiding his feelings became habitual for Alfred. His sister Kate remembered that, from this time on, it was never his way to speak of troubles, and she wrote: 'He was sensitive and easily wounded, but wounds he bore in silence.'

During her illness, Sarah Jane had withdrawn so much from the daily routine of the household that her death made little outward change. Edward Housman's younger sister Jane, who had come up for a while to help out, soon returned to Lyme Regis to look after their ailing mother,

whose mental control was now so poor that she more than once had to be
sent to an asylum for 'unbalanced condition of mind'.[5] Mary Housman
stayed on as housekeeper, and apart from a change of governess, family
life went on outwardly much as before. But the family was in mourning.
The children grieved silently, and wore harsh black stockings; while the
tolling bells of Bromsgrove Church, which continued to regulate the
hours, were another constant reminder of their mother's death.

During the next twelve months Alfred thought a great deal about his
mother and, in the light of her death, he began to change his ideas about
religion. He did not simply 'lose his faith' as Sarah Jane had feared. He
was too deeply religious not to believe that there was a God; but he
became less and less able to believe in the Christian Revelation. If Jesus
Christ was the son of God, and really could answer prayers and intervene
in the normal working of the Universe, then nothing so pointless and
unjust as his mother's death would have been allowed to happen. Alfred
wanted to believe in Christianity, but could not: years later he expressed
this feeling in a poem called 'Easter Hymn' which, because of its
controversial nature, he did not publish during his lifetime:[6]

> If in that Syrian garden, ages slain,
> You sleep, and know not you are dead in vain. . . .
> Sleep well and see no morning, son of man.
>
> But if, the grave rent and the stone rolled by,
> At the right hand of majesty on high
> You sit, and sitting so remember yet
> Your tears, your agony and bloody sweat,
> Your cross and passion and the life you gave,
> Bow hither out of heaven and see and save. (MP 1) (More Poems)

By the time that he was thirteen, Alfred had secretly abandoned
Christianity, and learned to think of himself as a Deist, believing that
there was a God, but no more than that. Since he was a boy of eight and
had looked into Lemprière's Classical Dictionary, he had been fascinated
by legends of the pagan gods and goddesses of Greece and Rome; and his
reading of these legends, together with his growing love for the beauty of
the countryside, brought him closer to being a pagan or pantheist, and
offered an escape for his sensitive mind from the bleakness of a Universe
in which God is present but indifferent.

Unlike his son, Edward Housman did not turn his back on Christianity;
but he did long to move from Perry Hall, where he could only forget his
dead wife by indulging in bouts of heavy drinking. However, his professional life tied him to Bromsgrove; and Perry Hall belonged to his
father's estate, so he was not really in a position to sell it. Then, in

February 1872, the tenant of Fockbury House died. Edward's childhood home now belonged jointly to Edward and to his brothers and sisters, Thomas, Mary, Jane and Joseph. Income from the tenancy of Fockbury House helped Edward, who was its Trustee, to run Perry Hall; and he should have found a new paying tenant as soon as possible. But the prospect of a move was too tempting for him, and he decided that he and his family would go to live at Fockbury themselves. He would lose his income, but he planned – almost certainly without the consent of his brothers and sisters – to raise an immediate mortgage of £1,500 on the property, which would provide him with plenty of ready money for the time being.

Edward was a charming man, liked and respected throughout his life by many of the most influential people in Bromsgrove, and he was a leading member of many local societies and governing boards. But in making this move, he had succumbed to his fatal weakness: the wish to live the life of a prosperous country gentleman. His father had been able to live that life, and Edward had been brought up fitted for nothing else. But although he hoped for a great deal of family money in the future, he was not at present rich enough for the role he wanted to play. He never earned much as a solicitor, and had no lands to provide him with the income needed to maintain a large household. However, he would rather have the illusion of prosperity than nothing at all; and, to achieve it, he was quite prepared to sacrifice the future to the present. Photographs of Edward reinforce the impression of a man who has inherited some of his father's intelligence, but more of his determination than of his judgment. The mouth and the jaw are firm, even obstinate, but the eyes are weak and uncertain.

So Edward felt that a move to Fockbury House would suit him very well; Perry Hall would have to be kept on, but he would continue to use part of it as his offices, and from time to time he managed to let out the main body of the house.[7] There remained the problem of his children: Mary Housman was a good housekeeper, but a poor substitute mother; and Edward was lonely after Sarah Jane's death. After a while he began thinking of Mary's younger sister, Lucy Housman, who had introduced him to his first wife, and had been Sarah Jane's bridesmaid at their wedding. Lucy was eight years older than Edward, so that in 1872 she was already forty-nine; but he knew that she had always admired him, and that she was a strong, sensible person who would make a good job of bringing up his children and running his household – and he proposed to her.

Lucy accepted, as Edward had hoped. He confided in Alfred, the only one of his children who had met her; and Alfred, taking on what was really too large a responsibility for a thirteen-year-old boy, wrote at once to assure his future stepmother that he would do everything he could to help her look after his brothers and sisters.

Early in 1873, Lucy visited the family, who were still at Perry Hall. She was not a great beauty, and at times looked rather too earnest; but the children liked her, and the visit was a success. Laurence, in particular, took to her at once; and in their first walk alone together, knowing nothing about his father's plans, he touchingly proposed marriage himself, telling her that he had five pounds in the Savings Bank, and choosing the small cottage in which they were to start life together. Soon after this visit, Edward moved out to Fockbury with his seven children, who were by now very excited at the thought of life in the country.

As the crow flies, Fockbury House was only a mile and a half from Perry Hall, but it was in a different, more peaceful world. When the day came for the move, most of the baggage and furniture had been sent on ahead in carts, and the family crowded into an open carriage. Their road lay westwards, away from the shadow of Bromsgrove Church and through a countryside of rolling farmland. Then they turned into Perryfields Road, and drove northwards to the slopes around Fockbury House. Up these slopes through narrow lanes the horses drew them, until on their right, at the head of the Valley Road, the children saw their new home. Soon their carriage drew up alongside a picturesque building dating back to the seventeenth century: the lower storey plain brickwork; the upper half-timbered with several gabled windows. Many local people still called it the Clock House, as one of the gables had once held a large clock which gave time to the neighbourhood.

Fockbury House, being an old, unmodernised country home, had no gas, no water taps, and no drainage; but, as Kate pointed out, 'it was a good place for children'. It was large and rambling and there was also a sizeable garden in which to roam, as well as a range of farm buildings to explore, with rickyards, barns and lofts. In the country round about there were 'woods and lanes, fields, pools and brooks . . . friendly farms dotted about the neighbourhood, part of our grandmother's property, affording us truly exciting playing places'. Close at hand, at the bottom of Fockbury field, they visited a poacher who lived with his four children in a small cottage under a wall of rock, and who told the children: 'When I can do no more ratting and rabbiting, then I hope the Lord will take me', while further away, a yeoman farmer named John Daffern, who had once been a family tenant, became a particular favourite — perhaps because they would sometimes be treated to a draught of fresh milk when they called at his farm.

When they first arrived at Fockbury, only a few hundred yards along the road from the house where Alfred was born, the children found on an attic floor the remains of a library dating from the time of Caxton. Most of this valuable collection had been destroyed through the astonishing carelessnesss of their grandmother, who had allowed her offspring to tear up the covers to use as wads for their muzzle-loading sporting guns; the insides of the books she had sold for butter paper.[8] Alfred later commented tartly that: 'our grandmother of course had no brains at all that I could discover; but our grandfather ought to have been ashamed of himself'. However, several works of interest had survived, including a botanical collection made by the Holdens in the 1690s, and 'an emblazoned pedigree showing two lines of Holden descent' dating back to the reign of Henry II.

Edward, relaxing into life as a country gentleman, greatly enjoyed the distinguished family connection with the countryside, which meant that he was sometimes spoken of locally as 'the Squire'. Alfred shared his father's enjoyment. He was fascinated by the pedigree, while the botanical collection stimulated his interest in nature; and he began to make walking through the surrounding countryside his chief recreation.

Towards the end of June, Edward, now aged forty-two, married his fifty-year-old cousin, Lucy, in London; and a month later he brought his new wife home. It was a nervous moment for Lucy, despite the success of her earlier visit; but the children, gathered in the entrance hall with their governess, greeted her warmly: only Laurence, remembering his earlier proposal, felt embarrassed when 'my father gave me a roguish look, which meant, I suppose, Cut you out, my boy!' That evening, Lucy discussed with the children what they were to call her – they decided upon Mamma.

Alfred had something more serious to discuss with his stepmother. The new governess, Mrs Cooper, had disgusted him by her immoral behaviour, behaviour which she had managed to conceal from his father. Alfred told Lucy plainly that Mrs Cooper was not fit to be looking after his sisters, and then had to explain about her promiscuity which must have embarrassed him considerably.[9] Mrs Cooper was livid with Alfred when she was forced to leave the household, spitting out vicious comments whose gist was that Alfred, though no longer a child, was not yet a mature adult. This unpleasant episode helped to make Alfred think of sex between men and women as something rather repulsive; an impression which was confirmed by the guidance of sexual matters which was given to him at about this time by his father, who appears to have concentrated on warning him about the dangers of giving way to sexual desires.[10]

Not long after this, at a time when Alfred was at least fourteen, Edward took it into his head to have all the boys in his family circumcised. Alfred's sister Kate later commented:[11]

I do not think it was to fulfil a scriptural rite that he sought, for there

was no Abrahamic tradition in our family; but on sanitary mosaic lines,
I think he considered it would contribute to their physical salvation – as
perhaps it did. He ought to have thought of it in their babyhood. It was
severe treatment, mentally and physically, for well-grown boys, and a
great mystery at the time to the younger ones who made open complaint, with a mixture of importance and resentment, of the ill-
treatment which had befallen them while my sister and I were staying
at Lyme Regis.

Severe treatment indeed, particularly traumatic for boys well out of
infancy, and treatment which once again must have helped to make
sexual activity seem dirty to Alfred.

Meanwhile, at Bromsgrove School, Alfred was doing well. Dr Blore,
who remained as headmaster until the summer of 1873, later described
Alfred as the sort of boy he was always afraid would ask him some
question which he could not answer; and although quiet and studious,
Alfred was not downtrodden by any of the other boys for long. On the
contrary, he developed into quite 'a determined personality, able to take
his own way, and yet to avoid troubles'.

In term time, his younger brothers and sisters saw comparatively little
of him. Robert was still away in Bath; and the other children were taught
by the governess who came to replace Mrs Cooper. Alfred had to be up
early for a six o'clock breakfast before walking to school, down the lanes
to Perryfields Road, across country to Bromsgrove, and through the town
to the school, where in the summer work began at seven.

When he was only fourteen Alfred, who had remembered his mother's
talent for writing verse,[12] entered the school verse competition with a
poem about Sir Walter Raleigh. He did not win but he felt pleased with his
efforts, and, as he afterwards protested, considered them much better
than his later prize poems.[13] Some of the lines are similar in form and in
imaginative power to the best of Tolkien:[14]

> From land to land like night he flies
> The playmate of the stormy breeze
> Before his prow the shade of fear . . .
>
> He flies to other lands afar
> The lands beneath the evening star
> Where fairer constellations rise
> And shed their light from bluer skies
> Where undiscovered treasure shines
> Locked in the dim and gloomy mines
> And red volcanoes howl and glare
> Like daemons on the midnight air.

While Alfred made no lasting friends at school, he got on well enough with his class mates. Much to his relief, as a day-boy he was not forced to take part in games or athletics like the boarders, and during the long mid-day interval on whole school days, he worked quietly in one of their study-rooms.

In the autumn of 1873, a new headmaster came to Bromsgrove, Herbert Millington, who was later said to resemble certain portraits of Matthew Arnold, with his handsome features and his eager, intellectual expression. Millington had some failings, of which the chief were his class prejudice, and his contempt for those who did not see things as he did. He was a forceful man, and in his dislike of 'the trade element' he made life hard for many of the day-boys, even encouraging the use of insulting nicknames such as 'Bacon' and 'Carthorse' for the sons of a grocer and a farmer. However, he was a good teacher of clever boys;[15] and he made his influence felt throughout the school, particularly in the way in which he encouraged his pupils to adopt his own interests. One of these was botany, for which Alfred had already shown an inclination.

Afternoon school was usually from 4 to 6 p.m., so that Alfred was not home at Fockbury until nearly seven; and then he dined late with his father and stepmother, and worked alone. But he had not forgotten his promise to help Lucy with the upbringing of the rest of the family: when on half-holidays the children met her in the drawing-room for their 'customary hour', Alfred would join them in cards, games and glee singing.

During the holidays, Alfred took a more active role, encouraging his brothers and sisters to draw, paint, take part in games, and write stories. He very much enjoyed the nonsense verse of Edward Lear and Lewis Carroll, and sometimes amused his brothers and sisters with nonsense rhymes of his own:[16]

> Little Miss Muffet sat on a tuffet
>    Opening her mouth very wide.
> There came a great spider; she opened it wider
>    And the spider ran down her inside.

He also encouraged them to write more serious verses, giving as much help as was needed, so that Laurence later wrote: 'When I was a small child he *did* persuade me that I had written a sonnet which was really his; and he wrote it down as mine in the family album.'[17] They were competitive and possessive children, and Alfred made use of this in the way that he taught them. When studying trees, for example, they each had to choose a favourite — Alfred's choice was the beech — but they all had to choose a different one. In the same way, he encouraged them to share his interest in Gothic architecture by making them choose particular

Gothic cathedrals as their favourites. 'We found great fun in all this', Kate wrote later, 'for Alfred had a way of making things he did amusing as well as interesting. Our gatherings were generally hilarious.' However, the extra responsibility which Alfred had assumed put a real distance between him and the other children, and made his family life anything but normal.

Lucy herself read to the family almost every day, especially during the winter months and school holidays: she began with the narrative poems of Scott, and eventually read her way through most of Shakespeare. In the evenings Edward sometimes read to them from Dickens, and he also encouraged his children to take an interest in one of his own numerous hobbies: shooting, fishing, music, photography, gardening, and even firework-making. Alfred did not join in with his father's arrangements, but spent the time instead in reading or walking; partly because he no longer felt that he was one of the children; and partly, as Kate later explained, because his 'sense of some pleasures was acute, and seemed exercised best alone. It was alone that he liked to tramp to enjoy the sight and smell of woodlands, or to gaze on a setting sun or a starry sky.'

From Fockbury House, he would often walk into narrow Worms Ash Lane, which, set between high banks of reddish rock and gnarled tree roots, leads up westwards over the side of a small hill. From the top of the lane, on a fine day, he could see as far as the Clent and Lickey hills. But usually he turned into a field at the side of the lane, and a few more paces brought him to the top of the hill. Southwards lay Bromsgrove, its church spire standing out clearly above the town; and to the west Alfred looked out over a peaceful land of small wooded hills and hamlets to the distant Shropshire hills. This beautiful view became for him a powerful image associated with some of his deepest feelings. In daylight, it was a symbol of hope: flowing with milk and honey, like the Promised Land of the Israelites; and in fact the other Housman children, remembering the story of Moses going up from the plains of Moab nicknamed the hill 'Mount Pisgah'. In the evening, Alfred came here to meditate upon his troubles and upon greater mysteries: a fifteen-year-old boy standing alone on a hill-top watching the last of the day, while:

> From hill and cloud and heaven
>    The hues of evening died;
> Night welled through lane and hollow
>    And hushed the countryside,
>    But I had youth and pride.
>
> And I with earth and nightfall
>    In converse high would stand,

> Late, till the west was ashen
> And darkness hard at hand,
> And the eye lost the land.          *(LP 39 (Last Poems)*

The scene is perhaps more Romantic than Biblical, with Alfred as the Romantic idea of the Bard, seeking the truth 'alone in a wide natural landscape high above the rest of humanity'.[18]

The Housman family now lived in the parish of Catshill; and summer and winter, they walked the mile to church twice every Sunday. They went in arm-in-arm pairs, with Edward and Lucy leading the way. Alfred and Robert should have followed, but even when Robert returned from Bath, he did not join his brother. They had grown apart in those three years of separation, and Alfred, unable to confide in him, kept Robert at a distance. Besides, at the age of thirteen Clem was not only taller, but cleverer than Robert, and a more entertaining companion for her eldest brother. Robert, aged fourteen, was left to walk with twelve-year-old Kate, who was cheerful, but hated lessons, and was therefore considered rather a dunce by the rest of the family. Then came an ill-assorted pair: ten-year-old Basil, who with his orderly studious mind was most like Alfred, and a favourite of his; and the irrepressible Laurence, who at the age of nine was always in one scrape or another – though Clem kept an eye on him when she could. Last came the governess, hand-in-hand with six-year-old Herbert.[19] They all walked down the Valley Road, past the house where Alfred had been born, and then north-eastwards over the fields to Catshill Church.

At Catshill, the rustic congregation consisted mainly of yeoman farmers and labourers, dressed in the clean smocks which they would wear for the rest of the week – some of them even sported old-fashioned beaver hats. The vicar of Catshill, the Rev. James Kidd, was a great countryman, and Alfred liked talking to him about botany, but in church he was very dull. The Housmans enjoyed listening to their father reading the Lesson, which he often did; but under Kidd's ministry, as Laurence later recalled, 'the bread of the gospel turned to stone'.

When the service was over, Alfred sometimes wandered down to the southern corner of the churchyard, where a decorated stone cross marked his mother's grave. She had been buried not far from the Rev. Thomas Housman; and, remembering the inscription on Thomas's more imposing monument, which began: 'To whom was first entrusted this church, this God's acre . . .', Alfred was later to write bitterly:

> There's empty acres west and east,
> But aye 'tis God's that bears the least:
> This hopeless garden that they sow
> With the seeds that never grow. *(AP 11) (Additional Poems)*

Lucy Housman had won the affection of her adopted family, but she was a stronger figure than they had at first recognised, and in time the children stopped calling her 'Mamma', and called her 'Mater' instead. She was rather puritanical, gradually weeding out the high-church tendencies which had been implanted by their mother. Lucy disapproved particularly of holidays on Saints' days, allowed by Sarah Jane, and kept watch until one Saint's day, out of term, they failed to go to church – and that was the end of the special holidays. She followed up this victory by reading on Sunday afternoons 'an awful life of Luther, in two big volumes, translated from the German'.

Alfred was unaffected by his stepmother's Lutheran teachings; but, as he was painfully aware in later life, he grew up with something of her class prejudice. Of course, there were in those days such inequalities between the various classes that is was easy to believe that the lower orders of society were naturally inferior. In church, the Housmans sat in the very front pew as a sign of their social status; and while the Housman children were getting a good education, other local children were being taught in a primitive dame school at Catshill. At Fockbury House itself, the servants were not overworked, and they were paid fair wages; but Lucy treated them as being in some ways less human than herself. When a weeping maid asked for permission to visit her dying mother, Lucy agreed, but then commented to her children: 'They make a great fuss, but they don't feel about these things as we do.'

Since his mother's death, Alfred had corresponded regularly with his godmother and with Sophie Becker, writing mainly on family matters, with family jokes such as references to the possibility of Mrs Wise becoming a Roman Catholic. Sometimes he would even write in French, addressing Mrs Wise as Madame Guise of Masion de Chestre à bois, and signing himself 'Alfred Edouard Maisonhomme'. He also went to stay at Woodchester whenever possible, though at least once he had to decline an invitation, regretting that: 'Mr. Millington has set his heart on some very wonderful achievements on the part of the school at next Midsummer . . . I am chained to my books.'[20]

In the summer of 1874, when Alfred was fifteen, the Wises and Miss Becker came to Fockbury House for a few days; and Miss Becker, Edith and Minnie posed for a photograph as part of a group in fancy dress, with Sophie Becker as Queen of the Night, Alfred as an archbishop, and his ten-year-old brother Basil in military uniform.[21] Miss Becker was judged 'shrewd, sensible, and brightly humorous'; but Alfred's family did not recognise the strength of his attachment for her. On the other hand, his friendship with Edith Wise was plain enough. Alfred's brothers and sisters decided that he was secretly in love with her; and, even when she became engaged to the curate of Woodchester, they teased Alfred with a reference to his rambles with her on Selsley Hill:[22]

> Alfred Edward solemn and wise
> Opens his mouth and rolls his eyes
> But when chasing Selsley slopes
> opes his eyes and eyes his 'opes.

They were not surprised when he failed to react angrily; his weapon in the family, when he needed one, was scorn and aloofness. Once, when Robert smacked his cheek, Alfred simply assumed an exaggerated air of superiority, and turned his face like a good Christian for another smack. When Robert hit him again, he did retaliate, but not fiercely, and Robert soon gave way – perhaps because, as Laurence later recalled, 'it would have been almost like fighting against a parent or an uncle to have stood against Alfred at that time as man to man'.

In school, good places in form, prizes and praise continued to come to him; and indeed, his success at school was an important factor in making him feel that there was something worth while left in life after his mother's death. He was proud of his successes; and years later, when Kate read an account by Laurence of Alfred's early life, she wrote rather crossly: 'It is news to me that he was ever a modest little boy . . . I never saw him troubled by modesty of any sort – as a boy or afterwards.'[23] It was in the summer of 1874, shortly before the Wises visited Fockbury, that Alfred won the school verse prize for the first time. In fact, his poem, on the Death of Socrates, was inferior to his imaginative verses about Raleigh the previous year. But he had produced what was required, a sort of conventional sub-Swinburnian echo, so perhaps he deserved to win for that alone.

During the Christmas holidays, Alfred's stepmother decided that it was time for his outlook to be broadened a little, and she sent him off to London for a few days, in the care of her sister Mary. The steam-engine which pulled their train into London brought Alfred and his elderly cousin to a thriving city of some four millions – a city much closer to nature than it is today. Sheep and cows were still driven through the mud to be slaughtered at Smithfield; in the suburbs pigs and goats were kept in back gardens, and even allowed on to the streets to forage for food. 'I am serenaded every morning by some cocks who crow as if their life depended upon it. If they were in my hands,' Alfred wrote with grim humour to his stepmother, 'their life would depend upon it.'

Alfred enjoyed himself tremendously. He saw Trafalgar Square, which as a provincial boy he found 'magical'; admired the view from Westminster Bridge; toured the main London streets, and visited Westminster Abbey, where he heard an anthem 'like a boa constrictor – very long and very ugly' – and visited Poets' corner. In St Paul's Cathedral, which he liked better than the Abbey, he went up to the Golden Gallery, leaving his nervous cousin safely behind on *terra firma*; at the Albert Hall he stood for a performance of Haydn's *Creation*; and in the British Museum he visited the zoological gallery, where he was reminded of a famous book by Jules Verne, and came to the conclusion, 'which you may tell the readers of *"The Centre of the Earth"*, that if the Mastodon and Megatherium were to fight it would decidedly be a very bad job for the Megatherium . . .'.

But in the British Museum Alfred's passion for the ancient world led him to spend most of his time 'among the Greeks and Romans'. As might have been expected, Alfred did not have any particular feeling for the female statues. He had hardly been encouraged to view sexual relations with women with joyful anticipation, and perhaps already harboured the distaste later to be intellectualised into his scornful attitude towards most of the female sex. However, he did find the male statues fascinating. At home in Worcestershire, he had read and enjoyed stories of Gods and heroes, and of firm friendships between comrades-in-arms; and he had looked in his imagination for a heroic friend:

> When I would muse in boyhood
>     The wild green woods among,
> And nurse resolves and fancies
>     Because the world was young,
> It was not foes to conquer,
>     Nor sweethearts to be kind,
> But it was friends to die for
>     That I would seek and find.                (*LP* 32)

Certainly, Alfred did not at all care for the Towneley Venus, which Lucy had recommended to him; instead, he wrote to her that 'what delighted me most was the Farnese Mercury'. Alfred had in his mind a picture of the Roman world, its civilisation bound together by marching legions, full of individual heroes. When he saw the finely uniformed men of the Grenadier Guards and the 1st Life Guards in St James's Park, he wrote: 'I think of all I have seen, what has most impressed me is – the Guards. This may be barbarian, but it is true.'

His trip to London was not Alfred's first contact with the larger world. His father subscribed to an illustrated weekly, the *Graphic*, which reported all the international and national news of any importance, from details of the Ashanti war to the clashes between Disraeli and Gladstone. Edward Housman particularly encouraged an interest in politics and, in the evenings, when the children joined him and Lucy for a sip of wine after dinner, he would sometimes call out a toast of 'Up with the Tories, and down with the Radicals!', which they would all shout together.

When Alfred returned from London, it was to find that some of his family had caught scarlet fever, so he boarded at school for a while. He had enjoyed his holiday, but this prolonged separation from his family made him homesick. One afternoon he walked across the town, and up the long slope to Bromsgrove churchyard. From here he could look northwards, beyond the gravestones and the young lime trees, in the direction of Fockbury. He could see his home clearly, 'especially', he wrote to Lucy, 'the window of your room'. He was in the churchyard

from two o'clock till three. I wonder if you went into your room between those hours. One can see quite plainly the pine trees, the sycamore and the elm at the top of the field. The house looks much nearer than you would expect, . . . Give my love to my Father, and to my brothers and sisters and believe me, your affectionate son Alfred.

A few days later, on a half-holiday, he followed up this letter by actually walking over to Fockbury, and calling to his family from an adjacent meadow.

Before long, the children recovered and Alfred returned home; when, a few months later, it was Lucy's turn to be away from Fockbury for a short holiday with her mother, Alfred wrote her an amusing letter in rhyming couplets. Alfred's Aunt Mary, Edward's sister, was staying with them; and he wrote that the weather had been:

> So hot and torrid, that my stout
> Aunt Mary has not ventured out, –

And would not, until the evening, when:

> . . . to the shadowy garden fly
> My relative and Clem and I.
> Clemence becomes a fancied knight
> In visionary armour dight . . .
> I turn into a dragon dire
> Breathing imaginary fire;

while the stout Aunt Mary became:

> . . . a hapless maid
> Imprisoned in a dungeon's shade.

Alfred was still busy organising his brothers and sisters; and was now making them contribute to a family magazine, that he wrote out himself and circulated among friends and relations. He also encouraged play-acting, and would announce in the morning what they were to perform that evening, tell them the plot and assign the parts. It was at about this time in the spring of 1875 that the children acted a parody of Hamlet.

Laurence, who used to complain that Alfred kept the best jokes for himself in these entertainments, later wrote:

> Alfred was Hamlet. He entered sniffing and holding his nose, preliminary to his first remark: 'There's something rotten in the state of Denmark.' When he killed Polonius he cried 'A rat, a rat, my kingdom for a rat'. That was about the quality of it; and as it came from him we considered it to be wit of the first order.

Alfred's successes continued at school, where during the summer of 1875 he again won the verse prize – this time with a poem entitled 'Paul on Mars Hill'. It was no worse than his 'Death of Socrates', but writing these prize poems badly affected the style of at least one private poem, in which the morbid and heavily laboured couplet

> Summer! and after Summer what?
> Ah! happy trees that know it not

comes perilously close to farce. But there is real beauty in some lines on 'The Ruins of Rome'; and one can find in them a less pessimistic attitude, showing that Alfred's inner gloom was lightening, and that he was coming to terms with his mother's death:

> The city is silent and solemn
>     That once was alive and divine
> And here stands the shaft of a column
>     And there lies the wreck of a shrine;
> But the wild bird still sings in the marshes
>     The wild flower still blooms on the lea
> And under its infinite arches
>     The river runs down to the sea.

But, before long, there were fresh worries to occupy Alfred's mind. The first of them concerned his friend Edith Wise. She had been happily engaged to the curate of Woodchester Church for some time now; but, when plans were made for their marriage, the curate, who had always thought of the Wises as a well-to-do family, was not at all satisfied with the marriage settlement, and broke off the engagement in disgust. It was humiliating for Edith to realise that the curate had been mainly interested in her money; and, to add to her unhappiness, shortly after this incident her father died. Very much to their surprise, the family found that they had been living off their capital, and they were not nearly so wealthy as they had imagined. Kate wrote later that her brother Alfred 'shared in the sorrows of that bitter time'.[24]

The other worry which affected Alfred was much closer to home, but was also pecuniary – in this case, with Edward Housman's financial mismanagement. The story is a rather complicated one, but worth telling for the light which it throws on Edward's character, and on Alfred's family life.

Edward, as Trustee of his father's estate, had failed to share out a sum of £1,000 which Thomas had left to be divided among his children; and Edward had also taken out mortgages on Perry Hall, and on his mother's cottage in Lyme Regis, neither of which properties he owned. When he moved to Fockbury, he had raised a further supply of ready money by mortgaging that property also; but the move had simultaneously reduced his income and increased his expenditure. Now, after two years of being a country gentleman, his funds were running low. With no more family properties to mortgage, he fell behind with interest payments, and when on 5 June 1875 he finally conveyed Roseville Cottage to his mother, he also passed on a mortgage debt of £1,500 for which he expected her to assume responsibility.

This was more than his brothers and sisters could stand; and within twelve days, Mary, Jane, and the Reverend Joseph had joined their mother to file a Bill of Complaint addressed to the Lord High Chancellor.[25] Soon afterwards, Edward received a summons.

Then on 26 June, the Court of Chancery ordered that Thomas Housman's will should be put into effect; but at the same time it ordered enquiries into fourteen related points, and adjourned the case indefinitely. The only really effective action which it took was to insist that the sum of just over £400 which Edward admitted that he still possessed of his father's money should be paid into Court pending a final settlement.[26]

This payment left Edward very short of money; and he was now being pressed for payment by Daniel Weaver, to whom he had mortgaged Perry Hall. Weaver was tired of receiving no interest, and on 11 August he informed Edward, through his solicitors, that he would exercise his power of sale unless the mortgage was paid off. Edward replied that Perry Hall, as a part of Thomas Housman's estate, was in Chancery, and that under those circumstances he was not prepared to pay; but he did not object to Weaver exercising his power of sale. Of course, as Trustee, Edward should have objected to a sale; but if no sale took place, he would still owe Weaver £1,100; and even if he raised this money, Perry Hall would still be in Chancery, and would probably be taken away from him. So he wanted the house to be sold; but this was part of a larger plan: he had already enlisted the help of the young Edward Wise of Woodchester, in an ingenious scheme to defraud Thomas Housman's estate.

Ted Wise attended the auction of Perry Hall in November 1875, and the property was knocked down to him for £1,275, but Wise was acting as Housman's agent. By the end of February 1876 the property had been conveyed to Wise as Trustee for Housman. Ted Wise did not have to dig into his own pocket, and could not have done so even if he had wanted to. £1,100 was found by agreeing a new mortgage with Weaver, who had found Housman an unsatisfactory client, but was prepared to deal with Housman and Wise together; while the balance came from Housman's pocket. Edward thus effectively removed Perry Hall from his father's estate and from Chancery and got it into his own hands for the sum of £175, less than a sixth of what the house was worth.[27] With his title to the property now secure, he was able to pay the balance of £175 and to cover his other immediate needs by taking out a second mortgage on Perry Hall for £500 with a certain Martha Perkins, who must have had more money than sense.[28]

Edward Housman had gained a breathing-space; but he must have realised that his days of living as the 'squire' of Fockbury were numbered; and, as the real world pressed in upon the illusion which he had created, and was still desperately trying to sustain, he again began drinking too much and his health suffered. The first sign of this was that his appearance at church became less regular, and Alfred agreed to read the lessons at Catshill when his father was feeling too ill to do so.

Alfred did not know the details of his father's financial dealings; but an advertisement for the auction of Perry Hall had been prominently displayed in the local press, and he must have been told something of what was happening. The long-term future was still quite hopeful, because whatever his father did with his share of the family money, there was a great deal more wealth in the wider family, and Alfred and his brothers and sisters were the only children of their generation, and so would presumably inherit it. But there would clearly be a period when the immediate family would become increasingly poor. The establishment at Fockbury was gradually reduced, until at last they only had one horse in the stables, and one maid in the house.[29] Luckily Robert and Laurence, who had joined Alfred at school, were both scholars; but their outfits were often shabby, and Laurence grew to hate and fear Mr Millington, who humiliated him in front of his class by telling him to come to school better dressed. Laurence solved this problem, at least for a time, by getting up very early and wearing his Sunday best to school without Lucy knowing; but as Alfred started to realise that the immediate future looked uncertain, he began to suffer from silent, introspective moods which alarmed the rest of his family.

Alfred's worries, about the Wises and about his own family, destroyed the delicate growth of optimism which had been appearing during the summer of 1875. Alfred, now aged sixteen-and-a-half, began to fill the first of several notebooks with copies of poems which were all about sorrow, separation, or death. He copied from Milton and Matthew

Arnold, as well as from many of the great Romantics: Wordsworth, Byron, Shelley and Keats. But the poet from whom he copied most often was G. A. Simcox,[30] a writer of sentimental romantic verse of which this is a fair sample:

> Men only have I tried
>> And they have shallow hearts and so have I.
>> I will be away from them before I die
> And be a little child, and taste the summer tide.
> I will away; the sunny world is wide, –
> 'And desolate', her aching heart replied.

Alfred's own aching heart was soothed by only one thing: academic success. In the New Year of 1876, he passed into the sixth form, where he came under the personal tuition of the headmaster. Alfred was clever, he was good at classics, and he found his headmaster's enthusiasm infectious; as did others.

For Alfred, an important moment came when, in the summer following his seventeenth birthday, he had won a prize; and Millington presented him with a copy of *Sabrinae Corolla* ('a small garland of the Severn'). This was a volume of translations into Latin or Greek verse from English, German, and Italian, edited and contributed to by the classical scholar B. H. Kennedy. He was the Headmaster of Shrewsbury School, and all of the eighty or ninety scholars who contributed to the book were former pupils. It was the gift of *Sabrinae Corolla* which Housman later said first turned his mind to classical studies, 'and implanted in me a genuine liking for Greek and Latin'.[31]

Among the first fruits of this liking were his own Latin poems, including a translation of Dryden's 'Fairest Isle, all isles excelling'.[32]

Alfred was not only writing Latin verse, but the most informal English verse. During summer visits to Woodchester, when Mrs Wise set him to work to cover jam pots, he would often write amusing couplets on the labels;[33] and when, this year, he spent part of his Christmas holidays at Woodchester House, he turned his attention to the Visitors' Book, and wrote in it a long prophecy for the year 1877, part of which runs:[34]

> And Minnie will look in the looking-glass,
>> And make herself quite ecstatic
> With her own tip-tilted loveliness,
>> And profile perfectly Attic:
> And Ted's moustache will grow on his face
>> With much procrastination,
> And Edie will go flying off into space
>> For want of gravitation.

> And poor Miss Becker must keep up her pecker,
>     And her heart mustn't sink in her shoes: –
> And it might be wise to advertise
>     In the matrimonial News: –
> And however the winds may rage in the skies,
>     And however the seas may foam, –
> Yet still Mrs. Wise, (to no-one's surprise)
>     Will take and go over to Rome.
> And her village pastor's prophetic soul
>     Will be in the seventh heaven: –
> 'I told you so, I knew she'd go
>     in 1877'.

Alfred made no prophecies about himself, though his schooldays were drawing to a brilliant close. By the summer of 1877, he was at the head of Bromsgrove School, and the winner of prizes for English verse, freehand drawing, and French, as well as for Latin and Greek verse. A photograph taken at the time shows him looking alert, self-confident – perhaps even a little arrogant. In January he had failed to win a scholarship to Corpus Christi College, Oxford,[35] but on 15 June, a telegram arrived at Fockbury House announcing Alfred's success in winning an open scholarship to St John's College, Oxford;[36] worth £100 a year, it would be just enough for him to manage on during term-time. Kate later recalled that this was 'one of the happiest events' in her brother's life.

Edward Housman had at last been forced into selling Fockbury House, and a few weeks after the news of Alfred's scholarship, the Housmans were returning to live in Perry Hall; although the family was poor, for the next few years Alfred's own position was quite secure; and in the long term he could reasonably assume that he would inherit enough family money to be comfortably off. He seemed to have had no more ambition to be a solicitor than his father had had; nor was he making the mistake of training for a career which he despised. Instead, he was going up to Oxford to study classics. This was not a course which Alfred intended should turn him into a teacher or a don; Oxford was simply to be a part of his education as a gentleman, and a natural extension of his successful career at school.

One of Alfred's last poems as a schoolboy was a song which he felt Lady Jane Grey might have sung in captivity. it is charming but melancholy, and begins:[37]

> Breathe, my lute, beneath my fingers
>     One regretful breath
> One lament for life that lingers
>     Round the doors of death

For the frost has killed the rose
And our summer dies in snows
And our morning once for all
Gathers to the evenfall.

Alfred's childhood had not been an easy one for a sensitive boy. The absence for three years of Robert, his brother and childhood friend; the death of his mother, to whom he had been so closely attached; the curious position which he had occupied in his stepmother's household, neither boy nor adult; these had driven him into a lonely inner world of lost faith and Romantic meditation in which he longed for a heroic friend. Yet his only real intimates were two women whom he saw infrequently: Edith Wise, already at twenty-one well on her way to becoming an old maid; and Sophie Becker, who was fourteen or fifteen years his senior, and wrote to him in maternal fashion as 'My dear boy'.[38] However, Alfred had much to be proud of, and, when he left Bromsgrove for his first term at Oxford, he had everything to hope for.

# CHAPTER 3

# A Scholar at Oxford

We one by one inscribed our names in a large book, in this
wise, 'Alfredus Eduardus Housman, e Coll.Di. Joh.Bapt.Gen.
Fil.Natu max.' which is, being interpreted, 'A.E. Housman, of
the College of St. John the Baptist, eldest son of a gentleman.'
A.E.H. in a letter home

If in spite of my reason I can believe that my will is free, in spite
of my reason I can believe that God is good.
*Is Life Worth Living?* by W. H. Mallock

In October 1877 Housman went up to Oxford to read classics. But for
him as for other freshmen, the University was at first only a vague
abstraction; they belonged less to Oxford than to their individual
Colleges, each of which was a separate community with its own teaching
staff, administration, endowment and customs. In St John's College,
which was particularly hostile to change, Housman became part of the
traditional world of chapel and High Table, a masculine world in which
compulsory celibacy had only just come to an end and where, even when
the first women's colleges were opened, there was no question of Alfred
or his friends entertaining or visiting unchaperoned young women.

However, in many respects Housman and his fellow undergraduates
were well treated. Apart from a few of the scholars they came,
necessarily, from the most prosperous part of society, and they were
looked after in what was considered to be a proper manner. Not only
were they waited on at table, but the College employed three laundresses
to keep their clothes clean, and, more important, six 'bedmakers' or
personal manservants.

There were twenty-two freshmen in Alfred's year; and in the afternoon
of Saturday 13 October they were all gathered together in the rooms of
one of the College tutors, Mr Ewing, who told them how to write their
names in Latin. Then he marched them off to New College for the
ceremony of Matriculation, by whbich they were formally admitted to the

Register of the University. One by one they inscribed their names, in Latin, in a large book; and then, after paying a fee of £2 10s. 0d., they were called up by the Vice-Chancellor who gave them each a violet-bound copy of the University Statutes, and told them – in Latin – that the Statutes must be obeyed. Alfred was clearly not impressed with any great respect for the University authorities by this proceeding, for he was soon writing contemptuously to his stepmother:

> As to keeping the statutes contained in the violet cover, you may judge what a farce that is when I tell you that you are forbidden to wear any coat save a black one, or to use fire-arms, or to trundle a hoop, among other things.

Despite the slightly arrogant strain which this letter reveals, Alfred intended to work hard, and to succeed, as he had done at school.

For his degree, he had to pass two sets of major public examinations: Mods, taken after two years, was mainly concerned with translation from and into Latin and Greek; Greats involved him in a quite separate course of work, and a further two years of study. These apart, there were regular College examinations, known as 'Collections'; and Alfred was also expected to write essays, and to attend tutorials and lectures. No individual College had enough tutors in every subject, and, to begin with, Alfred had three tutorials a week at Magdalen College. His tutor, T.H. Warren – later to become President of Magdalen – had already given him a list of suggested reading, which began with:

Plautus Aulularia (Wagner) Read Introduction carefully
Martial (Paley) Say 300 epigrams

Propertius Paley Read II I III 4, 17, 18 V II

Catullus 64 Peliaco etc
          66 Omnia qui magni

Cicero de Finibus Book II at discretion if possible with Madvig,

and implored him to 'read all good introductions you can find'.[1] Warren later wrote that Housman was 'certainly to me one of the most interesting and attractive pupils I can remember. He had even then, as quite a young student, a combination of force, acumen and taste which I shall never forget.'[2] Meanwhile, in St John's, Alfred had to follow a course of study based on attending nine lectures a week; and, in this connection, T.C. Snow, the Senior Tutor, recorded that from the very beginning Housman threw himself into his work 'with the most remarkable vigour and ardour, and in mature and original ways'.[3]

Many of the freshmen were from Merchant Taylors' School, which had strong links with St John's; and so they came up to Oxford with their friendships ready-made. Alfred had no such friends – though the son of a Bromsgrove doctor, a student of twenty-five, was kind enough to call on him soon after he first arrived in Oxford, to help him to feel at home. But St John's was not unsociable, and Alfred was soon being invited to breakfast by other undergraduates. During his first term, Housman struck up a particular friendship with Alfred Pollard, another freshman and an open scholar, whose rooms were on the same staircase as his in the Canterbury Quad. As they were both scholars, both reading classics, and neither came from Merchant Taylors' or was a great games player, they were thrown together a good deal, and found that they had several interests in common. The other scholar of their year, Moses Jackson, was a scientist and an athlete, and not surprisingly, they at first had little to do with him.

Housman did not limit himself to the requirements of his degree. In College, he joined a select group who read essays on Sunday nights in the rooms of Mr Ewing; and, in the wider University, he attended lectures by Ruskin, the Slade Professor of Fine Art. Ruskin was now devoting his energies to an attack on the social injustice and squalor produced by uncontrolled capitalism. Housman found his lectures stimulating and entertaining; and, as he wrote to Lucy, he particularly enjoyed one during which Ruskin produced a picture of Turner's, framed and glassed, representing Leicester and the Abbey in the distance at sunset, over a river:

> Then he said, 'You, if you like, may go to Leicester to see what it is like now. I never shall. But I can make a pretty good guess'. Then he caught up a paintbrush. 'These stepping stones of course have been done away with, and are replaced by a be-au-ti-ful iron bridge.' Then he dashed in the iron bridge on the glass of the picture. 'The colour of the stream is supplied on one side by the indigo factory.' Forthwith one side of the stream became indigo. 'On the other side by the soap factory.' Soap dashed in. 'They mix in the middle – like curds', he said, working them together with a sort of malicious deliberation. 'This field, over which you see the sun setting behind the abbey, is now occupied in a *proper* manner.' Then there went a flame of scarlet across the picture, which developed itself into windows and roofs and red brick, and rushed up into a chimney. 'The atmosphere is supplied – thus!' A puff and cloud of smoke all over Turner's sky: and then the brush thrown down, and Ruskin confronting modern civilisation amidst a tempest of applause.

For most students, there is a sharp break between life at University, and life at home, though one soon becomes accustomed to jumping from one to the other; within a week or two of being amused by Ruskin's lecture,

Housman the bright undergraduate had returned home for a family Christmas, and resumed his place as the leader and educator of his brothers and sisters. One of the activities which he arranged for them was a short story competition, and, for his own entry, he wrote 'A Morning with the Royal Family'. In this entertaining sketch, the King, clearly modelled on Edward Housman, is an eccentric personality who manages at one stage to get a doorscraper entangled in his necktie; and – pursuing this literary game – the king's mother is not inaccurately but less kindly described as a rather stupid old lady who probably couldn't even learn how to suck eggs. The humour of the piece is mainly in its elaborate play on words. At one point in the story the poet laureate has written the following apparently unflattering lines about the Queen's entry into the ballroom:

> The drums went rattle, the guns went boom,
> Head over heels she came into the room;
> The trumpets rent the air with squeals,
> In came her majesty, head over heels.

Now the King demands to see the poet laureate: and when he does:[4]

'What do you mean', shrieked the king, 'by saying that your most gracious queen came into the room head over heels?'

'Oh, well, you know', said the poet laureate, 'if you like I can alter it, and say she came into it heels over head. It wouldn't be true; but still, if you want me to, I'll say it.'

Alfred's relationship with his brothers and sisters naturally changed a little as they became older and wanted to be more independent of someone who had been like a second father to them; but he was still on affectionate terms with them all and, soon after the start of the spring term of 1878, his fourteen-year-old sister Kate sent him a charmingly teasing letter, which ends:[5]

If you make any comments on my chronology, etymology, orthography, syntax and prosody you need never expect another letter from *me*.

    I remain your affectionate and doting
sister
Kate

NB I always could spell affectionate ritely it shows my disposition.
    Mamma hates PS's so do I this is only a NB.

During his first two terms at Oxford, as well as writing to his family, Alfred kept up a busy correspondence with the Wises of Woodchester. Sophie Becker knitted him some socks, and sent them to him; and Alfred in his turn sent them all a copy of the first number of *Ye Rounde Table*.[6] Between February and June 1878, six numbers of this short-lived undergraduate magazine appeared, to which Alfred contributed no less than thirteen pieces, mostly skits and facetious verses. Here is part of a light satire on the romantic novels of 'Ouida', which Alfred entitled 'Punch and Jouida. A Novel':[7]

> She used to live in a garden with an old woman, who was her mother. . . .
>     But one day the old woman died. When the old woman began to do this, she called Jouida, and said, 'Povera infanta mia.'
>     Then Jouida said, 'How did you learn Italian?'
>     And the old woman said, 'If I must die, I should like to die with good taste, and so I have bought this Italian grammar. I must die, because you would never do for the heroine of a novel by a talented authoress unless I did. They all do it. Adieu my child. Always run away when you see a man, and mind and bury me nicely.'

Alfred wrote under the pseudonym of 'Tristram',[8] the legendary knight of sorrowful birth who had in 1852 been the subject of a long poem by Matthew Arnold. Housman's commonplace-book was still being filled with extracts from the English romantic poetry of Keats, Shelley, Tennyson, Christina Rossetti and others,[9] but Matthew Arnold was rapidly becoming his favourite poet. *Sabrinae Corolla* had included one of Arnold's poems, and now Housman was busy in his spare time reading and learning by heart much of Arnold's work. Their contemporary at St John's, E.W. Watson, later wrote that Housman and Pollard were as one in their admiration for Matthew Arnold, and that 'Housman would challenge us to cite a line the continuation of which he could not give. We never caught him out'.[10] In the grave, melancholy beauty of Arnold's best work, Housman found perfectly expressed many of his own deepest feelings, such as his sense of loss after his mother's death, and his questioning of religious faith.

Alfred was attending some church services in the city; but he wrote about the preachers with a rather cruel humour. Thus, on Canon King of Christ Church:

> The sermon was unconscionably long . . . at the end of an hour and a quarter, he concluded with an apology to his younger brethren for having bored them, and giving as his reason that Our Lord grieved Peter, which I did not quite see the force of.

On the Dean of St Paul's: 'He is very nice to look at . . . but he is certainly tedious. I thought so last term, and now I am confirmed.' And on the Bishop of Manchester: '[he] commenced operations by blowing his nose, which is a rhetorical device he has apparently just found out, and which in the first ecstasy of novelty he uses with injudicious profusion'. No doubt their sermons were particularly tiresome for someone who had abandoned Christianity, even if he had not yet abandoned Gȯd; and for someone who was still partly searching for the inspiration which might bring him back to the church again, but who, in his inward thoughts, echoed Arnold's cry in 'Dover Beach':

> The sea of faith
> Was once, too, at the full, and round earth's shore
> Lay like the folds of a bright girdle furl'd;
> But now I only hear
> Its melancholy, long, withdrawing roar,
> Retreating to the breath
> Of the night-wind down the vast edges drear
> And naked shingles of the world.

As well as religion, politics occupied Alfred's thoughts. He had learned an interest in politics from his father, and his 'Prophecy for year 1877' had contained the lines:[11]

> We shall probably have much sharpening of swords
>  And also much festive revel
> And Dizzy may go to the House of Lords
>  And Gladstone may go to the ——!

He had also joined the Oxford Union, and so in February 1878 he was able to attend a debate about the Conservative Government's pro-Turkish policy in the aftermath of the recent Russo-Turkish war. The Conservatives won the day; but the motion was framed in anti-Conservative terms, and as soon as it had been read out, there 'ensued seven good minutes of storm and tempest, and the cheering and groaning were such that neither could roar down the other, and they ceased from pure exhaustion'. Then the first anti-Conservative speech began. It lasted for more than an hour and a quarter, but Alfred reported in a letter to his father that the speaker's remarks did not take more than twenty minutes: 'they only cropped up as islets in the oceanic demonstration of opinion'.

Two days later, Alfred took part in an anti-Russian demonstration in the Corn Exchange, where they sang 'Rule Britannia', and the popular:

We don't want to fight
But by jingo if we do
We've got the ships, we've got the men,
We've got the money too!

and they listened to the poet Alfred Austin denounce the Liberals.

Housman, who had been enjoying himself, was annoyed when the Liberal speakers were not given a fair hearing, many of them being forcibly ejected from the Hall. Alfred tried to put a stop to this, but failed, and afterwards wrote:

> the result was a rather rowdy meeting. The motion – Conservative and Turk – was of course carried with acclamation, and then the meeting fought itself out of doors and culminated in the combustion of an effigy of Mr. Gladstone just outside our college.

Despite these diversions, Alfred was working hard; and in the second week of March he sat for the Hertford – a Latin scholarship open to undergraduates in their first or second year. He did not win, but succeeded in coming 'among the first six, which is better than anyone else thought I should do, and better than I myself fancied'.

Extra money from another scholarship would have been very useful; but Housman was already becoming accustomed to leading a modest and frugal life. He was very much helped by the fact that St John's had always been an economical College, noted for simplicity of living. Alfred's scholarship was worth only £100 a year; but he was part of a community in which it was felt that a commoner might maintain himself very respectably on £120. He had to pay the College for food, drink, and so on – which was included in his 'Battels' – and for tuition, rooms, coal, and furniture; and his quarterly account with the College for 1878 shows that at the end of the year he had managed to save £12 7s. 1d. of his scholarship money to cover other expenses:

1878 Housman
    To scholarship £100

| | | | | |
|---|---|---|---|---|
| Battels | 15/ 2/ 5½ | 16/15/ 9½ | 17/15/10 | 3/10/6 |
| Tutorage | 7/ 0/ 0 | 7/ 0/ 0 | 7/ 0/ 0 | |
| Rooms | 1/11/ 6 | 1/11/ 6 | 1/11/ 6 | 1/11/6 |
| Coals | 1/ 3/ 0 | 1/ 8/ 0 | 13/ 4 | |
| Furniture | 1/ 6/ 0 | 1/ 6/ 0 | 1/ 6/ 0 | |
| | 26/ 2/11½ | 28/ 1/ 3½ | 28/ 6/ 8 | 5/ 2/0 |

£ 87/12/11

Oct 26 Balance by cheque    £ 12/ 7/ 1

£100/ 0/ 0

For the sake of comparison, in the same year his friend Pollard received a balance by cheque of £3 9s. 3½d., and the science scholar, Jackson, a cheque for £9 5s. 11½d.[12] So Housman was being as careful as possible, knowing that – whatever their expectations in the future – his family's means were at present very restricted. When sending letters from the

Oxford Union, who supplied stamps for their members for letters up to a certain weight, he would even go to the trouble of splitting a long letter in half, and addressing two separate envelopes, in order to save himself the odd ha'penny.

It was fortunate that Alfred was cautious in his spending, for the situation at home was much worse than he can have realised. Edward Housman had long ago given up trying to put his financial affairs on a sound footing; his only concern was to survive from month to month; and before long his fecklessness had led to a split with the Wises, which cost Alfred the company of his closest friends; and to a financial crisis, which cost Alfred his future share of his grandmother's fortune.

When in 1867 Perry Hall had been cleverly removed from the jurisdiction of Chancery and placed in the hands of the young Ted Wise as Trustee for Edward Housman, it was understood that Housman would be responsible for paying the interest on the new mortgage which had been negotiated. But Edward Housman was not earning enough money as a solicitor to support his family *and* to pay interest on that mortgage, or indeed on the subsidiary mortgages which he had arranged. He had always despised his job; and, since Sarah Jane's death, something in his personality had been broken, and he had become genuinely and increasingly incapable of sustained effort. The time came when, once again, he failed to make his interest payments. This put Ted Wise in an extremely awkward position, since he was legally responsible for seeing that the money was paid; and, as March 1878 wore on, a first-class row was developing between the Housmans and the Wises.

Edward Housman, already in debt to others for at least £120, and desperately concerned to put off the day of reckoning, devised a scheme which brought him a few months' respite. On 1 April he made a formal agreement with Wise, to the effect that he, Housman, really would pay all the interest then or thereafter due on the main mortgage; but he also persuaded Ted Wise to advance him a substantial sum of money. Housman secured this on 16 April by signing a contract with Wise, by which Wise was to buy Perry Hall for £400, and was to be given 'a good marketable title to Perry Hall', subject only to the main mortgage. [13]

Having received his money, Edward Housman did absolutely nothing about fulfilling his part of the bargain. By 26 October Ted Wise had felt compelled to bring a legal action against Housman in the Chancery Division of the High Court; and he was joined in his complaints by Martha Perkins and others to whom Housman owed money. [14]

Edward's situation was now hopeless, and he and his family were only rescued from complete ruin by the kindness and generosity of Edward's youngest brother, the Reverend Joseph Housman. Joseph bought Perry Hall himself, in February 1879, paid off the existing mortgages, and gave a sum of £125 to Ted Wise, as some measure of compensation for the losses which he had suffered. Then Joseph took out a mortgage on the property himself, for £1,300 at 4½ per cent interest; and he paid this interest himself, and allowed his elder brother to stay on at Perry Hall, rent free. [15]

Edward Housman still had to earn enough money to feed, clothe, and educate his family; but he had just enough regular work for that. Joseph had cleared his debts, and had made sure that, whatever else happened, the Housmans of Perry Hall would keep a roof over their heads. For the present then, they were secure; but their great expectations had been dashed, when in January, just a few weeks before Joseph came to their rescue, Edward's mother, Ann Housman, drew up a new will.

The new will and the rescue were clearly part of the same unofficial family settlement. There were some small bequests which Ann Housman merely held in Trust for her grandchildren, and which she could not prevent them from eventually receiving; but she had control over the bulk of her still considerable private fortune, and in her new will she left it to be divided equally between her children Mary, Jane and Joseph. So far as was possible, Edward and his family had been cut out. [16] When Edward learned of this, he must have realised that, without the hard work of which he was now incapable, there was nothing but comparative poverty ahead. Yet he and Lucy did not let Alfred know about the new will. It seems that they were afraid that the bad news would depress him and stop him working hard; and no doubt they began to talk within the family of how,when Alfred had his degree,he would be able to help support them.

For the moment Alfred was chiefly affected by the dispute with the Wises. When he first went to Oxford, Edith Wise and Sophie Becker were his two closest friends; when he was away from them, he missed them a great deal – indeed, in the romantic fashion of the day, it would not be too much to say that he pined for their company. When in the spring term of 1878 Mrs Wise received the first number of *Ye Rounde Table*, with some of Alfred's work in it, under the name of Tristram, she replied in approving terms, [17] and invited him to go to Woodchester to spend part of the Easter vacation there. But before Easter, his father's dealings with Edward Wise had caused an awkward situation which made Alfred feel that he could not take up the invitation. That autumn, he was still writing to his godmother, with the usual jokes: [18]

here everyone is going over to Rome like wildfire . . . the Pope's Chamberlain asks men to breakfast & leads them into a private oratory where Mass is going on; and he says 'Doesn't it look grateful, comforting?' and they say 'yes it does' . . . if you would only come & pay me a visit you might go over with great éclat and quite a string of young men at your heels.

But when he learned of the legal action between the two families, and of how badly his father had behaved, even his correspondence with the Wises came to an end. It was another eight and a half years before he felt able to visit Woodchester House again.

The great sadness which he felt at the separation from his friends helped to shake his residual belief in God, and he became one of Matthew Arnold's 'vague half-believers of our casual creeds' from his 'The Scholar-Gypsy'. The shifting and uncertain state of his mind at this time is seen clearly in the poem, 'Iona', which he wrote in 1879 as an entry for the Newdigate Prize for English verse. Matthew Arnold had won it in 1844, but Housman – who stayed up all night to write his poem, and then heard in the College chapel the next morning the prophetic words: 'We have toiled all the night and taken nothing' – was not so fortunate. Indeed, he wrote most of 'Iona' in the rather turgid style of his Bromsgrove prize poems; but it gives a most interesting picture of his views.

The image of a Golden Age of long ago was a powerful one for Alfred, who often looked back to happier days in his own past; and, for 'Iona', he took as his starting-point some lines by the Latin poet Catullus which looked back to a Golden Age when the gods had involved themselves directly with human affairs and contrasted it with his present, when the gods were no longer revered. Housman's poem similarly contrasts a past age of simple Christian faith with a present in which the search for knowledge has undermined religious belief, so that would-be pilgrims to the sacred isle of Iona – pilgrims such as Housman – can no longer find the comfortable answers which traditionally reconciled man to his lot.

In his poem Housman studies for a moment what his intellect tells him is the truth: there is no God, and therefore there is no meaning or purpose in life; the Universe is indifferent, and man is no more than a speck of sentient matter doomed to a short and futile existence in a remote corner of the cosmos. Then, like many others who have reached the same conclusion, he turns away from it, unable to live with such a low opinion of himself and his race. He prefers to say to those who long for wisdom:

> Find ye the truth, if so divine it seems,
> But we will live our lives & die in dreams.
> It doth not seem so dear a thing to us
> That ye have left our temple ruinous,

and he can even hope that his intellect has misled him:

> is it surely night?
> Or are our eyes instead made dark, that we
> Walk in a daylight that we cannot see?

At any rate, he concludes, such speculation is pointless.

Two of the central ideas in 'Iona' – that reason leads man from God, but that reason may sometimes be a bad guide – are echoed in W. H. Mallock's book *Is Life Worth Living?* which Alfred now read with great interest. Mallock pointed out that modern philosophy declared belief in God to be 'a dissolving dream of the past'; but he also argued that human happiness was intimately bound up with morality and religion. He maintained that the intellect should not always be trusted; describing free will as 'a moral necessity, though an intellectual impossibility', and went on to say that: 'If in spite of my reason I can believe that my will is free, in spite of my reason I can believe that God is good.' Mallock concluded that, if a man wanted his life to be worth living, the only anwer for him was to say: ' "I believe, although I can never comprehend".'[19]

Alfred toyed with Mallock's ideas, which were a possible way back to his mother's church for him; but with his powerful intellect, he could not base his view of life upon Mallock's anti-intellectual arguments, and already in 'Iona' it is clear that his thoughts were impelling him, more than half unwillingly, towards atheism.

In May 1879, Housman was occupied with a more immediate secular problem: classical Mods. But the examination papers, mainly a matter of translation work, presented him with few difficulties. He stayed with his friend Pollard for five or six days in London while they were waiting for their results, 'and on four successive evenings', Pollard recalled, 'we went together to see Irving and Ellen Terry in revivals of plays they had performed during the season. I think Housman was the most absorbed member of the audience.'

From London, Alfred wrote a friendly letter in doggerel verse to his sister Kate. At one point, remembering their stepmother's strictness, he imagines that Kate:

> By her bed-curtain
> . . . reads my epistle
> When she ought to be reading
> A pious missal
> Or some such proceeding
> Or saying a prayer
> (Or combing her back-hair);

and then he lapses into a curious melancholic fantasy: Kate burns his letter, and then, because his pride has been wounded, Alfred dies. After his death, Kate begins to recall his good points, and to wish that she had other letters of his; and so, from beyond the grave, Alfred calls to her:[20]

> Then come, I ask it,
> When roses bloom

And put a basket upon my tomb
And honey-suckle
And roses rare
And do not chuckle
At putting it there. . . .

But Kate preserved his letter; and when the examination results were published, Alfred found that he had no other cause for screening wounded pride. He had not won the Hertford or the Newdigate, but those failures were burnt up in the light of his new success: he had taken a First in Mods.

* * *

Many years later, Housman wrote: 'The only proper place for the average undergraduate is in his mother's womb. He is not ripe for birth';[21] and there is no doubt that it is much more difficult for an immature mind to cope with success than to come to terms with mediocrity or even failure. The fact that he was able to have a good opinion of himself had helped to preserve the sensitive young Housman from despairing when things in his life went wrong; but, to have that good opinion publicly confirmed, for a while tipped the balance too far in the other direction; Alfred's total failure in Greats two years later was due not to an emotional crisis, as has often been suggested, but to the overconfidence and indeed arrogant attitudes which were confirmed and strengthened by his success in Mods.[22] It was this overconfident attitude which led Alfred to divert his energy into work which had nothing to do with the syllabus, and to treat part of his Greats course with contempt.

During his first two years at St John's, Alfred had become increasingly interested in what was then the chief problem of classical scholarship: the restoration of those remaining works of the Greek and Latin authors of antiquity to something approaching their original state. There were many of which several versions survived, and studying these, trying to decide what the Greek or Latin author had in fact written, and making emendations to the accepted text when necessary, was a laborious but intellectually satisfying task. It demanded not only a first-class command of the ancient languages, but also an imaginative sympathy with the dead author, and a sensitive understanding of his style of writing and the vocabulary which he would have used.

When in 1878 the great classical scholar H. A. J. Munro published his *Criticisms and Emendations of Catullus*, Housman bought a copy, and even wrote letters to Munro, who very kindly took the trouble of replying to this enthusiastic undergraduate.[23] Propertius was another Latin poet for whom much needed to be done; and during the year in which he took Mods, Alfred began to think that he might do for Propertius what the

great Munro had done for Catullus, and give to the world the first edition
of his chosen author's work which would meet the requirements of
modern critical science. Before long, Housman was spending a great deal
of time working on Propertius – time which would have been more wisely
spent in studying the Greats syllabus.

Greats – apart from some translation work – 'consisted of papers on
Ancient History, Logic, and Moral and Political Philosophy, reinforced by
others on a formidable array of prose authorities – Plato and Aristotle,
Herodotus, Thucydides and Xenophon, Plutarch and Cicero, Sallust and
Tacitus'. But Housman allowed his new interest in textual criticism to
play too important a part in his work. The Rev. H. J. Bidder, one of the
College tutors, spoke later on of Housman 'as a man on whom he had
done his best to make an impression – and failed', for the reason that,
when Bidder was teaching Greek philosophy, Housman refused to
consider Plato's meaning except in so far as it was relevant to the
settlement of the text.[24]

Housman did work for Greats; but although his preparation was
perfectly adequate in most subjects, he could never bring himself to work
seriously at philosophy. Not only was he chiefly interested in the text but,
as his poem 'Iona' showed, he condemned the sort of learning which
might destroy the illusions upon which he felt that man's happiness was
based; and, in his general dislike of philosophical disputation, he was
probably influenced by Matthew Arnold, whose 'Scholar-Gypsy' had
deserted his studies in Oxford largely to escape the 'infection of our
mental strife'.

One modern critic has suggested that Housman was 'not a very intelligent man', and that 'there is no evidence that he would have done well if
he *had* tried. Philosophy was obviously alien ground to him.'[25] But
Housman's detailed annotations in a book by A. E. Taylor on Greek
philosophy (now in the Library of St John's, Oxford, see p. 18), show that
he was perfectly capable of understanding philosophical problems. The
point was, that he despised them, as he revealed in this marginal
comment: 'Plato's doctrine of Forms or Universals is useless as a way of
explaining things – it is up to Science to show what is the reality of the
world.'

If all Housman's tutors had been really first-class men, he might still
have responded to their teaching; but, through his correspondence with
Munro, and in his work on textual criticism – when he pitted himself
against the scholars who had studied the text before him – Housman was
in contact directly or indirectly with some of the best minds who had
applied themselves to classical scholarship; when he compared them
with his College tutors, and even with the University Professors, he
generally found the latter to be inferior. T. C. Snow, who had taught

1  *The Rev. Robert Housman,*
   *Alfred's great-grandfather*

2  *The Rev. Thomas Housman,*
   *Alfred's grandfather*

3 *Edward Housman as a young man, Alfred's father*

4 *Alfred with his brother Robert, being held by their mother, Sarah Jane; probably photographed on Alfred's second birthday*

5 *Clemence aged four and Kate
aged three*

6 *Basil aged two*

7 *Alfred aged seven-and-a-half with his brother Robert aged six, standing outside Perry Hall with toy rifles, photographed by their father*

8 *Sarah Jane Housman*

9 *Perry Hall, Bromsgrove*

10 *Lucy Agnes Housman, Alfred's stepmother*

11 *Fockbury House, originally called The Clock House*

12  *Sophie Becker*

13  *Alfred Housman as a young man of eighteen*

14 *St John's College, Oxford* c. *1870*

15 *St John's Torpids crew 1880, with Moses Jackson on extreme right*

Housman for Mods, was rather an idle man, even though he was very able and enjoyed teaching the brightest undergraduates in his charge. Then, when Housman began to study Greats, the story goes that he heard 'Bobby' Ewing preach a sermon in the College chapel. Ewing pronounced a Greek word ἀκριβῶς instead of ἀκρῑβῶς; and Housman immediately 'vowed that he would not try to learn anything from such an ignoramus;[26] Then there was the Rev. H. J. Bidder: Housman probably admired him as a botanist, who had created a famous rockery in the College gardens; but Bidder was a tutor of the old style, who thought more of his port than his profession.

As for Jowett, the Regius Professor of Greek, Housman attended only one of his lectures, and came away 'disgusted' by his 'disregard for the niceties of scholarship'. Jowett enjoyed lecturing on philosophy, and made no secret of the fact that he thought making emendations to classical texts was a futile pursuit. The Corpus Professor of Latin was Henry Nettleship; and Housman did sometimes speak of him in later life – but apparently 'never in terms which suggested that Housman was indebted to his teaching'. Certainly, Housman's contempt for these men reinforced the strain of intellectual arrogance which led to his downfall in Greats.

When he was not working or attending lectures, Housman continued to delight in the Oxfordshire countryside, walking on one occasion as far as Bicester. Sometimes he was alone: a neatly dressed Scholar-Gypsy, watching the hay being scythed above Godstow bridge, or wandering the skirts of Bagley Wood. But, during their first two years at St John's, Pollard joined him many times on these walks.

Then in the autumn of 1879, at the start of their third year at St John's, Housman moved to rooms in a different Quad; although Pollard still walked with him occasionally, played 'elementary lawn tennis' with him, and even visited him at Perry Hall one vacation, the two young men saw less of each other than before. It was this year which saw the beginning of Alfred Housman's friendship with Moses Jackson, a relationship so important to Alfred that when he was an old man he recalled: 'Oxford had not much effect on me, except that I there met my greatest friend.'

Despite his first name, Moses John Jackson had no Jewish blood. He was an Englishman, born at Ramsgate on 14 April 1858, and educated at the Vale School, Ramsgate, of which his father was the Principal. A brilliant scientist, Jackson went up to University College London at the age of seventeen; and two years later he won an open scholarship to St John's which he entered at the same time as Pollard and Housman. Jackson was a scientist and an athlete, and Housman was neither. Pollard tells us further that Jackson was 'often lively, but not at all witty'; so what was the basis of their friendship? Pollard writes: 'I think it was the

simplicity and singleheartedness that attracted A.'[27] Jackson was indeed
an admirably straightforward character, as well as being intelligent and
extremely good-looking; and Housman gradually fell into an agreeable
companionship with him.

Housman was by now known to the Fellows as 'a quiet and reserved
man, wholly occupied with the study of the Classics, and taking little
interest in the general affairs of the College'.[28] However, he maintained
an interest in politics. There was a General Election in the spring of 1880,
which, much to Alfred's disgust, was won by the Liberals. But Sir William
Harcourt, who had held Oxford for the Liberal party, submitted himself
for re-election on his appointment as Home Secretary. He was opposed
by A. W. Hall, a Conservative undergraduate of Exeter College; and a
lively campaign followed. The campaign was opened, as Alfred wrote to
Lucy Housman

> by the Vice-Chancellor announcing that any undergraduate who
> should take part in any political meeting would be fined £5. . . . We
> had great fun with Mr. Ewing [the Ancient History tutor whom
> Housman despised], who is one of the pro-Proctors this year; we told
> him we knew of an undergraduate who had spoken at every Conserva-
> tive meeting during the election, which wrought him up to wild
> excitement till we mentioned the name Alexander William Hall, after
> which his ardour seemed to cool.

Hall won the election — though he was soon ousted by a commission of
enquiry into corrupt practices; and on the evening of his short-lived
victory, the men in St John's were forbidden to leave College after seven:
but, as Alfred reported

> a good many got over that by leaving before seven: and we were also
> forbidden to look out of the windows or in any way attract the attention
> of the mob; however, we blew horns out of the windows with great
> profusion, and on one of the dons coming round to demand the
> offending instrument he was presented with an aged and decrepit horn
> which had no inside and would not blow: so that in the morning he
> returned it with an apology, saying that he thought he must have made
> a mistake, as he could not make it give out any sound at all.

During their fourth year at St John's, it was customary for men to live in
lodgings outside the College; and so in the autumn of 1880 Alfred
arranged with his friends Moses Jackson and Alfred Pollard that they
should take 'five rooms together in a picturesque old house in St. Giles',
nearly opposite the College, now long ago displaced by academic
buildings. It was here that Housman finally became an atheist, and wrote
the first of his mature poems.

In the troubles of the last year or two – troubles which had included his father's declining health, his family's financial embarrassment, and the quarrel with the Wise family – Alfred had done 'a good deal of praying for certain persons and for myself'. Indeed, on his twenty-first birthday in March 1880 – when by a grim and symbolic twist of fate he came of age on Good Friday – Alfred had gone to church not just once, from a sense of what was thought fitting by his family, but twice.[29]

But at last his meditations led him to abandon the church. For a man whose emotions were as intense as his intellect was strong, there could be nothing simple about religious belief or disbelief, and for the rest of his life Housman remained emotionally attached to a past in which he had believed in God; but the intellectual break with any form of religious faith was complete.

Housman had now to renounce all conscious hope for the time promised in Revelation – to give up all hope that he would one day be reunited with his mother. He knew Matthew Arnold's *Requiescat*, in which the only comfort to be derived from a woman's death is that:

> . . . for peace her soul was yearning
> And now peace laps her round.

Now he placed these thoughts in a new setting: echoes from the famous hymn 'Abide with me', in which the Christian prays that God will remain with him even when 'Earth's vain shadows flee'. So, in the first of his mature poems, 'Parta Quies', published in the Oxford magazine *Waifs and Strays* in March 1881, Housman became emotionally reconciled to the idea that he would never see his mother again; and he wrote her a moving farewell:

> Goodnight; ensured release,
> Imperishable peace,
>     Have these for yours,
> While sea abides, and land,
> And earth's foundations stand,
>     And heaven endures.
>
> When earth's foundations flee,
> Nor sky nor land nor sea
>     At all is found,
> Content you, let them burn:
> It is not your concern;
>     Sleep on, sleep sound.          (*MP* 48)

Eight months later, *Waifs and Strays* published another poem by Housman. In 'New Year's Eve', with its nightmarish vision of a church filled with 'Ranks of dreadful faces/Flaming, transfigured in flame' he concentrated in a more dramatic way upon his break with religion.

In the religious doubts which had led to his final loss of faith, Housman had been 'a spectator of all time and all existence'; and, as he later wrote, 'the contemplation of that repulsive scene is fatal to accurate learning'. He spent valuable time in this contemplation, still refused to work at philosophy, and still used up precious working hours in studying the text of Propertius. But in no sense was he deliberately trying to fail in Greats: rather, he was greatly overconfident.

Housman never missed a lecture although he did not have any great respect for some of his lecturers; nor did he fail to write his weekly essays[30] – remembered by Pollard as very diverting – but he had seriously misjudged the amount of work which would be necessary in philosophy if he was to get his degree. Such a misjudgment was not so difficult in the atmosphere of the day as described by Pollard, who wrote: 'We went up to Oxford in a child-like belief that if we were good we should get a prize, and even if we weren't good, it would help.'[31]

After the Lent or summer Collections of 1880, the Senior Tutor, realising perhaps that Housman was in some danger, made a harmless remark of his 'the occasion for informing him before us all that he was *not* a genius'; but where a private talk might have had some effect, this public snubbing, not surprisingly, achieved nothing – except to make Housman still more hostile and unreceptive.

No doubt Alfred's attitude would have been very different had Edward and Lucy taken him fully into their confidence and had he realised that his future, and in some ways theirs, depended entirely on his degree. But Edward, who was now drinking more heavily than ever, did not relish the thought of explaining to his clever son just what a mess he had made of the family finances; while Lucy still hoped that, if she could keep Alfred from worrying, he would go on to get a good degree, and a well-paid job which would bring in badly needed money. They both did their best to keep up appearances, not only to local people in Bromsgrove, but also to Alfred himself. Indeed, one summer vacation, Alfred brought his friend Pollard home with him; and the story goes that they were both regaled with good food and good wine.[32] So Alfred did not fully realise the low ebb to which the family fortunes had sunk; nor, in his ignorance of Ann Housman's altered will, did he understand that the future would bring no answering flood-tide.

There was another more important reason why Alfred was living too much in the present: he had formed a delightful new friendship. The warmth which Alfred had been able to show Edith Wise and Miss Becker was now poured into his relationship with Moses Jackson. In this handsome and athletic figure he had at last found one of the 'friends to die for' (*LP* 32). In the evenings, Housman and Jackson and Pollard would all dine in Hall at St John's and then, after wandering back through the front Quad and out under the entrance Tower, they would cross St Giles' to their lodgings. Next, recalls Pollard,

> [we] . . . had our coffee (neither Housman nor Jackson smoked), I mostly retired to work by myself in the lower sitting room, leaving the other two on the first floor. Jackson's was an absolutely safe first in science in the schools, and [he] had no need to read much in the evening.

There is nothing remarkably suggestive about this picture of Housman and Jackson talking comfortably in the evenings. If theirs was a highly-charged friendship, this was not exceptional. As one writer put it:[33]

> In the old days a man's memories of his Oxford years had a sensual lilt to them: the emotional impact of the city itself was warm and vivid and often the friendships formed within the College were highly-charged – if not overtly homosexual, certainly shot through with rapturous undertones in an age torn between puritanism and the libidinous liberties of classical Greece.

However, there were special circumstances which helped to make this friendship a particularly important one for Alfred Housman.

Alfred had been brought up by a weak father and a powerful mother, and it is reasonable to suppose that his unusually strong relationship with his mother had led to an early development of the more feminine aspects of his psychological make-up – a development which may indeed be largely responsible for the sensitivity of his poetry and the imaginative insight of his textual scholarship. Later, when he began to mature and was given guidance on sexual matters by his father, guidance came, according to his sister Kate, 'in a form calculated to make sex in himself and in women repulsive'.[34] Other incidents in his teens, including the shock of circumcision, must have reinforced his attitude to sex; and his natural impulses had been channelled first into idealistic friendships with Edith Wise and Sophie Becker, and then – when their company was denied him – into a similarly close and idealistic friendship with a handsome, single-hearted companion, Moses Jackson. But at this time, although Housman admired and even adored his friend, he was probably unaware that he had any specifically homosexual feelings for him. Such an awareness would certainly have been disturbing in a society which condemned homosexuality so strongly. But, although gloomy pictures by Dürer adorned his walls – *Melancholia*, and *Knight, Death, and the Devil* – Housman was 'quietly happy', and Pollard remembers how, when he was in the mood, Housman would tell small audiences 'humorous stories of his own making'.

Only seven weeks before Finals, Alfred was writing this light-hearted letter to Kate, about the recent Census:

'Sir', said the census-taker, 'the first thing is to write your name in full'. I wrote down 'Albert Matilda Hopkins' & waited for further instructions. 'We will now have' proceeded he, 'your relation to the head of the house'. 'My relations with the President', replies I, 'are, I regret to say, rather strained. He makes me go to Chapel every day now I am in college, & I do not like it. No', I continued, taking out my handkerchief & howling, 'I can't abear it. I think I had better fill up that column with "down-trodden slave".' I did so.

'How old are you?' said he.

'303' responded I.

'You bear your great age well', he observed.

'I bear your great impudence well', I retorted.

'What restrains me, I wonder, from drawing my revolver from my breast-pocket & blowing out your apology for a brain? What restrains me?'

He trembled & was silent: yet this was not a difficult question to answer. What restrained me was the fact that there was no revolver in my breast-pocket.

Then on 21 May, only six days before the start of his Final Examinations, Alfred was warned by Lucy Housman that his father had suffered a stroke and was desperately ill.[35] No doubt this had some effect on the quality of the papers which he wrote; but the principal reason for Alfred's disastrous performance was that he had not done enough work on the syllabus. In some of the essays which he had written for his tutors on philosophical subjects, he had disguised his lack of knowledge by writing in a very amusing manner; but this was not enough to satisfy his examiners.

During some of the examinations, Housman had very little of substance to offer; once, when Pollard saw him go up for a second supply of paper, and 'congratulated him on having so much to say . . . he replied a little gruffly that he was tired of sitting still'.[36] One of the College lecturers, Canon Nance, later recalled that, on the philosophical side, 'his performance had been so ludicrously bad as to show that he had not made any effort, and to give the examiners the impression that he was treating that part of the business with contempt'.[37] The examiners – Bywater, Grose, Macan, Richards, and Bidder[38] – had only one course of action left open to them; when Alfred returned to Perry Hall at the end of the summer term it was with the news that his friend Jackson had a First in Science; that Pollard had a First in Greats; but that he himself was a total failure. Housman was bitterly humiliated by his failure; nor was there any consolation at home, where his stepmother chose this, the worst of all moments, to explain to him the true state of family affairs. Not only was his father ill, and their present financial discomfort acute, but there would be no large inheritance to look forward to when his grandmother died; and it was made clear to Alfred how much store had been set by what had seemed his own certain success. Shaken by this double disappointment, he became more silent and withdrawn, but his spirit was not broken. The academic world had rejected him, but he would not accept its verdict as final: 'Pride is one of the seven deadly sins; but it is an efficient substitute for all the cardinal virtues',[39] and Housman gradually became determined that, in time, the academic world should not only welcome him back, but should learn to respect him – as a great scholar.

# CHAPTER 4

# The Years of Poverty,
## 1881–92

For wel I woot my servyce is in vayn;
My gerdoun is but brestyng of myn herte
Chaucer, *The Franklin's Tale*, ll. 264–5

est aliquid quo tendis, et in quod derigis arcum?
Have you any goal in life? Is there any target at which you aim?
Persius, *Satire III*, l. 60

When Alfred first arrived home, there was not much time to worry about the distant future. Edward Housman remained dangerously ill until the end of July;[1] and on the thread of his life hung the income from some official work, which had just been enough to maintain his family for the last few years. Without that money, they would be not merely poor but ruined; Basil, Laurence, and Herbert would have to be withdrawn from Bromsgrove School, and Alfred might have to abandon his plans for returning to Oxford, where he hoped to prepare for a Pass degree which could still give him something to show for his years as an undergraduate.

At this extremely worrying time, Herbert Millington did his best for the Housmans. He had already visited Lucy to assure her that, if Edward died, he would see that the boys' education did not suffer.[2] Now he generously offered some part-time teaching to Alfred. This consisted only of taking the sixth form from time to time in Millington's absence, but Alfred accepted the job gratefully, and used it to earn a little money at the times during the next year when he was at home. Millington later described Alfred as 'a thorough and sympathetic teacher, warmly interested in his work and his pupils';[3] and it must have done Alfred good to feel that someone still had confidence in him, and that he had something positive to do while he tried to make plans for the future.

His failure in Greats had immediately lost Alfred the small allowance which a relative had been paying him since his success in Mods; and then on 18 October – although his scholarship at St John's still had a year to run – the President, James Bellamy, signed an order that 'Mr. Housman's . . .

Scholarship be sequestrated until he has passed all the Examinations required for taking the B.A. degree'.[4] The scholarship was not actually stopped until the beginning of 1882; and so Housman was able to go up to Oxford for the Michaelmas term. He attended the lecture on 'Aristotle's Ethics for Passmen' given by Canon Nance, who had taught him before his success in Mods, and who now felt very sorry seeing Housman, 'with his great Classical powers . . . having to prepare for a Pass Degree'.[5]

Alfred came home again on 13 December. He had left many of his belongings behind in his rooms at Oxford, perhaps still hoping that somehow it would be possible for him to stay on and continue his studies. But his father, who had now made a good recovery, made it clear to him that there would be no money available, and on 14 December Alfred 'returned to Oxford to fetch his things'.[6]

On Christmas Day 1881, Edward Housman walked up Adams' Hill to the early service at Bromsgrove Church, accompanied by his six eldest children,[7] the outward picture of a well-established Victorian paterfamilias; but he had failed to provide adequately for his family, and, unable to face his own shortcomings, Edward gradually forfeited the respect and admiration – though not the affection – of everyone in the house but himself.[8] He took things more easily than others could; and later it seemed to Laurence that – while Lucy struggled to make ends meet, and Clem worked into the early hours on complicated tax calculations – Edward Housman preferred not to know the efforts which others were making on his behalf.

Edward certainly did busy himself in some ways, but he had always had quaint ideas – in the summer after Sarah Jane's death, when there was a blazing July, he had actually persuaded the local fire-brigade to come along to cool down Perry Hall by spraying water on its roof![9] And now, instead of attempting to work at his job, he tried all sorts of unlikely ways of making money: growing camellias and pineapples; cultivating grapes which he then tried to preserve in bottles of water hung on a special frame, hoping that he could keep them until they were out of season, and could be sold for a huge profit; and once he had even bought a property in Wales, mistakenly thinking that he would find gold there![10]

So Alfred had to decide what to do to earn his own living. He had learned from his friend Moses Jackson that he intended to apply for a post in the Civil Service; and, for want of a better idea, Alfred decided that he would follow Jackson's lead. He then settled down for several months of hard work at home, preparing not only for his Pass degree, but also for the Civil Service examinations which would take place in London in July.

Meanwhile, Alfred was seeing more of his brothers and sisters than he had done for some time; but he did not draw closer to them. Certainly, he can have had little in common with Robert by this time. The latter's interests were scientific rather than artistic, and, at the age of twenty-one, he was still living at home – perhaps through a recurrence of poor health, perhaps because there was no money to send him to University – and he seems to have been unable to contribute anything to the household.

Clemence was nineteen, and had inherited her mother's good brain: even Millington – in general opposed to women receiving higher education – had said that 'he wished he had her in his sixth form'. Clem was busily occupied as her father's unofficial head-clerk; the main brunt of his clerical work had already fallen on her shoulders, and for two or three years she was to be 'the "expert" who worked out all the Income Tax calculations for half the County of Worcestershire'. But, although clever, the cast of her mind was too intensely religious for Alfred to confide in her.

Kate, aged eighteen, was also living at home. She had always liked and admired Alfred, but now found him, to her dismay, 'a stricken and a petrified brother', who from the time of his failure in Greats 'was withdrawn from all of us behind a barrier of reserve which he set up as though to shield himself from either pity or blame'. He met no word of reproach at home, 'but,' she commented, 'his own self-reproach was deep and lasting'.[11]

While Alfred had little to say to Kate, he may have had more time for his favourite brother Basil, a scholar with a string of prizes in French, geography, history and theology to his credit. During the time when Millington employed Alfred, Basil became head-boy of Bromsgrove School. He was in the classical sixth, and was actually taught by his elder brother, who later wrote: 'When Basil left school he had a sounder knowledge of Greek and Latin than I had at the same age, only he had no turn for composition.'[12]

Laurence, aged sixteen, was in the fifth form, with prizes for French, drawing, and recitation.[13] He had a good speaking voice, enjoyed acting in school plays, and went whenever he could to watch performances by travelling companies. Laurence's closest friend in the family was still Clem, to whom he would read his poems; but at this time he was also becoming very attached to his stepmother. Lucy, though sometimes troubled by his fondness for acting, called Laurence her comfort, knitted socks for him, and generally spoiled him; for his part he enjoyed the special attention which she gave him, and learned to admire her for her strength in the face of all the family troubles. 'When financial affliction fell on us', he wrote later, 'she rose to it heroically.'[14] For Laurence, Alfred was a slightly remote but very important figure, whose good opinion was highly valued. On one occasion Laurence had translated one of Ovid's odes, and was reading it to Clem. Alfred was sitting in a corner of the room, apparently deep in study; but when the poem was finished, and

Alfred commented with the single word: 'Excellent!', Laurence was so impressed that he remembered the poem for the rest of his life.

The youngest of the family, Herbert, was in the third form on the classical side. Though he was a scholar like his brothers, in that brilliant family his light shone rather more dimly than theirs. He was Kate's favourite,[15] and probably viewed Alfred with feelings similar to hers.

Perry Hall was no longer a comfortable place to live or work during the early months of 1881; in most of its rooms the family felt the authentic chill of poverty. But they could still afford to keep a fire going in the dining-room, and this was

> the room in which a good deal of the household activities went on, with constant comings and goings of various members of the family, and sometimes with conversation added. . . . Into this room, as soon as breakfast had been cleared, Alfred would bring his books, and sitting at the table would study for the whole morning, oblivious apparently to what went on around him.

Robert had also been thinking seriously about his future; and on 21 April he began at Mason's College, Birmingham – presumably with a scholar-ship – as one of its first students in engineering.[16]

Then, in June, came news which underlined the poverty of the Housmans of Perry Hall as compared with the rest of the family: Ann Housman died at Lyme Regis on 6 June, leaving not a penny of her still considerable fortune to Edward. Ann's body was brought to Catshill churchyard, where, after a funeral service attended by the son and grandchildren whom she had cut out of her will, she was buried along-side the Rev. Thomas Housman, not far from the grave of Edward's first wife Sarah Jane.[17] Subsequently there was another bitter moment for Edward: a sale at the Golden Cross Hotel in Bromsgrove of lands in the area which had belonged to his mother. These included fields and farms near the Clock House, Fockbury – a sale which realised a total of more than £5,000, none of which reached Edward's pockets.[18] There was only one consolation which – though comparatively small – was, in their reduced circumstances very important. On Ann's death, a sum of £200 each passed to the children through the bequest of an uncle.[19] Alfred never touched his share of this money, but generously gave it to his father.

At the time of his grandmother's death in June 1882, Alfred was in Oxford, retaking his degree examinations. He failed in one subject, political economy; but was judged worthy of a Pass degree, and on 24 June the President of St John's ordered that the third quarter of his scholarship money, £25, should be credited to his College account. Later in the year, after various fees and expenses had been deducted, Alfred was sent a cheque for the balance of £3 19s. 10d. – at a time when his friends Pollard and Jackson, having forfeited none of their scholarship money for the year, both received cheques of more than £60.[20] But Alfred does not seem to have been bitter about this. Just as he recognised that the examiners had been right to plough him in Greats, so he recognised that the President had acted justly towards him. Indeed, having accepted the punishment, Housman was already beginning to adopt the system of thought which lay behind it, and to feel that the setting and maintenance of high standards was something intrinsically important. He certainly wished to remain a member of St John's, and in the Register of 1881, alongside his final account, is a note explaining that Mr Housman 'wishes to keep name on books after expiry of scholarship'.

The Civil Service examinations were in July; Alfred passed them, and was presently offered a post in Dublin. Despite the fact that he was a burden at home – where he was still earning nothing except for occasional payments for taking the sixth form in Millington's absence – he refused the job. Lucy was upset by this, and insisted that he accept the next thing that was offered.[21]

Meanwhile, the summer term at Bromsgrove came to an end. Laurence had won another prize, and Basil three more – including the scripture prize. Lucy had promised that if Basil won this, he would not have to attend her week-day Bible readings at home any more; and she noted rather sadly in her diary: 'Our last reading in the Bible after 9 years. For the future Herbert only.'[22] Laurence and Basil now both left Bromsgrove School. Laurence, whose talents seemed to be more artistic than academic, began attending a local art school, where he was joined by his sister Clemence. Basil was thinking of becoming a doctor, and to make sure that this was really what he wanted to do, he spent several months apprenticed to a local GP. Then he tried for a scholarship at Cambridge – and won it, only to be told that the award would not be given to him, but to another candidate who was 'supposed to be more needy'! However, Basil soon won another scholarship, this time to Queen's College, Birmingham, and this one he was allowed to keep.

Alfred, still waiting to hear of another possible job in the Civil Service, passed the time by doing some of the academic work for which he felt that he was most suited. It was in fact during this year that he published his first classical paper, about some of the poems of Horace, in the *Journal of Philology*. This paper, 'Horatiana', was well received, and was later described by one of Housman's admirers as

an astonishing performance for a young man of twenty-three.
. . . The penetrating analysis of context, the familiarity with the way a poet talks, and a scribe copies, are all there – even the propensity

of scribes to shuffle the order of letters, of which much was to be heard thereafter – and there is at least a foretaste of his future incisiveness of style.

But then came news of another vacancy in the Civil Service – and for the next six years Housman published nothing except for a brief note on Ovid's 'Ibis'.

By what must have seemed great good fortune, the vacancy was for a job in the Patent Office in London, where his friend Moses Jackson had already been appointed to a well-paid position as Examiner of Electrical Specifications. Alfred applied at once; and towards the end of November heard that he had been accepted.[23] He was in a much less well-paid section than Moses, with a starting salary which only matched his Oxford scholarship of £100 a year, and gave no prospect of increase for three years. With this he would clearly be able to contribute nothing to his family: but at least he would no longer be a financial burden upon them. He had learned to live a frugal life at Oxford, and although it would be impossible for him to dress well, or to entertain friends, he would just be able to exist on his salary if he was very careful. Alfred did not delay at home any longer than was necessary, and by 4 December was established at lodgings in 15 North Place, Bayswater.

\* \* \*

The new town of Bayswater stood on an area of running streams and gravelly soil, noted for its springs, reservoirs, and conduits. The streets, squares, and terraces of the town had been built as recently as the 1840s, in the district which extended from the gravel pits to the north-west corner of Hyde Park.[24] Open countryside was not far away; nor was it a long journey from Bayswater to the Patent Office where Housman worked. Regular trains were already running on the southern part of what is now the Circle Line of the London Underground. From the station at Bayswater it took Housman fifteen minutes to reach the Temple Station in central London, and from there it was only a ten-minute walk up Arundel Street, across Fleet Street and up Chancery Lane to Southampton Buildings and the Patent Office.[25]

The south side of the Office bordered Quality Court, and it was at 4 Quality Court that the Trade Marks Registry had been established in 1876.[26] Here in a rabbit warren of a building, Housman's job was mainly investigating the claims of new marks as compared with those already registered: a time-consuming but intellectually undemanding task.[27] He later said that his job had been in 'the gutter',[28] and it did bring him into close contact with the market-place, and with the world – to him a quite alien one – of modern business. He dealt with applications relating not only to such conventional items as tea, tobacco, soap, wine and seeds, but

– to take two examples from the month in which he joined – relating also to such things as 'Clutterbuck's Chemical Closet Cleaner', or 'Dr. Scott's Electric Corset – A great boon to delicate ladies!'

Housman later liked to pretend that he did 'as little as possible' at the Patent Office; in fact he was efficient and conscientious. And for at least five years, from 1884 to 1889, everyone in his department was hard worked, largely as the result of a new Act of Parliament, which provided for the registration of the fancy words which were used in many trades.

The official letters which Housman wrote were always 'beautifully expressed quite surpassing those of his fellows: and I fear', wrote his superior, Ralph Griffin, 'that I used him too much as a scribe in consequence'.[29] He was recognised as a man of great ability – and indeed, for a short time he was to become Private Secretary to the Comptroller of the Patent Office. His letters continued to be excellent; but his outspoken criticisms, and his impatience of alteration to his drafts, were not appreciated by the Comptroller, who returned Housman to the Trade Marks Department. Here Housman remained, registering new trade marks, examining applications, writing letters – and deriving some amusement from his work on at least one occasion, when an elaborate new Index of Trade Marks was being compiled. 'It goes', he commented, 'on very remarkable principles which I do not quite understand. Under the head of "Biblical subjects" is included an old monk drinking out of a tankard; and the Virgin Mary and St. John the Baptist are put under "Mythical Figures".'

Generally speaking, the routine of Housman's life at the Patent Office was very orderly; but politics did intrude once, in the winter of 1884–5, when Irish terrorists campaigning for independence organised a series of explosions in London, and in January 1885 tried to blow up the House of Commons and the Tower of London. In June, Alfred wrote an amusing letter to his stepmother jokingly describing the commotion caused in his office after a local bomb scare, and claiming that his own room was considered the most likely setting for a further explosion.

Alfred was still living in Bayswater; but he had only stayed at his lodgings in North Place for a few months before moving, in early 1883, to another part of the district. This was because Moses Jackson was already living in London, and so was his brother Adalbert, a classics student at University College London. It had seemed a good idea for the three young men to find a set of rooms together. The cost would not be greater than what they were already paying; and they would have the advantage of pleasant company and probably a higher degree of comfort. So they all moved to lodgings in a narrow, porticoed house, four storeys high, at 82 Talbot Road, Bayswater.

For nearly three years, Housman lived here with the Jackson brothers.

He grew to like Adalbert, a good-looking man with a taste for literature. Alfred also resumed the close and delightful companionship with Moses which he had enjoyed so much in happier days at Oxford. At week-ends, the three friends often went out together for long walks through the nearby countryside; and, in the evenings, Alfred and Moses talked again, as they had done in their rooms overlooking St Giles'. Indeed, outside office hours Alfred seemed to wish to imagine that those earlier times had never been interrupted, and to turn away from reminders of the truth: even to shunning the friendship of his one-time companion Alfred Pollard. Pollard joined the Department of Printed Books at the British Museum in 1883, and for a while saw something of Housman and the Jacksons; but he was not made very welcome, and in the end, he writes: 'I got it into my head that the sight of me reminded Housman of his troubles and was unwilling to thrust myself on him more than he might welcome.'

Alfred had not forgotten his academic ambitions, and his proud wish to prove that, despite his Greats failure, he was a first-class scholar. So he began to go to the British Museum in the evenings, to work on his edition of the poet Propertius; but, all too often, the lure of Moses Jackson's company was stronger than Alfred's ambition, and he allowed his work to suffer. A poem written in the 1880s shows his keen awareness of this – and also his inability to do anything about it:

> Days lost, I know not how,
> I shall retrieve them now;
> Now I shall keep the vow
> 　I never kept before . . .
>
> How hopeless under ground
> Falls the remorseful day.　　　　　　　　　(MP 16)

As the months passed, Housman was less and less able to concentrate upon his classical studies. His affection for Moses Jackson was deepening into love, and his attention was more and more centred upon the world which he shared with the Jackson brothers, a world to which even his own family were denied access. Indeed, from this time onwards, Housman began to keep his friendships in separate compartments, so that one group would hardly know that another existed.[30]

Alfred wrote to his family occasionally, but told them nothing of importance. 'After he left home', wrote Kate, 'he was very much of a sealed book to us; and we should hardly have been surprised to find that he led some queer double life.'[31] Even when in the summer of 1884 two of them came to live in London, they saw little of him, and Alfred did not mention their presence in the city to his two friends.

It had been decided that Laurence should use his £200 inheritance to go to London to pursue his artistic career; and Clem was sent with him, 'released from the Victorian bonds of home', Laurence recalled, 'for the sole reason that it was considered too risky for me to go alone without someone of more stable character to look after me'. Always a dutiful brother, Alfred met them at Paddington, and took them to lodgings at a friend's house, where they spent their first fortnight. But as they parted, Alfred, anxious to have no intrusion into his private life, made a point of saying: 'I don't want you to come and see me at my lodgings: I shall be out or too busy.'[32]

Clem and Laurence soon moved to rooms in Kennington, where Alfred dutifully visited them whenever he was invited to do so – but they were never asked to his rooms in return.[33] They had chosen Kennington because they could live near an Arts and Crafts centre where Clem could study wood-engraving, and they also joined the Miller's Lane Art School in South Lambeth.

It was about a year later, in 1885, that Clem and Laurence met Moses Jackson for the first time, when they paid a visit one Sunday to Alfred Pollard. Pollard introduced Jackson to them; and Jackson expressed surprise at meeting them, since he had never heard that Alfred Housman had a brother and a sister living in London. Afterwards, still feeling rather puzzled, he wrote to Edward Housman, and mentioned the incident, perhaps to find out if there was some family quarrel of which he was unaware and which he might help to resolve. Edward at once wrote to ask Jackson 'whether he thought Alfred was living an irregular life'; but Jackson replied, 'that he was sure he was *not*'.[34] He was able to be so positive because he lived in very close contact with Alfred; but he may well have had no idea of the deep emotions which he had aroused in his friend.

Alfred's family, somewhat reassured by Jackson's letter, had to attribute Alfred's self-imposed seclusion to the fact that he was still suffering from the shock of his failure in Greats; and for his twenty-sixth birthday, in March 1885, he received a postcard from Clem and Laurence with a drawing representing the Cherubim and Seraphim continually crying; his father wrote to him as well; and from his stepmother he received some violets, and a long comforting letter. Alfred was not too withdrawn from his family to reply that Lucy's letter was 'quite the best epistle I have ever seen, with the possible exception of the second of the apostle Paul to the Corinthians'. Alfred also mentioned that he had heard that Basil was coming to town, and hoped that he 'will not be too much occupied to go to a theatre with me some evening'. In the same letter, he wrote amusingly about the Oxford and Cambridge Boat Race. Oxford had won by a length and a quarter; but he had noticed that there were fewer people than usual, and little wearing of colours:

Palm branches seemed to be the commonest decoration among the lower orders. The blue which they wore was a very artful shade, which could be made out to be either Oxford or Cambridge with equal plausibility, whichever might happen to win.

Edward Housman may have been reassured by his exchange of letters with Moses Jackson that all was reasonably well with his eldest son; but Jackson himself began to look with fresh eyes at his friendship with Alfred, perhaps cooling towards him a little as he tried to understand why Alfred should have found it necessary to exclude Clemence and Laurence from the household at Bayswater.

But then, in the autumn of 1885, something went badly wrong between Alfred and Moses. No doubt it was true, as Laurence Housman later wrote, that the emotional element in Alfred's friendship for Moses had been Alfred's alone, and at last this became clear to him. Suddenly, and without any warning, wrote Laurence,[35]

my brother, after something which must have been of the nature of a quarrel, disappeared for a week; and an anxious letter from Jackson came to my father to say that he did not know what had become of him. Whether the worst was feared I do not know.

What Alfred did or felt during his absence remains something of a mystery, but William Blake once wrote: 'If any could desire what he is incapable of possessing, despair must be his eternal lot',[36] and no doubt there was despair in Alfred's heart – and even thoughts of suicide, given a place in his thinking by Matthew Arnold's poem 'Empedocles on Etna', in which the disillusioned hero commits suicide, and which Housman had in Oxford days praised as containing 'all the law and the prophets'. Later, Alfred wrote some verses referring to this unhappy time:

> The world goes none the lamer,
>   For ought that I can see,
> Because this cursed trouble
>   Has struck my days and me. . . .
>
> Oh worse remains for others
>   And worse to fear had I
> Than here at four-and-twenty
>   To lay me down and die.                    (*MP* 21)

(He was in fact twenty-six, but the age had been changed at least once in draft for the sake of the sound.)

Whatever the pain of his realisation that his feelings for Moses Jackson would never be reciprocated, he decided to continue, sustained certainly by pride. 'Mother, you bore a Man',[37] one of his unfinished poems began; and manful he would be. So, after a week's absence, he returned to Talbot Road.

He only remained there for a short time. Knowing that there could be no resumption of the old way of life, in that closed delightful world which he had shared with the Jackson brothers for nearly two years, he was soon looking for lodgings in another part of Bayswater. When he moved out to 39 Northumberland Place in the late autumn of 1885, he took with him a few mementoes of the household which he was leaving; a card which had once invited Adalbert to a meeting of the West London Debating Society, and another which had asked Moses to play against Swindon Rangers for the Ealing Rugby Club: both of these Housman treasured for more than fifty years.[38]

Alfred and Moses still saw each other often, and they remained friends: but with a difference. Alfred still loved Moses; but Moses kept him at a greater emotional distance, treating him with kindness and consideration, but making it clear that their relationship would not advance in the direction which Alfred had hoped for.

Rejected by Moses, Alfred was forced not only to learn something more of the bitterness of love, but also to recognise and come to terms with the fact that he was homosexual. This was a painful process, for although he had lost his faith he still clung to the moral teachings of the church, and these told him that homosexuality was sinful. Oppressed by the feeling that his character was permanently flawed, he longed for the very spiritual consolation which he knew that his leanings denied him, and among the poetry which he wrote into his notebook during the next few years there is a single, symbolic line:

> Bow hither out of heaven and see and save.          (*MP* 1)

And the next lines in his notebook, in the form of an epitaph for himself, clearly state a belief that only in death will he find peace and wholeness again:

> I never sigh, nor flush, nor knit the brow,
> Nor grieve to think how ill God made me, now.
> Here, with one balm for many fevers found,
> Whole of an ancient evil, I sleep sound.          (*AP* 12)

In another poem, written not long after this, Housman wrote that he had given away not only his heart, but his soul: isolated and alone, there could be no salvation for him until the Day of Judgment:

> There pass the careless people
> That call their souls their own:
> Here by the road I loiter,
> How idle and alone.
>
> Ah, past the plunge of plummet,
> In seas I cannot sound,
> My heart and soul and senses,
> World without end, are drowned.
>
> His folly has not fellow
> Beneath the blue of day
> That gives to man or woman
> His heart and soul away.

and he concludes:

> Sea-deep, till doomsday morning,
> Lie lost my heart and soul.   (*ASL* 14) (*A Shropshire Lad*)

Alfred must have felt that belief in God meant admitting that he was damned. His own recourse was to a pride which allowed him to deny God – and so deny damnation – and he soon passed into a more absolute and rigorously maintained atheism in which, if he believed that there was any guiding or controlling influence at work in the Universe, he believed that it was strictly impersonal. Lacking anything very positive to live for, he badly needed to construct or adopt a solid philosophy which would give him some purpose for continuing to exist.

Housman slowly acquired such a philosophy. It underwent some change and development, but its basis was always to be a strange blending of the sentiments of the preacher in Ecclesiastes with some aristocratic ideas of his own. The preacher, describing worldly existence, wrote: 'all is vanity and vexation of the spirit' (Eccl. 1:14); but he also suggested that life was not always as bad as it might be, and that man should not be afraid to enjoy whatever he could. The preacher wrote another sentence which was now perfectly suited to Housman's temperament. 'Whatever thy hand findeth to do, do it with thy might; for there is no work, nor device, nor knowledge, nor wisdom, in the grave, whither thou goest' (Eccl. 9:10). Alfred had for some time been arrogant in his view of life and his fellows; after his failure in Greats he had a particular need to excel, and came to feel that the setting and maintenance of high standards could in itself provide a satisfactory purpose for existence. If there was no God, then to excel was at least to hurl back defiance at an unfriendly Universe, and to impose one's own order and meaning upon it.

In fact, having moved away from the Jacksons, Housman immediately began to rechannel his energies, working hard at his planned edition of Propertius, covering new ground, and also drawing together the work which he had done at various times over the last five years. By 11 December he had completed work on the text and apparatus criticus, and wrote to the publishers, Macmillan and Company:

Gentlemen,
     I propose that you should, if you think fit, publish my recension of the text of Propertius. . . . The collection and arrangement of materials for the commentary will naturally demand further time and labour; and I therefore judge it best that the text with its apparatus criticus should be issued separately, especially as I annually find not a few of my corrections anticipated by German scholars in philological journals.

But much to Housman's disappointment Macmillan were not prepared to gamble on an unknown scholar; and it was some months before Alfred resumed his serious classical studies with much enthusiasm.

In the meantime, in 1886, he changed lodgings again, moving right away from Bayswater to the village of Highgate. In Housman's day, the village was described as romantic rather than picturesque, with its main street, although so near to London, having about it 'that appearance of quietude and sleepiness which one is accustomed to meet with in villages miles away from the busy metropolis'.[39] Alfred moved into 17 North Road, which his landlady, Mrs Hunter, called 'Byron Cottage'. It was a small, three-storeyed Georgian house, and Housman was the sole lodger. The best rooms were on the ground floor, but these were used by Mrs Hunter, and Alfred had rooms on the floor above.[40] Clemence Housman considered that this arrangement must have suited her brother very well. Not only would it have been cheaper: and although his salary had been increased in 1885 from £100 to £137 10s. 0d. per annum he was still a poor man; but also the bathroom and lavatory were on the first floor, and, as Clem said: 'He would not have cared to go upstairs, from down, for either. . . . He was exceedingly bashful about being seen in dishabille.'[41] From his sitting-room, Alfred could look out over a patch of garden towards the grounds and buildings of Highgate School; while Highgate Wood and Hampstead Heath were both within easy walking distance.

     Moses and Adalbert Jackson also moved away from Bayswater in 1886, when Moses found rooms in Bloomfield Street more convenient for his work at the Patent Office. Alfred continued to adore Moses, and to see him as often as he could; and he also kept up a warm friendship with Adalbert, who had since graduated, and was now teaching at a preparatory school for boys.

The following year, there were two alliances which touched Housman. One of them he knew about: his Oxford friend Alfred Pollard made what was later described as 'a venturesome but happy marriage'.[42] The other alliance concerned Housman much more closely, but was kept secret from him: Moses Jackson had fallen in love with a young widow, Mrs Rosa Chambers. Moses, who had himself found time to pursue his academic career, and was now a Doctor of Science and a Fellow of University College London, decided that he would be better able to afford marriage if he left the Patent Office and took up a new career as a teacher. A post abroad would give him the chance of more rapid advancement, and in the autumn of 1887 he was offered an appointment in India, as Principal of Sind College, Karachi. He sailed at the end of December in the *Bokhara*,[43] leaving behind in London the two who loved him best. Mrs Chambers could at least look forward to his return and their wedding; but Alfred Housman felt, rightly, that in this move to the other side of the world there was an element of final rejection of his own love. Some years later, Alfred recalled his parting from Moses in two poems. One of these begins quite plainly:

> Because I liked you better
> Than suits a man to say,
> It irked you, and I promised
> To throw the thought away.          (*MP* 31)

and goes on to describe how they parted 'To put the world between us', and how Moses asked Alfred to forget him. The other, much finer poem, concludes with the moving declaration of love which Alfred would have liked to make to his departing friend and runs:

> Shake hands, we shall never be friends, all's over;
>     I only vex you the more I try.
> All's wrong that ever I've done or said,
> And nought to help it in this dull head:
>     Shake hands, here's luck, goodbye.
>
> But if you come to a road where danger
>     Or guilt or anguish or shame's to share,
> Be good to the lad that loves you true
> And the soul that was born to die for you,
>     And whistle and I'll be there.          (*MP* 30)

Alfred's diaries for the next three years contain few entries: but most of them are about Moses. The 1888 diary contains brief details of Jackson's passage to India, beginning with the dates when the *Bokhara* arrived at Gibraltar, left Naples, and arrived at Port Said.[44] Then Jackson joined the

*Mongolia*, which left Suez on Friday 13 January, and, despite this unlucky starting date, reached Bombay safely at midnight on the 24th. Three days later, according to Alfred's diary: 'He gets to Karachi at "8 o'clock".'[45] There are no further entries about Moses until Sunday 8 July, when Alfred, who had himself received no word from Moses, records rather sadly: 'He wrote this day to Nightingale [a comrade at the Patent Office], having seen his name in the paper as called to the bar. "My dear Nightingale" "Yours very truly".' It was the middle of November before Alfred could write in his diary: 'This afternoon, at Off: I receive letter. . . .'

Alfred posted one letter to Moses in December, and another the following June; he received no reply, and then even Nightingale, when questioned, said that he had not heard from Moses for a long time. At last, in October 1889, Moses came back to England for two months of home leave. Alfred's entry for Tuesday 22 October reads wistfully: 'He came to the Office: lunch he, I, MCK, Nghtgle. Afterwards he went with MCK into City. He dined at Nghtgle: K also –'. On the Friday evening, Alfred went to pay a call on Moses: but was told that he had just gone out to Camberwell; and he did not see Moses until three weeks later, when, on 18 November he records in his diary: 'He came to me at the Office a little after 3.'

This must have been an awkward meeting for Moses. He had come home to marry Rosa Chambers, but had not dared to mention this to Alfred, fearing no doubt that his old friend would find the news deeply disturbing. Even now, he could not bring himself to reveal his plans; and, when the wedding took place on 9 December at St Saviour's Church, Paddington, Housman was not invited, and knew nothing about it. By the time he was told, in January 1890[46] perhaps by Adalbert Jackson – Moses and his new wife were safely back in India.

Whatever Alfred's private feelings of loss, he at once sent Moses a letter of congratulation.[47] Perhaps he realised that, now Moses was securely married, there was a chance that their friendship could after all continue in a way which Moses would not find emotionally awkward. Years later, Housman was even to write for his friend a wedding-poem remarkably lacking in bitterness and generous in spirit. Although it includes the lines:

> Friend and comrade yield you o'er
> To her that hardly loves you more.          (*LP* 24)

As his diary testifies, of the two further letters which Alfred wrote to Moses in 1890, one was another of congratulation: on the first of the sons who was born to Rosa and Moses in October.

Alfred's thoughts had not centred exclusively on Moses for the past three or four years. From 1886 onwards, away from the closed world of

Talbot Road, he had renewed contact with his old friends, the Wises of Woodchester. It was then nearly nine years since Edward Housman's unprincipled behaviour had caused a rift between the Housmans and the Wises. In the interim, Edward had suffered from a stroke; while Alfred was no longer a young student, but a man of twenty-six – and, anyway, he had had no part in the original dispute. It was time enough to forget the past; and when in 1887 Alfred wrote to his elderly godmother, she invited him to stay at Woodchester House for a few days in April.

Arriving again in Woodchester, and revisiting some of the haunts of his own and his mother's youth, was for Housman a delightful experience. He wandered round the village and its environs with thoughts of nostalgic regret for times past, and for the innocence of his childhood; and he also had the great pleasure of renewing old friendships.

Edith Wise was thirty-three, and unmarried. Alfred had now suffered his own rejection; and at this new meeting, he re-established with Edith 'a serene and steadfast friendship, that', in his sister Kate's words, 'may have been founded on renounced love on both sides', and was 'a solace to his other unhappinesses'.[48] Minnie, aged thirty, was also unmarried; and Alfred was soon on good terms again both with her and with her elder brother, Ted Wise, now aged thirty-five.

Although the Wises had found themselves poorer than they expected when Mr Wise died, they had managed to survive (partly by taking in paying guests), and Sophie Becker was still living with them. She was now in her late forties, as warm-hearted and intelligent as Alfred remembered her; and his love for her was in no way diminished.

Alfred's visit to Woodchester was a great success; and before long a stay there became an annual event. The area fed his romantic longing for the past without – as at Bromsgrove – reminding him of the unpleasantnesses of the present. He was able to relax in the company of old and dear friends, to shake off some of the cares of London life, and to revert to some of the happier customs of his undergraduate days. On this occasion, for example, he wrote an amusing set of verses for Edith, which began:[49]

> Oh decorate the station
>  And paint the village red:
> Express exhilaration
>  By standing on your head

and, after his departure, he sent Mrs Wise some lines, describing his inconsolable journey to Paddington, where:

> From attics and sky-touching flats
> Folks put out their heads through the casement
> And said, 'What's that noise? Is it cats?'

> And wiping the tears from my features
>         I said, in a dolorous key,
> 'Go to bed, go to bed, my dear creatures,
>         It is not the cats: it is me.'

Alfred had also been seeing more of his family. His father's strange and sometimes even outrageous behaviour had not always encouraged closer ties with home: for example, Edward developed the idea that, as their father, he was part-author of anything which his children produced;[50] and he stole poems by Laurence and Alfred, made a few alterations, and then submitted them to the local paper for publication under the initials 'EHB', or 'Edward Housman, Bromsgrove'. In 1884 one of Alfred's schoolboy productions, a translation of an ode by Horace, appeared in the *Messsenger* under these initials.

But Alfred had forgiven his father for this theft; and he actually went home for Christmas 1886, for the first time since the merry 'feasting'[51] of a holiday at Perry Hall four Christmases in the past.

Alfred found his stepmother 'in a wonderfully matrimonial frame of mind'.[52] This was because Alfred's sister Kate was being courted by Edward Symons – and Lucy thought it a most desirable match. Symons, a scholar of University College, Oxford, who had been lecturing in mathematics at St John's during Alfred's final year there, was now, at only twenty-nine, the Second Master of Bromsgrove School. Kate, who was not a great beauty, was flattered by his attentions. She could see that he was a decent, kindly man; and, at twenty-four, this might be her last chance to get away from the home in which she had nothing to look forward to but poverty and hard work. When he proposed to her in February, Kate accepted. On hearing the news of their engagement, Alfred wrote to her:

> I rather expected this . . . I am very glad to hear it and I should think you have every prospect of being happy with Symons. Being in love and engaged is the best thing that ever happens to anyone in this world, and it makes them good as well as happy.

Then, with an elder brother's insight, he added: 'The great thing is to make sure first that one really is in love and not deceived by the pleasure one naturally feels at being paid the greatest compliment possible.'[53] He had guessed correctly that Kate – as she later confessed – was *not* really in love;[54] but his concern was unnecessary. Her wedding to Edward Symons on 13 August was the start of a most happy and successful marriage, during which Kate grew to love her husband very deeply.

Besides renewing contact with the Wises, and seeing something of his family, Alfred had become more friendly and agreeable to his Patent

Office colleagues since Moses Jackson left for India. There had been less activity than usual at the Trade Marks Branch where, since 1888 the number of new registrations had dropped by nearly a quarter; and by October 1890 the amount of comparison work was not sufficient to occupy the ordinary staff. At this moment, an Administrative Principal took up work, and, on behalf of three of his senior colleagues, it was Housman who drafted a letter of protest to the Registrar. He complained that there was already too little work to go round; and that the new man's position as Principal 'would give him a status not justified either by length of service or by acquaintance with the details of the work of this Branch'.

Housman had struck up something of a friendship with Hodges, the staff clerk, whose salary of over £300 a year – at a time when Housman was still earning less than £180 – enabled him to lead a moderately comfortable family life. Hodges had thought Housman 'lethargic' in earlier days; but was surprised when Housman attended a debating society meeting, and spoke out against the socialists in a manner which was 'scathing and witty'. After this, Housman spent an occasional evening with Hodges and his wife; and Hodges recalled:[55]

> His great abilities were not incompatible with joy in small and trifling things. Once, for instance, he had spent part of an evening lying on the floor playing with a cat and a piece of string, and this was commented on somewhat sharply by our maid. When my wife told him of this later, he was greatly delighted and laughed heartily. . . . [On another occasion] he said, in a reference to his taste for sweet champagne, that what he best remembered about his visit was that he had had three helpings of a most delicious cheese soufflé.

Housman also became friendly with another clerk at the Patent Office, John Maycock. Maycock rowed for one of the crews of the Thames Rowing Club, and shared lodgings with another rowing enthusiast, M. H. Eyre, in Putney. On Sundays, Maycock and Eyre often went for long walks in the most beautiful parts of Surrey; and now, wrote Eyre: 'Housman on many occasions, came with us, & was a most delightfull companion, in conversation generally, & particularly in pointing out, what was most charming, & interesting.' He recalled that Housman had 'a deep appreciation of the beauties of nature, as regards landscape, & the wild flowers, birds & animals which one comes across in the course of a long day's walk over fields, & commons & through woods'. Housman also seems to have been a fount of amusing anecdotes; and they talked about Shropshire, as Eyre's mother had lived there, and Eyre himself had had many walks in the south of the county. The day would generally end up with dinner at an inn – their favourite haunts were the Greyhound at Carshalton, the White Horse at Shere, the Angel at Guildford, and the Seven Thorns, an old coaching inn near Hindhead – after which they would get back to town by train.[56]

The company of these friends was pleasant for Alfred; and in July 1890 he spent another brief holiday with the Wises at Woodchester, enclosing with his thank-you letter to Mrs Wise 'a cloak room ticket for Miss Becker and also a poem which I have written in her own beautiful language: please tell her this, because otherwise she may not know it: I assure her that it is the fact'. But his closest friend at this time was probably Adalbert Jackson.

They had become friends when they shared lodgings in Bayswater; and afterwards had corresponded regularly,[57] meeting from time to time. During school holidays, Adalbert occasionally called at the Patent Office and went out to lunch with Alfred;[58] and they went walking together. Adalbert was also Alfred's main source of information about Moses Jackson during the first years of Moses's absence in India. There is no evidence as to the nature of their relationship; but some years later Alfred wrote two poems about Adalbert which suggest a deep affection; and when Alfred's brother Laurence was an old man, he told an American biographer that Alfred was physically attracted to Adalbert, and that his feelings were warmly returned.[59]

There were times when Housman preferred to be alone, and then, after a pint of beer at luncheon, he often walked from Highgate along a footpath which led up past woodland and ponds towards Hampstead Heath, with its undulating turf and long avenues of limes. Here Housman would walk along, 'thinking of nothing in particular, only looking at things around me and following the progress of the seasons . . '.[60] The few diary entries made between 1888 and 1891 which did not refer to the Jacksons were indeed about the changing seasons, showing how he had maintained that interest in botany which had been his since early school-days. The complete entry for the day in October when Moses Jackson's eldest son was born, reads:[61]

Epping Forest
Hornbeam shows some yellow
One honeysuckle bloom
A tree with red berries and leaves turning partly yellow
heather mostly faded
His son born.

Housman wrote that sometimes, during these walks, 'there would flow into my mind, with sudden and unaccountable emotion, sometimes a line or two of verse, sometimes a whole stanza at once, accompanied, not preceded, by a vague notion of the poem which they were destined to form part of'.[62] By 1892, Housman had added eighty pages of poem drafts to a notebook which he had first used for classical notes of reference. Among the poems or lines of Housman's which have been mentioned in this chapter, were included, 'Today I shall be strong', 'Bow hither out of heaven and see and save', 'I never flush, nor sigh, nor knit the brow' and 'There pass the careless people'.

Apart from a passing reference to the land of Moses Jackson's 'exile' in the lines 'And up from India glances/The silver sail of dawn', it was not until years later that Alfred wrote the more explicit poems about his friendship with him. In September 1890 he wrote 'The Merry Guide', which begins charmingly enough; but Housman then imagines that he meets a Mercury/Hermes figure, who must on one level be identified closely with Moses:

> With mien to match the morning
> And gay delightful guise
> And friendly brows and laughter
> He looked me in the eyes.
>
> Oh whence, I asked, and whither?
> He smiled and would not say,
> And looked at me and beckoned
> And laughed and led the way.

Later comes the sinister realisation that he is being escorted to the regions of the dead; and the 'delightful guide' continues to lead him on:

> With lips that brim with laughter
> But never once respond, . . .                    (*ASL* 42)

More important for his future popular success as a poet, Housman had been inspired by a deeply-rooted longing for the past, the longing which filled him with a vaguely pleasurable melancholy when he revisited Woodchester, or remembered the countryside westward of Bromsgrove which he had roamed as a child. He had written a draft of the poem in which 'Stourbridge' later became Wenlock:

> 'Tis time, I think, by Stourbridge town
> The golden broom should blow;
> The hawthorn sprinkled up and down
> Should charge the land with snow;                 (*ASL* 39)

and also: 'Far in a western brookland', in which he imagines that a wanderer hears the poplars trembling in the windless night-time ('long since forgotten', and was to become 'no more remembered'):

> He hears: long since forgotten
> In fields where I was known,

> Here I lie down in London
>   And turn to rest alone.
> There, by the starlit fences,
>   The wanderer halts and hears
> My soul that lingers sighing
>   About the glimmering weirs.          (*ASL* 52)

Most poignant of all, because it so closely identifies the countryside of his youth with a lost innocence which he feels that he can never recapture:

> Into my heart an air that kills
>   From yon far country blows:
> What are those blue remembered hills,
>   What spires, what farms are those?
>
> That is the land of lost content,
>   I see it shining plain,
> The happy highways where I went
>   And cannot come again.          (*ASL* 40)

None of these were submitted to poetry magazines for possible publication; though Housman did have a hand in two volumes of verse which were published while he was at the Patent Office. One was Herbert Millington's *Translations into Latin Verse*, published in 1899; in the foreword, Millington wrote:

I wish to acknowledge with gratitude the debt I owe to my old pupil and distinguished friend, Mr A. E. Housman, for his valuable criticism of these verses, which have been submitted to him before publication. His keen eye and sound learning have detected not a few blemishes which might have disfigured these pages.

The other was Alfred Pollard's *Odes from the Greek Dramatists*, published in 1890, which included translations by Housman of poems by Aeschylus, Sophocles, and Euripides. The Sophocles contains a gloomy quatrain which, apart from the antiquated language which Housman deliberately chose for the translations, might have been one of his own private poems:[63]

> Thy portion esteem I highest,
>   Who wast not ever begot;
> Thine next, being born who diest
>   And straightway again art not.

While Housman had been writing some poetry, his main efforts for a number of years had been connected with his classical studies. In the closing months of 1887, when he knew Moses was leaving for India for the first time, Alfred had once again said to himself:

> Days lost, I know not how,
> I shall retrieve them now;
> Now I shall keep the vow
> I never kept before. (*MP* 16)

Once again, partly to give some meaning to his life, and perhaps partly to show Moses what sort of a man he was, Alfred began another attempt to carve out a classical career for himself. Once again, when he had finished his work at the Patent Office, he would go to the British Museum, spending the evenings there, reading 'a great deal of Greek and Latin'. This time, his efforts were sustained. Early in 1888 he published a short article with remarks on Isocrates and Aeschylus in the *Classical Review*; and then, more important, he contributed to the *Journal of Philology* the most interesting of his conjectures on Propertius, and a commentary on the *Agamemnon* of Aeschylus. These articles, 'models of accuracy and thoroughness and exceptionally brilliant critiques', were the first of a rich harvest. Herbert Millington was so struck by the work which his former pupil was producing that as early as February 1888 he wrote a letter to the *Journal of Education* in which he referred to Housman's career, and concluded:[64]

> I can only hope that there are still in Oxford men of influence who read the *Journal of Philology*, and that, having read a certain article therein on the *Agamemnon* of Aeschylus, they will speedily take steps to call this wandering son of theirs, who wrote it, home.

Housman's philosophy insisted that he should set and maintain the highest standards; and in 1889 the quality of his work brought him an invitation to join the distinguished Cambridge Philological Society, and the friendship of one of its leading members, Henry Jackson, Fellow of Trinity. By 1890 his confidence in his own opinions on classical literature meant that he was writing reviews expressing himself with a force and authority which commanded and received attention and respect.

Housman's work in the British Museum was still producing a stream of first-class papers when, in 1892, the Professor of Greek and Latin at University College London died. After the death of the overworked Professor Goodwin, the Professorship was split in two; and on 19 April 1892, Alfred Housman, aged thirty-three, applied to the Council of University College for the Latin Chair. The high quality of his classical work, and the impact which he had made upon the academic world was such that – to let John Carter take up the story:[65]

> the candidature of this obscure young man, whose application proclaimed his failure at Oxford and who had never held a university post

of even the humblest kind, was endorsed in the most respectful terms
by fifteen of the foremost scholars of the day: among them the
Professors of Latin at Oxford, Cambridge and Dublin, the Professors of
Greek at Dublin and St. Andrews, and those two Cambridge paragons,
A. W. Verrall and Henry Jackson; not to mention Gildersleeve from
America and Wecklein from Germany. 'Mr. Housman's position is in
the very first rank of scholars and critics', wrote Arthur Palmer; 'I
regard him', said Tyrrell, 'as holding a place in the very van of modern
scholarship'; Nettleship considered that 'his peculiar gifts . . . deserve,
in an especial way, public recognition in England'; 'I can say without
hesitation', wrote Verrall, 'that there is no-one for whose judgement I
have more respect.' Perhaps only those conversant with the trades-
unionism of Academe can appreciate to the full the exceptional
character of such a volley of endorsements.

Needless to add, Housman was appointed Professor of Latin; and the
calling which he had taken up he followed until his death, spending
nineteen years at University College London before moving to
Cambridge in 1911 for a further twenty-five years as Professor of Latin in
that University.

When he left the Patent Office, after ten years of comparative poverty
and obscurity, his superior presented him with a Wedgwood medallion
of Wedgwood's partner Thomas Bentley; and this 'lay on his writing desk
to the end of his life'. From his fellow-clerk and walking companion John
Maycock he received a more personal tribute, which he also preserved:

I am as delighted with your success as though I had got something for
myself. Now mind, that's saying as much as one can say for anyone
else's good fortune. W[ebb]'s remark that your success was a score for
the Office excited my anger. I told him that it was a score for you, and
that it was nothing at all for the infernal Office. It is funny to think how
I used to chaff you about your work producing no money, and all the
time you were working silently on, with that strength of purpose which
I can admire but can't imitate. . . . As a rule English people never allow
themselves to say or write what they think about anyone, no matter
how much of a pal he may be. Well, I am going to let myself loose. I
like you better than any man I ever knew. There is, as far as I could ever
discover, absolutely no flaw in your character as a man. I don't say this
only on my own account, but I have seen how you can stick to a friend
like you have to Jackson. I mean not stick to him in the sentimental
sense of not forgetting him although he is right out of your reach. I have
always, besides liking you so much, had a great respect for your learning. I always do respect a man that can do anything well. Now your
work has produced for you substantial honour, I feel proud of your

success, and I hope that you will be much happier altogether. I know you must naturally feel proud. If you don't, you are a duffer. One doesn't get too many moments of elation in this life, so don't check the feeling when you have it. The testimonials are wonderfully good. At one o'clock or thereabouts Kingsford and I will drink a glass of the old Falernian to your long life and increasing prosperity. Dear old pal, I'm as pleased as if I'd done something good myself.

Housman always felt a special attachment to University College, for having, as he put it, 'picked him out of the gutter, – if I may so describe His Majesty's Patent Office';[66] but his immediate satisfaction was overshadowed by a serious personal loss. Housman began his work at University College London in October; and in November Adalbert Jackson contracted typhoid, and died in hospital after a short illness.[67] Alfred had now lost a close friend, perhaps even a lover; and this prompted all kinds of melancholy reflections such as those which, a year later, inspired him to write:

> Oh, many a month before I learn
>   Will find me starting still
> And listening, as the days return,
>   For him that never will.
>
> Strange, strange to think his blood is cold
>   And mine flows easy on,
> And that straight look, that heart of gold,
>   That grace, that manhood gone.          (*MP* 42)

In another poem, Housman recalled meeting a beggar whose eyes and voice reminded him of his dead friend, now lying buried 'at the sea's brim' in Ramsgate. With a bitterly ironic reference to Hardy's poem, 'The Return from First Beholding her', Housman wrote:

> He looked at me with eyes I thought
>   I was not like to find,
> The voice he begged for pence with brought
>   Another man to mind.
>
> Oh, no, lad, never touch your cap;
>   It is not my half-crown:
> You have it from a better chap
>   That long ago lay down.
>
> Turn east and over Thames to Kent
>   And come to the sea's brim,
> And find his everlasting tent
>   And touch your cap to him.          (*MP* 41)

Before Adalbert's illness and death, Alfred had given his first major lecture at University College. One passage of the lecture is breathtakingly autobiographical, and might describe Housman at the end of his disastrous Oxford career:[68]

> man stands today in the position of one who has been reared from his cradle as the child of a noble race and the heir to great possessions, and who finds at his coming of age that he has been deceived alike as to his origin and expectations; that he neither springs of the high lineage he fancied, nor will inherit the vast estate he looked for, but must put off his towering pride, and contract his boundless hopes, and begin the world anew from a lower level.

Housman had begun the world anew from a lower level; but now, after ten years in the Patent Office, he had found his way back. The great possessions to which he stood heir were intellectual possessions, his high lineage was that of the great classical scholars who had preceded him; and he could once more have hope and pride; if there was no moneyed future, he might still be an aristocrat of the intellect.

In other ways, also, he had come through these years with a measure of success. His sense of justice, his intellect and his pride had separated him from God; but he had acquired a philosophy which gave some purpose to his life. His passionate desire for Moses Jackson had brought him suffering, and led him to hide and repress his longings; but these same repressed longings of his melancholy spirit, for love, and for the innocence of his childhood, were already breaking through into his conscious mind in the form of verses of haunting beauty. Nor was Housman from this time a wholly divided man: the outward life of the austere classical scholar nourished and sustained the inner life of the broken-hearted romantic poet, who might otherwise have drifted downhill towards suicide; while the inner life of the poet gave insight and understanding and elegance of thought to the great classical scholar. It is fortunate that this relationship existed and worked so well, because in 1892 Alfred Housman was at the very start of the most important and productive years of his life.

# CHAPTER 5

# An Academic Life,
## 1892–1911

By bridges that Thames runs under
In London, the town built ill,
'Tis sure small matter for wonder
If sorrow is with one still.

*A Shropshire Lad*, 50

Man goeth forth to his work, and to his labour: until the evening.

Psalms, 104:17

On hearing the news of his appointment as Professor of Latin at University College London, Housman had little time for self-congratulation. As the new junior Professor, it was his task to deliver a lecture to mark the opening of the academic year in October. It would be his first public oration, and he was determined that it should be remembered: its composition took him much time and trouble during the summer months.

Housman set himself to answer the question: 'What is the good of learning?' First he dealt with the aims of learning usually put forward by scientists, and then by those on the Arts side. Scientists, said Housman, define the aim of learning as utility; and then, to the accompaniment of shocked tut-tuts from some students, he made slighting references to the utilitarian views of Herbert Spencer, his philosophical *bête noire* since Oxford days. 'Our business here is not to live, but to live happily'; so the aim of studying science must be something other than utility. As for those on the Arts side, he considered that they defined the aim of learning as being to 'transform and beautify our inner nature by culture'; but he did not believe that studying, say classics, would especially transform or beautify the inner nature of a large proportion of the human race. Although the study of classics might refine a student's literary discrimination, so great a classical scholar as Richard Bentley had made an ass of himself trying to emend Milton's poetry. Housman's personal view was

81

that man can only be truly happy and fully alive when his craving for knowledge is gratified: so learning is good in itself. Adding that the pleasures of the intellect were 'the least perishable of pleasures', and that a man should study whatever attracted him, he concluded that the only rivalry between science and the arts should be the rivalry of fellow-soldiers whose honour it was 'to search out the things which God has concealed'.

Later Housman was to describe this lecture as rhetorical and not wholly sincere. He certainly believed that excellence in learning was of importance in itself; but he had long felt that knowledge does not always lead to happiness. He seems to admit this in his lecture: 'the pursuit of truth in some directions is even injurious to happiness, because it compels us to take leave of delusions which were pleasant while they lasted': thus 'the light shed on the origin and destiny of man by the pursuit of truth in some directions is not altogether a cheerful light'. But then he states that: 'The house of delusions is cheap to build, but draughty to live in, and ready at any instant to fall; and it is surely truer prudence to move our furniture betimes into the open air. . . .'[1] This was not perhaps the sincere view of a man who had once written:[2]

> Find ye the truth, if so divine it seems
> But we will live our lives & die in dreams.

At any rate, his lecture had been well aimed to please an academic audience. Housman's new colleagues were impressed by the authority with which he spoke; and the Council of University College, feeling satisfied that they had been right to take this clerk from the Patent Office and install him as a professor, paid him the rare compliment of printing and distributing his Introductory Lecture.

\* \* \*

University College London had first opened its doors to students in October 1828. Thus in Housman's day it was a relatively new establishment; and it was also a progressive one: women were admitted to its classes, considerable emphasis was placed on the teaching of science; and, from the first, students had been admitted without religious or political tests.

When Housman joined University College, the Classics Department was in poor condition. Alfred Goodwin, a much respected man, was appointed Professor of Latin in 1867; but then in 1879–80 he taught Greek as well. He found this too great a burden, the work of the department suffered, and from 1880–9 he gave up the Latin Chair, and was solely Professor of Greek. Sadly, in 1889 Goodwin was allowed once again to combine the two professorships: his health broke down under the strain, and it was his death which had left the way open for Housman's appointment.

Now, at least, the Latin and Greek Chairs were separated again, with Housman as the Latin Professor, and with the Greek Professorship taken up by William Wyse, a Fellow of Trinity College, Cambridge, whom Housman knew from the Cambridge Philological Society. The two new Professors found that their classes were not large; but there were some ten hours of teaching a week. Moreover, they 'seldom had pupils who possessed a native aptitude for classical studies or intended to pursue them far';[3] and the teaching terms were twelve weeks long, which Housman, remembering the eight-week terms at Oxford, found 'not nice'.[4] Some of the teaching was very basic, with exercises in grammar, Latin composition, and unseen translation, so that each student's work needed individual attention. With the obligation to give eight or nine lectures on Latin literature each spring, Housman was more occupied with teaching than he might have wished.

The college was not residential, and there was at first little social life among the teaching staff. In the evenings and at weekends Housman returned to his lodgings in Highgate where he worked, wrote poems, and on one occasion in 1894 wrote a splendidly ironic letter about Highgate Wood which was published in the *Standard* on 14 March; it began:

Sir,

In August 1886 Highgate Wood became the property of the Mayor and Commonalty and Citizens of the City of London. It was then in a very sad state. So thickly was it overgrown with brushwood, that if you stood in the centre you could not see the linen of the inhabitants of Archway Road hanging to dry in their back gardens. Nor could you see the advertisement of Juggins's stout and porter which surmounts the front of the public house at the south corner of the wood. Therefore the Mayor and Commonalty and Citizens cut down the intervening brush-wood, and now when we stand in the centre we can divide our attention between Juggins's porter and our neighbours' washing. Scarlet flannel petticoats are much worn in Archway Road, and if anyone desires to feast his eyes on these very bright and picturesque objects, so seldom seen in the streets, let him repair to the centre of Highgate Wood.

Writing letters to the paper – however amusing – is a rather lonely pursuit. But later in 1894 there was a change at University College which considerably added to Housman's enjoyment of his years in London. That patient and exact scholar, William Wyse, disillusioned by the generally low calibre of his students, and the elementary nature of the teaching they required, returned to his Fellowship at Cambridge. His successor, whom he told 'not to expect too much', was a married man of about Housman's age, called Arthur Platt.

Platt had been educated at Harrow and Cambridge where, rather like Housman at Oxford, he had failed to get a First through not sticking closely enough to the syllabus. But at least he had gained a Second and, though he did not have Housman's genius for conjectural emendation, he was a fine scholar, and an expert on the subject of Greek metre. Platt and Housman respected each other's work, and also shared an enthusiasm for literature: 'Greek was his trade', wrote Housman of Platt, 'but the home in which he dwelt was great literature.' Platt's tastes were wide-ranging: he seemed to have read everything, from the *Divine Comedy* to *Jorrocks's Jaunts and Jollities*,[5] and he knew the novels of Jane Austen practically by heart.[6] Housman's tastes in literature were also broad, and his reading included not only Matthew Arnold, Mark Twain, and Thomas Hardy – but lesser-known writers of detective novels and ghost stories.

Arthur Platt was a convivial man, and it was largely he who created social life among the University College dons, by persuading them to gather after lunch in a room which had been given to him, but which he turned over for general use. It was during these informal meetings that Housman was drawn into friendship not only with Platt but with W. P. Ker, the Professor of English, a man endowed with a dry sense of humour, who naturally shared their love of literature.

A bachelor now in his late thirties, Ker came originally from Glasgow. He had won a scholarship to Balliol College, Oxford, and had then been elected to a fellowship at All Souls. Even now, after five years as Professor at University College, he regarded Oxford as his real home, and returned there every week-end during term-time. He was very learned in European as well as in English literature and it was said of him that he knew all the languages of Europe as far as the Slav borders.

Ker often went to London Zoo. As a student wrote, this devotion sometimes had unfortunate consequences for Platt, who at one time was going about 'with three distinct wounds inflicted by the mistaken enthusiasm of his dumb friends'. The same student told Professor Housman how he had visited the Zoo and gone to the giraffe house, where he saw a crowd of children watching a man remove his hat 'while the giraffe, its neck stretched to the fullest capacity, was rubbing its head backwards and forwards, upon the bald crown. When the object of this somewhat embarrassing affection turned his head, Platt's features were revealed.'[7]

For seventeen years, from the time that Housman was in his early thirties to the time that he was a middle-aged man of fifty-one, the three friends worked together at University College. Students would crowd to the Arts Dinners to hear their three speeches, each so different and each delightful, and to meetings of the Literary Society – a Society which

Housman compared to a Minotaur:

> This monster [he wrote] does not devour youths and maidens; it con-
> sists of them, and it preys for choice on the Professors within its
> reach . . . in the hopes of deserving the name [of a Literary Society] it
> exacts a periodical tribute from those whom it supposes to be literate.

Housman himself read a number of papers to the Society, his subjects
including Burns, Tennyson, Swinburne, Campbell and Matthew Arnold.
Burns he provocatively declared to be a great critic but not a great poet;
and as Ker was present at the meeting, Housman introduced a number of
teasing references to Scots and Scotsmen in general. Ker, however,
refused to be drawn, announcing only: 'Forgiveness is the last refuge of
malignity. I will not forgive Professor Housman.' Tennyson he attacked
for unfounded optimism, saying that if God had read 'In Memoriam',
which contains lines like:

> Oh yet we trust that somehow good
> Will be the final goal of ill

he would have said to Tennyson, as he had once said to Job: 'Who is this
that darkeneth counsel by words without knowledge?' Swinburne's early
work Housman admired greatly, and he was especially fond of the
Prologue to 'Tristram of Lyonesse', which begins:

> Love, that is first and last of all things made
> The light that has the temporal world for shade.

But Swinburne's later work he detested, on one occasion describing it as
nothing but 'a clattering noise'. The sound of a poem was certainly as
important to Housman as its sense, and for this reason he had a fondness
for some minor poets: Christina Rossetti, for example, whose beautiful
verses he declared to be 'the sort of nonsense that is worth writing'.

Again, in one of his papers to the Literary Society, Housman was very
kind to Thomas Campbell, a minor poet but a man with an expert control
of sound, who wrote the famous 'Hohenlinden'.

The other poet to whom Housman gave nothing but praise was his old
idol, Matthew Arnold, whom he now described as 'the great critic of our
land and time'; and, comparing him with some well-known Victorian
critics, he wrote:[8]

> I go to Mr. Leslie Stephen, and I am always instructed, though I may
> not be charmed. I go to Mr. Walter Pater, and I am always charmed,
> though I may not be instructed. But Arnold was not merely instructive
> or charming nor both together: he was what it seems to me no one else
> is: he was illuminating.

Unfortunately, only memories and a few fragments of most of these papers survive. 'In their kind they were excellent', wrote A. S. F. Gow of Trinity College, Cambridge, who heard several of them. But Housman was determined to let nothing but his best work outlast him, his high standards leading him to comment on his Swinburne, one of the papers which he intended to have destroyed: 'I do not think it bad; I think it not good enough for me.' One oration, delivered to the University College Union Society, he actually tore up page by page as he was speaking, so that it could not be printed afterwards. His literary papers were allowed to survive a little longer, as he intended to read them more than once; but he ordered them all to be destroyed on his death, and his instructions were obeyed.[9]

After the papers had been read, there was a debate. Housman would argue fiercely enough with older members of the Society – if his pistol missed fire, wrote one of them later, he could knock you down with the butt end – but he took a more lenient and encouraging line with the younger ones. The discussion was often enlivened by good-natured leg-pulling between Housman, Ker and Platt; and it became something of a challenge for one of the students to make a bold attack on one of Housman's papers, a favourite line being to compare Housman with God. While Housman looked ominously down his nose, 'The assailant was warmly cheered – then there was an icy silence as Housman rose to reply, the assailant began to wish he hadn't, and the audience waited in delighted expectation of seeing him butchered . . .'.[10] There was only one assailant against whom Alfred declined to defend himself: his brother Laurence, who came to speak in favour of woman's suffrage. It was obvious to all those who knew him that Alfred must disagree strongly with his brother's views, and when Laurence had finished speaking, 'there were loud cries for Alfred Housman'. He rose and said, with disarming good humour:

> Birds in their little nests agree
> And 'tis a shameful sight
> When Children of one family
> Fall out, and chide, and fight.

So, some of the students at University College met Professor Housman's brother; but, of course, there were large areas in his life about which they knew nothing. The sustained importance of his feelings for Moses Jackson, the shock of Edward Housman's death in November 1894, the period of 'continuous excitement' in 1895 during which Housman wrote so many fine poems, all these were locked away. When in March 1896 the man whom they knew as a reserved academic published a volume of romantic poems, *A Shropshire Lad*, they were unable to

reconcile the academic and romantic facets of his life, and he became
something of a mystery to them. One of his students, R. E. Mortimer
Wheeler, wrote of Housman as[11]

> the austere and aloof Professor of Latin. He had very little liaison with
> his students, who came and went at their own individual discretion
> . . . his tongue could on occasion be as biting to all of us as his pub-
> lished prefaces. In spite of this, we all liked him in a kind of way, and
> felt a certain awe of him as a man of mystery and of manifest ability.
> The Shropshire Lad never emerged: but when he interpreted a page of
> Latin text, his precise and incisive translations, free from all ambiguity
> and humbug, are remembered still.

Housman took his teaching seriously, and set high standards for the
men and women whom he taught. For the intellectual capacity of women
in general, he had a low regard, once writing, rather waspishly:[12]

> Man regards woman with intellectual contempt and sexual passion,
> both equally merited. Woman welcomes the passion but resents the
> contempt. She wishes to be rid of the discredit attached to her little
> brain, while retaining the credit attached to her large bosom.

But he did not single them out for attack: he simply made no allowances
for them. His caustic comments would sometimes reduce the women to
tears, perhaps because they still expected special treatment; and some of
them were deeply wounded when, like many teachers, he found it
difficult to remember their names from week to week. But at least one of
his women students later wrote: 'We did not mind his making us cry,
because we knew he was just.'[13] And when he came across a woman
whom he considered exceptional, he made every effort to help her, as the
recollections of another student testify:[14]

> My first impression would have been of a reserved and rather
> unapproachable man, & of a lecturer of high scholarly attainments who
> could nevertheless make every detail clear and understandable to an
> attentive student. I wanted to 'get on' so his lectures were a joy and
> satisfaction to me.
> I never met him outside the classroom, but I often had a few words
> with him about my private reading before the MA exam, & he even
> volunteered to teach me the elements of making Latin verses – & did.

There was another student whom Housman met in less formal
surroundings. For a period during the 1890s he often went for Sunday
supper to the home of Dr George Fletcher, whose daughter attended his
classes three or four days a week. There was a simple reason for
Housman's visits: he had few friends in Highgate, and Fletcher, though

ten years his senior, was an Old Bromsgrovian, while his father had been the Housmans' family doctor for many years. Sadly enough, the Fletchers, noticing how often Alfred called on them, and not knowing of his homosexual inclinations, decided that their pretty daughter was the object of his visits. Worried that she was in some danger from his attentions while she was unchaperoned during the day, they stopped her from attending University College at the end of her first year. [15]

Otherwise Housman met few of his students outside the classroom, except at meetings of the Literary Society; or in the lunch room, where 'the great man used to surprise us by his immense appetite for beef and beer';[16] but he did enliven some of the college magazines which they read, by contributing a number of his humorous verses. These included a clever skit on the sometimes laborious way in which the action unfolds in classical Greek drama. Entitled 'Fragment of a Greek Tragedy', it ends:[17]

> ERIPHYLA (within). O, I am smitten with a hatchet's jaw;
>     And that in deed and not in word alone.
> CHORUS. I thought I heard a sound within the house
>     Unlike the voice of one that jumps with joy.
> ERIPHYLA. He splits my skull, not in a friendly way,
>     One more: he purposes to kill me dead.
> CHORUS. I would not be reputed rash, but yet
>     I doubt if all be gay within the house.
> ERIPHYLA. O! O! another stroke! that makes the third.
>     He stabs me to the heart against my wish.
> CHORUS. If that be so, thy state of health is poor;
>     But thine arithmetic is quite correct.

More typical of the pieces which he contributed is 'The Parallelogram, or Infant Optimism', a delightfully nonsensical set of verses, one of which runs:[18]

> Wherever placed, it matters not
> In how unsuitable a spot,
> - The parallelogram must stay:
> It is too weak to crawl away.

Among his colleagues, Alfred Housman built up a considerable reputation as an after-dinner speaker. This dated from an occasion in March 1895. The Professor of Chemistry at UCL, William Ramsay, had discovered the inert gas argon. A dinner was held in honour of this, but the speaker who was to have made the principal toast could not be present. F. W. Oliver, the Professor of Botany, who had heard of Housman's abilities in this field 'from an Oxford source', persuaded him to make the toast instead. Housman's speech was the success of the

evening. Not only did Ramsay show 'the utmost kindliness and friendliness' to his young colleague for the rest of the many years during which
they both worked at UCL, but[19]

> from that time he was the refuge of those at University College who
> had to organise formal dinners. One, to W. P. Ker, was enlivened by
> Housman's imaginary Biography of his victim. Ker, Housman
> asserted, being determined to teach English, had begun by learning to
> speak and write it: 'And I must say that he learnt it very well; in fact, if I
> could speak and write Latin as well as Ker speaks and writes English, I
> should hang myself in despair of ever finding a sufficiently appreciative
> audience.'

Housman enjoyed belonging to a community. He was a proud and
ambitious man, and was now highly regarded not only by his immediate
colleagues but by many important figures in the literary and classical
field; but he did not wish his personal life to be in any way remarkable or
remarked upon, and as a member of an academic community he was able
to conceal as much of his private life and emotions as he wished beneath a
respectable and unremarkable disguise. When the publisher Grant
Richards met Housman for the first time in 1898, he found him 'agreeably
precise' in speech, bearing and dress. In fact, in 1898, Housman had a
particularly good reason for wishing to appear just like everyone else, for
in that year Moses Jackson came home on leave for a short while, apparently without his wife and family. Alfred was still devoted to him, but
had, through correspondence, established a more relaxed personal relationship. Alfred Pollard and his wife, who were now living in Wimble-
don, invited Jackson and Housman to dinner, offering to put them up for
the night afterwards. 'When I retired to rest', wrote Pollard later, 'I found
an apple-pie bed awaiting me and I think the Professor of Latin was a
fellow-victim, though I'm not quite sure that he wasn't an aggressor.
Anyhow, we became very youthful and light-hearted.' One can imagine
the shock which would have spread through University College if it had
become known that their Professor of Latin had recently made an apple-
pie bed for a man with whom he was in love. No wonder Housman had
'an air of preferring to pass unnoticed through the streets'!

Two years after this, there was a real crisis at University College. The
Honorary President of the College was now Lord Reay, an able adminis-
trator who had been Governor of Bengal and then Under-Secretary of
State for India. But he had no hand in the day-to-day running of the
College; and there was still no proper academic head. Not only was the
administration in need of reorganisation, but the financial position of the
College had become extremely serious. By the summer of 1897, the
College owed its bankers £30,000; and the situation deteriorated still

further during the next few years, when to the existing difficulties were added the illness of Horsburgh, the College Secretary. Housman was staying at Henley for regatta week when the crisis broke in July 1900. As a member of the Council of University College, he was summoned back to London by an urgent telegram from Miciah Hill, the Professor of Mathematics; and the Council meeting which followed was a dramatic one: 'though all else may fade from memory', Housman wrote, over thirty-five years later, 'the meeting of July 1900, when Horsburgh was dismissed, is branded on my soul.'

For some time there had been a group of Professors who had felt that the Constitution of the College needed reforming. Housman had not been one of these 'convinced reformers'; though, as one of the Deans himself between 1894 and 1896, he was aware of the weaknesses of the existing system of administration, and had tended to take the part of the reformers in a discussion.

The meeting was attended by most of the Council, including Arthur Platt, Professor Oliver, and Mr Ashburner. There was a tedious delay while minor problems were discussed, then they moved on to the main business. A report had been prepared advising that a Principal should be appointed. This was read,[20] and, in the discussion which followed, Housman acted as the spokesman of the reforming group. He demanded from Lord Reay a new Constitution in which there would be a proper academic head of the College; and he asked for the dismissal of the present Secretary. Horsburgh was sent out of the room, and it was decided to sack him. Lord Reay then asked Housman to take the Minutes of the rest of the meeting, which he did, tactfully glossing over what had happened.

Afterwards, Housman had to stay behind to enter the Minutes into the official Minute Book, while Oliver kindly took a telegram to the Post Office to let his friends in Henley know that he would be back later than expected. But everything had gone very well: Lord Reay had been quick to see that Housman had the Council solidly behind him; and that his proposals made sense. The meeting was the start of an important set of reforms which put the Constitution of the College on a firm basis. Less than seven years later, College circumstances were so improved that Housman was able to write nonchalantly: 'One does not discover the difference, except that the Senate is now called the Professorial Board.'[21]

After the crisis of 1900, Housman did not play a large part in College affairs. However, he did serve for a time on the finance sub-committee, where he drew up entertaining reports, one of which describes the 'varying degrees of reluctance of Professors and Fellows to pay their dues'; and he was an energetic Treasurer of the Dining Club, of which his appreciation of good food and his growing knowledge of wine made him a valuable member.

For the most part though, Housman concentrated upon his teaching and his classical researches. In 1903, he published the first volume of what was to be his great classical work, a revised text of the Latin poet Manilius. This was prefaced by one of the biting commentaries on the failings of other scholars for which he was becoming well known; and the work as a whole was dedicated to 'M.J.J.', his friend Moses Jackson.

Most years, Housman managed to get away for a few days' holiday to Woodchester; and he also kept in good touch with his family, writing long letters to his stepmother about the continental holidays which he had begun in 1897; and corresponding with his brothers and sisters. But for some years, family news was very gloomy: his youngest brother Herbert died fighting in the South African war in 1901; and in 1905, after a short illness, his brother Robert also died. Two years later, Lucy herself died; and no doubt these three deaths contributed to the silences which some-times made Mrs Hunter think that her lodger should see more people.[22] In some ways, Housman had made himself less accessible than ever when in 1905 he had moved with his landlady from Highgate to a country hamlet near Pinner. But by this time he had also built up a modest social life in London.

Like many sincere and serious people, he had no small talk, and therefore disliked the sort of mixed party at which serious conversations are considered anti-social. He would occasionally go to dinner at the houses of friends like the Platts, but even among friends he sometimes felt ill-at-ease. Accepting one dinner invitation, he wrote to Mrs Platt:

> The reason why you so seldom see me is that when the weather is bad on Sundays I am afraid to come so far, and when the weather is good, the country, being both nearer and larger, drags me north. Platt, who knows everything, even Greek, will explain to you that every particle of matter in the universe attracts every other particle with a force directly as their masses and inversely as the square of the distance which separates them.
>
> Moreover, at the last at-home I came to, you treated me very ill. I had hidden under the piano, or in it, I forget which; and you came and pulled me out.

In an effort to dissuade another hostess, whom he disliked, he wrote much more firmly:

> People are asking me out a great deal too often, and you are one of the chief offenders. I am not a social butterfly like you: nature meant me for solitude and meditation (which frequently takes the form of going to sleep): talking to human beings, whether 'lovely ladies' or not, for

any length of time leaves me in an state of prostration, and will finally undermine my health unless I take care.

Housman managed to kill the idea of having women admitted to the Professors' Dining Club;[23] and his favourite social activity outside the College was to enjoy a good dinner in the company of two or three of his male friends, followed by a visit to a music hall.

When he was a child Housman had enjoyed some serious music, but in London he avoided it entirely. Serious music demands a serious response and, with his underlying melancholy, what Housman required was something light-hearted which he could simply enjoy. In a good music hall, one could drink a pint of beer or a glass of wine, talk to one's friends, and keep half an eye on the continuous entertainment which was provided – often of a very high standard. There were jugglers, magicians, animal acts, short dramatic scenes, and, most important of all, vocalists. The best of the lyrics were witty and urbane, like Charles Coburn's 'The day I broke the bank at Monte Carlo'; there were also songs about the Empire and patriotism – a theme close to Alfred's heart in view of his brother Herbert's career; and nostalgic songs, sung by men like Harry Lauder, which brought tears to the eyes of all those who, like Alfred, were far from their childhood home.

Apart from his publisher, Grant Richards, the chief of the friends with whom Housman visited the halls was William Rothenstein, who made three portrait drawings of Housman in 1906. The following year Housman invited Rothenstein, who at the age of thirty-five was about thirteen years his junior, to dine at the Café Royal. 'The form which these orgies take', he wrote to Rothenstein, 'is that after dinner we go to a music hall, and when the music hall closes, as I have no club, we are thrown on the streets and the pothouses: so you know what to expect.' Rothenstein accepted the invitation, and afterwards made Housman a present of one of the drawings which he had made of him. After this they lunched or dined together from time to time, and Housman took him to see his brother Laurence's play *The Chinese Lantern* when it opened in June 1908 at the Haymarket Theatre.

Alfred found Mrs Rothenstein rather tiresome, and several times declined her invitations to dinner-parties and other entertainments. On one occasion she tried actually telephoning him at the College, and the next day he had to write apologetically: 'I hope that my conversation through the telephone yesterday did not sound brusque. I am very little accustomed to using that instrument. I was very sorry not to be able to come to the theatre with you. . . .' On another occasion she tried to persuade him to spend part of the summer with her family at a French seaside resort; she cannot have been very flattered by his reply, which was charming, but which suggested that he would 'store his mind' more profitably by visiting some cathedral towns which he had not yet seen!

Despite all this, he kept up his friendship with Rothenstein, and was pleased to go to a private view of an exhibition of his drawings in May 1910. He wrote to Mrs Rothenstein that he liked

> particularly and extremely the picture 'Night', though I fear that the subject may have something to do with this . . . a dark tree with the moon rising behind it . . . I suppose that a picture which is praised by the *Standard* and admired by me must have something wrong with it, and that Rothenstein will reel under this double blow.

Housman lured Rothenstein and Ashburner to the music halls without much difficulty; but Gilbert Murray, the Professor of Greek at Glasgow University, took rather more persuading. Housman first asked in April 1900, 'When are we going to the music-hall?' Several unsuccessful attempts and four-and-a-half years later he wrote firmly: 'You cannot deny that you are now in London, therefore your long-impending music-hall can no further be delayed.' Even then, Murray seems to have escaped him. A fortnight later, instead of enjoying dinner and a music hall, Housman spent an evening at the Court Theatre, sitting through Murray's translation of a play by Euripides. He had enjoyed reading the translation much more than he enjoyed watching it performed; and although he afterwards wrote to thank Murray for the ticket, he could only find wholehearted praise for the 'statue of Cypris standing there quiet all the time'. At any rate, Housman and Murray appreciated each other's scholarship. They corresponded on classical matters – on one occasion Housman was kind enough to send Murray some unpublished conjectures which he was able to use – and Housman was pleased when in 1908 his friend was appointed Regius Professor of Greek at Oxford, congratulating him 'on having survived a Scotch professorship long enough to obtain what I hope will be consolation even for that'. Housman also thought it worth while to tell Murray some of his general views about life, as in this letter:

> I rather doubt if man really has much to gain by substituting peace for strife, as you and Jesus Christ recommend . . . do you really think you can outwit the resourceful malevolence of Nature? God is not mocked, as St. Paul long ago warned the Galatians. When man gets rid of a great trouble he is easier for a little while, but not for long: Nature instantly sets to work to weaken his power of sustaining trouble, and very soon seven pounds is as heavy as fourteen pounds used to be. Last Easter Monday a young woman threw herself into the Lea because her dress looked so shabby amongst the holiday crowd: in other times and

countries women have been ravished by half-a-dozen dragoons and taken it less to heart. It looks to me as if the state of mankind always had been and always would be a state of just tolerable discomfort.

If Alfred's view of the state of mankind was not very cheerful, at least he kept something of an open mind on the subject; and although he had abandoned his own religious beliefs, he would readily quote scripture, and maintained a keen interest in things which touched upon religion. In the summer of 1900 he went for a walk in Buckinghamshire one week-end with Karl Pearson, the Professor of Eugenics at University College, 'to find a farmer who lays a particular kind of eggs, which tend to prove that there is no God'. A few years later Housman was writing to his friend Walter Ashburner, a former colleague at University College London who was now living abroad, and reported to him with a certain wry amusement, that Lord Kelvin had announced in the Botanical Theatre 'that the vegetable kingdom requires a God, though the mineral could do without him'.[24] More seriously, he wrote to Rothenstein in 1907 about a short story by W. H. Hudson: 'A piece [like this] . . . hateful characters and harrowing events, showing God and man at their worst, is good to some extent if it is true, because then it is a weighty indictment of the nature of things.'

While he was at University College, Housman seems to have taken less of an interest in politics than he had as a young man, but he generally welcomed a Conservative victory, saying that it would 'vex the kind of people I don't like'.[25] Indeed, Alfred was just as sceptical as his father had been about the benefits of democratic government. An aristocrat at heart, he was even prepared to believe, with the Greeks, that a class of slaves was the 'essential' foundation of 'a well-governed state'. The one real advantage of democracy, as he saw it, was that it was difficult to betray a government you had chosen, and so there was less likelihood of revolution. ' "Democracy does save you from horrors like that",' he said at a College debate, 'and at the word "horrors" a shudder seemed to pass over him.'[26] He was certainly a great patriot, and his patriotism was strengthened by his brother's part in the South African war. When one day a pro-Boer professor – who, unfortunately, knew nothing about Herbert Housman's death – made some disrespectful remarks about the English private soldier, the result was a display of Housman's invective which surprised even his colleagues.

Besides seeing friends in London, Housman made occasional journeys to Cambridge where he was on good terms with a number of leading scholars, including Henry Jackson and J. G. Frazer. Henry Jackson had introduced Housman to the Cambridge Philological Society, and published his classical papers in the *Journal of Philology*, back in the days when Housman was a clerk at the Patent Office; and now Housman continued to visit him regularly, on one occasion taking Platt with him. From 1906, Jackson was the Regius Professor of Greek at Cambridge; and when in 1908 he was awarded the Order of Merit, Housman wrote to him in the most friendly way.

James Frazer, only five years older than Housman, was half way through *The Golden Bough*. Housman, with his deep interest in religious truth, was fascinated by Frazer's work; and it was at a dinner-party in Frazer's house that Housman first met Andrew Gow, the outstanding young classical scholar who was later to be his friend and biographer: though on this particular occasion Gow took away 'little . . . except a disappointing answer to the question where he spent his vacations; he went, it seemed, not to Shropshire but to Paris'.

Housman had made a success of his years as Professor of Latin at University College London; but although he had continued to publish papers every year, he had never had as much time as he would have liked for his own classical researches because his teaching programme was so demanding. He had once written with some feeling that he had hoped a friend would get a certain Greek Chair 'in order that you might cease to sit up till four in the morning preparing lectures and looking over essays'; and when in 1910 the Kennedy Professor of Latin at Cambridge died, Housman was delighted to be asked to stand as a candidate for the post, which would involve much less formal teaching. It was not at all certain that he would be elected, especially as the forcefulness of his attacks on other classical scholars had made him distrusted in some quarters; and, in view of this, Henry Jackson at once began a benevolent intrigue on Housman's behalf.[27]

In the meantine, there was what must have been an irritating and somewhat unpleasant incident. The writer and adventurer, Frank Harris, then editing a weekly journal, decided that he would interview the author of *A Shropshire Lad*, perhaps hoping to get permission to publish some of his poems; and, as Housman wrote, he 'came down on me at the College like a wolf on the fold'. Harris dragged him off to an impromptu lunch, at which a gang of Harris's friends were present, including the writer Richard Middleton with his 'huge felt hat' and his 'enormous black beard'.[28] Housman felt and looked ill-at-ease among this unconventional group. Middleton, who had no doubt expected the author of *A Shropshire Lad* to be more obviously a poet in his dress and manner, later wrote rather unkindly:

He looked elderly and insignificant and suggested in some subtle way an undertaker's mute, the kind of man who wears kid gloves too long in the fingers, and generally has a cold in the head . . . [his] eyes might be rather fine in repose, but the whole body and speech of the man were twittering with nervousness.

In their own way, Frank Harris and his friends did their best to set Housman at his ease; but they cannot have struck the right chord when they 'sympathised with him over his luckless environment': after all, he was proud of his professorship and his classical work in London. Nor did they flatter him as they hoped, when they 'quoted his poetry without stint': they simply made him feel – probably quite rightly – that they were not being wholly sincere. At the end of the meal, thoroughly exasperated by his companions, Housman stood up and bluntly accused them of having arranged the lunch solely in order to extract some poems from him. This was unnecessarily rude, even if true, and later Housman did not like to recall the incident; but he would be less than human if he had never lost his temper, and on this occasion he had been considerably provoked by patronising efforts to 'find him worthy of his own work', as Middleton put it.[29]

Then, in January 1911, Alfred Housman heard the good news for which he had been waiting. The electors at Cambridge, waiving the customary trial lectures, wrote to offer him the appointment of the Kennedy professorship. Housman accepted, and was given a home in Cambridge by Trinity College, who promptly elected him to a fellowship. As the letters of congratulation poured in, Housman wrote to Ashburner (*Fifteen Letters to Walter Ashburner*: 30 January 1911), modestly attributing his election as professor to the fact that *he* was personally unknown to the majority of the electors, and the other candidates – who included such men as J. E. Sandys, J. P. Postgate and J. E. Reid – were not. The *Oxford Magazine* simply stated:[30]

> Mr. Housman is the greatest living critic of Latin poetry; and it is fitting that such a man should fill the Chair of Munro. . . . If we bred a great man, yet it took us a long time to find it out . . . Cambridge has invested in genius.

Mrs Rothenstein was among those who sent Alfred letters of congratulation; and he wrote back: 'To have less work and more pay is always agreeable, and that will be the case with me.' But the real gain for Housman was that at last, at the age of nearly fifty-two, he could look forward to having sufficient time to devote to the classical studies at which he excelled. He celebrated privately by dining at the Café Royal with Arthur Platt and Grant Richards. Later on, Housman attended several more formal dinners given in his honour at University College.

One of these, held just before Easter, was given by the students.[31] They had gained much from Housman: contact with his mind, his love of truth, perhaps even 'his grim courage in facing a world, the evil of which he felt more keenly than most'.[32] As well as his present students, some of his former pupils at University College had turned up for the occasion, and they presented him with a silver loving cup on which was inscribed his own couplet:

> . . . malt does more than Milton can
> To justify God's ways to man.                    (*ASL* 62)

Housman stood up to thank them, and in a short speech he apologised for sometimes forgetting their names, but joked that if he had concentrated on their faces, he might have forgotten the Latin which he was meant to be teaching them.[33] Then he talked about Cambridge, describing his predecessor, Mayor, as: 'a man who drank like a fish . . . if drinking nothing but water may be so described! When I come to Cambridge with this loving cup, things are going to be changed!' Finally, he claimed one title to fame at University College: 'as Augustus found Rome brick and left it marble, so I found the Easter Vacation four weeks, and leave it five!'

The Professors' Dining Club also held a farewell dinner for Housman. In his speech to his colleagues, Alfred mentioned a recent decision that professors at University College should retire at the age of sixty-five. This was not to apply to professors already appointed, but Housman said that he would have felt morally bound to retire at sixty-five, and that he had been kept awake at night wondering how he would survive from then until his seventieth birthday, when he would be eligible for an old age pension of ten shillings a week. However, his appointment at Cambridge had provided him with a refuge: 'Death, raving madness, or detected crime', he rejoiced, 'are the only enemies I now have to fear.'[34] It was either at this dinner or a later one that he again 'referred to the extreme abstemiousness of his predecessor, Mayor, and (practically) said that he should have to eat and drink all the time he was at Cambridge to restore the balance'.[35] Then he added: 'Cambridge has seen many strange sights. It has seen Wordsworth drunk; it has seen Porson sober. Now I am a greater scholar than Wordsworth, and a greater poet than Porson, so I fall betwixt and between.'[36]

# CHAPTER 6

# A Literary Life (1)

Despising the bourgeoisie, and yet belonging to it, they add to its strength and glory. . . . The lives of these infinitely numerous persons make no claim to the tragic, but they live under an evil star in a quite considerable affliction; and in this hell their talents even ripen and bear fruit.

Herman Hesse, *Treatise on the Steppenwolf*

Joys impregnate. Sorrows bring forth.

William Blake, *The Marriage of Heaven & Hell*

## *Poems 1892–July 1894*

While Alfred Housman had been a clerk at the Patent Office, he had steadily filled some eighty pages of a notebook with the drafts of poems. These had flowed into his mind – usually when he was out walking – 'with sudden and unaccountable emotion, sometimes a line or two of verse, sometimes a whole stanza at once, accompanied, not preceded, by a vague notion of the poem which they were destined to form part of .[1] Now that he was a professor of Latin, he continued to enjoy walking; and a small but steady flow of poetry continued to well up into his consciousness.

Not that his poems were pure inspiration: at least part of each usually had to be worked at, and work at it Housman did, with enormous skill and patience. He once complained that one stanza of 'I hoed and trenched and weeded' (*ASL* 63), had to be consciously composed, 'and that was a laborious business. I wrote it thirteen times, and it was more than a twelvemonth before I got it right.'[2] And in other poems, there would be points at which Housman might try eight or nine words before he found exactly what was wanted.

Many of the poems which he wrote during the first two years of his professorship were self-pitying and morbid. This is not really surprising. In the world's eyes, Housman was now a successful man; but his

98

emotional life had been unhappy, at times desperately so. The loss of his mother and, later, the loss for many years of the companionship of Edith Wise and Miss Becker, the woman to whom he had transferred some of his love and affection when his mother died, were combined with the loss of what could have provided a spiritual anchor – a firm religious belief at which he might have rested during his other academic and financial troubles. Later, he had been rejected by Moses Jackson, and any hope of finding lasting consolation in the arms of Adalbert Jackson vanished with the latter's death from typhoid fever only a few weeks after Housman's Introductory Lecture at University College.

It was during his first two years at University College that Housman wrote the extremely self-pitying verses of 'The farms of home lie lost in even' (MP 14) in which he declares that, if he returns home, not even a dog will run down the yard to greet him; and in 'By shores and woods and steeples' he wrote gloomily:

> Now who sees night for ever,
> He sees no happier sight:
> Night and no moon and never
> A star upon the night.                    (MP 38)

On one or two occasions, Housman allowed the publication during his life-time of thoroughly inferior poems like these – for example, the heavily sentimental·

> With rue my heart is laden
> For golden friends I had;                 (ASL 54)

and occasionally, self-pitying lines found their way into poems which were on the whole worth preserving, and rather spoiled them. But, generally speaking, Alfred recognised his failures, and kept them to himself; it was only after his death that a number of them were published by his brother Laurence, who sometimes failed to distinguish between what had been left unpublished because it was controversial, and what was simply inferior.

Besides a number of morbid verses, Housman wrote several deeply personal poems about the Jackson brothers, including 'Shake hands, we shall never be friends, all's over', 'Because I liked you better/Than suits a man to say', and 'Strange, strange to think his blood is cold'. Alfred was also writing poems in which his private emotional experiences have been transformed into a general comment on the nature of existence, as in the haunting lines:

> From far, from eve and morning
> And yon twelve-winded sky,

> The stuff of life to knit me
> Blew hither: here am I. (*ASL* 32)

Other poems written at this time show that Housman had come to believe that the Universe was seriously flawed. This belief did not stem simply from his recognition of his homosexuality, and his feeling of being shut out from God, though this was undoubtedly an important factor. He had long ago rejected God with his intellect, but he was still emotionally attached to his mother's church, and it was during this period that he wrote a verse of homosexual guilt, set in a religious context by a clear reference to one of the Psalms, in which he describes how he 'cleansed his heart/And washed his hands in innocence in vain' (*MP* 28); now, too, he wrote 'Easter Hymn', in which he urged Christ to 'Bow hither out of heaven and see and save' (*MP* 1), if he really was the son of God.

He examined the world's suffering, and could find no reason for it, and no remedy either. In one bleak and bitter poem, he wrote:

> The toil of all that be
> Helps not the primal fault;
> It rains into the sea,
> And still the sea is salt. (*MP* 7)

In another, Housman finds a personal remedy, even if rather a negative one:

> Be still, be still, my soul; it is but for a season:
> Let us endure an hour and see injustice done. (*ASL* 48)

Later, he strikes a rather different note, in a poem about the Biblical story of Lot's wife being turned into a pillar of salt:

> Half-way, for one commandment broken
> The woman made her endless halt,
> And she to-day, a glistering token,
> Stands in the wilderness of salt.
> Behind, the vats of judgment brewing
> Thundered, and thick the brimstone snowed;
> He to the hill of his undoing
> Pursued his road. (*MP* 35)

The general message of this poem is clearly that God, or the Universe, is unjust; but there is something more: in spite of the terrible destruction of the cities of Sodom and Gomorrah, in spite of the pointless execution of his wife for simply looking back at the scene of that destruction, Lot does not complain, or abandon himself to self-pity. Instead, he pursues his road with quiet determination even though he knows that it will eventually lead to his own death. There is something a shade more positive about this than the idea of 'enduring'; and Housman was to develop this theme of doing what can be done, even when one knows that everything is in vain, in later more heroic poems such as 'The Oracles' (*LP* 25), and 'As I gird on for fighting. . . . My sword that will not save' (*LP* 2).

## Poems August–December 1894; the background to the writing of A Shropshire Lad

Alfred Housman was proud of his poetry; and although, as he later told a friend, he had sometimes been anxious in case his inspiration dried up, by the summer of 1894 he was clearly thinking in terms of eventually having a selection of his verses published. At this stage, he had only worked on sixteen of the poems which were finally included in his first publication, so it might not have been ready for many years. But during the next few months a combination of circumstances produced a flood of poems, 'and a ferment so terrific that the nervous reaction was well-nigh insupportable'.

The belief that his poems were worth publishing must have been in itself a powerful stimulus. In his introduction to *A Shropshire Lad*, Alfred once mentioned a period of 'continuous excitement', and his brother Laurence wrote that this excitement was 'literary and poetic over A having at last found his metier'.[3] More important, perhaps, was the manner in which Alfred intended the poems to be presented. By August 1894 he had already written a few couplets from 'Terence, this is stupid stuff', in which he explains that his poetry has a bitter taste in order to prepare people for the bitterness of life (*ASL* 62); and a month or two later he wrote a Shropshire ballad in which a murderer says: 'Terence, look your last at me/For I come home no more' (*ASL* 8). The Greek dramatist Terence was brought to Rome as a slave, and lived there in exile; no doubt Housman, thinking of his own exile in London from the world of his childhood, saw some similarity in their situations. At any rate, he began to think of a cycle of poems, incorporating the best of what he had written, in which there would be descriptions of Shropshire life, and in which the central character would be a Shropshire lad, Terence Hearsay, who would come up to London and live there in exile as Housman had done. When published, the poems would be called simply 'The poems of Terence Heresay', and there would be nothing to connect them with the Professor of Latin at University College London. Having invented this 'fig-leaf of a fictitious character', which, as his brother Laurence wrote, 'he *pretended* was not his own', Alfred was able to 'let himself go'.[4] This use of 'Terence Hearsay' as a mouthpiece for his ideas helped to remove any inhibitions which had restrained Alfred's output of poems in the past; but an equally important factor was the death of Edward Housman in November 1894.

Alfred can never have admired his father, indeed he had many reasons for despising him; but he also remembered Edward as a loving, good-natured, easygoing parent, a part of the precious lost world of childhood; and at least for that he loved him still. He returned home for the funeral, and afterwards stayed on at Perry Hall for the Christmas holidays, 'settling things and looking over books & papers'. Kate wrote that her brother 'did not feel grief, beyond the inevitable poignant memories of youth';[5] but for Alfred, those memories were one of the most important parts of his life, and he wrote sadly:

> Around the huddling homesteads
> The leafless timber roars,
> And the dead call the dying
> And finger at the doors.
>
> Oh, yonder faltering fingers
> Are hands I used to hold;
> Their false companion drowses
> And leaves them in the cold.                     (*LP* 19)

So Alfred mourned his father; but Kate believed that their father's death was, in general, a liberating influence: 'the removal of a burden & a distress, for our father had become broken and infirm, though his age was only 63'.[6] More than this, Alfred became conscious of the fact that he was now head of the family, but had no sons to succeed him; and when his poems began to flow more rapidly, he became excited by the conviction that he was producing 'immortal progeny';[7] an excitement which in itself stimulated the creation of more poems. Certainly, in later life his regard for his first volume of verse was 'like that of a mother for her first-born. Over and over again he showed a special, a tender, affection for it.'

It is perhaps not surprising, given the part which Housman's feelings for Moses Jackson had played in shaping his outlook on life, that, when Housman's poems were published, sensitive critics began to 'nose about on a false scent for a hidden lady',[8] feeling, quite rightly, that the poems had been written by someone who had had an unhappy love-affair. Housman's ambivalent feelings about his homosexuality were certainly an important part of his inner, emotional life. He seems to have felt guilt at his homosexual desires; while, at the same time, he believed that homosexuality was not utterly wrong. He was all too aware that the society of his day condemned homosexuals, and perhaps had this in mind when he wrote: 'This is why most men will go to hell: because, when they cannot enjoy a thing themselves, they try to prevent others from enjoying it.'[9] In December 1894, he actually wrote a poem in which he stated clearly that he did not wish to obey all the laws of God and man; but other people would not let him do as he pleased. The solution, as he put it:

> I, a stranger and afraid
> In a world I never made.
> They will be master, right or wrong;
> Though both are foolish, both are strong.
> And since, my soul, we cannot fly
> To Saturn nor to Mercury,
> Keep we must, if keep we can,
> These foreign laws of God and man.     (LP 12)

On another occasion – perhaps when feelings of guilt were more predominant – he remembered Christ's sayings (Matt. 18:6), and wrote the following bitter couplet:[10]

> Lock your heart & sink the key
> With the millstone in the sea.

It may well be that the flow of his poetry was further stimulated during 1895 by the publicity given to these issues by the trial of the most notable homosexual of his day, a man only five years older than himself, the playwright Oscar Wilde. Six years before this, public condemnation of homosexuality had been strengthened by the sensation of the Cleveland Street scandal, which centred round a homosexual brothel where Lord Arthur Somerset, among others, had committed acts of gross indecency, some of them with telegraph boys from the Post Office;[11] and when in 1890 Wilde's story of youthful corruption, The Picture of Dorian Gray, was published in Lippincott's Monthly Magazine, one of the reviewers wrote:

> Mr. Wilde has art, brains, and style, but if he can write for none but outlawed and perverted telegraph boys, the sooner he takes to tailoring (or some other decent trade) the better for his own reputation and the public morals.

Oscar Wilde ignored this suggestion; but in April 1895 he brought an ill-advised libel action against the Marquess of Queensberry, who had objected to Wilde's homosexual association with his son, Lord Alfred Douglas. Instead of clearing Wilde's name from the 'libel' of 'posing as a sodomite', the case against Queensberry quickly collapsed, and led to Wilde's own arrest for homosexual practices. On this, the National Observer reported:

There is not a man or a woman in the English-speaking world
possessed of the treasure of a wholesome mind who is not under a deep
debt to the Marquis of Queensberry for destroying the High Priest of
the Decadents. The obscene imposter. . . .

and soon it was impossible to open a newspaper without reading some
reference to the case. On 25 May, Wilde was convicted and sentenced to
two years' hard labour. In his final speech he had defended himself with
the words: 'It is in this century misunderstood, so much misunderstood
that it may be described as the "Love that dare not speak its name", and
on account of it I am placed where I am now.'[12]

After Wilde's conviction, other homosexuals feared for their own
safety, and some men of letters fled to the Continent. For his part,
Housman wrote a bitterly satirical poem, never published during his
lifetime, in which a man is taken to prison 'For the nameless and
abominable colour of his hair':

> Oh a deal of pains he's taken and a pretty price he's paid
> To hide his poll or dye it of a mentionable shade;
> But they've pulled the beggar's hat off for the world to see and stare,
> And they're haling him to justice for the colour of his hair.          (AP 18)

In the same year, there was another incident which struck Housman
forcibly: a young naval cadet at Woolwich, realising that he was
homosexual, decided to shoot himself rather than give in to his 'evil'
impulses. Housman, whose personal reaction to the event is described in
Laurence Housman's *Encounter* article of October 1967, wrote both
sympathetically and ironically:

> Shot? so quick, so clean an ending?
>     Oh that was right, lad, that was brave:
> Yours was not an ill for mending,
>     'Twas best to take it to the grave.          (ASL 44)

To these strands contributing to the 'continuous excitement' which
produced so many fine poems in 1895 – his father's death, the release
from inhibition which adoption of the guise of Terence Hearsay afforded
him, and the emotions aroused by the suicide of the Woolwich cadet and
the Wilde trial – two more may be added. Housman told Sir Sydney
Cockerell that the flood of poems had come to him 'partly perhaps as a
reaction from a learned controversy [on the manuscripts of Propertius] in
which he was then engaged'. Certainly, Housman's poems came to him
most easily when his conscious mental control had been relaxed with a
pint of beer at lunchtime, and it is quite reasonable to suppose that a tiring
controversy may have had something of the same effect. In addition,
during the harsh February of 1895, Alfred had an unpleasant sore throat

and felt rather run-down for a while; this would also have weakened his conscious control; and indeed, once Alfred teased a gushing young lady who had asked, 'and when, Mr. Housman, will you give us some more of your charming poems?', by replying: 'When next I have a relaxed throat'. For the rest of his life it amused him to attribute his poetry solely to a physical condition, and when he was nearly seventy-four he wrote to an admirer: 'my poetry, so far as I could make out, sprang chiefly from physical conditions, such as a relaxed sore throat during my most prolific period, the first five months of 1895'.

In the same letter, Housman explains why he made Terence Hearsay a Shropshire rather than a Worcestershire or even a Gloucestershire lad: 'I had a sentimental feeling for Shropshire', he wrote, 'because its hills were our western horizon.' This remark takes one right back to Alfred's childhood and the evenings when, as a fifteen-year-old boy, he would leave Fockbury House and walk up Worms Ash Lane to 'Mount Pisgah', from where he could look to the distant Shropshire hills. Whether or not he had actually visited Shropshire since then, Alfred had certainly heard some first-hand descriptions of it: in his Patent Office days when out walking with Maycock and Eyre he had often talked of Shropshire, as Eyre's mother had lived there, and Eyre himself had had many walks in the south of the county. Housman did once confide in a friend that he wrote six of the 'Shropshire' poems before being in the county, adding that he then set foot there, 'to gain local colour'. This visit, which he probably made while he was staying at Perry Hall after his father's death, he later described in a letter to his brother Laurence, in which he mentions that he 'was in Bridgnorth for several hours. In the churchyard there I remembered having heard our mother describe it and the steps up to it, which I had absolutely forgotten for more than 25 years.'[13]

But Housman's Shropshire is largely an imaginary land; and the real place-names were often used for romantic colouring rather than because Housman had a particular feeling for a real place. One of the poems already written when he made his visit to Shropshire was 'Hughley Steeple'; and when the poems were published, his brother Laurence visited Hughley and then sent Alfred a letter accusing him of romantic falsification: Alfred had written:

> The vane on Hughley steeple
>     Veers bright, a far-known sign;                    (ASL 61)

and he had also described how the suicides were buried to the north of the church tower, away from more respectable people. Laurence pointed out that the 'far-known sign' was buried away in a valley; and that most of the 'suicides' to the north of the tower were respectable church wardens and wives of vicars! Alfred replied that, on his visit to Shropshire, he had ascertained by looking down from Wenlock Edge that Hughley church could not have much of a steeple. But as I had already composed the poem and could not invent another name that sounded so nice, I could only deplore that the church at Hughley should follow the bad example of the church at Brou, which persists in standing on a plain after Matthew Arnold had said that it stands among mountains. I thought of putting in a note to say that Hughley was only a name, but then I thought that would merely disturb the reader. I did not apprehend that the faithful would be making pilgrimages to these holy places.

## Models and influences

Having discussed the background to the writing of *A Shropshire Lad* in terms of the influence which stimulated Housman, it is worth looking briefly at the models upon which the form of what he wrote was based.

Alfred told a friend that, while he was writing his poems, he was conscious of three models, which he described as 'fortunate influences': the Border Ballads, Heine, and Shakespeare's Songs. The Ballads had a particular appeal: their combination of clear, precise form with often rather sinister tales in which some vital part of the story is left unexplained until the last possible moment, echoed something of his own emotional make-up. As a boy, he had read and enjoyed *Ballads from Herodotus*,[14] and his interest in the ballad form was probably reawakened by his colleague Professor Ker, a man described as having a head in which one ballad or another was always running.[15] Heine also fascinated Housman, who read him in the original, having learned enough German to be able to compose verses in that language for Miss Becker. Like Housman – though not homosexual – Heine had suffered from an unhappy, one-sided love-affair which had tinged his work with romantic melancholy; like Housman, he found some consolation in the natural beauty of the countryside; and he developed a simple, direct poetic style, writing lyrically about nature and ironically about man. Shakespeare's Songs, with their simplicity, their haunting beauty, and their direct call to the emotions, also appealed to Housman and influenced him. Sometimes, he would virtually quote a line of Shakespeare in his own poetry: 'How that life was but a flower' from *As You Like It* (V, iii. 30), became in one of Housman's poems' – Ah, life, what is it but a flower?' (*ASL* 5); and there are several references to Shakespeare's lines from a song in Cymbeline: 'Fear no more the heat o' the sun,'. 'Fear the heat o' the sun no more' (*ASL* 43), writes Housman; and again, 'Dust's your wages, son of sorrow' (*ASL* 44); and perhaps it is from these lines that he drew the 'golden friends' of his poem 'With rue my heart is laden' (*ASL* 54).

But if the Border Ballads, Heine, and Shakespeare's Songs were the 'fortunate influences' of which Housman was himself chiefly aware, careful study of his poems shows that his mind was well-stocked with the work of other writers. 'Echoes' of these writers in Housman's poems have been the subject of at least one major study;[16] but even a brief and incomplete account tells an interesting story. Of the 123 clearest references in Housman's *Collected Poems*, twenty-five refer to the Bible – mostly to the Old Testament, with no less than five references to Ecclesiastes, and several to the Psalms; eighteen to Shakespeare, with references to at least seven of the plays, ranging from *King Lear* to *As You Like It*; seventeen to Matthew Arnold; ten to classical authors, such as Lucretius, Catullus, and Sappho; eight to Milton; seven to Christina Rossetti; six to Robert Louis Stevenson; four to Tennyson; three each to Heine, the Border Ballads, and hymns; and one or two references each to Thomas Moore, Goldsmith, Sir Walter Scott, Blake, Pope, Gray, Browning, Lang, Wordsworth, Simcox, Byron, W. H. Davies, Robert Bridges, and D. G. Rossetti. The many references to Matthew Arnold are not surprising – he was the poet whose work Housman claimed to know by heart when he was an undergraduate. But Housman's poems have been praised for their classical purity and pagan spirit, and it is therefore interesting to see that the Bible had remained the greatest single influence upon his thought, while he showed a high regard for the work of several authors overtly Christian in thought and expression, authors such as Milton and Christina Rossetti. What is clear also from this list is that although Heine and the Border Ballads were an important general influence on the form and style of his verse, they were – except in one or two notable instances, such as the translation of one of Heine's poems[17] – very little responsible for their individual content.

But whatever the influences upon a man, it is his innate talent or genius which, in the light of his own experience, combines and refashions them into something new; and during 1895, Housman wrote all or part of nearly seventy poems. Fifty of these form the chief part of *A Shropshire Lad*, which is still in print, and popular, over eighty years after first publication. The strain of composition was intense, and years later, talking to a friend, Housman 'reverted spontaneously to the cost entailed, and . . . the pained look showed only too clearly how heavy it had been'.

## *1895: composition; and 1896: publication of* A Shropshire Lad

It was the first five months of 1895 that were the most prolific period, producing twenty-five of the poems destined for his Terence Hearsay collection. Another twelve were written between June and August, and nine between October and December. During those first five months, Alfred wrote the bitter poem about love, 'When I was one and twenty' (*ASL* 13); the nostalgic 'The winds out of the west land blow' (*ASL* 38), and the pleasant pastoral lines which begin:

> 'Tis spring; come out to ramble
> The hilly brakes around,
> For under thorn and bramble
> About the hollow ground
> The primroses are found.                    (*ASL* 29)

He also wrote two of the poems for which he is, deservedly, best known: one of them, 'Is my team ploughing', a poem of deep romantic melancholy which begins with a dead man asking his friend:

> Is my team ploughing,
> That I was used to drive
> And hear the harness jingle
> When I was man alive?

and ends – after he has been reassured that all is well – with a savagely ironic twist:

> Yes, lad, I lie easy,
> I lie as lads would choose;
> I cheer a dead man's sweetheart,
> Never ask me whose.                    (*ASL* 27)

And the other, that beautiful poem, at once melancholy and philosophical, which begins:

> Loveliest of trees, the cherry now
> Is hung with bloom along the bough,
> And stands about the woodland ride
> Wearing white for Eastertide. . . .                    (*ASL* 2)

Two more fine pieces were written, but not included in the collection: the lines referring to Adalbert Jackson 'He looked at me with eyes I thought/I was not like to find' (*MP* 41); and an equally excellent poem about courage in the face of a hostile Universe, 'As I gird on for fighting' (*LP* 2). This last poem was probably omitted by Alfred from his first collection of verses because he had already included several poems about fighting and soldiering, and did not want to tip the balance too far in that direction. The poems on being a soldier are, indeed, an important element in his work.

'A homosexual', wrote Proust, 'is not a man who loves homosexuals, but merely a man who, seeing a soldier, immediately wants to have him for a friend.'[18] As a boy on his first trip to London, Alfred had been, above all, impressed by the Guards. His fascination with soldiers had continued, and was given a new dimension when his own brother Herbert gave up his medical career in 1889 and joined the King's Royal Rifles as an ordinary private.[19]

Alfred now viewed soldiers with a complex mixture of emotions, of which a homosexual interest was only part, though it is shown very clearly in the poem which begins:

> The street sounds to the soldiers' tread,
>     And out we troop to see:
> A single redcoat turns his head,
>     He turns and looks at me.              (*ASL* 22)

Housman also felt a romantic admiration for their courage and self-sacrifice, and described how

> To skies that knit their heartstrings right,
>     To fields that bred them brave,
> The saviours come not home tonight:
>     Themselves they could not save.         (*ASL* 1)

and this admiration led him to use military symbolism when he wished to describe the sort of courage which he felt every man needs if he is to face up to life:

> So here are things to think on
>     That ought to make me brave,
> As I strap on for fighting
>     My sword that will not save.             (*LP* 2)

Alfred felt great compassion for those soldiers who died young, soldiers who had perhaps joined the Army merely to escape from the scene of an unhappy love-affair; and his compassion was tinged with a degree of envy for those who would 'carry unspoilt into safety the honour of man/The lads that will die in their glory and never be old' (*ASL* 23).[20]

During the last seven months of 1895, Housman's 'continuous excitement' abated; but it was now that he wrote several of his most popular poems, including 'Her strong enchantments failing' (*LP* 3), 'The lads in their hundreds to Ludlow come in to the fair' (*ASL* 23), and 'On Wenlock Edge'. This last poem is one of Housman's finest achievements, not least because it contains a mature, unself-pitying acceptance of the troubles of life, by setting them in a long historical perspective:

> On Wenlock Edge the wood's in trouble;
>     His forest fleece the Wrekin heaves;

> The gale, it plies the saplings double,
>     And thick on Severn snow the leaves.
>
> 'Twould blow like this through holt and hanger
>     When Uricon the city stood:
> 'Tis the old wind in the old anger
>     But then it threshed another wood.
>
> Then, 'twas before my time, the Roman
>     At yonder heaving hill would stare:
> The blood that warms an English yeoman,
>     The thoughts that hurt him, they were there.
>
> There, like the wind through woods in riot,
>     Through him the gale of life blew high;
> The tree of man was never quiet:
>     Then 'twas the Roman, now 'tis I.
>
> The gale, it plies the saplings double,
>     It blows so hard, 'twill soon be gone: .
> Today the Roman and his trouble
>     Are ashes under Uricon.                    (*ASL* 31)

Some of the poems which Housman now composed, he never published. These include the poems about Moses Jackson, 'Shake hands, we shall never be friends, all's over' (*MP* 30), the bitter satire relating to the trial of Oscar Wilde, 'Oh who is that young sinner with the handcuffs on his wrists?' (*AP* 18), and a poem in which two rather indifferent verses prepare the way for these majestic lines about the courage of man:

> When God would rear from earth aloof
> The blue height of the hollow roof,
> He sought him pillars sure and strong,
> And ere he found them sought them long.
>
> The stark steel splintered from the thrust,
> The basalt mountain sprang to dust,
> The blazing pier of diamond flawed
> In shards of rainbows all abroad.
>
> What found he, that the heavens stand fast?
> What pillar proven firm at last
> Bears up so light that world-seen span?
> The heart of man, the heart of man.          (*AP* 15)

By the end of 1895, even after rejecting those poems which were too controversial or which fell below his usual standard, Alfred had enough to consider publication. Eventually he selected around sixty poems, most of them written during the previous sixteen months, though several were two or three years old, such as 'If truth in hearts that perish' (*ASL* 33); and some, including 'There pass the careless people' (*ASL* 14), and 'Into my heart an air that kills' (*ASL* 40), dated back more than five years. Putting them under his chosen title, 'The poems of Terence Hearsay', he offered them to Macmillan. Macmillan, however, rejected them, apparently on the advice of the biographer, John Morley, who was then their reader. Housman now asked his old friend Alfred Pollard to visit him. According to one story, they had lunch together in University College, and then went back to Byron Cottage, where Housman went out for a walk leaving Pollard to read the poems and form an impression of them. When Housman returned, apparently very depressed, Pollard soon cheered him by saying that the poems would still be read in two hundred years. He also had two important suggestions to make, both of which Housman adopted: the title should be changed to 'A Shropshire Lad' – and Housman should acknowledge his authorship. [21]

Pollard then introduced Alfred Housman to the publishing firm of Kegan Paul, which had offices at Paternoster House, Charing Cross Road, just above the Garrick Theatre. Their manager, Spencer Blackett, was so taken with the military poems that, as Housman wrote, 'he wanted me at first to make the whole affair, with Herbert [Housman]'s assistance, into a romance of enlistment. I had to tell him that this would probably take me another thirty-six years.' However, Blackett did not insist too strongly; Kegan Paul had what another publisher called a 'strongly engrained . . . habit of publishing verse for which the authors would pay'; and when Housman had agreed to pay them £30, they agreed to print an edition of 500 copies. A few last-minute changes were made to the table of contents; but by the week of Housman's thirty-seventh birthday, in March 1896, *A Shropshire Lad* had been printed with sixty-three poems, and was ready for publication.

Housman's friends and family reacted with mixed feelings to the slim volume. Millington, who was sent a presentation copy, was flattered by the gift, but disliked the poems; though, as Alfred said years later: 'Well, of course, the only poetry that Millington was able to admire was Tennyson's.' Alfred's sister Kate wrote to say that she liked the verse better than the sentiments. 'The sentiments, she then goes on to say, appear to be taken from the book of Ecclesiastes', Alfred reported to his brother Laurence. 'To prefer my versification to the sentiments of the Holy Ghost is decidedly flattering, but strikes me as a trifle impious.' Laurence, who was himself trying to build up a reputation as a poet, immediately recognised that Alfred's poems were superior to his own, and would overshadow them; but he later wrote, generously

the day when I first opened *A Shropshire Lad* and found there more than thirty very good poems awaiting me, was one of the great events of my life . . . its quality came on me like thunder out of a clear sky. Before the end of the day I knew a dozen of the poems by heart, and before the end of the week nearly all of them.

But Laurence's reactions were not entirely uncritical. He approved of the title 'A Shropshire Lad' – after all, Alfred's nostalgia for the countryside of his childhood was an important element in the poems, and he had associated this with Shropshire names. But Laurence recognised that the specifically 'Shropshire' poems are not always the best. In fact, when they are dissociated from Alfred's own experience, they are often the worst. Many of them, such as 'Ned Lear and I were drunk last night', the unhappy romance of Nancy and Ned, and a poem about a dead man waking up Terence, had already been abandoned in the notebooks;[22] but others which did find a place in *A Shropshire Lad* were almost equally poor: one thinks of 'Farewell to barn and stack and tree' (*ASL* 8), and of the other verses which begin:

> This time of year a twelvemonth past,
> When Fred and I would meet,
> We needs must jangle, till at last
> We fought and I was beat.           (*ASL* 25)

As Alfred used to write in books opposite poems which he disliked: 'Ugh!', Laurence rightly pointed out that the Shropshire lad, just as fictitious a character as Terence Hearsay, was 'a quite impossible combination of light-hearted rustic and deeply-feeling highly-learned thinker, on whom the burden of life lies heavy . . .'. Laurence went on: 'I would commend to all readers of these poems . . . this truth: that wherever they are least like "A Shropshire Lad" they are most deeply and truly like the man he really was who wrote them. . . .'[23]

Thirty years or more after publication day, Alfred was reading a book about contemporary poets in which his own work was discussed. At one point, the author was busy looking for 'a clue to the discovery of why *A Shropshire Lad* was immediately, and has been continuously, popular'. Housman wrote in the margin, quite accurately, 'it wasn't'.[24] This was not altogether the fault of the reviewers. The *Athenaeum*, then 'the recognised organ of the literary world', ignored the book altogether; but those reviews which did appear were favourable enough, beginning with *The Times*, which on 27 March wrote under 'Books of the week, shorter notices', that Mr. A. E. Housman had struck 'a decidedly original note'; and they also praised 'his gift of melodious expression'. During the course of the year, friendly reviews appeared in numerous journals and newspapers, including the *Bookman*, the *Star*, the *Daily News*, and the

16 *Katharine Housman as a
young woman of twenty-two*

17 *Edward Housman as an
elderly man*

18 *Patents Office, Southampton Building, Chancery Lane, where Housman worked as a clerk*

19 *Fleet Street in the 1890s*

20 *Moses Jackson*

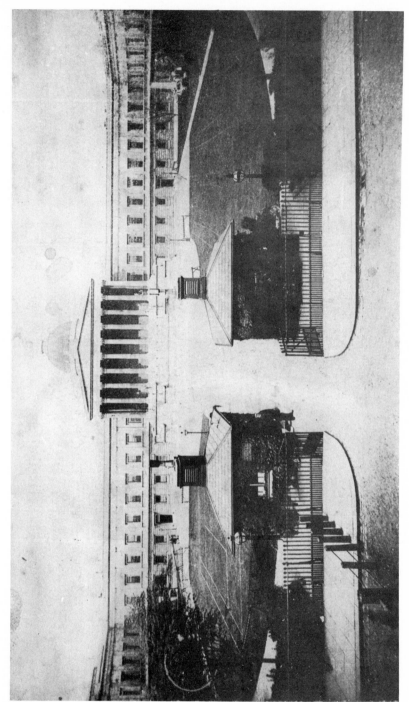

21 *University College London in 1880*

22  *A view from Wenlock Edge looking across the Wrekin*

23 *Alfred Housman in London, 1896, the year in which* A Shropshire Lad *was published*

24  *W. P. Ker, Professor of English at University College London*

25 *Arthur Platt, Professor of Greek at University College London*

*Guardian.* Even the well-known poet and critic Edmund Gosse, who 'began by asking sneering questions about this houseboat person', was later to be found 'chattering appreciatively in three columns'. The review which apparently gave Alfred most pleasure was the one written by Hubert Bland, which appeared in the *New Age* on 16 April, part of which ran:

> The little volume before us contains, on well-nigh every page, essentially and distinctively new poetry. The individual voice rings out true and clear. It is not an inspiring voice, perhaps; it speaks not to us of hope in the future, of glory in the past, or of joy in the present. But it says and sings things that have not been sung or said before, and this with a power of directness, and with a heart-penetrating quality for which one may seek in vain through the work of any contemporary lyrist. . . . This direct expression of elemental emotions, of heart-thoughts, if we may be permitted the phrase, is the dominant note of all Mr. Housman's work, as it was of Heine's alone among modern singers.

Bland added that, as the poems were wanting on a note of gladness, they could not be called the highest poetry; but they came astonishingly near the highest: and this has been the verdict of those who have loved Housman's poetry ever since.

However, the publishers did little to 'push' the book. One hundred and sixty-two copies were sent to John Lane for publication in America; but despite this, only 381 copies had been sold by the end of 1896; and two years after publication there had been no new edition, and in fact six copies of the first remained unsold.

Oscar Wilde was in prison when *A Shropshire Lad* was published; but his friend Robert Ross learned some of the poems by heart, and recited them to him when he visited him; and when Wilde was released after his two years of captivity, Alfred sent him a copy of the poems himself. On 9 August 1897, Wilde wrote to Laurence Housman, praising a book of his, and adding: 'I have lately been reading your brother's lovely lyrical poems, so you see you have both of you given me that rare thing, happiness.'[25] In his next letter, of 22 August, Wilde again praised *A Shropshire Lad*, and also told Laurence that he was writing the 'Ballad of Reading Gaol', which he described as 'Terribly realistic for me . . . a sort of denial of my own philosophy of art'. Since *A Shropshire Lad* contains a number of 'terribly realistic' poems – take for example the poem of which one verse runs:

> They hang us now in Shrewsbury jail:
> The whistles blow forlorn,

And trains all night groan on the rail
To men that die at morn.                    (*ASL* 9)

– it may well be that Wilde, whose sufferings had inspired Alfred
Housman, had in turn been inspired by Housman's poems to write one of
his most remarkable works.[26]

## A literary life, 1896–1911

Wilde's praise was flattering, but Housman received more real benefit
from the enthusiastic interest of an unknown book reviewer called Grant
Richards. Richards, a handsome young man of twenty-three, was the son
of an Oxford don, and the nephew of Herbert Richards, one of the
examiners who had ploughed Housman in Greats. He was no scholar
himself, but an engaging rascal with an eye for the main chance. When *A
Shropshire Lad* was first published, Richards was working for the *Review of
Reviews*, in which he praised Housman, with more spirit than brilliance,
as 'a very real poet, and a very English one at that'. Then in the autumn of
1896, when he was planning to set up his own small publishing company,
he wrote to Housman proposing to publish the successor to *A Shropshire
Lad*; 'but as they don't also offer to write it', Alfred wrote to Laurence, 'I
have had to put them off'. Richards, not the sort of man to be discouraged
by a refusal, tried again in February 1898, though with a rather different
request. By this time his publishing firm, Grant Richards Ltd, had been in
business for just over a year; and Richards himself had scraped up
enough of an acquaintance with Alfred's brother Laurence to be able to
approach him from that quarter. His idea was that he should take over the
remaining copies of *A Shropshire Lad* from Kegan Paul, and publish a
second edition at his own risk.

Alfred treated this proposal very cautiously. 'I suppose', he wrote, 'no
author is averse to seeing his works in a second edition, or slow to take
advantage of an infatuated publisher; and it is impossible not to be
touched by the engaging form which your infatuation takes'; but he
insisted that the price and form of the book should be the same, which
would mean that Richards would be out of pocket. Richards, undeterred,
replied on the following day:[27]

Dear Sir,

I confess you rather clash with my ideas about 'A Shropshire Lad'
when you say that you would not like the second edition to be sold at a
higher price or to differ from the first in form. I hardly thought it likely
that you would want to make any alterations in matter or to add – the
book is there complete now as it stands for every reader to see. But,

somehow, I don't think as much was made of it on its appearance as might have been, and the only chance of again attracting the reviewer to it is to reissue it with an entirely new type and in a new form – not at a higher price if that could be avoided, but I am afraid it couldn't.

I don't know, of course, whether Messrs. Kegan, Paul would object to the transfer.

There the matter rested until July, when Richards wrote again. This time Housman weakened, and as soon as he had found out from Kegan Paul that 'their feelings would not be lacerated', he agreed that Richards should publish a second edition. Richards was delighted, and followed up his victory by asking for one or two new poems to include in the new edition;[28] but on this point Housman was adamant: 'I think it best', he wrote rather magisterially, 'not to make any alterations, even the slightest, after one has once printed a thing. It was Shelley's plan, and is much wiser than Wordsworth's perpetual tinkering, as it makes the public fancy one is inspired.'

Soon after this, Alfred met Grant Richards for the first time, in Laurence's company, at the Globe Theatre;[29] and a few days later he called on Richards in his London offices, where he repeated that Richards might produce a second edition. Richards said that he should take a share of the profits, but Housman replied: 'I am not a poet by trade; I am a professor of Latin. I do not wish to make profit out of my poetry. It is not my business'; and he added: 'If the book proves the success you anticipate then use what you would normally pay to me to reduce the price of subsequent editions.' Perhaps he felt that to accept money at this stage would throw a rather ridiculous light upon the fact that he had had to pay for the book to be published in the first place; more likely, he felt so sensitive about the success or failure of *A Shropshire Lad* that he wished to hide this by acting as though it was of no importance to him whether the book made a profit or not; and in any case, after so many years of poverty, it must have pleased him to appear as a gentleman for whom money, in some things at least, was a sordid irrelevance. Richards entered in his ledger: 'No agreement. No royalty to be paid'; and he printed 500 copies which were published at 3s. 6d. on 14 September 1898.

Most reviewers paid little attention to this new edition; but the *Athenaeum* wrote a friendly notice, and the *Manchester Guardian* called it 'the most interesting volume of verse published in this country for some years past'. Richards worked hard to sell the book, and by the end of the year nearly four-fifths of the edition had been sold. Housman was delighted, and wrote: 'It does you infinite credit that the sale should be so good: I wonder how you manage it.' In February 1899, Richards wrote to Housman to ask him again if he would accept a royalty of 10 per cent of the published price;[30] but Housman still refused. Sales in 1899 were in fact rather disappointing, and it was not until February 1900 that Grant Richards was ready to publish a third edition of 1,000 copies, 300 of which were sent to John Lane in New York. At the end of 1902, there was another new edition of 2,000 copies; but, as Richards pointed out, by this date, after seven years in print, the book had only sold 1,475 copies in England. However, he trusted his judgment, continuing to bring out new editions, and Housman's reputation as a poet grew steadily.

As he became a recognised literary figure, Housman began to circulate a little in the literary world. He never played the part of a literary man, remaining conventional in dress and manners, and since he was also a shy man in company he did not find it easy to make himself liked. Max Beerbohm, who met him in 1907 among a group of literary and artistic people, wrote rather rudely about him: 'He was like an absconding cashier. We certainly wished he would abscond – sitting silent and then saying only "there is a bit of a nip in the air, don't you think?" '[31] At some time in the early 1900s he also met one of his admirers, the young John Masefield, at the tavern in the Temple, London, which had once been one of Dr Samuel Johnson's haunts; and this was the start of a lifelong friendship.[32] More important, he was taken up by the critic Edmund Gosse, who lived at the very hub of London's literary life. Gosse admired his poetry and was himself tortured by homosexual longings, which may have secretly endeared Housman to him.[33] It was probably at one of Gosse's dinner-parties in 1899 that Housman first met Thomas Hardy, whose work he had read with much admiration since he was an undergraduate. Both men were usually shy and reserved in company, but their meeting was a success: and Housman, who had visited Dorchester the previous summer during a holiday tour of the West Country, was now invited to return there for a stay at Max Gate, the Hardys' home. Alfred seems to have got on rather well with Hardy's ageing wife, Emma, who confided in him that her husband's favourite poem among the Shropshire Lad collection was 'Is my team ploughing'; but Housman never discussed his poetry directly with Hardy. Indeed, the conversation between these two men who had both stared bravely into the heart of the Universe, and found it flawed, was probably a great deal less exciting than one might have imagined. They did not see each other for some years after this visit; but Alfred met Emma from time to time at the Gosse's when she was staying in London.

Housman's reputation as a poet was particularly strong among composers. One music historian states: 'The brevity of the lines, their essential Englishness, their pastoral atmosphere, their rhythm, and their simple spontaneity of feeling were contributing factors';[34] but the real attraction of the poems to composers must have lain in their combination of beautiful lyrical phrases, perfect for picking out in the foreground of music, with the great emotional strength of the underlying thought, in which there could often be found a background of that universal melancholy which music can express so well. Housman put no difficulty in the way of those who wished to set his verses to music, and would not even charge them a fee, writing, on one occasion, 'Vanity, not avarice, is my ruling passion'; and on another 'I always give my consent to all composers, in the hope of becoming immortal somehow'. It was certainly not because he admired modern music; his taste in music, as we have seen, was unashamedly popular.

Among those who set his poems to music was Ralph Vaughan Williams, who published 'On Wenlock Edge' in 1909. In November of that year he called on Housman; they had a friendly meeting, and Housman agreed to allow him to print some of the verses on his programmes. Some years later, Housman was very annoyed to discover that: 'composers in some cases have mutilated my poems, – that Vaughan Williams cut two verses out of "Is my team ploughing" (I wonder how he would like me to cut two bars out of his music) . . .'; and when a friend of his, knowing nothing of this, made the mistake of playing him some gramophone records of Vaughan Williams's song cycle, he was surprised to see the author sitting bolt upright in his chair, his face flushed with anger.

Housman continued to allow composers to set his words to music; but he usually objected to their inclusion in anthologies. He made one or two exceptions, as when in 1903 he allowed H. E. Butler, then a Fellow of New College, to reprint '1887' in *War Songs of Great Britain*; but he refused Arthur Quiller-Couch permission to print any of his poems in the *Oxford Book of English Verse*, not wishing to be included in an anthology with poets such as W. E. Henley, whom he despised;[35] and years later he wrote angrily and rather arrogantly, to Grant Richards: 'You must not treat my immortal works as quarries to be used at will by the various hacks whom you may employ to compile anthologies.' He also, as a general rule, refused requests for contributions from magazines, writing to one editor: '. . . my reputation, such as it is, I will preserve intact, and not injure it by writing verse to order. I have never done so for anyone, even when offered bribes, literature not being my trade.'[36]

Housman's relationship with Grant Richards had been friendly, but was for some time confined to business. In addition to the requests of composers and anthologists, their correspondence concerned the sending of review copies, problems about costs and all other matters which concern an author and his publisher while a book is being seen through the press. Housman, with his insistence on high standards, was often exasperated by the way in which printers introduced errors into his work, writing for example in the autumn of 1902:

> When the next edition of the *Shropshire Lad* is being prepared, it would save trouble to the compositor as well as to me if he were told that the third edition is almost exactly correct, and that he had better not put in commas and notes of exclamation for me to strike out of the proof, as was the case last time.

It was in this letter, when he had corresponded with him regularly for over four years, that Housman began 'Dear Richards, If I may drop the Mr.'; and nearly two years later, in July 1904, Alfred asked his publisher to dine with him for the first time, at the Café Royal.

When Richards, a married man, ran up the stairs at the Café Royal an hour late, dressed in tweeds, after spending the day motoring in the country with 'a lady', who was certainly not his wife, he found that Housman and Housman's other guest were already eating a *canard à la presse*. As a *bon viveur*, Richards was soon impressed by the realisation that

> this was or had been, no dinner automatically suggested by a maitre d'hotel, but . . . had been ordered carefully and with experience by my host . . . a man to whom good food and the wines that should go with it were a matter of more than ordinary importance.

Grant Richards was something of a rogue, but a man with an engaging personality. Housman had always appreciated his enthusiasm for *A Shropshire Lad*, and was prepared to forgive Richards for his tweeds and his late arrival when he found that he made a delightful companion at the dinner table. Indeed, the two men shared a great relish for good living. Housman's father had always enjoyed good food, even taking up cooking as a hobby when he could no longer afford a first-class cook; and he had also introduced Alfred to excellent wines from an early age. Once his days of comparative poverty at the Patent Office were over, Alfred had been able to develop his taste for what was best in food and wine, and was now something of a gourmet. After Richards and Housman had dined together many times, Richards wrote admiringly that the

> white-haired and priest-like *sommelier* at the Café Royal of that period . . . treated him with respect. A Madeira of distinction would begin the meal, and with the fish would come . . . a Johannisberger '74, and then a superb Burgundy. Burgundy, white or red, was ever A.E.H.'s favourite wine. Port and old brandy followed in their proper places.

Housman could also appreciate what it meant to have financial troubles, and was sympathetic and helpful when, later in 1904, Grant Richards's publishing business ran into serious difficulties. Richards had

been, in his own words, 'tempted beyond prudence by too much credit,
. . . [and] overtrading and spending too much money . . . I am not
prepared to say that I did not deserve it . . . It was, however, a bitter
experience'. Alfred wrote to him as soon as he heard of his difficulties,
and did what he could for him by inviting Richards to dinner at the Café
Royal, together with his brother Laurence, 'a person', as Richards
described him, 'whose goodwill counted in the commonwealth of letters'.
After dinner they went to a music hall and the Criterion Bar, where Alfred
ordered him a cocktail and Laurence promised to send him a bottle of
mead. In the heat of the moment Richards, who was soon to be declared
bankrupt, decided to repay their kindness by inviting the brothers to
dinner. Laurence then made Grant Richards a bet that he could not
produce hedgehogs at a London restaurant within twenty-four hours;
and so, twenty-four hours later, the three men were dining together
again, this time at the Carlton restaurant. The hedgehogs – obtained from
Scotland, and apparently tasting rather like haggis – were washed down
with whisky, and followed by snails with white wine. Richards later
confessed, rather ingenuously: 'I should not at that moment have been
dining out at the Carlton at all, and so A.E.H. told me. But I made up for it
by other economies.'

Richards's firm was sold; but since he had never made a formal
agreement with Housman, Richards owned no rights in *A Shropshire Lad*,
rights which, if they had existed, would have had to be sold with his other
assets. Housman was kind enough to leave the book for the time being in
the hands of Richards's Trustees, and before long Richards had resumed
business, initially under the name of his wife, E. Grant Richards.
Retaining control of *A Shropshire Lad* proved to be very valuable for
Richards. Sales in 1905 only amounted to 886 copies; but in 1906 the book
at last began to sell really well, and from then until 1911 the average
annual sale was more than 13,500 copies, on which the 10 per cent royalty
which Richards had once offered to its author would in itself have been
worth at least £150 a year.[37]

The friendship between Housman and Richards prospered. Housman
wrote a sympathetic letter when Richards's father died in 1905. The
following month, hearing that Richards wished to see him on some
matter, Housman sent him a theatre ticket, with a note that 'If you go, I
shall be there about 9 o'clock, just drunk enough to be pleasant, but not so
incapable as a publisher would like an author to be'. They dined together
many times in London, and at least once in Paris; and, whether for
reasons of business or friendship, Housman often visited the office in
Carlton Street, on the corner of St Alban's Place, where, when times grew
better, Richards leased five or six rooms. His private offices – as described
by another of his authors – were[38]

on the second floor, up a small dingy staircase, and the room itself was
so small that it surprised me by its cosiness. I could not call it dingy. It
was quaint rather, Georgian in atmosphere, with a small open fire
glowing in one corner, a great roll-top desk entirely out of keeping with
the place in another, a table, a book-case, a number of photographs of
celebrities framed, and the rest books.

During the summer of 1909 Richards decided to invite Housman for a
week-end to his home at Cookham Dean. The children's nurse was
ordered to keep them away, in case Alfred should dislike their company;
and on the Sunday Richards and Housman walked along the banks of the
Thames as far as Sonning, where they lunched at the White Hart, and
Richards was impressed by Housman taking the ingredients from the
waiter and making a good salad. The following February, Housman was
invited again; this time Richards found that he need not have worried
about keeping the children away from his guest. After an accidental
confrontation between Housman and 'a Red Indian . . . pursued by three
young ruffians', the Richards children found that he was not the ogre
whom they had feared, and indeed, his friendly interest soon made him a
great favourite with them.

Grant Richards had been helped back towards modest prosperity by
revenue from sales of *A Shropshire Lad*; but Housman still refused to
benefit from them. Nor did he make any effort to protect his interests in
America, where the firm of John Lane had published copies of *A
Shropshire Lad* sent to them by Kegan Paul, and by Richards; and from
where Housman had already begun to receive admiring letters. One of
these letters arrived in June 1903 from a young man of twenty-two named
Witter Bynner. Alfred replied to him:

> naturally there is a pleasure in receiving such ardent letters as
> yours. . . . My chief object in publishing my verses was to give
> pleasure to a few young men here and there, and I am glad if they have
> given pleasure to you.

Bynner, as the poetry editor of *McClure's Magazine*, was an influential
figure, and it was his enthusiasm which was largely responsible for
stimulating American interest in Housman's poetry. By the end of 1905
this interest was such that John Lane were anxious to come to a formal
agreement by which they could publish their own edition of *A Shropshire
Lad*; but surprisingly Housman showed no interest, although he stood to
gain a good deal of money from such an agreement. In the end he more or
less suggested to John Lane that, as his poetry was not protected by
copyright in the United States, they should go ahead and bring out a
'pirated' edition; this they did.

Housman continued an occasional correspondence with Witter Bynner, and in February 1910 he wrote a letter to him in which he answered a question which all admirers of *A Shropshire Lad* must have been asking for years: how many more poems had Housman written which might be published? In fact, since the publication of *A Shropshire Lad* in 1896, only five more of Housman's poems had appeared in print: 'Diffugere Nives', his translation of some lines by Horace; and four which might be loosely described as 'soldiering' poems: 'Illic Iacet', 'The Olive', 'The Oracles', and 'Astronomy'.[39] 'The other day', Housman now told Bynner, 'I had the curiosity to reckon up the complete pieces, printed and unprinted, which I have written since 1896, and they only come to 300 lines, so the next volume appears to be some way off.' If the complete pieces came to only 300 lines, the incomplete ones certainly doubled and may even have trebled this total; but Housman was right that the next volume was some way off – twelve years, as it turned out.

Some of the poems which he had been writing were similar in theme to those which he had written earlier, verses about Moses Jackson ('He would not stay for me; and who can wonder?' (*AP* 7)); and about the bitterness of existence. But there is one group of poems which Housman was writing during these years which belongs particularly to this time: his cycle about fighting, courage, and the Boer War.

## A poet of the Boer War

The complex mixture of emotions with which Housman viewed soldiers in general has already been outlined: the homosexual interest, the admiration for courage and self-sacrifice, the compassion, tinged with envy, for those who died young and with honour; and the special interest which stemmed from his brother Herbert's enlistment in the King's Royal Rifle Corps, and the vivid letters he sent home about the often appalling conditions which ordinary soldiers were expected to endure.

When the South African war broke out in 1899 Herbert was among the soldiers sent out to fight; and Alfred soon began to write more poems about soldiering. The first of these, 'Illic Iacet', was published in the *Academy* in February 1900, and describes the death of a soldier. It begins in a straightforward, heroic fashion:

> Oh hard is the bed they have made him,
>     And common the blanket and cheap;
> But there he will lie as they laid him:
>     Where else could you trust him to sleep?;

but then goes on to suggest that soldiers, however brave, are in a sense in love with death, and the poem ends sadly, almost reproachfully:[40]

> And thin is the quilt, but it covers
> A sleeper content to repose;
> And far from his friends and his lovers
> He lies with the sweetheart he chose.          (*LP* 4)

'Grenadier', the next poem which Housman worked on, looks with compassion at the ordinary soldier, asked to fight for his country for 'thirteen pence a day'. A dead Grenadier records how:

> For thirteen pence a day did I
> Take off the things I wore,
> And I have marched to where I lie,
> And I shall march no more.
>
> My mouth is dry, my shirt is wet,
> My blood runs all away,
> So now I shall not die in debt
> For thirteen pence a day.          (*LP* 5)

For this miserable sum he has lost his life, and everything he could ever expect is lost forever: 'For in the grave they say', writes Housman, alluding to a sentence from Ecclesiastes (9:10), 'Is neither knowledge nor device/Nor thirteen pence a day.'

Six pages further on in his notebook, after some verses for Moses Jackson, Housman was drafting one of his best-known poems about courage, 'The Oracles'. In this, a man comes to believe that death is the end of everything; but he is fortified by recalling the courage of the Spartans at Thermopylae. Death was certain, and final; but they faced it bravely and with dignity, even making sure that they were smartly turned out before the battle began:

> *The King with half the East at heel is marched from lands of morning;*
> *Their fighters drink the rivers up, their shafts benight the air.*
> *And he that stands will die for nought, and home there's no returning.*
> The Spartans on the sea-wet rock sat down and combed their hair.
>
>                              (*LP* 25)

These poems, taken together, show the complexity of Housman's attitude. On the one hand, he writes admiringly of bravery; on the other, he cannot but feel the tragedy when brave men die, and that they have missed their real purpose in life. After 'The Oracles', the very next page in the notebook contains a few lines which were later used as the basis for 'The Deserter':[41]

> Ay, kiss your girl, and then forget her;
>     'Tis like the brave.
> They love the leaden bullet better
>     To lie with in the grave.

Here Housman concentrates upon the tragedy of war which, he says, compels men to desert their lovers, and go to seek their death. And here too there is a mixture of attitudes. In the line 'Tis like the brave' – the only line to survive unaltered into the later poem – there is resentment, but also a grudging understanding of the power within a brave man that obliges him to take such a course. And in the final version, in lines such as:

> But my day is the day of battle,
>     And that comes dawning on,

Housman conveys once again something of the courage and resolution with which a man can face his destiny.

The next poems which he wrote were less sombre: 'Star and coronal and bell' (LP 16), in which he talks of the reviving power of the spring: and a draft of 'Fancy's Knell' (LP 41). But then came a family tragedy, perhaps half-expected, but still very bitter: the death in battle of Herbert Housman on 30 October 1901. Alfred immediately wrote for his brother a personal lament, which began:

> Farewell to a name and a number
>     Recalled again
> To darkness and silence and slumber
>     In blood and pain.                                    (MP 40)

Within the next few months came 'The Use of the Globes', later renamed 'Astronomy', haunting and sad, about the brother who died without gaining for himself the name that he desired. Alfred looks up at the stars, and recalls that his brother, in Africa, would have seen different stars in the sky:[42]

> The Wain upon the northern steep
>     Descends and lifts away.
> Oh, I will sit me down and weep
>     For bones in Africa.
>
> For pay and medals, name and rank,
>     Things that he has not found,
> He hove the Southern Cross and sank
>     The pole-star underground.

And now he does not even see
Signs of the nadir roll
At night over the ground where he
Lies buried with the pole.          (*LP* 17)

In the last verse, the stars have come to seem an image of inescapable fate, an image which Alfred carried on in his next poem, which began: 'The stars have not dealt me the worst they could do' (*AP* 17).

The theme of fatal destiny was taken up in another poem written during the first few months of 1902: 'The rainy Pleiads wester', a new version of a love poem about Moses Jackson, based on a Sapphic original. Sappho, the Greek poetess, had written:[43]

The moon has set and the Pleiads.
It is far into night and the hours
Pass on their way. I am left
Lying alone.

Housman, knowing these lines, also recalled the words from the book of Job: 'Canst thou bind the sweet influences of Pleiades, or loose the bands of Orion?' (Job 38:31); and he wrote:

The rainy Pleiads wester,
Orion plunges prone,
The stroke of midnight ceases,
And I lie down alone.

The rainy Pleiads wester
And seek beyond the sea
The head that I shall dream of,
And 'twill not dream of me.          (*MP* 11)

Soon after this, Housman drafted four verses of 'The Land of Biscay', whose theme is that things are foredoomed (*MP* 46); 'The sigh that heaves the grasses', a poem about the cold indifference of the Universe, which, in the lines:

The diamond tears adorning
Thy low mound on the lea,
These are the tears of morning,
That weeps, but not for thee,          (*LP* 27)

related directly to his brother Herbert's death; and 'The Olive', inspired by the end of the war in South Africa, and published in the *Outlook* on 7 June 1902, comments with bitter irony on how peace should flourish on the cess of war:[44]

Shading the bloody trenches
  Its dressers dug and died
The olive in its orchard
  Should prosper and abide.

Close should the fruit be clustered
  And light the leaf should wave,
So deep the root is planted
  In the corrupting grave.                    (*AP* 23)

This remarkable group of poems, beginning with 'Illic Iacet', and ending with 'The Olive', must entitle A. E. Housman to be described as a poet of the Boer War. Not many years later, the First World War inspired others to write bitterly about the misery of war. Housman had been there before them, and set that misery within the broad philosophical context of a flawed Universe, in which such evils are inescapable, and all man can do is to bear them as bravely as he may.

# CHAPTER 7

# Mainly Family,
## 1892–1929

A friend loveth at all times, and a brother is born for adversity.

Proverbs 17:17

When in 1892 Alfred Housman became Professor of Latin at University College London, the news of his appointment soon circulated round his large family: it reached Clem and Laurence, living not far away across London; and it travelled up to Edward and Lucy in the Midlands; to Stockport, where Alfred's brother Basil was practising as a doctor;[1] to Huddersfield College, where his sister Kate lived with her husband Edward Symons; to Glasgow where his brother Robert worked as an electrical engineer; to his Uncle Joseph in the West Country; and finally, after many weeks, the news reached a distant corner of the Empire where, at Thayetmo in Upper Burmah, Alfred's youngest brother Herbert, the soldier, read about his new appointment in *The Pioneer*.

Basil, Alfred's favourite brother, had managed in 1891 to qualify as a Fellow of the Royal College of Surgeons – a rare achievement among Birmingham students in those days. Herbert had originally followed Basil to Queen's College, Birmingham, to study medicine; but he was not really enthusiastic about becoming a doctor, and as soon as he was free from parental control, at the age of twenty-one, he had thrown up his medical studies and joined the King's Royal Rifles as a private.[2] To enlist as an ordinary soldier was a bold move for a man with Herbert's family background, who would normally have considered it a disgrace to join the Army without a commission. However, Herbert had been supplied by his father with the names of distant relatives whom he could mention to establish his standing as a gentleman, and he was led to believe that he would eventually come into enough money to enable him to take up a commission.

Herbert wrote frequently and with great warmth to Lucy, addressing her as 'My dearest Mater', and signing himself 'ever your most affectionate boy' and she passed on his letters to her other step-children.

Alfred, with his romantic interest in soldiering, must have been particularly impressed by the contrast between moments of excitement and heroism – as when Herbert and a few of his comrades faced a body of rebels ten times their number – and the dreadful privations which they suffered, not all of them due to natural causes: during one expedition in the rainy season, the soldiers had been reduced to a ration of half a pound of meat and four biscuits a day, and then, when they returned home with their clothes rotted, they were expected to replace boots and uniforms at their own expense, as they had worn them out before the regulation time! Herbert also corresponded directly with his brothers and sisters, especially with Kate; and was pleased when, for his twenty-fourth birthday in July 1892, Alfred sent him, appropriately, a copy of Rudyard Kipling's *Barrack-room Ballads*. He wrote to the Mater:[3]

> The book that Alfred sent me has been the delight of myself and my comrades ever since I got it. . . . There never was a man, and I should think never will be again, who understands 'Tommy Atkins' in the rough, as he does.

Kate, aged thirty, had a difficult time in 1892. She now had two small children to look after, and in the early part of the year her husband's health broke down. For a while Edward was extremely ill. When he had recovered he had no wish to stay on at Huddersfield, and after successfully applying to become Headmaster of Banbury Secondary School, he moved there with his family in 1893.[4] Kate, tied up with her growing family, saw very little of Alfred; and, with Herbert out of the country, she was probably closest to her stepmother, though she did also see something of Laurence, who was one of her sons' godparents, and of Robert. His scientific interests had separated him from Alfred, Laurence, and Clem, for whom science was largely a closed book; but he kept in touch with Kate and Herbert, and the Christmas of 1891 found him at Perry Hall.

Meanwhile, in London, Clemence aged thirty-one, and Laurence aged twenty-five, had moved from Kennington and were living with their landlady in a house in Marloes Road, Kensington, facing the workhouse gates. For some years now Clem had been earning a modest income from wood-engraving for the *Graphic* and other illustrated papers; but there was only a limited commercial future for her, because new printing techniques were making her method an expensive way of reproducing pictures. She had also written a short novel, *The Were-Wolf*, which had appeared as the Christmas number of the magazine *Atalanta* in 1890. It was a strange story of horror and self-sacrifice, beautifully told; and on its publication Alfred wrote her a letter of warm appreciation beginning 'Capital, capital, capital!'

Laurence had always been very close to Clem, and since moving to London he had allowed her to take the place of his stepmother, who as a result became increasingly jealous of their relationship. Laurence had spent five or six years as an art student, but had failed 'to get set in the right direction', and although he found some work as an illustrator, he had spent more and more time writing. Alfred Pollard, a family friend since Alfred Housman's undergraduate days, now went out of his way to help Laurence, giving him introductions to editors and publishers through whom he gradually began to get some of his work into print: a selection of Blake, some books of fairy stories, and a story in the *Universal Review*. Like his brother Alfred – though they never discussed it – Laurence had grown up with homosexual tendencies; and the *Universal Review* story, *The Green Gaffer*, led to a friendly meeting with Oscar Wilde, in the days before Wilde's persecution. Laurence continued to write stories, and to illustrate books, but his earnings were still very small, and he sometimes doubted whether he would ever be able to make a real living.

Laurence also had religious doubts. He never became an atheist, like Alfred; but for much of his life he was occupied in searching for a religious framework which could accommodate him, and at this time he was flirting with Roman Catholicism, which had a deep emotional appeal for him, but which he was unable to accept intellectually. At Perry Hall, he was suspected of high-church tendencies, by Edward 'with secret satisfaction', but by Lucy, who had of course done her best to weed out such tendencies, 'with stern disapproval'.

Meanwhile Edward Housman still managed to retain his post as clerk to the Commissioners for Income Tax in the Droitwich district, which brought in a small annual income. Though it was well known that he drank too much and worked far too little, he still retained the love of his wife, and the affection if not the respect of his children; he wrote comic verses, enjoyed pottering about in the kitchen, and could still grow flowers in the garden, even though the greenhouse had had to be let long ago.[5] He remained a weak but charming character, and if he drank too much, well, as his son Alfred was later to write,

> . . . malt does more than Milton can
> To justify God's ways to man . . .      (*ASL* 62)

Lucy, as always, 'very courageous and staunch to her duty as she saw it',[6] remained loyal to Edward, and kept a close eye upon her stepchildren. But as she grew older, she became more and more inflexible in her ideas, being particularly intransigent on the matter of retaining Perry Hall. She refused to acknowledge that now the family were gone its upkeep was an unnecessary financial burden. For the sake of harmonious relations Laurence eventually had to drop his attempt at getting them to move somewhere more suitable.

In 1894 Edward's health broke down for the last time. He was confined to bed, and died on 27 November 1894 when his heart failed. Herbert, who was home on leave, was able to comfort his stepmother and saw to the registration of the death and other urgent formalities. Alfred travelled up to Bromsgrove to be present at his father's funeral, and watched as the coffin was lowered into a grave in Catshill churchyard, beside Sarah Jane, and not far from Thomas and Ann Housman. Alfred had to go back to London almost immediately, but returned to Perry Hall and spent the Christmas holidays at home, settling things and looking over books and papers.[7] In the meantime, Lucy had seen to the setting up of a tombstone on which, to keep Edward from joining Sarah Jane,[8] she had had engraved: 'Here rests waiting for the Resurrection Day, Edward Housman.' Alfred's most personal tribute to his father was a poem full of grief at his passing:

> They shall have breath that never were,
> But he that was shall have it ne'er;
> The unconceived and unbegot
> Shall look on heaven, but he shall not.
> The heart with many wild-fires lit,
> Ice is not as cold as it.
> The thirst that rivers could not lay
> A little dust has quenched for aye;
> And in a fathom's compass lie
> Thoughts much wider than the sky.       (*AP* 11a)

Alfred was deeply aware that he was now the head of the family, and had acquired a new and important set of responsibilities towards its members.[9] His first task was to see Lucy happily settled. She still wanted to stay on at Perry Hall, but at last realised that this was out of the question, and in the spring of 1895 went to live with one of her sisters in Hereford, where she made the Cathedral the centre of her life. Until she made this move, various members of the family took turns to keep her company at Perry Hall.

But Alfred's responsibilities did not end with his stepmother. From this time on, he kept up a much closer interest in the lives of all his brothers and sisters. In particular, he spent some time helping and advising Laurence, who, not long after their father's death, sent Alfred the manuscript of his first volume of poems, *Green Arras*.

Alfred sorted through the poems, putting them in a rough order of merit, offering some sound general advice, and writing long critical notes, 'both kind and caustic', on individual poems. For example, he wrote:

> What makes many of your poems more obscure than they need be is that you do not put yourself in the reader's place and consider how, and at what stage, that man of sorrows is to find out what it is all about. You are behind the scenes and know all the data; but he only knows what you tell him.

And then, applying this to a particular poem, 'The Great Ride', he asked:

> how soon do you imagine your victim will find out that you are talking about horses? Not until the thirteenth of these long lines, unless he is such a prodigy of intelligence and good will as I am: there you mention hoofs, and he has to read the thirteen lines over again. 'Flank' in line six is not enough: Swinburne's women have flanks.

Nevertheless, *Green Arras* was successfully published in 1895 by John Lane, and Laurence began to feel that he was quite well established. As well as earning money as an art critic for the *Manchester Guardian*, he could now count on a public of a thousand for his prose and half as many for his verse, and his reputation was steadily growing. But then

> like a bolt from the blue out came *A Shropshire Lad*, and straightway [Laurence records] as an author with any individuality worth mentioning, I was wiped out. I became the brother of the 'Shropshire Lad'; and for the next five years I laboured under the shadow of that bright cloud.

Literature was Laurence's trade; and it was hard to be overshadowed by a brother whose single slim volume of poems had been written as a side-line to his academic career. But Laurence's first reaction was to be genuinely delighted with the poems, and later in the year he even visited some of the places in Shropshire associated with them. From now on there was a more or less amiable rivalry between Alfred and Laurence, a rivalry stimulated by the fact that people were sometimes muddled about which brother had written what. This led to some amusing incidents. In December 1896 Alfred met a Greek Professor, who was interested to learn that he was talking to the brother of Laurence Housman. Alfred wrote to tell Laurence of this, because he thought Laurence would like to hear that the Professor:

> said that he had got *Green Arras*, and then he proceeded, 'I think it is the best volume by him that I have seen: the *Shropshire Lad* had a pretty cover.'
>     I remain
>         Your affectionate brother (what a thing is fraternal affection, that it will stand these tests!)

Alfred wrote to Laurence about reviews of Laurence's books, wrote appreciatively about the ingenuity of his stories, and – though he teased him for writing faster than anyone could be expected to read – he was always interested to see what new work Laurence was going to produce. Awaiting Laurence's *Spikenard*, a volume of devotional poems which was to be published in 1898, Alfred wrote to their stepmother 'Perhaps I myself may write a Hymn-book for use in the Salvation Army', and he enclosed two comic examples, of which one runs:

> 'Hallelujah!' was the only observation
> That escaped Lieutenant-Colonel Mary Jane,
> When she tumbled off the platform in the station,
> And was cut in little pieces by the train.
> Mary Jane, the train is through yer:
> Hallelujah, Hallelujah!
> We will gather up the fragments that remain.

*Spikenard* was, in fact, the cause of some bad feeling between Laurence and Alfred. Alfred described the poems to Laurence as 'nonsense verse' – which he intended as a compliment, since he also applied that description to beautifully written poems such as those by Christina Rossetti which he admired a great deal. But Laurence was hurt by what he took to be a condemnation, and it was some years before the misunderstanding was cleared up. Despite this, Laurence generously accepted that Alfred's poems were superior to his own; and if in later years he ever got a little jealous of his eldest brother, he contented himself with reflecting that Alfred's life had been, in general, much less happy than his own.[10]

Certainly, while Alfred continued to live a respectable but emotionally repressed life at University College London, Laurence was learning to be outrageous and unrestrained in the company of the man who for many years was to be one of his closest friends: Herbert Alexander, known affectionately as 'Sandro'. With Sandro, Laurence learned the pleasures of bicycling, tenting, sun-bathing, and wearing scanty Greek costume for dinner – with Sandro dressed up as Cupid. On one occasion, Laurence even posed for photographs sitting naked in a tree with Sandro and some other friends. When Sandro's enraged father found out about this, they could only explain that they were posing as 'arboreal men'. Laurence also went on holiday to Italy with Sandro and another young man; and he was carrying on a correspondence with Oscar Wilde, who wrote to him in December 1898: 'Your soul has beautiful curves and colours.' When he was in London, Laurence frequented the Café Royal with George Bernard Shaw, Frank Harris, and others; and when, in the last year of Wilde's life, they decided to do something to help Wilde, who was now living in Paris under the name of Sebastian Melmoth,[11]

Shaw took round the hat and the proceeds were given to Housman (as the youngest) with instructions to go to Paris to find Wilde, pay his rent and outstanding debt to the café proprietor, give no cash to Wilde, and report back to the Café Royal. Several times he made this journey before Wilde's death.

In 1900 Laurence found popular favour with *An Englishwoman's Love-Letters*, which was published anonymously and pretended to be a true account of a failed love-affair. The first edition sold out within a week, and the profits from this and successive editions of the book brought Laurence real prosperity for the first time. Alfred had a low opinion of the highly sentimental love-letters; and when Laurence followed it up with the autobiographical *A Modern Antaeus*, he told Laurence that 'he thought I had mistaken my vocation, and that I ought to have been an accoucheur, because of my "too great interest in the process of gestation"'.[12] However, Alfred was pleased that Laurence and Clem were more affluent. Clem – who on first reading *A Shropshire Lad* had apparently cried out, with a mixture of sorrow and relief, 'Alfred has a heart!' – had now made two contributions herself to the family bookshelf: first in 1896 when *The Were-Wolf*, sensitively illustrated by Laurence, was published in hard covers by John Lane; and then in 1898, when her novel *The Unknown Sea* was published by Duckworth. It is a haunting and haunted tale of self-sacrifice: with its echoes of the Victorian household at Perry Hall, perhaps even of her brother Alfred's troubles – 'the incurable wounds of a proud spirit', writes Clem of her hero, 'gaped and bled hot and fresh'.[13]

Neither book brought in a great deal of money; but with the success of *An Englishwoman's Love-Letters*, Laurence and Clem were able to move from their rooms opposite the workhouse in Marloes Road, to a high flat overlooking Battersea Park, with a view all the way to Hampstead.

If Alfred was pleased to see Laurence and Clem more comfortable, he had been delighted at the news that his brother Basil was to marry Jeannie Dixon, an attractive girl whose family lived at Tardebigge not far from Bromsgrove. Alfred was asked to be Best Man, and his speech was a great success. Laurence, who was present at the wedding, in July 1894, later recalled that Alfred 'commended the custom of a certain African tribe, which, he said, made a religious practice of eating the mother-in-law at the wedding feast. It was a good instance of his humour, which had always a bite in it. . . .'

Other family news in the years up to 1900 was that Kate and Edward Symons had moved from Banbury to Bath, where Symons had been appointed Headmaster of King Edward's School. After lecturing in Birmingham, Robert became scientific adviser at Kynoch's, a gun-making firm in Birmingham, where he became an expert in the theory and

practice of ammunition and shooting.[14] As for Herbert: he continued with
his career in the Army, and had been made a sergeant when the Boer War
broke out in 1899. Before he was sent with his Regiment to the field of
action, *An Englishwoman's Love-Letters* was published, and he expressed a
great desire to read it. 'After which', commented Alfred, 'the Boers will
have no terrors for him.'

Herbert was certainly brave, 'always to the fore when there was any
fighting to do'; and he was also a fine soldier. His Lieutenant later wrote:
'I got to know him very well and formed a very high opinion of him as a
soldier. [He did] extremely well the whole time . . . and has been
mentioned in despatches'; and the officer in command of his Company,
called him 'quite the *best* sergeant in my Company'. Alfred, reading
reports of Herbert's bravery, must have remembered the lines which he
had written for anyone who was thinking of becoming a soldier:

> Oh stay with company and mirth
>     And daylight and the air;
> Too full already is the grave
> Of fellows that were good and brave
>     And died because they were.            (*LP* 38)

For on 30 October 1901, his youngest brother was killed in action.

Herbert's body lay all night in the rain: and these lines of Alfred's,
though they were drafted before Herbert's death, are strangely appro-
priate:[15]

> But oh, my man, the house is fallen
>     That none can build again;
> My man, how full of joy and woe
> Your mother bore you years ago
>     Tonight to lie in the rain.            (*LP* 18)

And now, remembering perhaps one of Herbert's letters from Burmah, in
which he had written about the stars, 'very large and numerous.
. . . The falling stars are very beautiful . . . I have seen nothing of the
Southern Cross',[16] Alfred wrote:

> For pay and medals, name and rank,
>     Things that he has not found,
> He hove the Southern Cross and sank
>     The pole-star underground.             (*LP* 17)

But Alfred's real sense of loss and waste were expressed most bitterly in:

> So ceases and turns to the thing
>     He was born to be

A soldier cheap to the King
And dear to me;
So smothers in blood the burning
And flaming flight
Of valour and truth returning
To dust and night.                    (MP 40)

The Housman's had lost an open, honest warm-hearted brother – Kate's favourite, and a very devoted stepson to Lucy. They put up a plaque to commemorate Herbert in Bromsgrove Church, and Alfred's poems have ensured him another kind of immortality.

Herbert was only thirty-three when he died; but his death must have been half-expected. Four years later Robert Housman's death at the age of forty-five came as more of a shock to the family, though Robert's health had always been delicate. He had plunged into the Bristol Avon to get a good photograph of the surrounding countryside, the cold was said to have been too much for him, and three days later 'a chill on the kidneys' brought to a tragic end the life of one who was described in his obituaries as having been a fine scientist with a brilliant future.

The Housmans were all very shaken by Robert's death. All five of the surviving brothers and sisters: Alfred, Clemence, Kate, Basil, and Laurence, were present at the funeral which Edward Symons arranged at a local church in Bath.[17] The most religious among them, Clem, will have been comforted by the words of the Anglican service 'Order for The Burial of The Dead': 'Behold, I shew you a mystery: we shall not all sleep . . . (for the trumpet shall sound,) and the dead shall be raised incorruptible.' Alfred and the others may have responded with more emotion to: 'Man that is born of a woman hath but a short time to live, and is full of misery. He cometh up, and is cut down, like a flower; he fleeth as it were a shadow, and never continueth in one stay.' Not long after this, Clem dedicated her new book to 'Robert Holden Housman – Thanks be to God for my good brother, who has blessed this life of mine';[18] and the family as a whole had a sundial memorial put up in the cemetery where Robert was buried, with the inscription upon it: 'Our days on earth are like a shadow, and there is none abiding.'

Lucy, now in her eighties, was not well enough to make the journey to Bath. Indeed, the shock of Robert's death nearly killed her. Laurence went up to visit her, and found her terribly upset, even attacking Kate, her favourite stepdaughter, and blaming her for allowing Robert to wade through rivers when she knew how poor his health had been. After this Lucy's own health rapidly deteriorated, and at the beginning of August, feeling that she had not much longer to live, she drew up her will. Despite her outburst against Kate, the will went heavily in Kate's favour. Alfred,

Basil, and Laurence also benefited, while Clem, who had stolen Laurence from her, was cut out of the will altogether. [19] But Lucy did not die at once; by the end of September she had begun to recover some strength, and for the next two years she clung precariously to life. Alfred visited Lucy in February 1907; and, wishing to spare her any financial worries, he afterwards wrote to Laurence:

> I have induced Dr. Morris to tell me, on condition that Mamma does not hear that he told, the amount of his bill for last year. It is about £70. 0s. 0d; and I want to find out, if possible, what this will mean to Mamma. I have no clear notion what her income is and what margin it generally leaves her; and perhaps you or Clemence can give me some notion. I am anxious to prevent her feeling any severe pinch for the bill, but on the other hand I don't want to be extravagant or ostentatious; so if you can help me to judge what I should give her in order to effect these two ends I should be much obliged.

Lucy died in November the same year. She had said in her will: 'I wish to pass out of this world with as little public notice as possible'; and, according to her instructions, she was enclosed in an 'elm box without any shape and laid in the same grave with my dear husband, with charcoal to assist decay'. [20] Alfred attended the funeral, but there was no cause for great mourning over Lucy's death. She had lived to be eighty-four, after a useful life, in which she had not only stood by Edward Housman through thick and thin, in the most staunch and loyal manner, but also done her best to bring up seven stepchildren, often in difficult circumstances. All the same, hers was the third death in Alfred's immediate family circle in the last six years; and after the funeral he wandered off alone through the south of Shropshire, no doubt revolving many memories of childhood in his mind, exactly as he had done after his father's death thirteen years previously.

In 1903, Laurence and Clem had moved from their flat overlooking Battersea back to Kensington. Soon after the move, Laurence was busy helping Somerset Maugham to edit a new annual, *The Venture*; and when he asked Alfred for a contribution, his brother kindly let him print 'The Oracles'. Alfred added, in his accompanying letter to Laurence:

> I hope you won't succeed in getting anything from Meredith [who had earned Alfred's dislike by calling *A Shropshire Lad* an 'orgy of naturalism'], as I am a respectable character, and do not care to be seen in the company of galvanised corpses. By this time he stinketh: for he hath been dead twenty years.

*The Venture* was not a commercial success; and Laurence was also having little luck with his plays. *Bethlehem* had been refused a licence on the ground that the Holy Family might not figure in a stage play; and a light opera based on *The Vicar of Wakefield* was first rearranged by an American star (who began appropriating all the best dialogue), and was finally so hacked about that Laurence had to withdraw his name from the production to protect his reputation. Rather unwisely, he still insisted on going to the first night; when the manager, on hearing of his arrival, was so enraged that he ordered him out of the theatre, threatening to attack him if he had not left by the end of the first Act. Laurence prudently withdrew, only to find that the incident was blown up out of all proportion by the press, who interviewed the manager and then carried an untrue story about Laurence having got up and booed the actors during the performance! In between these two disasters, he wrote *Prunella*, a 'grown-up fairy tale play' on which he collaborated with Granville Barker. On its first run, in the winter of 1904–5, the play was mauled by the critics, and was a failure with the audiences. However, Alfred came to see it, and at the end of the second Act he turned to Laurence and said '"Good", which was', records Laurence, 'perhaps the most unconditional praise I ever had from him.'[21] Alfred's judgment was right. When the play was revived two years later it began to pay its way; and eventually it crossed the Atlantic and was an enormous success in New York.

In the meantime Clem, writing in the small hours after Laurence had gone to bed – she apparently drank whisky to get through the nights[22] – had completed and published her strange and complex tale, *Sir Aglovale de Galis*. Laurence thought this her greatest work. Clem's message, that Arthurian honour was a sham, and that the real reason for the break-up of Arthur's Court was Arthur's incest and Lancelot's adultery, was not one likely to appeal to a public brought up on Tennyson's *Idylls of the King*. The book was written with her usual moral fervour:

In the days of his youth Arthur sinned with Morgause, King Lot's wife, not knowing that he and she were sprung from the same womb. With knowledge of the fatal truth and the measure of his guilt came dread of doom to follow oppressing his soul. Then came Merlin and foretold that the fruit of incest should prove his bane . . . the laws he had broken were the laws of God given to man, and sooner or later the hand of God would bring him to account (pp. 233–5).

If one contrasts the last part of this extract with Alfred Housman's 'The laws of God, the laws of man', in which he writes:

> let God and man decree
> Laws for themselves and not for me,                        (*LP* 12)

it shows us something of the huge gap in outlook which had opened up between Clem and her brother. Clem's religious beliefs were intense, even fanatical, and made any real intimacy between her and Alfred out of the question. At any rate, *Sir Aglovale de Galis* was a commercial failure, and Clemence wrote no more books.

Alfred continued to take an interest in Laurence's plays, going in 1908 to the unsuccessful *The Chinese Lantern*, a play with incidental music which made him complain that he was left 'faint and weak from the effort of straining to hear the human voice through the uproar of pussy's bowels'; and though he would not attend Laurence's defiant public reading of *Pains and Penalties*, a censored play based on the marital difficulties between George IV and Queen Charlotte, Alfred attended the first night of Laurence's translation of *Lysistrata*.[23] Laurence's translation was very free – though he wrote to Alfred: 'There is more of Aristophanes in it than you believed when you saw the play';[24] and it was also very timely.

For some years, there had been an increasing interest in the problems of women in society. As early as 1902 Laurence had made Marcia, his portrait of Clem in *A Modern Antaeus*, say:

> I'm too strong for my sex. . . . There are so many things I *can* do, and mayn't. It never strikes a man, I suppose, what a prison that is? You don't want to thread needles, and darn stockings, or wear your hair long; all things you could do if you wished. If you want to break out, you break out, and that's the difference. But look at me! (p. 296).

Now the women's suffrage campaign was in full swing, and Clem and Laurence were in the thick of it.

The summer of 1909 saw Clemence working hard as banner-maker-in-chief for the Women's Social and Political Union; and when Mrs Pankhurst led a delegation to Parliament to present a petition to the Prime Minister, and was arrested, and the crowds of women outside made attempt after attempt to storm the doors, the voice heard in the Central Lobby, shouting above the din: 'The women of England are clamouring to be admitted!', was that of Laurence.[25] After being converted to votes for women by one of Mrs Pankhurst's speeches, Laurence had become an ardent advocate for the movement. He discovered that he could make effective public speeches, and became an important figure on lecture platforms in London and the provinces, at one time even wondering whether he should not totally abandon his literary career and become an itinerant preacher for suffrage, taking only his living expenses.

For his part, Alfred shared his father's doubts about the virtues of democracy. He certainly saw no reason for extending the franchise still further by giving votes to women, and he did not attach a great deal of importance to their other complaints. When in August 1909 Lily

Thicknesse sent him a copy of her husband's suffragist pamphlet, *The Rights and Wrongs of Women,* he replied with a letter of teasing irony:

> My blood boils. This is not due to the recent commencement of summer, but to the Wrongs of Woman, with which I have been making myself acquainted. 'She cannot serve on any Jury'; and yet she lives bravely on. 'She cannot serve in the army or navy' – oh cruel, cruel! – 'except' – this adds insult to injury – 'as a nurse'. They do not even employ a Running Woman instead of a Running Man for practising markmanship. I have been making marginal additions. 'She cannot be ordained a Priest or Deacon': add *nor become a Freemason.* 'She cannot be a member of the Royal Society': add *nor of the Amateur Boxing Association.* In short your unhappy sex seems to have nothing to look forward to, except contracting a valid marriage as soon as they are 12 years old; and that must soon pall.

The following summer Laurence asked Alfred to sign a declaration in favour of women's suffrage, but Alfred declined, giving two or three excuses before making it clear that he was not on his brother's side:

> Even if I were actually in favour of women's suffrage in the abstract I think I should like to see some other and less precious country try it first: America, for instance, where the solution ought to be just as urgent as here.

Alfred knew that Clem had become involved in active tax-resistance, and he finished by sending his love to her, adding that he hoped she had read, or would read, H. G. Wells's book *Ann Veronica,* in which the heroine of that name is sent to prison as a militant suffragette. Clem took no notice of her brother's friendly warning. She was refusing to pay house duty on a cottage which she had rented and stocked with furniture not her own, so that there was nothing for the bailiffs to seize. Finally, on 30 September 1911, she was arrested, sentenced, and sent to Holloway Prison. That night the *Evening Standard* carried a picture of Clem and Laurence standing in front of the prison gates – 'a lovely portrait of my disreputable relatives', as Alfred described it to Grant Richards.[26]

Alfred's other brother and sister had been living less dramatic lives. In 1908 Basil had successfully applied for a job as an Assistant School Medical Officer in Worcestershire, and he moved with his wife to Tardebigge, where they spent the rest of their lives in the area where they had passed their childhood; while Kate had been working hard supporting her husband's efforts at King Edward's School, Bath.

Kate had become the 'family-bureau correspondent' after Lucy Housman's death in 1907, and from then on she frequently wrote to Alfred.[27] She passed on family news to him, and they also corresponded about the Housman family tree, in which Kate and a distant cousin of theirs had become interested.[28] Alfred, sharing her love for the family, grew very much more attached to Kate as the years passed; though Kate for her part always remembered that Clem had been his favourite sister when they were all children, and never quite forgave him for it.[29]

\* \* \*

When in August 1914 England declared war on Germany, Alfred's generation of the Housman family were all in their fifties and past fighting age. Only Basil found an official appointment: in 1915 he served in Birmingham, where he worked at one of the special war hospitals, and also gave medical examinations to recruits. The heat and burden of the day, so far as the Housmans were concerned, fell upon Kate's children. Her eldest son, Herbert, was already serving in the Navy; and now as Alfred reported to a friend, the other three were 'being inoculated for typhoid and catching pneumonia on Salisbury Plain and performing other acts of war calculated to make the German Emperor realise that he is a very misguided man'. The light-hearted tone in which Alfred wrote disguised the profound concern which he felt for his nephews. On hearing that they were enlisting, he had immediately sent £100 to Kate so that she could kit them out as well as possible for the war. Then at the beginning of December, when Denis was ill at home after reacting badly to the inoculation, and Jerry was home on leave, Alfred went down to Bath for a few days to see them both,[30] and to be some support for Kate, who was keeping 'a brave face over a heart of too little hope' as, one by one, her sons prepared to leave for the battle-fields.

On this occasion Alfred did not see the fourth son, Clement, to whom he had already given some very personal encouragement. When he enlisted, Clement, who was in love with a girl whom he hoped to marry, and who had every reason for wanting to live, found that he was 'in deadly fear of getting killed'. Alfred, hearing of this, sent him these verses, which according to Laurence Housman, describe 'a man in fear of death who conquers his fear':[31]

> Her strong enchantments failing,
>   Her towers of fear in wreck,
> Her limbecks dried of poisons
>   And the knife at her neck,
>
> The Queen of air and darkness
>   Begins to shrill and cry,
> 'O young man, O my slayer,
>   Tomorrow you shall die.'

O Queen of air and darkness,
    I think 'tis truth you say,
And I shall die tomorrow;
    But you will die to-day.                    (LP 3)

Clement told Kate that this poem had helped him overcome his own fears, and he copied it out, and left it with his mother, saying that it would console her if he *was* killed. [32]

When Alfred went down to Dulverton to enjoy a few days' holiday with Kate and Edward Symons in August 1915, the news about his four nephews was reasonably good. Jerry had been invalided home in February; Herbert had been present in the naval action off the Falkland Islands;[33] Denis and Clement were still 'somewhere in France'. But only a few weeks later, Clement was killed in action. Clem, who was his godmother, wrote sadly to one of her friends; 'I can't help thinking of the blessing and consolation it would have been had he before he went out married his dear little Vera, and if now there were hope of a coming life.'

Alfred, a 'brother born for adversity', wrote directly to his sister:

My dear Kate,
    I have been scanning the casualty lists in these last days, and when I saw your card this morning I feared what the news must be. Well, my dear, it is little I or anyone else can do to comfort you, or think of anything to say that you will not have thought of. But I remember your telling me at the beginning of the war that he had almost a hope and expectation of dying in battle, and we must be glad that it was a victorious battle in which he died. I do not know that I can do better than send you some verses that I wrote many years ago; because the essential business of poetry, as it has been said, is to harmonise the sadness of the Universe, and it is somehow more sustaining and healing than prose. Do assure Edward of my feeling for you all, and also, though I do not know her, the poor young girl.
    Your affectionate brother      A. E. Housman

The poem which he sent to Kate was 'Illic Iacet', which ends:

Oh dark is the chamber and lonely,
    And lights and companions depart;
But lief will he lose them and only
    Behold the desire of his heart.

And low is the roof, but it covers
    A sleeper content to repose;
And far from his friends and his lovers
    He lies with the sweetheart he chose.        (LP 4)

Kate lost no more of her sons to that cruel sweetheart, though Jerry came close to being killed on more than one occasion. After an incident which meant the surgeons had to amputate his left arm, Alfred wrote to him as soon as he heard what had happened, and told him to get the best artificial arm made that he could, and to send him the bill;[34] and not long after this Alfred posted to *The Times* his famous poem, 'Epitaph on an Army of Mercenaries', praising the courage of the British troops:

> These, in the day when heaven was falling,
> The hour when earth's foundations fled,
> Followed their mercenary calling
> And took their wages and are dead.
>
> Their shoulders held the sky suspended;
> They stood, and earth's foundations stay;
> What God abandoned, these defended,
> And saved the sum of things for pay.          (*LP* 37)

This poem is in part an ironic comment on the popular hymn 'Abide with me', in which God is asked to 'Abide' even 'When earth's foundations flee'; but God does not abide, says Housman: he abandons. This provides the context for the real message of the poem: which is a celebration, in general, of the huge courage of man, holding the sky suspended like an Atlas when he knows that he must rely solely on his own strength; and, in particular, of the bravery of the British troops who, for a few shillings a week, faced death while defending the interests of their country.

Although Alfred and his brothers were not involved in the fighting, Laurence took his own gamble with death during the war, travelling to New York and back in the early months of 1916, risking the German submarines, in order to make speeches about the setting up of a League of Nations after the war. Reacting to the dangers and horrors of the war, Laurence wrote the first of his well-known *The Little Plays of St Francis*, commenting later: 'in the serene sanity of St. Francis I found such blessed escape from a world gone mad'.

At least there was some good news for Laurence and Clem in the last year of the war: on 11 January 1918, Laurence wrote to some close friends, 'Clem and I fell into each other arms on the stairs this morning when we learned that the Lords had climbed up to Woman's Suffrage. I almost do believe it is sure and safe at last.'

\*     \*     \*

After the war, Alfred frequently visited Basil at Tardebigge. Basil had found great contentment as a country doctor;[35] and indeed Alfred once described him as 'the most normal member of the family'. He had no children, but lived happily with his wife, respected by his neighbours, and liked by his servants. According to Laurence, Jeannie was one of the people with whom Alfred got on 'well and easily. A typical case of a sincere, quite non-intellectual character, with an easy flow of speech which left Alfred free from conversational effort himself, and yet sufficiently interesting to give him entertainment.'[36] Clem found Basil and Jeannie *too* non-intellectual, and was not much interested in them.[37] But Alfred found their company pleasant and relaxing. 'He always seemed to enjoy things and to be happy', wrote Jeannie later, 'and enjoy amusing others with his clever nonsense. I have known him and Basil laugh until they cried.' Basil was no longer so fit as he had been, but he liked watching County Cricket, and could still enjoy a game of croquet; he particularly delighted in Alfred's nonsense rhymes, though he had no time for *A Shropshire Lad* or indeed any serious poetry,[38] and in the evening he and Alfred would drink claret, or perhaps listen with amusement to those 'fools on the radio', as Alfred contemptuously called the broadcasters.[39]

The two brothers also went out for drives together, until in the summer of 1926 Basil's health suddenly began to deteriorate, so that for a while he was unable to leave the house. Alfred now began making excursions on his own, getting Basil's man to drive him over to the Bromsgrove area, where he retraced the walks which he had enjoyed as a child.[40] Basil's health continued to be poor, so that it was difficult for him to earn his living as a doctor; and from now on Alfred sent him £50 a year to help make ends meet.

Meanwhile, in the summer of 1921 Edward Symons had retired as Headmaster of King Edward's School, Bath. To celebrate his retirement, the Symonses had arranged a holiday in Monmouth, where they were joined first by Clem and then by Alfred. Alfred had been chauffeur-driven all the way from Cambridge, an extravagance which greatly shocked Clem. But it was pleasant to have a car at their disposal, and one day the party drove over to Tintern Abbey, lunching nearby before wandering round the ruins. Clem, still 'a strikingly handsome woman, with . . . dark luminous hazel eyes', was flattered when Alfred chose to walk with her, pointing out all the architectural details in which he knew she was interested; but she was also irritated when he told her – as she reported to Laurence – that, on a particular issue, 'he has not yet been able to vote against my "wretched sex" at Cambridge, as he was left off the lists by mistake. But for the next occasion he will be qualified.'

The following summer, Alfred, Clem, Kate and Edward spent another holiday together. Once again, Laurence kept away, writing an unkind letter about Clem's companions in which he suggested that Kate was the

only one whom he greatly admired; her husband ate more than necessary, and 'Alfred, her other companion, has intellect too lofty to be
domestic. He prefers to be interested in things he does not have to talk
about.'

Nevertheless, Alfred continued to show a practical concern for the
well-being of the family. Within a few years of Edward Symons's retirement, Edward and Kate found that they were much poorer than they had
expected to be; and when Kate was reduced to asking Alfred for a loan of
£200, he sent her a cheque for that amount by return of post. Later, she
worried about not being able to repay him, but he wrote kindly:[41]

> There is *not* the least hurry about repaying. . . . You are quite at liberty
> to look upon me as one of the ancient Gauls, who were quite willing to
> lend money on a promise to pay it back in the next world: such was
> their belief in the immortality of the soul, until Christianity under-
> mined it.

He had been helping her for several years with research for a history of
King Edward's School, Bath, which she was writing, and he generously
paid for her to become a Life Member of the London Library.

In 1926, Alfred and the other Housmans heard of the death of their
uncle Joseph Brettell Housman, the man who had helped to save their
father from financial ruin in 1879. Joseph was nearly eighty-four years old
when he died. Kate had always been devoted to her 'Uncle Joe',[42] and he
in his turn had taken a friendly interest in her and her children. He died
childless, leaving his money to his wife, with the provision that, on her
death, it should go to Kate or Kate's children.[43] So when Joseph's widow
died only two years later, Kate inherited a house in Exeter, and a good
sum of money to go with it. She and Edward soon moved into the Exeter
house, and she repaid £200 to Alfred, who wrote, thanking her: 'I am glad
that you have come to comparative opulence, and that you like your last
new mansion.' One of her sons later said of Kate that she 'spent her whole
life giving'; she had worked unceasingly over the years for her husband
and her children, and now that she had inherited some money she very
unselfishly offered to share it with Basil and Jeannie, and so helped to put
an end to their financial worries as well as to her own.

Despite those worries, Kate had found time, over the years, to keep
Alfred very well informed about the activities of her children. Herbert had
been continuing with his successful career in the Navy, and was now
married. Denis had been for some years an assistant medical officer in
Shropshire; but he and his wife Phyllis had lunched with his uncle Alfred
in Trinity on at least one occasion;[44] and they now had three sons, so that
Kate was a grandmother and Alfred a great-uncle. Jerry, with his usual
bravery and good humour, had made light of his artificial arm; and was

also happily married. Alfred, who took a special interest in the nephew who had suffered so badly on his country's behalf during the war, was always pleased to see Jerry's letters to his mother; and once Jerry stayed in Cambridge for a few days when he was home on leave.[45]

Between Alfred and his brother Laurence, there was a continuation in these years of the same more or less friendly rivalry which had characterised their earlier correspondence; and people were still confused about which brother had written what. On one occasion, for example, Laurence wrote to tell Alfred that he had made a great deal of money by selling some copies of *A Shropshire Lad* which he had persuaded Alfred to sign. Laurence offered Alfred the proceeds; but Alfred declined, replying that the Dean of Westminster had recently thanked him for the amusement he had derived from Alfred's writings, 'especially about Queen Victoria and her Ministers – so if I bring you money, you bring me fame'. Laurence had indeed been writing a popular series of one-Act Victorian plays, later collectively known as *Victoria Regina*; and he had also published several series of his *Little Plays of St Francis*.

The sales of these plays had kept Laurence and Clem in reasonable prosperity. At the end of the war, they had moved from Kensington and retired to their cottage on the edge of the New Forest, where Clem 'planted herself ferociously in the soil'. But Laurence was hoping from the beginning of 1919 that he could persuade her to move to Street, the home of their Quaker friends, the Clarks. Laurence had been strongly drawn towards the Quakers during the last years of the war, admiring their pacifism, and feeling that they had 'a sort of spiritual liberty' which was lacking in the Churches of England and Rome. At last, in 1923, Clem was persuaded to move, and they had a house built for themselves in an orchard which they purchased from the Clarks.

Alfred was pleased by Laurence's popular success; but his comments on Laurence's work were not usually very flattering: after coming down to watch some of the *Little Plays of St Francis* at the Glastonbury Festival which Laurence was now directing, he commented only: 'Not so bad as I expected.'[46] But in 1922 he thought highly enough of Laurence's judgment to ask him to look through the poems which he was then preparing for publication;[47] and Laurence was later delighted to find that, although he had only sent Alfred those of his books which he thought would particularly interest him, Alfred had collected all his books in their various editions, and had 'said kinder things about them behind my back than he did to my face'.

As Alfred approached his seventieth birthday in March 1929, he could reflect with pride that he had done his duty as head of the family since Edward Housman's death over thirty-four years in the past. Before then, his brothers and sisters had regarded him as an isolated and withdrawn figure; but since that date he had in various ways and at various times given most of them encouragement, help, comfort, or companionship. Over the whole of Alfred's life, his loving concern for his family had often brought him sorrow: sorrow for his mother's tragically early death, for his father's premature physical collapse, for the deaths in battle of his brother Herbert and his nephew Clement – a sorrow which had been an important influence upon his poetry and his philosophy of life. But there was another side to all this: one of his nephews remembers Alfred, on a picnic with Kate and Edward, 'very much one of the family';[48] and his sister-in-law Jeannie wrote: 'He always seemed to enjoy things and to be happy.' Among his family, he had found a degree of happiness which had usually eluded him elsewhere.

\* \* \*

During all these years, from 1892 to 1929, there was one family which, though not his own family, was closer to Housman than any other: the Wises of Woodchester. His godmother, Mrs Wise, died in 1892; but Alfred continued to visit Woodchester House almost every summer. Indeed, Woodchester was more than a second home for Alfred: it was in many ways the real home to which, like a boy coming back from boarding school, he returned to find the love and easy affection which had been denied him during the long weeks of the term.

The Wises were not poor, but they were no longer prosperous; they continued to take in paying guests, and they also reduced their staff. So Alfred's visits were reminders for him as well as for them of happier days; and something of the cheerful atmosphere when he was staying with them bubbled over into the comical verses which he wrote into the Visitors' Book, such as:[49]

> This is the house where Perkins dwelt
>     Lord of the mill of pins;
> And here, where Radical Dissent
> Once pitched its pure and pious tent,
> Atrocious Tories make their lair
> And use the Book of Common Prayer
>     And swelter in their sins.
> Oh, home of Perkins, can it be
> That things like this are done in thee?

There was one major change in the household at Woodchester during the pre-war years. Although Sophie Becker had lived as a member of the family for over forty years, Ted and Edith and Minnie had to tell her that they could no longer afford to keep her; and she returned to Wiesbaden in

Germany.[50] From there, she continued to correspond with Alfred, but he never saw her again.

Indeed, during the war years he lost touch with her altogether; and he was only able to renew contact with her when she was an old lady of ninety. Strangely, he avoided travelling to Germany to meet her face to face. Perhaps his feelings for her were so intense that it was easier and less painful to be in touch through the controlled medium of correspondence – just as he maintained contact with the distant Moses Jackson.

After the war, Housman kept up his visits to Woodchester, where Edward Wise was now in his seventies, with Edith and Minnie, like Alfred, in their sixties. Despite their reduced circumstances, the Wises had managed to stay on at Woodchester House – and even to be charitable to the really poor families of the village, who in the winter months would go to their kitchen once or twice a week, 'to receive a large jug of meat and lentil and pea soup, according to the size of the family'.[51] Now they were forced to sell their old home, and move into a much smaller dwelling in North Woodchester. Here there was no longer even a spare bedroom for Alfred, who had to lodge nearby in Selsley Road when he visited them.[52]

Not that he ever felt like a visitor. He knew all the Wises' friends, and wrote about newcomers to the village with the curiosity and slightly suspicious interest of an old inhabitant. At Woodchester, he certainly became a very different person from the reserved and distant Cambridge Professor, as is shown in this charming account of one of his visits, written by Ellinor Allen, a close friend of the Wises:[53]

> The Professor always took the greatest interest in the famous Roman pavement which is uncovered in the old churchyard at intervals. When that happened in 1926 he wrote that he would be very willing to help in any way, selling picture postcards or taking money at the entrance etc, in fact helping in *any* way, but he would not give talks which we were having at intervals. He arrived one afternoon to be greeted by Edith with 'Now hurry up Alfred with your tea, as your first talk is due at half past five' & it was no use protesting; he gave the most interesting lectures during the fortnight that the pavement was on view, he described how the Romans would have lived here, with the villa of the governor of this district, the farm buildings &c – we were all thrilled by him.

Housman's friendship with the Wises, like most happy and straightforward friendships, was not at all dramatic or exciting; but there is no doubt that it was one of the happiest and, for him, one of the most important elements in a life which was too often lonely and withdrawn.

# CHAPTER 8

# Travelling Abroad,
# 1897–1929

This yearning for new and distant scenes, this craving for freedom, release, forgetfulness – they were, he admitted to himself, an impulse towards flight, flight from the spot which was the daily theatre of a rigid, cold, and passionate service. That service he loved, had even almost come to love the enervating daily struggle between a proud, tenacious well-tried will and this growing fatigue . . .

Thomas Mann, *Death in Venice* (1911)[1]

He enjoyed a glass of port. That is something. One wishes he could have enjoyed the happy highways which he resigned in the body and possessed so painfully in the imagination. Perhaps he had a better time than the outsider supposes. Did he ever drink the stolen waters which he recommends so ardently to others? I hope so.

E. M. Forster on A. E. Housman[2]

As a classical scholar at St John's, Alfred Housman must sometimes have wished that he could go abroad to visit the classical sites of Italy or Greece. But he had no money to do so and, in any case, this was after the age of the Grand Tour, and in the 1870s and 1880s Continental travel was not as fashionable as it had been in the previous century.[3]

After his failure in Greats, Housman remained comparatively poor for another eleven years, and it was during this period that his confinement in England became really galling. As he fell in love with Moses Jackson, and came to realise the homosexual nature of that attachment, Housman also came to realise that he was effectively trapped in a land whose moral codes and attitudes were extremely hostile to men of his kind. Preserving his reputation depended upon Housman disguising his real nature even from his friends. He wrote bitterly about this in 1894:

> Please yourselves, say I, and they
> Need only look the other way.

> But no, they will not; they must still
> Wrest their neighbour to their will,
> And make me dance as they desire
> With jail and gallows and hell-fire.

The Continent meant a large measure of toleration for homosexuals, and a real escape for all sorts of people from the bonds of Victorian respectability. But the Continent was as far away for a poor man as the Saturn or Mercury which Housman mentioned in the last lines of his complaint:

> And since, my soul, we cannot fly
> To Saturn nor to Mercury,
> Keep we must, if keep we can,
> These foreign laws of God and man.    (LP 12)

It was not until Housman had been a Professor at University College London for five years that he felt financially secure enough to spend money on foreign travel. Then, in August 1897, at the age of thirty-eight, he crossed the Channel for the first time, and travelled by train to the Paris of the Impressionists, with its little music halls and cafés chantants and yellow fiacres.

No doubt Housman enjoyed the good living, the low prices, and the entertainment. The Bible had taught him: 'There is nothing better for a man, than that he should eat and drink, and that he should make his soul enjoy good in his labour' (Eccl. 2:24); and by getting some pleasure out of life, Housman felt that he was doing something positive to set against the indifference of the Universe. Later he expanded this feeling into a principle of his philosophy: 'I am a Cyrenaic or egoistic hedonist, and regard the pleasure of the moment as the only possible motive of action.' To his stepmother Alfred wrote admiringly about the architectural excellence of Paris; about the beauty of the Seine as it flowed beside handsome quays and beneath handsome bridges; and about the wild and picturesque Bois de Boulogne, which he preferred to the more formal London parks. He also visited Versailles; and then, after a week in Paris, he decided to venture further afield, and boarded a train for Rome and Naples.

Italy was hotter than usual for late September, and the damp and enervating Sirocco was blowing for part of the time; but this did not mar Housman's enjoyment. In Rome, the classical scholar stood among the ruins of the Forum, and the romantic poet searched for the graves of Keats and Shelley. From Naples, he travelled up and down the coast, visiting the islands of Ischia and Capri, seeing 'cyclamens blooming as thick as wood anemones in April', and going out to the Roman town of Pompeii.

Alfred also travelled to Vesuvius, from where, much impressed, he wrote to Lucy a detailed letter describing his ascent, the sight of molten lava and of the crater's edge.

On this first trip abroad Housman had behaved very much like any other tourist, and there is no hint of anything which might have caused unfavourable comment at home. On his next journey three years later, things turned out very differently; and he then began to make foreign travels a regular part of his annual routine.

It was in fact in September 1900, shortly after the second edition of *A Shropshire Lad* had been launched, that Housman went abroad for the second time. After a windy and rainy crossing to Calais, he travelled by train across the flatlands of northern France. He went on through Switzerland, past Lucerne, and along the shores of Lake Zug, admiring the Alpine scenery. Then through the St Gotthard tunnel, and finally down to the plains of Lombardy and the city of Milan.

Milan did not impress Housman. Apart from its old stained glass windows, he found little to appreciate in the cathedral, and was glad to find that 'The inside is very dark, a fault on the right side, and so the defects in details do not trouble one much'. As for the city in general, Housman commented disparagingly: 'It considers itself the intellectual capital of the country, and probably hopes to go to France when it dies.' After a short stay Alfred took the train for Venice. He reached that city on a romantic evening, describing his arrival to Lucy:

> As the sun went down we came to what is called the dead lagoon, where the sea and land begin to mix, but there is more land than sea: the live lagoon, where there is more sea than land, is what Venice stands in. The scene was very dreary at that hour: pools and canals, and marshes all overgrown with that purple flower I sent you; and the last touch of mystery and desolation was provided by three large staring red tramcars about a quarter of a mile away which were being rapidly drawn, by one very small horse apiece, into the Adriatic sea. . . . Then the railway runs out on to the water to Venice over a bridge two miles and a half long. . . . Entering Venice itself, especially at nightfall, when most of the canals are empty, the first impression is its stillness: you get a gondola at the landing place by the station, and are taken to the other end of the Grand Canal, where the hotels are, chiefly by short cuts through lesser canals. . . .

Thomas Mann wrote evocatively:[4]

> Is there anyone but must repress a secret thrill, on arriving in Venice for the first time – or returning thither after long absence – and stepping into a Venetian gondola? That singular conveyance, come down

unchanged from ballad times, black as nothing else on earth except a coffin – what pictures it calls up of lawless, silent adventures in the plashing night; or even more, what visions of death itself, the bier and solemn rites and last soundless voyage!

Venice was the home of several English families; and Walter Ashburner, Housman's colleague at University College London, would have given him an introduction to his friend Horatio Brown, one of the leaders of the English colony.[5] Brown, an expert in Italian art and history, had been for twenty-five years a friend of the homosexual writer John Addington Symonds – 'Mr Soddington Symonds' as he was apparently described by the poet Swinburne. Symonds had been in the habit of visiting Venice, where he had befriended a young gondolier – an attachment which did not, in that tolerant city, with its notorious homosexual underworld, prevent him from being invited to official functions.[6]

Housman, following in Symonds's footsteps, had soon befriended a gondolier of his own. Andrea was a young man of twenty-three who had been blinded in one eye in an accident. This injury, though it made him less obviously handsome, was a sure way to Alfred's sympathy – as were Andrea's tales of the wife, two sisters, mother, mother-in-law and paralysed uncle whom he was expected to support. Soon Alfred was enjoying a double love-affair; with Venice and with his gondolier. Perhaps, like another visitor to Venice, he felt[7]

as if I were dreaming, or as if this was some exquisite holiday of my childhood. One could talk for years of these passages in which, amidst the shadow and sunlight of cool, gray walls, a gleam of colour has shown itself. You look down narrow courts to lovely windows or doors or bridges or niches with a virgin or a saint in them. . . . Unexpected doorways, dark and deep with pleasant industries going on inside, bakerooms with a wealth of new, warm bread; butcheries with red meat and brass scales; small restaurants where appetising roasts and meat-pies are displayed.

At the heart of Venice lies the Piazza San Marco, overlooked by the Basilica of St Mark, which Housman, who was drawn to visit it almost daily during his stay, described with some justice, as the most beautiful building in the world. Alfred also toured the palaces, the churches, and the art galleries. 'The painter best represented in Venice', he wrote, 'is that lurid and theatrical Tintoret, whom I avoid, and Paul Veronese, whom one soon sees enough of.' He preferred the paintings of Giovanni Bellini.

Often at sunset Housman would go up the Campanile in the Piazza. From here, with Venice looking 'like one large island', he watched the sun go down and the stars come out. Now, rather to his surprise, he tasted some of the pleasures which he had longed for so intensely since childhood:

> Ho, everyone that thirsteth
> And hath the price to give,
> Come to the stolen waters,
> Drink and your soul shall live.
>
> Come to the stolen waters,
> And leap the guarded pale,
> And pull the flower in season
> Before desire shall fail.
>
> It shall not last for ever,
> No more than earth and skies;
> But he that drinks in season
> Shall live before he dies.                    (*MP* 22)

The following September, after revisiting Paris, Housman went to Italy again. He travelled down to the 'rather handsome and very sleepy town' of Pisa, and also spent a few days in Florence before making his way for a second time to Venice and the intimacy of Andrea. On his first visit to Venice, Housman had admired the work of Giovanni Bellini; now he travelled out to Castelfranco to admire the 'Enthroned Madonna' of Giorgione. While in Venice he stayed at the Hotel Europa which, he wrote later, had 'absolutely the best possible situation. . . . In dignity, according to my gondolier, it ranks next to Danieli's, where the food and drink are better, but which is noisy, and not central enough, and dearer.'

Horatio Brown had just returned from staying with their mutual friend Walter Ashburner in the Engadine,[8] and soon invited Housman to have Sunday lunch with him and his wife. Housman was pleased to accept.

Housman was now forty-two years old; and during the next seven years, until the autumn of 1908, he continued to make fairly regular visits to Italy, visits which usually ended with a few days in Venice with Andrea. In 1903, he stayed on the shores of Lake Garda before travelling on to Venice;[9] two years later he was staying in Milan at the Cavour, where Ashburner introduced him to the wine 'Camastra, an acquaintance which has materially alleviated the sorrows of the Italian table d'hote';[10] in 1906 he went first to Rome and Capri, a trip which led him to comment rather condescendingly on 'the South-Italian character, which is interesting but rather vile';[11] and then in 1908 he was planning to stay on the shores of Lake Garda again. Ashburner had been hoping to see him in Venice, but Housman wrote to him at the end of August:[12]

I am afraid I am hardly likely to be in Venice as late as the 18th, unless

Brown or Andrea or the weather is quite extraordinarily fascinating or unless Garda detains me on my way there longer than I expect.

They were not extraordinarily fascinating, nor did Garda detain him long: in fact the holiday was for various reasons a great disappointment. For one thing, the scenery did not live up to Alfred's expectations. He stayed at Garda itself, which, as he wrote to his sister Kate, 'on the former occasion struck me as the prettiest part of the lake, when viewed from the steam-boat in which I was coming away'. But he complained petulantly:[13]

On land it is not so satisfactory, as the cypresses and olives which ornament the hills are mostly in private grounds, and there is the usual Italian lack of real open country. Also the food and cooking did not suit me, and when I got to Venice, as sitting all day in a gondola is not the best thing in the world for restoring one's digestion, I was more uncomfortable, for about five days, than I have been for a long time.

It was not only Housman's digestion that was upset; he was falling out of love with Andrea.

Housman subsequently wrote a letter to Grant Richards in which he advised him about where to stay and to eat in Venice – ('The best restaurant to my thinking is the Vapore, and my gondolier tells me that all foreigners say the same. From the Piazza you go under the clock and along the Merceria . . . '); but, although he made one more fleeting visit to Venice in the autumn of 1912, his own regular visits to that city had now come to an end. Housman's passion for his gondolier had evaporated; and at a later date, after writing a bitter verse about Moses Jackson, in which he complained:

> But this unlucky love should last
> When answered passions thin to air;
> Eternal fate so deep has cast
> Its sure foundation of despair.                    (*MP* 12)

He drafted a poem in which he made his farewell to Andrea. In his letter to Kate of November 1908, he mentioned that the Campanile 'has now risen to half its old height and the work is going on more briskly, so that they expect to finish it . . .'.[14] Now he used the phallic image of the 'tower that stood and fell' in a poem about his gondolier:

> Far known to sea and shore
> Foursquare and founded well,
> A thousand years it bore,
> And then the belfry fell.
> The steersman of Triest
> Looked where his mark should be,

> But empty was the west
> And Venice under sea.
>
> From dusty wreck dispersed
> Its stature mounts amain;
> On surer foot than first
> The belfry stands again.
> At to-fall of the day
> Again its curfew tolls
> And burdens far away
> The green and sanguine shoals.
>
> It looks to north and south,
> It looks to east and west;
> It guides to Lido mouth
> The steersman of Triest.
> Andrea, fare you well;
> Venice, farewell to thee.
> The tower that stood and fell
> Is not rebuilt in me.                    (*MP* 44)

Even before the rift with Andrea, Housman had not confined his foreign travels to Italy. Rather surprisingly, for a classical scholar, he never visited Greece; but in the summer of 1904 he took the Orient Express from Paris all the way to Constantinople. As other travellers have been, Alfred was impressed by the immense extent of the old Roman walls; a romantic impression of the fallen might of the Empire was heightened by: 'the loneliness around. Inside, the skirts of the city are thinly peopled, more market gardens than houses; outside, the country is rolling downs and graveyards, with cultivation only here and there.' He sketched details of city life for his stepmother: the carts drawn by white oxen or black buffaloes, 'pretty frequent in the streets; and once my carriage was stopped by a train of camels'; the fighting rams kept by the Turks as pets, which 'may sometimes be met in the streets, invading the greengrocers' shops and butting at the boys, who catch them by the horns'; the plague of sick dogs; the fire service, which would happily 'gaze at the conflagration: if the owner of the property likes to hire them, they will put out the fire for him, but not otherwise'. Housman was also struck by

the handsomest faces I ever saw. . . . Some of the Greeks make you rub your eyes; their features and complexions are more like pictures than realities: though the women unfortunately bleach themselves by keeping out the sun. The Turks, when they are good-looking, I like even better; there is an aquiline type like the English aristocracy very much improved: if I could send you the photograph of a young man who rowed me to the Sweet Waters of Asia, and asked you to guess his name, you would instantly reply: 'Aubrey de Vere Plantagenet'.

Alfred delighted in the city's famous sunsets, and later told his brother Laurence that Constantinople was the world's finest site.[15]

As well as visiting Constantinople, Alfred made several journeys to Paris, where he found that he very much preferred French cooking to Italian. In the late spring of 1907 Housman invited Grant Richards, who happened to be in Paris at the same time, for dinner at the Tour d'Argent. This restaurant was managed by Frederic, described in the contemporary *Gourmet's Guide to Europe* as[16]

the one great 'character' in the dining world of Paris. In appearance he is the double of Ibsen, the same sweeping whiskers, the same wave of hair brushed straight off from the forehead. He is an inventor of dishes, and it is as well to ask for a list of his 'creations' which are of fish, eggs, meat and fruit, and generally named after some patron of the establishment.

At the Café Royal in London Grant Richards had been impressed by the skill and understanding with which Housman ordered food and wine; and now he found that, at the Tour d'Argent in Paris, 'the name of Housman commanded immediate respect'. After a 'characteristic but simple' soup, the two Englishmen enjoyed *Barbue Housman*,[17] the dish of fish and small new potatoes which Frederic had named after his discriminating customer. This was followed by *canard à la presse*, a dish for which Frederic was so famous that he presented each guest who ordered it with a card stating the number of the duck so prepared since Frederic had taken over the restaurant. Richards wrote fondly

that duck was the richest, and the most succulent, that I have ever eaten; and with it went the richest sauce. With the food a fine white Burgundy, followed by a great old red Burgundy! And Coffee . . . and a *fine* dating back to the beginning of the last century . . . that 1907 meal was the finest that he ever gave me . . .

When Grant Richards subsequently wrote his entertaining and light-hearted novel *Caviare* (1912), he gave his central character, Charles, something of the approach to good living which he admired in Housman

Charles not only ordered good dinners himself, but he was the cause of good dinners in others. With him as guest, somehow or other, even the most careless host didn't push the carte across the table, as if to say, 'Order what you like: *I* shall have steak and kidney pudding.' There was something about his attitude as he sat at table that suggested

that he expected to lunch or dine as the case might be, and not simply
to feed (p. 103).

After the break with Andrea, Housman went more frequently to Paris.
Not only was it the gastronomic capital of the world, but it offered a rich
diet of sexual adventures. When in August 1909, at the age of fifty,
Housman wrote to Mrs Rothenstein saying that he would prefer not to
holiday with her family at a French seaside resort, he explained:

> I don't expect to come to France much before September, and then I
> shall not stay very long; and all the time that I can spare from the vices
> of Paris (as to which, consult William) I expect to spend in visiting
> cathedral towns which I have not yet seen.

This joke about the vices of Paris concealed a truth which would have
astonished the Rothensteins and his other friends in London: Housman
had begun to make use of the less well-advertised services of the French
demi-monde. The details of this may surprise even those who have
accepted Alfred's devotion to Moses Jackson, his attachment to Adalbert
Jackson, and his friendship with Andrea.

Among a private collection of Housman's papers, there exists a small
document in Housman's handwriting, found in a book when part of his
library was sold at Blackwell's after his death. On this document are what
would seem to be references to a number of male prostitutes, including,
sailors and ballet-dancers, together with a note of the price paid on
various occasions for their services, and a marginal note in which Alfred
refers with some satisfaction to the large number of these homosexual
encounters which he had enjoyed in the space of a little over a fortnight.[18]

Paris offered other erotic possibilities. Housman took a keen interest in
books which were banned in Britain as pornographic, and here he was
able to buy some French and German works described by his brother
Laurence as classics of their kind;[19] he also read a number of English
novels, including the then notorious *Fanny Hill*.

Pursuing his own pleasures, Housman spent a week or a fortnight in
Paris each autumn for the next four years. In the spring of 1912 he also
took a spring holiday in Sicily, where 'the weather and the wild flowers
were all that could be desired', and in 1913 he went to France earlier in the
year than usual, spent only a few days in Paris, and then hired a chauffeur-
driven car and motored around the west of Normandy. That autumn he
wrote to Grant Richards: 'No, I shall not be in Paris. I am staying at home
and being good'; and in the spring of 1914 he once again hired a car, and
went off for another motor-tour, this time in the south of France, in the
area of Marseilles and Avignon.

Less than two months after Housman's return to England from this pleasant sight-seeing and gastronomic interlude, the murder of the Archduke Franz Ferdinand of Austria set in motion the train of events which led to the First World War.

On one level, Housman was appalled by the suffering and the waste of lives; but his philosophy had prepared him for a world in which the most terrible things were likely to happen, and had taught him that it was his duty as a human being to defy ill fortune as courageously as possible. So he decided, when considering what to do with his spring holiday in 1915, to go abroad quite normally and ignore the dangers of travelling to the Continent in war-time. By the beginning of March, Alfred had persuaded or shamed Grant Richards into accompanying him to France; and he wrote to a friend, with some bravado: 'On the 16th I shall be beyond the Channel or beneath it: more probably the former, for steamers seem to ram submarines better than submarines torpedo steamers.' And he added, softening an arrogant thought with a characteristic stroke of very dry wit: 'Hitherto I have always refused to go the Riviera, but now is my chance, when the worst classes who infest it are away.'

Not surprisingly, the boat on which Richards and Housman embarked at Folkestone carried few passengers. These two civilians, one in early and one in late middle age, had a deck cabin to themseles. 'There was, we supposed, some danger of the ship being mined or torpedoed, but I recall', wrote Richards,

> that Housman neither expressed nor showed any nervousness on that score. He went to our cabin, exchanged his hat for the very small and out-of-date cricket cap that he so often wore, stretched himself out and, before we had left the harbour he was, or appeared to be, asleep. I was more curious, stopping on deck until we were well away from England.

They arrived safely at Dieppe, and travelled down to Nice, where they found everything unusually sober and deserted. There were few of the regular visitors to the town, so they were given an especially warm welcome by one of Richards's acquaintances, the author Ernest Belfort Bax, who lived on the Riviera with his wife. Housman enjoyed talking to Bax, a man of 'persistent curiosity . . . old-fashioned scholarship and ponderous humour'; and both the travellers were amused by his wife's 'Germanic domesticities and her fussy preoccupations with her lord's comforts and dignities'.

The place of the usual tourists in Nice had been taken by a few Allied troops, most of whom were Blacks from the Colonies; and their presence gave a sinister edge to the holiday: each morning, Housman and Richards would be woken in their hotel rooms 'by funeral music on the Promenade des Anglais, for influenza was rife in the town', reported Richards, 'and the blacks went down like flies. There would be marching soldiers on the way to the burial ground.'

From Nice the two men made excursions along the coast: eastwards to Monte Carlo, and westwards to Antibes or Cannes. Even at Monte Carlo, there were few people about, but a number of good restaurants were still open, and they tracked down some good Burgundies including a particularly fine La Tâche. One evening they went in to see the gambling tables. Alfred, after so many years of being careful with his money, was amazed and rather shocked at the risks which gamblers took. He watched with distaste while Grant Richards lost a couple of *louis* at roulette; and they did not visit the tables again.

Once they travelled beyond Monte Carlo to Ventimiglia, just the other side of the Italian frontier, where Housman was disappointed by a lunch consisting mainly of 'small envelopes of paste enclosing mincemeat', which they followed by a walk 'through the town and under some trees by the shore to a rough breakwater'. Closer to Nice, they visited Beaulieu, where they ate at the Reserve – 'one of the half-dozen best restaurants in the whole of the world we knew'. Not far from Beaulieu, at Cap Ferrat, they strayed into an area out of bounds to civilians. They were challenged by a soldier but, to Grant Richards's great relief, Housman's 'presence of mind, his good humour, his readiness and his lack of embarrassment impressed the officer before whom we were brought, and we were immediately released'.

In the following year, 1916, Housman and Richards planned another journey abroad; but at the end of March the SS *Sussex* was torpedoed by a German submarine off the French coast, and Richards's wife, on hearing of this, refused to let her husband cross the Channel again during wartime. Housman commiserated with his friend, writing:

The sinking of the *Sussex* is no deterrent to me; quite the reverse. I argue thus: only a certain number of steamers are destined to sink; one of that number has sunk already without me on board; and that diminishes by one the number of my chances of destruction. But women cannot reason, so I suppose your designs are knocked on the head.

Housman himself still intended to go 'at least as far as Paris'; and applied for leave to go through Folkestone and Dieppe, commenting to Richards (who had advised taking the less direct route by Southampton–Le Havre): 'After all, a quick death is better than a slow journey; and as I am only an author and not a publisher I am comparatively well prepared to meet my God.' But the Folkestone route was closed, and so Alfred abandoned his holiday – 'Not on account of mines or torpedoes, which I despise as much as ever', he wrote to Grant, 'but because . . . the voyage by Southampton–Havre, without the solace and protection of your company, is a long and weary subtraction from the short holiday I meant to take.'

In the summer, another attempt to reach France came to nothing; and then in 1917 the War Office refused to grant him a passport, so that he was confined to England for the rest of the war. Housman felt this restriction keenly, describing it as 'much to the detriment of my health and spirits'. On another occasion, when he was trying to find the right words for an obituary, he told Grant Richards: 'It is one of several proofs that I am suffering from confinement in these islands mentally as well as physically, that . . . I have not got hold of any sentence that will hit off your uncle.'[20]

The Great War ended in November 1918; and the following September, despite worries about visas and permits, Housman was back in France, motoring through 'beautiful country in the Limousin, where I had not been before. Things were cheap, and they were yearning for the return of the English tourist.' Before and after his tour, he spent a few days in Paris, where he was unexpectedly visited by Grant Richards, who had kindly arranged his visa and given him other help and advice in preparing for the journey. Alfred sent him a note saying:

It will be no good looking for me here this evening, and I am also engaged tomorrow evening and Monday evening: otherwise I have no tie. Usually I leave the hotel not long after 9 a.m., and tomorrow I will look you up at the Normandy soon after that time.

From now on, Housman visited France at least once every year for as long as his health permitted. He had experienced a certain perverse enjoyment tempting fate when he crossed the Channel in war-time; and perhaps it was to recapture something of that excitement that in 1920 he decided to 'attempt Paris by the aeroplane route in September'. There was now a regular service between Croydon and Le Touquet, with several small companies taking passengers for around £20 a seat. It was only eleven years since Blériot had first crossed the Channel in an aeroplane, since when there had, of course, been many developments, but the pilots still sat in open cockpits, there were no proper brakes, so that an aeroplane had to be slowed down by flapping the wings, the ailerons even the back doors; and there were many forced landings and a number of serious crashes. One pilot's total of forced landings climbed to seventeen during the first few years of passenger flights; while an aeroplane was still in the air, an experienced pilot would keep a close eye on the landscape below him, so that he always had in mind the position of at least one field which he could reach quickly if a forced landing became necessary. Flying under such circumstances certainly required just that sense of adventure with which Housman approached it.

Cook & Son, the travel agents, booked a seat for Housman with 'Air Express', one of whose aeroplanes crash-landed in the middle of August. Predictably enough Housman was not alarmed, writing philosophically: 'My inclination to go by the Air Express is confirmed by the crash they had yesterday, which will make them more careful in the immediate future.' However, on the eve of his first flight he made sure of at least one more first-class dinner at the Café Royal, inviting Grant Richards and Grant's son Charles to join him for 'two admirable grouse', and 'lashings of caviare'. As for the flight itself, Alfred sent this account to Kate:

> Well, I flew there, and am never going by any other route in future. Surrey from overhead is delightful, Kent and France less interesting, the Channel disappointing, because on both days there was too much mist to let both shores be seen at once. It was rather windy, and the machine sometimes imitated a ship at sea . . . but not in a very life-like manner. Members of your unhappy sex were sick, however. The noise is great, and I alighted rather deaf, not having stuffed my ears with the cotton-wool provided. Nor did I put on the life-belt which they oblige one to take. To avoid crossing the 60 miles of sea which a straight flight would involve, they go from Croydon to Hythe, Hythe to Boulogne, Boulogne to Paris. You are in the air 2½ hours: from Leicester Square to your hotel in Paris you take little more than four; though on the return journey we were two hours late in starting because the machine required repairs, having been damaged on the previous day by a passenger who butted his head through the window to be sick. My chief trouble is that what I now want is no longer a motor and a chauffeur but an aeroplane and a tame pilot, which I suppose are more expensive.

For the next four years, Housman flew across the Channel at the start of his holidays in France; and it came to be said of him at Cambridge 'that he was more proud of having travelled so many times by aeroplane than he was of being Kennedy Professor or of having written *A Shropshire Lad*'. As each year passed, the flights grew more comfortable. Housman particularly enjoyed his 1923 experience in a Handley-Page which 'crossed the Channel 7000 feet high, higher than the piles of clouds which lay over both shores, and both coasts were visible at once, which I have not found before'.

He stayed in Paris for part or all of each holiday; though to what age he continued to seek out homosexual prostitutes is uncertain. In 1922 he wrote to Grant Richards that he knew something of the 'Paris *Bains de vapeur*'; but his comment that he was flying to Paris, 'though not necessarily to those haunts of vice', is enigmatic to say the least. If he had more than a week to spare, he liked to engage a chauffeur-driven car and tour in the provinces; and so in 1923 he visited Brittany, where he was impressed not only by the coastal scenery – especially the impressive headland of Finisterre – but also by the churches and cathedrals, 'better than I had any idea of'; and in 1925 he travelled as far as the Pyrenees.

Then in 1926, at the beginning of June, Housman had an unexpected message from Venice. Andrea, his gondolier, sent word that he was dying, and that he wished to see his old friend again. Alfred hurried out to Venice, where he found that revisiting that city was a strangely emotional experience, as he later described in a letter to Kate:

> I was very surprised to find what pleasure it gave me to be in Venice again. It was like coming home, when sounds and smells which one had forgotten stole upon one's senses; and certainly there is no place like it in the world: everything there is better in reality than in memory. I first saw it on a romantic evening after sunset in 1900, and I left it on a sunshiny morning, and I shall not go there again.

Andrea was ill, but not so ill as Housman had expected. The summer weather had revived him somewhat, but Alfred reported to Kate, that though Andrea seemed better, he personally, expected him to 'go steadily downhill'.

In fact, Andrea lingered on for another four years until 1930; and it would be interesting to know whether he had really been at death's door, or whether the desperate call for Housman had been engineered by his improvident relatives. If so, their plan was a success – at least for the time being. Alfred, with his usual generosity, regularly sent money to Andrea to help make his last illness as comfortable as possible. But when at last Andrea died, Housman was infuriated to receive begging letters from Andrea's family, and they had nothing more from him.[21]

The summer following Housman's last visit to Venice, he spent a month in France, half of it on a motor-tour through Burgundy, Franche-Comte, the Jura, Lyons and Clermont Ferrand, in the company of Grant Richards. It was twelve years since their war-time holiday together on the Riviera; but although Housman was now an elderly man of sixty-eight, he had lost none of his relish for good food and drink. Richards later wrote of this:

> His passion in life was, I should say, accuracy in Latin and in Greek, and he had also pleasure in architecture, but he liked his meals. Do not mistake me. He did not eat a great deal. When at table he was of the Edwardian school rather than that of Victoria or the Georges. Nor did he, save on the rarest occasions, drink too much. *He enjoyed*. That is the truth: he enjoyed, appreciated, was happy with good food and

with fine wine. . . . His spare, wiry frame was good evidence that he did not indulge to excess.

Housman had also learned to enjoy travelling in style. When they arrived at the first hotel of their tour, the Épée in Auxerre, he astonished Richards 'by ordering two rooms and *two* bathrooms with that note of assurance which suggested that he was certain that such accommodation would be available. Don't you wish you may get it! I said to myself.' They did. 'It was', wrote Richards, '. . . but a foretaste of the milord manner in which A. E. H. journeyed.'

From Auxerre they motored on to Chablis, where they explored the vineyards before enjoying, at the Hotel de L'Étoile, a luncheon of *écrevisses à la crème* and *ballottine de pigeonneau*, washed down by a Vaudésir 1915 and a Clos des Hospices 1921. So excellent was the food and wine that, after travelling some distance in the afternoon, Housman suggested returning to Chablis for dinner; at which Richards smiled, and said that he had been thinking the same thing ever since they finished coffee. 'Monsieur Bergerand showed himself flattered by our return', wrote Richards later; and he provided them with '. . . *potage santé, soles au beurre d'écrevisses, andouillette du pays grillée*, and *fondue de poulet à la crème*, to which, in our special honour, truffles had been added.' With this feast they drank 'Chablis Grenouilles 1921 . . . Nuits Vieilles Vignes 1919, and an exceptional Marc.'

The Englishmen travelled on to Dijon, where they drank a Romanée 1904 – rather disappointingly for them, 'the oldest wine we encountered in a fortnight'. Then to Béaune, and a story of expertise at first unrecognised and then discovered which will warm the heart of any romantic, gourmet or not. After seeing the sights, Housman and Richards arrived at the Hotel de la Poste informally, and on foot, with Housman wearing his very undistinguished-looking cloth cricket cap. The two men entered the dining-room unwelcomed, and had to find their own seats. A waitress casually brought them the menu for the lunch of the day, asking whether they would like red or white wine to go with it. Housman, admirably controlled in the face of what was, for a gourmet, a terrible insult, asked to see the wine list, and quietly ordered two wines towards the foot of the list. No sooner had the astonished girl disappeared through one door with her order for a Meursault Perrières and a Montrachet 1919 'than through yet another there entered almost at a run but with considerable circumstance, a veritable *maître d'hôtel* and an impressive *sommelier*. The demand for rarer, more expensive wines, had set the machine going.' They were asked to pardon the girl's mistake; a more imposing menu was at once placed in Housman's hands; and the proprietor arrived to compliment him on his choice of wines. Soon they were settling down to a happy meal of *écrevisses à la crème, pâté de foie gras maison,* and *truffes-en-serviette.*

For several days they remained in the general area of Dijon. Then, on the road back from Arbois to Dijon, they stopped in Dôle; and Housman rather reluctantly accompanied Richards to the jeweller's shop of a M. Alfred Perrier, on whom Richards had promised to call. Inside the shop they were welcomed by a smiling, comely Madame, who said that Monsieur should be fetched at once. Perrier himself, the soul of hospitality, was soon inviting them to dinner, mentioning that he had an old bottle or two, at which his wife added: 'Ah, Alfred – he loves his wine!' Grant looked at his friend rather doubtfully, knowing as he wrote later, that Housman 'was not a man whom you could carry off to the house of a stranger at a moment's notice'. But all was well. 'Visibly, he was pleased at the invitation. He did not wait for me to speak, but accepted for us both. These, he afterwards told me, were people very much after his own heart.' Together, they enjoyed an evening of conversation and laughter, of admirable cooking and of rare and excellent wines. Housman, usually so reserved with strangers, became 'interested and quite voluble'; and the two men walked back to their hotel, in the light of a crescent moon, jolly and a little unsteady.

After Dôle, they drove eastwards to Poligny, and then on towards the Swiss border; but their plans to drive into Switzerland were thwarted by their chauffeur, Louis, who explained at the frontier that he had forgotten to have his passport endorsed with a visa for Switzerland; so they turned back, and drove south-west to Lyon and Clermont Ferrand before heading for Paris. Grant Richards was depressed, when the day came on which he was due to board a train at the Gare de Lyon; for him, the north meant 'grey skies and the pavements of London and work'. Housman stayed on in Paris for a day or two (where he caught food poisoning), and then flew home

> by the new 'Silver Wing' aeroplane, which is more roomy and steadier, and contains an attendant to supply you with cheese and biscuits and various liquors, and to point out objects of interest on the route: also an emergency door in the roof, which ought to be very tranquillizing.

The two men had enjoyed each other's company for most of the tour; though Housman was sometimes upset by his friend's tendency to embroider stories – at Dijon, he had fixed Richards with his eye, and asked him directly 'Why do you tell these bloody lies to these unsuspecting French people?'; and after dinner a few days later he had commented: 'Your talent for conversation, on which I have already remarked, is always making me drink more than I ought.' But in general he thought highly of Grant Richards as a travelling companion, writing to him in

January 1928: ' . . . if I were a capitalist I should not set you up as a publisher, but engage you as a courier, salary unlimited'. And later in 1928 Housman invited Richards to join him for a few days at St Germain-en-laye, where he was holidaying in a hotel with a magnificent view, the luxurious Pavillon Henri Quatre.

Housman enjoyed travelling abroad as though he were a wealthy man: which of us would not? But his foreign visits meant, above all, freedom – a temporary escape from the conventional sexual morality by which, even in the Cambridge of Forster, Brooke and Keynes, he felt imprisoned.

# CHAPTER 9

# *Trinity College, Cambridge,*
## 1911–29

. . . resuming his search for his tutor. He found him without
trouble in the tower room which he had chosen when he
arrived. All philosophers prefer to live in towers, as may be
seen by visiting the room which Erasmus chose in his college at
Cambridge . . .

T. H. White, The Once and Future King

We talk sometimes of a great talent for conversation, as if it
were a permanent property in some individuals. Conversation
is an evanescent relation – no more. A man is reputed to have
thought and eloquence; he cannot, for all that, say a word to
his cousin or his uncle. They accuse his silence with as much
reason as they would blame the insignificance of a dial in the
shade. In the sun it will mark the hour. Among those who
enjoy his thought he will regain his tongue.

R. W. Emerson, Friendship

### *Arrival and the pre-war years, 1911–14*

The journey across London to Liverpool Street Station, and then by
train to Cambridge, was one which Housman had often made before –
first as a clerk at the Patent Office, attending meetings of the Philological
Society, and then as a Professor of Latin at University College London.
But when he made this journey for the first time after being elected
Kennedy Professor of Latin, and a Fellow of Trinity College, Cambridge,
it was with a keen awareness that his status in the academic world had
been dramatically improved. 'He gives himself airs now as a Fellow of
Trinity', wrote his old friend and colleague, Arthur Platt, only half in jest,
'and tells me not to look down on him any longer . . .'.[1]

The train ran on, through Essex and into the flat fen-lands of
Cambridgeshire, past Stapleford and Cherry Hinton, and finally into the
station on the outskirts of Cambridge itself. Here, from the station yard,

Housman and his fellow-travellers could take a horse-drawn tram or a hansom to the town centre. The market-place was the heart of the town; and Cambridge would have been no more than a small market-town without the University. Colleges lay north and east and south of the market; and to the west, from Bridge Street in the north to Silver Street in the south, St John's, Trinity, Clare, King's, Queens' and other Colleges were ranged impressively together, with their backs to the River Cam.

At the time of Housman's arrival, Trinity contained more than sixty Fellows, and provided for some six hundred undergraduate and seventy post-graduate students. As a residential College, it was most unlike University College London; but the way of life was not new to Housman. Apart from the difference in scale, it was similar in many respects to the life in which he had himself taken part, as an undergraduate at St John's College, Oxford. As at St John's, the social and intellectual lives of the undergraduates centred largely on the College;[2] and there was a similar round of tutorials and lectures. As at St John's, the Fellows dined together each evening at High Table.

But Housman had grown used to solitude at Highgate and Woodridings, and he was apprehensive about College life, replying to Lady Ramsay's congratulations on his election: 'Joy does predominate over sorrow, as I am fond of money and fond of leisure; but, as I am also fond of solitude, and shall not have it at Cambridge, there is some sorrow mingled with the joy . . .', and he had even complained to his landlady at the prospect of being forced into the society of others. In fact, for the summer of 1911 he was nominally Professor in two Universities; so he delayed moving into Trinity, taking temporary lodgings at 32 Panton Street in the south of Cambridge.[3] As for the problem of doing two jobs at once: he remembered that it had been Oliffe Richmond, a young classical Fellow of King's, who had first urged him to stand for the Kennedy Professorship; and he repaid that favour by putting Richmond into his own post in London for the summer term.[4]

At Cambridge, Housman's first major public duty as the new Professor of Latin, was to introduce himself to the University in an Inaugural Lecture, which he did on 9 May, to a large and enthusiastic audience. 'Brilliant is the only epithet', wrote one scholar, '– flashing and scintillating with dry humour'; and Henry Jackson, the elder statesman of Trinity, wrote to Arthur Platt: 'Housman's discourse was excellent. He smote with all his might two tendencies of modern scholarship – on the one hand, aesthetic criticism; on the other hand, the slavish mechanical methods of the Germans.' Interwoven with his important arguments on these subjects was 'another theme on which', said Housman, 'it is natural and proper that I should speak today'.

Mentioning that the Chair of Latin, founded to honour B. H. Kennedy, had been held already by two of his pupils, Housman added

> it has now fallen, I might almost say, to a third, though a pupil who never saw him and whom he never saw. What first turned my mind to those studies and implanted in me a genuine liking for Greek and Latin was the gift, when I was seventeen years old, of the most delightful, at any rate to me, of all volumes of translated verse – the third edition of *Sabrinae Corolla*, having Kennedy for its editor and chief contributor.

Housman then praised his two predecessors, Hugh Munro, who had written to him kindly when he was an undergraduate, and whose edition of Lucretius was 'a work more compact of excellence than any edition of any classic which has ever been produced in England . . .'; and John Mayor, who had produced 'no work having even the air of completeness', but who had sensibly recognised his own bent as an antiquarian and lexicographer, and followed it.[5]

The kind and genuine sentiments about Cambridge scholarship sounded well coming, as they did, from an Oxford man, and helped to confirm Housman's reputation in his new home. His old College at Oxford had recently elected him as an Honorary Fellow,[6] finally wiping out the disgrace of his failure in Greats; and his old friend from Oxford days, Alfred Pollard, had travelled to Cambridge to hear the Inaugural Lecture, and was 'richly rewarded by the cry of pleasure with which I was greeted when he caught sight of me after it. I think that somehow my presence seemed to him a recognition that he had reached his haven at last.'[7] A sense of having arrived came to Housman not long after this in another, and a more curious fashion. Walking near Cambridge with a colleague, he came to a long narrow field, where the trees made a broad, grassy avenue: 'Suddenly Housman paused and, looking about him said: "Now this *is* strange. I have dreamt often of this very place – and now I am here. This is the exact place of my dreams."'

Immediately after the Inaugural Lecture, Housman travelled to Paris for a few days' holiday, and when he returned to his lodgings, he found that he had no very definite work to do for the rest of the summer term.[8] Instead, he spent his time getting to know Cambridge: he was shown over the Fitzwilliam Museum by its Director, Sydney Cockerell, and he found that he was 'much occupied with social duties . . . and either from the climate or the heat was generally tired when I was not occupied.' In August he went to Woodchester, where his godmother Mrs Wise had died earlier in the year; and then he went back to his old lodgings at Pinner, to work on his lectures for the autumn term, and to arrange for the removal of the bulk of his belongings to the rooms which he was to occupy in Trinity.

Eastwards of the older parts of Trinity College, on the other side of

Trinity Street, an archway led into Whewell's Court, built in the romantic neo-Gothic style which Housman had favoured since he was a child. It was in the Gothic tower at the eastward end of the second courtyard that Housman had chosen to live. This was one of the most secluded parts of the College; to reach his rooms he had only to come in through the Sidney Street entrance, turn in to the doorway in the north side of the tower, and climb the stone steps. He had several rooms: a study, which looked out over Sidney Street; and on the other side a small bedroom, and also a larger and more comfortable room which he used as a sitting-room, and where he also kept a dining table so that he could entertain guests.

As Kennedy Professor of Latin, one of Housman's chief duties was 'to give lectures in every year'; and when the autumn term began, he conscientiously lectured twice a week on the Satires of Persius.[9] Afterwards, he wrote with some pride to his sister, Kate:

> The attendance at my lectures was from 20 to 30 (which, though not large, is from 20 to 30 times greater than the attendance at my predecessor's) several of whom were lecturers themselves. I believe the lectures are considered good (as indeed they are.)

The lectures were, in fact, extremely scholarly expositions of the classical text. More suitable for other lecturers than for any but the most brilliant undergraduate, they nevertheless set a standard by which all other classical work in the University could be measured. Andrew Gow, then a young colleague of Housman's at Trinity, describes what it was like to listen to

> the level, impassive voice setting out, without enthusiasm but with an athletic spareness and precision of phrase, just so much commentary as was necessary for the interpretation of the passage under discussion. To call his lectures inspiring would perhaps be to convey the wrong impression, for they were austere both in matter and in manner, and they made a severe demand upon their audience, but certainly nobody with tastes at all akin to his own could witness that easy command of the relevant learning, that lucid exposition and dispassionate judgment, without setting before himself a new standard of scholarship . . . one was in contact with a mind of extraordinary distinction.

Apart from lecturing, Housman's other principal duty was 'to devote himself to research and the advancement of knowledge in his department'. This was what chiefly interested him, and he made full use of the time available. His reputation when he arrived in Cambridge was already considerable, based not only upon the great number of his published papers, but also upon his editions of Juvenal, and of the first book of Manilius. Now Housman gradually increased his reputation with more scholarly papers, and he also found time for some hard work on the second book of Manilius.

Safeguarding his public image seemed more important than ever to Professor Housman now that he had reached such an eminent position, and there is no indication that he ever became involved with any of the Cambridge homosexual groups of his day. During his first months at Trinity he was particularly cautious, and was very annoyed when Grant Richards sent a pornographic book to him through the post. It was one which Housman had read in Paris, and then passed on to Richards; and he now wrote: 'I am horrified at your bringing back a Tauchnitz and sending it to a respectable person like me. I gave it to you because otherwise I should have left it in France.' Something of the distance which Housman deliberately put between himself and most other people when he first arrived at Cambridge may be measured in the reaction of G. U. Yule, who had been Housman's assistant at University College London until 1899, and who came to take up a post at St John's College, Cambridge, in 1912. 'When I came here', he wrote, ' . . . I was shocked: he seemed a different man, walking solitary and alone with unseeing eyes that recognised none and repelled advance. When we did speak he was cordial but tongue-tied.'

There were other reasons why Housman sometimes appeared distant and aloof during those early days at Trinity. For one thing, he was rather out of sorts during the hot summer, and did not feel quite well again for some months, writing to his sister as late as December: 'I don't know that the climate exactly suits me.' For another, there was some news which depressed him. He had not been the only one to make a move in 1911: the friend closest to his heart, Moses Jackson, had also moved, and decided on where to settle permanently; instead of returning from India to England, as Housman must have hoped, Jackson had travelled on with his family to the province of British Columbia, in the far west of Canada. Here, at Aldegrove near New Westminster, he bought some land and took up farming.[10] He and Alfred continued with their friendly correspondence; but Alfred now recognised that, in all probability, he would never again see the man whom he still deeply loved.

However, during the autumn and winter of 1911 Housman found that, as a newcomer, he was 'much asked out to dinner. People', he wrote to Kate, 'are very hospitable and friendly.' No doubt he was entertained by James Frazer who he had known for several years; though Housman did not like Frazer's wife, and had written to Mrs Platt: 'the prospect of exchanging you for Mrs. Frazer is one of the clouds on my horizon.' Oliffe Richmond of King's College – back from London again – attended all Housman's lectures and saw much of him;[11] and it was perhaps through his hospitality that Housman first met the Provost of King's, M. R. James, who shared Housman's love of ghost stories, and himself wrote some of the most chilling ever printed.

Housman had also remained on good terms with Henry Jackson, the Professor of Greek and editor of the *Journal of Philology*; and he would sometimes join a group of men in Jackson's rooms after Hall. Here he was not so much at ease as he had been at University College in the company of Ker and Platt; and he sometimes overcompensated for his feelings of awkwardness by employing a wit so biting that he must have hurt the feelings of those with whom he was trying to be good humoured. On one occasion, the Irish composer, Sir Charles Villiers Stanford, was telling a story about Robert Louis Stevenson when he lost the thread of what he was saying, and paused. Housman at once stepped in: 'With the characteristic inaccuracy of your race, Sir Charles', he announced, 'you have mixed up two entirely different stories and have missed the point of each of them.'

Among those in the College whom he did not already know, Housman wished above all to be a respected figure; so that 'he was sometimes apt, from shyness, to suspect a liberty where none was intended, and to be sharp-tongued in answer'.[12] But he gradually made some new friends among his colleagues in Trinity, even if they were not very close. He took an interest in Andrew Gow, a young Fellow in his twenties who greatly admired his scholarship; Alfred took him out to the Cambridge theatre from time to time, and was genuinely sorry when in 1914 he left to become a master at Eton. Housman also became attached to Reginald Laurence, a Fellow in his mid-thirties who shared his taste for good wine; and he enjoyed seeing something of the philosopher Bertrand Russell, then a College lecturer with rooms in Nevile's Court. Russell, like Housman, was a friend of the Rothensteins, and Housman could also remember when Russell's mother and father had lived on the hill just opposite Woodchester. But the most exciting moment in College during these years probably came in the winter of 1912–13, when, as Housman wrote in mock horror, Trinity College became like

> a besieged city. A week ago there came a telegram to say that one of the junior Fellows, Pearse, . . . had left his home, mad and armed, and would probably make his way here. All entrances to the College have therefore been closed, except the Great Gate, which is guarded by a double force of Porters. Cambridge was perplexed at first, but has now invented the explanation that it is the Master who has gone mad, and has made these arrangements in order that he may shoot at the Fellows from the Lodge as they come through the Great Gate. The Provost of King's gives imitations of the Master thus engaged: 'Ah, there is dear Dr. Jackson!' bang!!

What makes matters worse is that the College evidently sets no value on my life and even on that of the Archdeacon of Ely; for Whewell's Court is left quite unprotected and I have to look under my bed every night.

The Master of Trinity College, H. M. Butler, was of course far from mad: and Housman appreciated his virtues. In 1913 Housman was asked by the other Fellows of the College to write an address congratulating Butler on his 80th birthday, a request with which he was glad to comply.

Outside the College, Housman made more friends. In particular he enjoyed the sparkling company of Arthur Benson, a Fellow of Magdalene College, only three years his junior, a prolific and popular author who talked brilliantly, despite suffering from periods of depression.[13] Housman, as a fellow-sufferer, sympathised with him and admired him for his achievements; though he would not be flattered by him into joining a Committee, as he made clear in a reply of May 1913:[14]

> You write me a very kind letter, but your suasions fall upon the deaf ear of an egotistic hedonist – I suffer a good deal from life, and do not want to suffer more; and to join the Academic Committee, or any similar body, would be an addition to my discomforts, not overwhelming, but still appreciable.

Despite this refusal – or perhaps because the suggestion of suffering intrigued Benson – a friendship grew between them, and in February the following year Benson was to be found lunching with Housman and Grant Richards in Housman's rooms and drinking 'some rather particular hock'.

Not long after his move to Cambridge, Housman met W. S. Blunt. He was introduced to him by Sydney Cockerell, with whom he had talked about the writing of *A Shropshire Lad*; and he accepted Blunt's invitation to spend the last weekend of November 1911 in company at his house in Sussex. On the first evening, Wilfred Meynell read them George Meredith's long series of poems, 'Modern Love', the tragic story of the breakdown of a marriage. Blunt recorded in his diary that, with Meynell's 'running commentary', this made 'excellent entertainment'. Then, on the Sunday, wrote Blunt:

> I took Housman for a walk and asked him how he had come to write his early verses and whether there was any episode in his life which suggested their gruesome character, but he assured me it was not so. . . . He shows no trace now of anything romantic, being a typical Cambridge Don, prim in his manner, silent and rather shy, conventional in dress and manner, learned, accurate, and well-informed . . . with Meynell's help we got him to discuss his own poems, though he

refused absolutely to read them out. . . . We had much pleasant talk
all day, and sat up again till twelve at night telling ghost stories. He
takes an interest in these. Housman's personal appearance is one of
depression and indifferent health. He does not smoke, drinks little,
and would, I think, be quite silent if he were allowed to be.

In describing his personal appearance as one of depression, Blunt had
penetrated as far as Housman's underlying melancholy; but Alfred had
not of course been entirely honest when he said that there was no episode
(or episodes) in his life which had suggested the character of his poems.
Indeed, fearing where investigations of this sort might lead, Housman
discouraged his new colleagues at Trinity from discussing anything to do
with his poetry.

Among his older friends, Housman continued to see something of the
Rothensteins; but now he saw them more often in Gloucestershire than
he did in London. They had bought a country house not far from Woodchester, and when he visited the Wises, which he did every summer, he
would walk over to see them.

Back in Cambridge after holidaying with the Wises, or with one of his
own family, Housman continued with his scholarly and unemotional
lectures. One of his students, a woman, later recalled how:

At five minutes past 11 he used to walk to the desk, open his manuscript, and begin to read. At the end of the hour he folded his papers
and left the room. He never looked either at us or at the row of dons in
the front.

Only once was there a change from this routine:

One morning in May, 1914, when the trees in Cambridge were covered
with blossom, he reached in his lecture Ode 7 in Horace's Fourth Book,
'Diffugere Nives, redeunt iam gramina campis'. This ode he dissected
with the usual display of brilliance, wit, and sarcasm. Then for the
first time in two years he looked up at us, and in quite a different voice
said: 'I should like to spend the last few minutes considering this ode
simply as poetry.' Our previous experience of Professor Housman
would have made us sure that he would regard such a proceeding as
beneath contempt. He read the ode aloud with deep emotion first in
Latin, and then in an English translation of his own:

> Thaw follows frost; hard on the heel of spring
>   Treads summer sure to die, for hard on hers
> Comes autumn, with his apples scattering;
>   Then back to wintertide, when nothing stirs. . . .

Torquatus, if the gods in heaven shall add
  The morrow to the day, what tongue has told?
Feast then thy heart, for what thy heart has had
  The fingers of no heir will ever hold.

Night holds Hippolytus the pure of stain,
  Diana steads him nothing, he must stay;
And Theseus leaves Pirithous in the chain
  The love of comrades cannot take away.      [MP 5]

'That', he said hurriedly, almost like a man betraying a secret, 'I regard as the most beautiful poem in ancient literature' and walked quickly out of the room.

Afterwards another undergraduate, a scholar of Trinity, commented: 'I felt quite uncomfortable. I was afraid the old fellow was going to cry.'

## The war years

With the start of the Great War in August 1914, Cambridge rapidly assumed its military responsibilities. By the end of November, Housman was writing to an old London friend that

> The thirst for blood is raging among the youth of England. More than half the undergraduates are away, but mostly not at the front, because they all want to be officers. I am going when they make me a Field-Marshal.

Although Housman himself, at the age of fifty-five, was too old for military service, he still made a real sacrifice, sending the bulk of his savings to the Chancellor of the Exchequer as a contribution to the war effort;[15] and then he settled down to live as normal a life as possible. He continued with his scholarly papers; and with his lectures on Persius and on some of the longer poems of Catullus; though Cambridge soon had '1000 undergraduates and 20,000 soldiers', with, as he told a friend, '500 of them billeted in the building in which I write these lines, and one of them doing a quick-step overhead'. To Grant Richards, whom he asked to visit him in the spring of 1915, Alfred explained that feasting and guest-nights were suppressed, but that on Tuesdays and Thursdays the dinner was better than on other days; and he later warned him not to be surprised if a sentry tried to keep him out with a bayonet, as Whewell's Court was 'now a barracks, sparsely inhabited by four Fellows of Trinity. We do not dress for dinner.'

But despite all the military activity in Cambridge, the city came to be seen by some people as a centre of unpatriotic pacifism. In Trinity there were four conscientious objectors, and thirteen members of the Union for Democratic Control. The UDC was in fact primarily concerned with the post-war settlements; but many of its members quite rightly felt by the end of 1915 that the best result would be a drawn war and a compromise peace, and so were labelled pacifists. There were also a number of the academic staff, including Bertrand Russell, who were strongly opposed to conscription; and, at the time, Housman agreed with them, believing that people should only fight for their country if, like his three young nephews, they had volunteered to do so. But the majority of the senior Fellows favoured conscription, and loathed any ideas which they felt smacked of pacifism, so that during 1915, although no one descended to outright rudeness, differing factions conspicuously avoided one another.

Bertrand Russell was more seriously affected by the bad feeling than most. The Council were about to make him a Fellow of the College, but because of his political views they changed their mind, and instead renewed his lectureship for a further five years. Those Council members who opposed Russell must have felt that their decision had been right when in April the following year, 1916, Russell published a controversial pamphlet about Ernest Everett, sentenced to two years hard labour for being a conscientious objector: 'He is only fighting the old fight for liberty, and against religious persecution. . . .'.

The Government decided against making a stand for those who were defending conscience, and prosecuted Russell, who was found guilty of making a statement likely to prejudice recruiting; and although he was not imprisoned, he was fined £100 costs. At this stage, Housman felt neutral: he believed that Russell had acted as a bad citizen, but he also agreed that people should not be persecuted for holding minority views.[16]

Now the Council of Trinity College renewed its attack on Russell, and when they met in July they agreed that he ought to be removed from his post of lecturer. When this decision was announced, there was a storm of protest. Gilbert Murray, now the Professor of Greek at Oxford, stated publicly that the action which the Council had taken was incredible; and before long twenty-two Fellows of Trinity, Housman's friend Andrew Gow among them, sent a formal letter to the Council to record their dissatisfaction. Housman did not sign it, though he felt that the Council's action was unwise. But when Russell petulantly asked for his name to be removed from the books of the College, Housman turned against him, feeling that this was an unnecessary insult to an institution of which he himself was proud to be a member.

Housman had little to say to the soldiers who were billeted in College. One of them, Evan Pughe, an old Trinity man, approached Housman and said how much he had enjoyed his poems, only to be told, before

Housman turned his back on this admirer, that 'the kindest action the Dons have ever done me has been never to mention my poems'. Housman felt that any discussion of his poetry posed a threat to his privacy, and since Pughe lived directly opposite him on the same staircase in Whewell's Court, the threat was greater than usual; no doubt it was this which led to an otherwise unnecessarily sharp reply.

That Housman took a real interest in the welfare of soldiers in general is shown by a letter which he wrote attacking the Dean of Lincoln for suggesting that soldiers should be deprived of their natural appetites during the war;[17] and at the end of September 1915, he allowed Sir Walter Raleigh, Professor of English at Oxford, to print some of the poems from *A Shropshire Lad* in one of *The Times'* Broadsheets which were issued to keep up the morale of troops in the trenches.

In February 1916, Housman once again invited Grant Richards to visit him at Trinity College; but put him off only a few days later because of an outbreak of cerebro-spinal meningitis among the soldiers quartered in the College. Later in the month, Housman wrote to Grant Richards again, this time to commiserate with him on the death of his uncle Herbert Richards, one of the examiners, who, long ago, had ploughed Housman in Greats. Housman had never nursed a grudge against Herbert Richards for this; and now he wrote, appreciatively: 'There are far too few severe and thorough scholars of his sort.'

In the meantime, news about the war came in, some of it serious, some less so. In June Housman wrote a teasing letter to Mrs Platt, having heard that 'Ladies in Cambridge are getting into closer touch with war: they are to be allowed to paint shells. I greatly fear that patriotism together with feminine unscrupulousness will lead them to poison the paint.'

The printing of some of Housman's poems in the Broadsheets for the trenches had given the sales of *A Shropshire Lad* a new lease of life; they climbed to over 14,500 in 1916, and although they dropped a little in 1917, in 1918 they reached nearly 16,000 copies – the best figure for nine years.[18] Alfred was pleased to think of the young men in the trenches reading his book; and when in the summer of 1916 he heard that Grant Richards had doubled the price of *A Shropshire Lad* from 6d to 1s. 0d., he wrote, with characteristic irony:

> I do not make any particular complaint about your doubling the price of my book, but of course it diminishes the sale and therefore diminishes the chance of the advertisement to which I am always looking forward: a soldier is to receive a bullet in the breast, and it is to be turned aside from his heart by a copy of *A Shropshire Lad* which he is carrying there. Hitherto it is only the Bible which has performed this trick.

Housman never heard of a man being saved from a bullet by a copy of his poems; but later he preserved among his papers the letter of an American who had looked after a wounded British soldier in France after the war. The American wrote that he had brought his copy of *A Shropshire Lad* for the man to read; at which the wounded soldier had smiled, and taking from under his pillow his own copy, tattered, torn, and bloodstained, had told him how he had carried the little volume in his pocket all through the war.

Since he was unable to get abroad during the last years of the war, in the summer of 1916 Housman was very pleased to join Grant Richards and his family for a holiday in Cornwall. Grant had married again in the previous year, to a Hungarian widow with a daughter, so the party consisted altogether of Housman, Richards, his Hungarian wife, five children (including the four from Grant's first marriage), a nurse, and maids, all crowded into an ancient cottage called Caerleon, which looked over the Channel, about half-way between Cadgwith and Ruan Minor, and about two miles from the Lizard. It was in many ways a children's holiday, but Alfred thoroughly enjoyed it, only showing signs of impatience when the children became a little too boisterous. He particularly liked Grant Richards's young wife Gioia, who was only twenty-seven, and talked to her for hours about Grant's work, about the children's future, and about the war; and once he even came to her rescue, dashing barefoot to help her down from a cliff on which she had climbed too high. Grant Richards later recalled that they often picnicked on the beaches, and that when they did, Housman – whose principal task was to look after the wine – was 'unusually cheerful, scrambling down to the remoter coves as if he were again an undergraduate, watching the rest of us bathe with amused eyes or going off on a stroll of his own'.

Once, Housman and Richards were out with the children when they stumbled on an adder which turned and hissed as if about to spring; Richards recalled that

> For a matter of seconds the children with their almost bare feet and legs were in some danger. Housman was on it in a flash. Three blows of his stick and it was dead – with so much energy had he attacked that the stick was broken.

That autumn, Grant sent his friend a walking-stick to replace the one which had been broken, and Alfred replied: 'I only hope the new one may make as good an end.' The Cornish holiday had been a great success, and in the following year, 1917, Housman spent two week-ends at the Richards's home.

Earlier in the war, Housman had been much amused when he heard that a letter from Edmund Gosse to the author Compton Mackenzie, then living in Capri, had been delayed by the censor for a week, and then sent on with a note advising Mackenzie that in future, his correspondent should write 'shortly and clearly'. Housman had written

> My dear Gosse . . . if the Censor finds your letters long, it is not that they are long by measurement, but that they take a long time to read when most of the words have to be looked out in the dictionary. . . . And considering that one of you writes from Hanover Terrace, while the other resides in Capri, a place of which the Censor never heard except in connection with Krupp, I think he treats you very handsomely in taking the more lenient and less probable view and allowing the letter to pass.

Now, in the spring of 1917, Gosse had provided him with entertainment of another sort: a biography of Swinburne, whose early poetry had strongly influenced Housman's own writing as a schoolboy and undergraduate.

Housman had always despised most of Swinburne's later work, and so he was particularly pleased to find that the only two poems he admired in Swinburne's later volumes, 'Ave atque Vale' and the prologue to 'Tristram of Lyonesse', had both been written early; but he was still more interested in the clandestine side of the poet's life. Knowing that Swinburne had been a drunkard, and obsessed with flagellation, Housman wrote to Gosse: 'Perhaps we should both blush if you unfolded the awful inner meaning of "a way which those who knew him will easily imagine for themselves".' And he asked whether Swinburne was the author of some poems in a collection of flagellant writings, *The Whippingham Papers*, which he had bought on one of his trips to Paris. Later, Housman sent these to Gosse, adding that the author of the poems – who was not in fact Swinburne – was said to have written another work, *The Romance of Chastisement*, which he had not come across and as a result 'my library is sadly incomplete, and not at all worth leaving to the British Museum when I die'. Gosse had been depressed when Housman had pointed out a number of small mistakes in his biography, but Housman made up for this now by writing to him

> I always feel impertinent and embarrassed when I praise people: this is a defect of character, I know; and I suffer from it, like Cordelia. The chief fault of your book is one which I did not mention, that there is too little of it.

Trinity College was still full of soldiers in 1917; the terrible slaughter continued on the Western Front, and the end of the war seemed as far away as ever. The year was enlivened for Housman by the visit of a young soldier whom he had met the previous year, but who had been lost to his sight in the ranks of the RAMC;[19] and in March 1917 he allowed *The*

26  *Sir William Rothenstein; self portrait*

27 *Drawing of Alfred Housman by Sir William Rothenstein*

28  *The Café Royal*

29  *Sergeant George Herbert
    Housman*

30  *Katharine Elizabeth Symons*

31  *Clemence Annie Housman in 1920*

32  *Laurence Housman* c. 1930

33 *The Rev. Joseph Brettell Housman*

34 *A Venetian canal*

35  *Paris in the 1890s*

*Blunderbuss,* a local war-time magazine edited by one of the soldiers stationed in Trinity, to publish his poem about courage which ends:

> What evil luck soever
>      For me remains in store,
> 'Tis sure much finer fellows
>      Have fared much worse before.
>
> So here are things to think on
>      That ought to make me brave,
> As I strap on for fighting
>      My sword that will not save.                    (*LP* 2)

In October, Grant Richards asked Housman to look up the ailing Percy Withers, a middle-aged doctor who very much admired Housman's poetry, and who had been wanting to meet him for some time. Withers had been transferred in the early summer of 1917 to war service in Cambridge where – like Alfred's favourite brother Basil in another part of the country – his job was to examine recruits to see whether they were fit for army life. But his own health was very poor, and when, one late autumn afternoon, Housman called on him in his rooms overlooking the Fitzwilliam Museum, he was still recovering from months of illness. Withers describes the scene as his landlady opened the door of the room in which he sat reading, huddled over a fire, and announced: 'Professor Housman.'

> I rose with difficulty from my lounging position to greet him; he was
> already halfway down the longish room, and as I faced him my
> confidence was further restored not only by his winning smile, but
> by noticing, from his flushed face and shy hesitant manner, that it was
> he, not I, needed encouragement. Percipience is apt to be swift and
> comprehensive at such times, and while he completed his two or three
> steps towards me, I further remarked his erect soldier-like figure,
> slight and of medium height, his small but shapely head, the cropped,
> carefully-brushed hair, touched with grey, and the blue eyes, once
> doubtless capable of fire, but now rather disappointingly dull – not, I
> felt, the eyes of a poet.

This meeting was the start of a curious friendship, often close but never really intimate, which lasted until Housman's death nineteen years later. Ever since the months when he had watched his mother dying, any illness had been a sure way of arousing Alfred's sympathetic interest, and the fact that Withers was often a sick man – he was later diagnosed as a diabetic – prepared the ground for their friendship. But its solid foundation was the enormous admiration which Withers felt for literary men, and particularly for Housman, to whom he was attracted on this first meeting by a feeling that there was something unexplained about him. Withers was intrigued by 'the sadness of his expression in all moments of repose'; Mrs Withers had joined the two men, and at the end of the visit, after showing Housman out, she remarked: 'That man has had a tragic love-affair!'

Before he left, Housman had invited Withers to dine with him in Hall one evening and he had also carried off a volume of *Georgian Poetry*. This had been pressed upon him by Withers, partly because it contained some verses by John Drinkwater, a young poet whom Withers had befriended; partly because he wanted an excuse for calling on Housman at his rooms in Trinity. This he did some days later. Housman, who had recently written to Grant Richards that Withers 'seems an agreeable man', gave him a cordial welcome. He had been sitting reading in his study at a table strewn with books, and Withers was interested to notice that a pair of dumb-bells lay on the floor beside the chair. Housman explained that he used them for ten minutes every morning after his cold bath, and again at night, whenever he felt drowsiness coming on as he sat by the fire reading.

They talked about Withers's work on the National Service Board, putting through sixty recruits a day, many of them in apparently poor condition. Then Withers asked whether he would one day publish a successor to *A Shropshire Lad*. At this, Housman waved a hand at his desk, and said that there were a few poems in one of the drawers, and that he might think of writing more – 'for posthumous publication, he added . . . with a laugh determined and full of meaning, but its meaning escaped me, so mocking it was, so sardonic and so evasive'. The meaning is clear enough when one knows the full story of the poems which Housman had written about Moses Jackson, and on other subjects which he did not feel he could safely publish during his life-time; but he would never do more than hint at this side of his life, and Withers was not perceptive enough to guess at it.

When Withers was leaving, Housman returned the volume of *Georgian Poetry* which he had borrowed; and, asked whether he had anything to say about it, he replied: 'No . . . Yes, one opinion I have formed: that your friend John Drinkwater is not a poet.' When Withers ingenuously asked how he could be so sure, Housman flushed, and was unable to speak for a moment; but then, growing calmer, he told Withers: 'You feel poetry in the throat, in the solar plexus, or down the spine. Drinkwater's verse touches neither spine, belly nor throat.'

For the next twelve months, while the war dragged on into 1918, and Withers remained at Cambridge, he saw a great deal of Housman, visiting him every few weeks in his rooms, dining with him in Hall, or meeting him there or in the Combination Room when he was dining in College as the guest of another Fellow. Housman was pleased that Withers praised his poems, and once told him self-deprecatingly: 'People don't want any more of my poetry. It is only a few like you who care anything about it; the rest neither anticipate nor desire more.' When Withers told him that he was wrong, and asked how he could justify letting his rare gift fall into disuse, Housman, in a most unusual moment of revelation

> told me what *A Shropshire Lad* had cost him [with] a staccato and troubled utterance, a voice striving ineffectually for composure, a tormented countenance, and all the evidence of an intolerable memory lived over again. There was no doubting the savagery of the experience. . . . He told me he could never face such self-immolation again, and as he said it a shudder passed over him.

But, in spite of this, Withers continued to badger him for more poems, and from time to time Housman would announce that he had written one.

The two men had an interest in common besides literature: they both liked studying the architecture of old churches and cathedrals. Not long before their first meeting, Housman had spent a holiday touring Rochester, Canterbury, Winchester and Salisbury. But the great difficulty for Withers in his friendship with Housman was that, although Housman loved listening to gossip, especially anything slightly malicious, he never initiated any small-talk himself. Despite this, he hated silences, so Withers found that he had to do a great deal of talking himself, and that the only certain way of having a conversation with Housman was to ask him a series of questions.

This taciturnity – which Housman may have learned in part from his old friend, Ker, who was famous for his silences – was also evident in the meetings after Hall in Henry Jackson's rooms, some of which Withers attended. He found that Housman would, on occasion, say nothing the entire evening, and yet appear to have enjoyed himself. On the other hand, when he did speak:

> His utterance, like all else he was or did, had in singular degree the arresting quality of distinction. His phrases were apt to their purpose like a burnished rapier. . . . The effectiveness of his talk lay in its fastidious precision – not a casual or unnecessary word, and every word the fittest possible. Interest and more than interest – excitement – was kept at stretch, and the range widened, by constantly recurring references and quotations, literary and historical, poetry and prose . . . [he would say] 'something like this' – and then reel off a lengthy sentence, perhaps Selden, perhaps Macaulay, or it might be some lesser known author.

In the right company, and on the right subject, Housman could talk brilliantly; and if some men found him difficult, others such as John Drinkwater – despite Housman's dislike of his verse – found 'nothing but charm, amiability, friendliness and responsiveness; and the last quality he should suspect in Housman was taciturnity'.

A much more distinguished writer whom Housman met during 1918 was André Gide, who was visiting Cambridge during the summer and autumn of 1918, and who had been given a letter of introduction to Housman by their mutual friend William Rothenstein. Gide had then written several of his best-known works, including *Les Nourritures Terrestres* and *L'Immoraliste*, an exploration of man's growing awareness of his suppressed homosexuality. After Housman's first meeting with Gide, he wrote to the Rothensteins that he hoped to see him again but there is no record of any further communication between them, and this is not really surprising. A real friendship between the French prophet of rebellion, and the English poet and Professor who had decided that it was impossible for him to rebel, would have been difficult, to say the least!

At last the fighting in Europe stopped, and those who had survived returned home to resume their normal lives, if such a thing was possible. Some of them returned with honour: two of Moses Jackson's sons had been decorated, [20] and Housman's nephew Jerry Symons had been awarded a Military Cross. But Jerry's brother Clement lay dead in a foreign grave; as did both of Alfred Pollard's sons, [21] and too many other 'fellows that were good and brave/And died because they were' (*LP* 38).

## An established figure

Professor Housman had tried to lead as normal a life as possible during the war, despite the fact that the University was drained of under-graduates and the younger dons. Now, life in Trinity College and in Cambridge as a whole resumed much of its pre-war pattern – though for a while there was a strange contrast among the undergraduates, between men straight from school and those who were veterans of the trenches.

Soon after the end of the war, Housman was delighted to be asked to join an exclusive Cambridge dining-club, limited to twelve members, who met once a fortnight in term-time and took turns to entertain each other. [22] Housman was by this time a great connoisseur of food and wine, so the Club had an obvious appeal for him; and the romantic side of his nature may have enjoyed knowing about the origins of the Club: it had been started two centuries ago by men who favoured the cause of the exiled King James II, and in Housman's day members still passed wine-glasses over their finger-bowls as a silent toast to 'The King over the water'. [23] The Club was known as 'The Family', a pleasant description, and one especially apt for those who, like Alfred, were unmarried, and for whom the regular meetings made up to some extent for the lack of a real family.

When Housman joined 'The Family', its most distinguished member was Sir J. J. Thomson, who had been elected Master of Trinity on the death of H. M. Butler in the previous year. Thomson was the Nobel Prize-winning physicist who had discovered the electron, and he looked and sometimes behaved like everyone's idea of an absent-minded Professor. Where Housman took great pains to be neat and presentable, Thomson – with his long iron-grey hair – was eccentric and unkempt in appearance, 'far too importantly occupied to bother about tailors and hairdressers'. But he liked Housman, sharing his love of walking and his relish for detective stories,[24] and he later wrote:[25]

> I always found him excellent company, and was very glad when I could sit next to him. . . . It is true that from time to time he had fits of silence and depression; but these were rare. . . . He usually, in my experience, talked freely, and, as might be expected, incisively. He held strong opinions on many subjects, and expressed them strongly, and he was not fond of strangers.

Andrew Gow could not have been a member of 'The Family' at this time, as he was away teaching at Eton; but he was at least once a guest of Housman's at a Family dinner in 1924, and later became a member himself; and he wrote about Alfred at these dinners:

> He liked good cheer and good wine . . . and, responding to their tonic, would draw upon surprising stores of knowledge in unexpected fields and show himself as vivacious as any member of the party. He would illuminate the conversation with flashes of wit, heralded by a slight arching of the wrist as it lay idle on knee or table, and by a charac-teristic downward glance . . .; [he] would pour out from his accurate and retentive memory anecdote and reminiscence with a felicity and economy of language which made him an admirable raconteur; and would greet the contributions of others with bursts of silvery laughter . . . something boyish and infectious.

When it was Housman's turn to entertain the other members of 'The Family', his dinners, as Sir J. J. Thomson records[26]

> had, like everything else he did, the air of distinction. There was always some dish which few, if any of his guests had met with before, and over which he had taken a good deal of trouble to instruct the College cook in all the details of its preparation. All the wine was good, and there was pretty sure to be some of special interest or rarity.

And, as a final and personal touch, just before the guests arrived, Alfred would usually make the salad himself.

Stephen Gaselee, Fellow and Librarian of Magdalene College, was not a member of 'The Family', but a friend of Housman's who shared his enthusiasm for good food and wine. The two men had a particular preference for Hock and Burgundy – Housman had built up a small but excellent cellar of both – and before wine sales of departed old dons they would sometimes arrange that one or the other of them would stand down for certain lots, so that they should not bid against each other. Gaselee invited Housman to dine occasionally, and was delighted in return to be invited to Trinity, where, in the Combination Room, there was 'a fair selection of the best port vintages from 1875 onwards'. Sometimes they shared their meal with Housman's friend Arthur Benson, and Gaselee remembered that 'The port, which was taken in strict moderation, seemed to loosen their tongues, and nowhere and never in my life have I listened to better talk . . .'. Alfred also made a custom of enjoying oysters and stout on New Year's Eve, as he wrote to Mrs Platt one December: 'I and other choice spirits here always see the New Year in on oysters and stout, to do what we can for the cause of human progress and the improvement of the world'; and another year, to his brother Basil: 'I have had a terrible shock from a telegram today from a London fishmonger. All the native oysters have been torn from their beds by tempest, and I shall have to eat the New Year in on Dutch.'

So Housman had gradually extended the circle of his acquaintances at Cambridge to include a number of agreeable companions. He talked enthusiastically to Percy Withers about Benson, though 'less of the man than the good companion and raconteur'; and probably his closest friend was R. V. Laurence, the Junior Bursar at Trinity. When he spoke of Laurence, his 'voice and manner disclosed more of affection than I ever heard from Housman's lips but once'. But despite his membership of 'The Family', and his friendship with men like Gaselee, Benson, and Laurence, Alfred was still extremely reticent about himself, even to his intimates. So reticent, in fact, that Laurence Housman found, when preparing his biography of Alfred, that 'some of them (Gow for instance) consider that he had *no* intimates'.[27] Gow himself wrote: 'we knew him as one of those who deliberately choose to restrict their friendships to the surface, neither giving nor asking for confidences.' Another man who knew Housman explains:[28]

He was often solitary because any substitute for perfect intimacy seemed to him too poor a thing . . . he had a passion for perfection. . . . Anything imperfect was torture to him. Conversation that fell short of what he felt to be worthwhile he instinctively avoided.

This last comment is not altogether true: Housman liked being talked to, as Percy Withers had noticed when they first met; and Laurence Housman once heard his brother 'quite amiably enduring a chatter-box of a man ("distinguished", a recipient of the O.M.) whom I found insufferably boring'.[29] But there is no doubt that Alfred's manner was often forbidding – not because he wished to restrict his friendships to the surface, but because he was afraid that he would be rebuffed. He once read a passage from T. E. Lawrence's *Seven Pillars of Wisdom*, and wrote 'This is me' alongside a passage which began:[30]

> I was very conscious of the bundled powers and entities within me; it was their character which hid. There was my craving to be liked – so strong and nervous that never could I open myself friendly to another. The terror of failure in an effort so important made me shrink from trying; besides, there was the standard; for intimacy seemed shameful unless the other could make the perfect reply, in the same language, after the same method, for the same reasons.

When someone whom he liked made some advance towards him, Housman's reserve could soon fade, as one of his acquaintances, Edward Marsh, observed in a touching little story:[31]

> Arthur Benson told me of a little incident which threw a faint but perhaps appreciable light on Housman's shy reserve. Arthur was spending the copious gains of his pen on a new Hall at Magdalene [where he had become Master in 1915], which was the pride of his life. He delighted to stand in the street and watch the masons at their work, and one day, catching sight of Housman, he did on impulse what as a rule he would never have dreamt of – seized him by the arm and dragged him into the building 'for to admire and for to see'. Something seemed to melt under his touch, a barrier fell, and for the first time Housman became entirely human. It was borne in upon Arthur that if people could only take to slapping him, so to speak, he would become a different person; but I never heard of anyone carrying the experiment further.

Housman would certainly not have welcomed a general invasion of his privacy; but, as he was now a very well-established figure in the academic world, he could have been less reserved without worrying that this would lead to people treating him with less respect. Quite apart from the excellent papers which he continued to produce, he had by September 1920 published the fourth volume of his Manilius, and it was becoming generally recognised that this attempt to edit the whole of Manilius was one of the great scholarly enterprises of the day.

Because of this, Housman's life in Cambridge was often solitary. In the afternoons he set out alone on his walks, 'clutching a walking-stick and attired in a nondescript grey suit, elastic-sided boots', which, incidentally, hardly anyone else had worn in England since Queen Victoria had died, 'high stiff single collar and close fitting cap, with a button top like a schoolboy's'.[32] His favourite route led past the Botanic Garden; but whether one met him here, or, just as likely, out in the countryside miles from Cambridge, 'he walked with a visibly abstracted air and often failed to notice one as he passed'. He entertained less often than most of his colleagues; and in the evenings would often retire to his Tower rooms to work alone, or to amuse himself with reading poetry or detective stories.

But although few of Housman's Cambridge friendships were really intimate, they still gave him pleasure, and a sense of belonging; and although he remained reticent about his own life, he was less reserved than at first. Indeed, he was well known by his friends as a man who would tell entertaining and often very bawdy tales which he had come across when reading the Latin and Greek authors;[33] and occasionally he wrote ribald limericks which he passed around for their amusement,[34] much as his mother had once passed around satirical verses for the amusement of her close friends at Woodchester.

Professor Housman felt warmly towards his colleagues – so warmly that according to Gow, he was 'deeply affected by the deaths of men on the very fringe of his acquaintanceship' – and he was very loyal to the community of which he and they were members. His reaction to the Bertrand Russell affair shows clearly that he would not tolerate any behaviour which he felt was a slight to the College, while he strongly desired the good opinion of the other Fellows. In November and December 1919 there was a forceful campaign to have Russell reappointed to a lectureship. In a letter to Hollond, one of the young organisers of the campaign, Housman said that he would not support it:[35]

> Russell is a great loss to the College, not merely for his eminence and celebrity, but as an agreeable and even charming person to meet; . . . what prevents me from signing your letter is Russell's taking his name off the books of the College. After that piece of petulance he ought not even to want to come back. I cannot imagine myself doing so; and my standard of conduct is so very low that I have a right to condemn those who do not come up to it.
>
> I am writing this, not to argufy, but only in acknowledgement of your civility in writing to me. I hope I shall not be able to discover 'conscious effort' in the amiability of yourself or Hardy when I happen to sit next to you in the future. I am afraid however that if Russell did return he would meet with rudeness from some Fellows of the College, as I know he did before he left. This ought not to be, but the

world is as God made it.

Your party has a clear majority, and you ought, quite apart from this question, to vote yourself on to the Council as opportunities arise. There is not nearly enough young blood in it.

Housman's letter was so warm that his failure to support the campaign did not lead to any bad feeling against him; and, in any case, the campaign succeeded, and Russell was offered a lectureship. He accepted it, but then resigned without taking up the appointment, perhaps secretly agreeing with Housman's estimate of his behaviour. It is interesting that Housman should have referred to his own standard of conduct as being 'so very low'. Presumably he was simply intending to make his opposition to Russell seem less intolerant than it might otherwise have done; but the words strike a surprisingly personal note. At the most, they hint at something of Housman's feelings about his own behaviour abroad; at the least, they reinforce the view of Housman as a man for whom loyalty to institutions was a very important element in life.

Housman was now sixty; and, wishing to devote as much of his time and energy as possible to his classical studies, he would not normally accept duties within the University; in 1920 he wrote: 'Not if the stipend were £150,000 instead of £150 would I be Public Orator. I could not discharge the duties of the office without abandoning all other duties and bidding farewell to such peace of mind as I possess'; and in 1925 he refused the offer of the Clark lectureship, saying that he regarded himself as a connoisseur of literature, but not as a critic; and that the time spent on preparing the required six lectures would give him anxiety and depression, and would be 'the more vexatious because it would be subtracted from those minute and pedantic studies in which I am fitted to excel and which give me pleasure'. Nor would he even appear at a meeting of a Queens' College society at which a paper by his old friend Sir James Frazer was to be read, in case on the strength of this appearance he might subsequently be worried into reading the society a paper himself.

But his affection for Trinity meant that Housman was prepared to take on a number of extra tasks on its behalf. In July 1919 it was Henry Jackson's eightieth birthday, and the Master and Fellows of the College gave him a replica of the tobacco-jar which had been owned by Jackson's most famous predecessor as Professor of Greek, Richard Porson. Although Housman disliked prose composition, and later said that the task had 'laid waste three whole mornings', the first of them occupied in wishing for death, he agreed to write the accompanying letter to Jackson, in which he emphasised that: 'Our tribute carries with it the personal affection of friends, and the gratitude of a community.' The letter was written to Housman's usual high standards; an exacting task, and perhaps he disliked doing it the more because it reminded him of the days when he was 'used too much as a scribe' at the Patent Office.

Housman was also a member of the College Wine Committee for many years. This involved pleasant duties for a connoisseur, such as occasional trips to London for wine-tasting sessions. As the years passed, Housman became rather discontented by the quality of the Burgundy which was offered for sale, and was glad that his private cellar contained a reasonable supply of pre-war vintages, as he was told that standards of wine making had deteriorated. But he carried out his duties with a keen palate for excellence; and on one occasion so much enjoyed a Madeira which cost rather more than the College had allowed for, that he ordered it and made up the difference out of his own pocket.[36] At the same time, he kept an eye on the quality of the food which was served at High Table, and the Suggestions Book contains many of his entries, such as this one, which dates from war-time:[37]

As venison is now about half the price of mutton it is our duty to have it sometimes in the interests of economy

or this, written in January 1928, not long after the College had engaged a new chef, a man who had worked at the great Café Royal in London:

The *sauce aux huitres* which we had last night with the cod was not oyster sauce but sauce *Hollondäise* into which an oyster or two had been dropped, combining no better than the Duke of Clarence with the Malmsey.

Housman had maintained his interest in botany, on his daily walks, and he also joined the Trinity College Garden Committee, and served on it for many years. For a part of that time he took on the considerable responsibility of being Secretary, which meant that he had to supervise the gardens and the gardeners, and to see that the recommendations of the Committee were properly carried out.[38] The Master, Sir J. J. Thomson, later wrote that Housman was 'very active and useful' in this post. He certainly had very decided views, liking flowers to have bright and definite colours, and 'very contemptuous of what are called in florists' catalogues "art shades", and which he called muddles'. It was Percy Withers who noted that he also loved their scent, as he had done since he was a child, and was very outraged if a new variety had sacrificed the fragrance of the parent stock. He took his interest in botany seriously, so that it sometimes seemed to a friend that he was more interested in the rarity than the beauty of a particular tree or wild flower; but there were moments when he could not disguise his love for natural beauty, as when he was crossing a field entirely ringed with the gleaming whiteness of the hawthorn, 'and then he stopped, and gazed, and exclaimed'. And at

Trinity Housman particularly admired the breath-taking flock of purple crocuses on the lawns at the back of the College, by the river; and a beautiful avenue of flowering cherry trees (for which Housman was not, in fact, personally responsible). The depth of his feeling for nature is most poignantly recorded in a poem written in 1922, which begins:

> Tell me not here, it needs not saying,
>    What tune the enchantress plays
> In aftermaths of soft September
>    Or under blanching mays,
> For she and I were long acquainted
>    And I knew all her ways.                  (*LP* 40)

Although he was prepared to serve on a number of committees, there was one major College institution with which Housman would have nothing to do – at least, nothing open. This was the chapel. Housman was still interested in religious questions, but would never attend chapel, not wishing to show any trace of allegiance to the God whom he had long ago rejected. Even if there was a preacher whom he particularly wanted to hear, Alfred would not sit in the main body of the chapel, but would steal up to the organ loft, out of sight of the congregation, so that he could hear the sermon without taking part in the service.[39] Outside the chapel, it was another matter, and once, when a leading Anglo-Catholic scholar, Bishop Charles Gore, was dining at Trinity, Housman particularly asked to be introduced to him.[40] Indeed, Housman was aware of his own ambivalent approach towards Christianity. In 1920 Geoffrey Grant Morris, the classical tutor of Corpus Christi, invited him to be his guest at a college feast, and in the course of the evening dared to ask Housman about his religious opinions. Alfred replied: 'I think I should describe myself as a High-Church atheist', and explained that the qualification 'High-Church' was a tribute to his mother's memory and his own early upbringing.[41]

In general, Housman had very little direct contact with the under-graduate members of the College, though when he was invited to a meeting of the Trinity Classical Society he would sometimes spend an evening reading a classical work with them. His main efforts were concentrated at this time upon pure scholarship: in 1925 he was working not only on the fifth volume of Manilius, but on a full-scale edition of Lucan; while by that year he had already published more than one hundred and forty reviews, articles, or critical comments on Latin and Greek subjects.

Only once, in 1926, did Housman supervise a research student, W. H. Semple, who later became Professor of Latin at Manchester University. And he did not do any individual teaching, or hold any seminars. But he continued to lecture, term by term, in the Examination Schools near

Cambridge Market Place, even if the number of those who attended was never very large. One student who attended some of Housman's lectures between 1919 and 1920 was R. M. Simkins, who recalls[42]

> that he was dealing with the Epodes of Horace among other subjects. These were not immediately connected with the classical Tripos syllabus and in any case what he said was far above our heads . . . our College tutors left it to us whether we went or not. . . .
>
> My memories are of a middle-sized grey-moustached man who at once gave two impressions – that he was completely master of the situation (misbehaviour or inattention would have been out of the question) and that his words were infallibly correct. The Housman we saw was the Housman who wrote the Introductions to Juvenal and Manilius. But in spite of the concentrated erudition we were constantly expecting some dry witticisms. These served to break any possible monotony and were by no means spoilt by the imperturbable serenity with which he uttered them. I only ONCE saw any semblance of a smile. I do not think he ever addressed any individuals and I am sure I should never have dared to approach *him*. In fact one felt that it would be impossible for anyone to express disagreement – unless it was in writing. Even now, after half a century, it gives me a shock if I find a modern scholar querying any of his 'readings' or explanations.

Geoffrey Carlisle was another student who found that the level of scholarship was far above his head; but when he also complained to his classical tutor that Housman did not seem to appreciate the Latin poetry, he was directed to *A Shropshire Lad*, and later wrote: 'I was immediately captivated, and the person of AEH took on a glamour it has never lost.'[43]

Any undergraduate who dared to call on Professor Housman uninvited was kindly received; but most of them, like Simkins and Carlisle, were too much in awe of him to do so – though Carlisle did arrange to sit next to Housman at Trinity High Table on two occasions after he had graduated, even if he was too shy to talk to the great scholar, and the increasingly famous poet. For the sales of *A Shropshire Lad*, which had revived during the war, climbed to record heights in the early twenties, when the nostalgic mood of many of the poems perfectly matched a widespread longing among people for a return to the days before the Great War – days which seemed in retrospect to have been an Indian summer of prosperity and tranquillity.

## Mainly friendships

Above the fireplace in Housman's rooms in Whewell's Court hung the photographs of Adalbert and Moses Jackson. While the picture of Adalbert showed a young man – and of course Adalbert had never grown old – the picture of Moses, which hung as a pendant to the other, was that of a man in late middle age.[44] Moses and Alfred were now elderly men, and with Moses and his family living in Canada, they were far apart; but their friendship, based on a lively correspondence, continued; and Alfred was as much in love with his old friend as he had been thirty-five years earlier. Alfred realised what a toll this friendship had taken on his happiness and peace of mind: in one poem, unpublished during his life-time, he described it as an 'unlucky love' (*MP* 12); and in another, also unpublished, he looked forward to death, when he would be freed from the painful burden of his love:

> Crossing alone the nighted ferry
>> With the one coin for fee,
> Whom, on the wharf of Lethe waiting,
>> Count you to find? Not me.
>
> The brisk fond lackey to fetch and carry,
>> The true sick-hearted slave,
> Expect him not in the just city
>> And free land of the grave.          (*MP* 23)

His efforts to ease his continuous sorrow, by writing to 'My dear Mo',[45] only prolonged the years of hopeless suffering. He had managed to disguise it enough to become quite a family friend, sending nonsense verse to his godson Gerald Jackson,[46] and even writing to Moses's wife, on one occasion sending her an illustrated edition of *A Shropshire Lad* together with a letter in which he commented: 'I do not admire the illustrations as much as I admire the poems!' Even when in 1922 Alfred sent Moses his newly-published *Last Poems*, the four-page letter which accompanied it was written in an amusing way. But among the poems in this volume was 'Epithalamium', the wedding poem written in Moses Jackson's honour which Housman had only recently completed, and which contained the lines:

> Friend and comrade yield you o'er
> To her that hardly loves you more;          (*LP* 24)

and the dedication to Moses was serious enough, written as it was from 'a fellow who thinks more of you than anything in the world', and who told his friend: 'you are largely responsible for my writing poetry and you ought to take the consequences'.[47]

Moses Jackson had himself known some sadness. In 1919, shortly after returning from the war, his second son had been killed in a bicycling accident in Vancouver; but, generally speaking, he had thoroughly enjoyed life on his farm near Aldegrove, where he had now been settled for eleven years. But by 1922 he was beginning to show symptoms of some serious illness; and less than a year later, suffering from cancer of the stomach, Moses was very close to death. Lying in a hospital bed in Vancouver, he pencilled a last, faint letter to his old friend, whom he addressed as 'Dear old Hous'. Alfred received the letter; and, soon afterwards hearing of Jackson's death, he endorsed the envelope 'Mo's last letter', carefully went over the writing in ink, and treasured it for the rest of his life.[48] Later, the Jacksons sent Housman a photograph of Mo's tombstone;[49] the picture of Moses remained on the wall above the fire-place. One day Alfred's brother Laurence noticed it; although he had met Jackson as a young man, he did not recognise the middle-aged man of the photograph, and he asked Alfred who it was. His brother answered, 'in a strangely moved voice . . . "That was my friend Jackson, the man who had more influence on my life than anybody else." '[50]

Moses Jackson was the only one of Housman's Oxford friends with whom he had kept in regular communication. True, he had been pleased to see Alfred Pollard at the Inaugural Lecture in 1911, but by then they seemed to have little in common, and if he did meet Pollard again, it was at very infrequent intervals; though, remembering that Pollard had helped him with the publication of *A Shropshire Lad*, Housman may have asked his advice about *Last Poems*. However, Housman was now an Honorary Fellow of St John's College, Oxford, who in 1925 commissioned Francis Dodd to make a portrait drawing of their prodigal son. Housman had always taken a friendly interest in his old University, feeling pleased, for example, when Oxford won the Boat Race; and in the post-war years he enjoyed meeting groups of Oxford men from time to time, whether informally, as when he lunched with Professor Adcock of King's College and several Oxford graduates,[51] or formally, at dinners of the inter-University club 'The Arcades'. In November 1921 he even agreed to propose the toast 'Oxford' at the annual dinner of Oxford men in Cambridge. The dinner was held in the Combination Room of St John's College, where, after addressing the company as 'Fellow-exiles', Housman entertained them with 'an elaborate comparison between the Ivy at Magdalene, which was said to be clinging to and destroying the fabric, and the women members of the University'.[52]

Housman's links with the Patent Office were even fewer than his links with Oxford. Having registered so many of them as Trade Marks, he still had an eye for advertisements; and when he wrote to Percy Withers about his New Year's Eve stout and oysters, joking that he took them 'medicinally to neutralise the excesses of Christmas', he finished: 'When you give Mrs. Winslow's soothing syrup to a baby, "the little darling wakes up as bright as a button"; and so do I on New Year's Day.' On his writing desk lay the Wedgwood medallion which his superior had given him when he left the Patent Office in 1892, and among his papers was John Maycock's letter of congratulation on his appointment as Latin Professor; but the only fellow-clerk with whom he had any contact at all in later years was Hodges, the married staff clerk at whose home Housman had long ago spent an occasional happy evening.[53]

Housman always felt a special gratitude towards University College London. When he left, he had asked to continue his membership of the Professors' Dining Club,[54] though he did not actually dine with them again until 1925, at the special invitation of H. E. Butler, his successor there as Professor of Latin. But, during that evening in October, he went over to Professor A. V. Hill, a Nobel Prize winner in physiology and medicine, who had been a Fellow of Trinity until 1916, and was now teaching at University College. 'Housman looked through me at Trinity', A. V. Hill remembered, 'but welcomed me warmly at University College, coming over to me in the most friendly way; as it was University College which had first recognised his academic brilliance after his years in the Patent Office.'[55]

Housman had kept several good friends from his days at University College, chief among them Walter Ashburner, W. P. Ker, and Arthur Platt. Occasionally Housman dined in London with Ashburner, and when in 1926 Ashburner went to Oxford as Professor of Jurisprudence, they still kept in touch – perhaps because they shared so many of the same fairly harmless prejudices: in January 1929 Alfred wrote to his friend: 'I met yesterday a man who had been entertained, as I never have, at Pembroke in your University, and who spoke well of its wine and its anti-feminism.'[56]

W. P. Ker retired as Professor of English at University College in the summer of 1922; and, although he soon afterwards left for a holiday in the Alps, Housman was glad to think that he would be able to show Ker the proofs of *Last Poems* on his return. Ker had been elected Professor of Poetry at Oxford in 1920, and still had several years of those light duties to occupy him; but in July 1923 he returned to the Alps again, where he fell dead from heart failure while enjoying one of his favourite mountain walks.

Two years later, Arthur Platt was also dead. Housman had continued to visit the Platts regularly, and he and Arthur had enjoyed a lively and uninhibited correspondence. Unfortunately, only one of these letters survives – in which Alfred wonders whether St Paul's experiences in the third heaven could be explained in the same way as those of Don Quixote in the moon. The rest were destroyed by Mrs Platt on her husband's death, as 'too Rabelaisian'. The friendship between Housman and Platt had always had an element of friendly banter in it: 'I congratulate you on having managed to live with Platt so long', wrote Housman to Mrs Platt in December 1920, adding 'This is a compliment of the season'; and a favourite theme was the fact that Housman preferred drinking, and Platt smoking. When Housman first went to Cambridge as Professor in 1911, Platt had written to their mutual friend Henry Jackson, mentioning Housman's boast that he would drink double to make up for Mayor's abstinence, and adding: 'so I hope you'll keep your eye on him; he'll drink only too much without any sense of duty to spur him on – comes of not smoking, I believe'.[57] Now Housman, after working hard to collect and edit the best of Platt's Essays for publication, added a Preface in which, after paying full tribute to Platt's good nature, his versatility, and his scholarship, he added: 'In conclusion it is proper to mention his vices. He was addicted to tobacco and indifferent to wine, and he would squander long summer days on watching the game of cricket.'[58] In the main body of the book, Housman added notes to explain simple references to cricket, such as 'that arts had had an unconscionably long innings', later explaining that his object was 'to win a smile from Platt's beatified spirit and mitigate the tedium of Paradise'.

William Rothenstein and his family had returned to London, and Alfred saw them from time to time. But he had always disliked Rothenstein's drawings of him, and was pleased to be able to write to Mrs Rothenstein in January 1927:

> You might tell William that he has lost his monopoly in my features, as I have been drawn this last year for my two Colleges by two artists named Dodd and Gleadowe. The two drawings are very unlike, but neither of them makes me look as nasty as the portrait which this College bought from William, and so prevented him, to my great relief, from exhibiting it any more in public and from adding malignant touches from time to time, as he used to do when he was out of temper. But I have a beautiful and forgiving nature, and I wish him as well as you a happy new year. . . .

The drawings were certainly very unlike; the Dodd portrait, commissioned by St John's College, shows Housman sitting beside a desk piled high with books; he is neatly dressed, with a tie and wing-collar; and his face is that of a man who has suffered, but who gazes proudly, almost defiantly, out of the picture, with a look of aristocratic challenge. Gleadowe's portrait, commissioned by Trinity, shows a different aspect: the face rather soft and sensitive; and the droopy moustache, which seems only incidental in Dodd's portrait, here becomes an important feature, reinforcing a general impression of sensuality. Gleadowe, who was Slade Professor at Oxford when he drew the portrait, later recalled that Housman[59]

chatted easily most of the time, and was so lively that I felt I had a good chance of getting something of his true character into the drawing. As I started drawing I said to him 'What about your time?' He thought I said 'tie', and replied 'Ready-made, half-a-crown, fastens with a clip behind. I'll take it off, if you like.' When I was drawing his ear, I remarked on its interesting shape. 'Ordinary criminal type, surely', said he.

Rothenstein made one more attempt to draw Housman. In January 1928, Alfred was one of a group of distinguished pall-bearers at Thomas Hardy's funeral in Westminster Abbey.[60] Rothenstein wanted to paint them as a group, but Housman would only agree to sit on the condition that all the other pall-bearers agreed first, telling William bluntly: 'You are much too great an artist to catch a likeness'; though he softened this remark by adding that 'a journalist present in the Abbey says that my person proved as polished as my verse, after which I desire to be for ever invisible.' When J. M. Barrie also held out against the project, it came to nothing, much to Housman's relief. Indeed, he disliked the portrait which Trinity had bought from Rothenstein so much, that in the end he gave the College another of himself by Rothenstein, one which he found less offensive, and then he removed the first one, and destroyed it.

One of the pall-bearers, Sir Edmund Gosse, died himself only four months later. Alfred had been very pleased to see him again, and find him looking 'as young as ever', for although they had seen each other fairly often before the war, their friendship had been continued only by occasional correspondence since then. But Gosse had written a very favourable review of *Last Poems* for the *Sunday Times*: and he had also pleased Housman – who had earlier complained that his biography of Swinburne did not reveal enough – by sending him a typewritten account of Swinburne's addiction to drink and flagellation. Gosse wrote about Swinburne's excesses in a way which may have struck an answering note in Housman's mind, when he thought of his own homosexual encounters;[61]

They existed, as it were, outside his morality, which was in all essentials (strange as it may seem) unaffected by them. He was totally without the vicious desire to cause other persons to accept his conduct in these matters as admirable. He never excused, or boasted, or expressed any remorse or regret for these excesses. I never heard him, and I never heard of anyone else who heard him, recommend them to others. He was a perfectly safe companion for youth, and to those who were temperate and innocent he seemed to have himself preserved both temperance and innocence.

Housman was certainly interested to note that, while his writings were influenced by de Sade, Swinburne's private inclinations were those of Sader-Masoch. On his own shelves in Whewell's Court there were a number of serious books about sexual matters; and he also read with interest German and French classics, such as Balzac's bawdy *Contes Drolatiques*,[62] and books which were banned in England, including James Joyce's *Ulysses* – which he had received from Grant Richards, to whom he wrote that he had 'scrambled and waded through [it] and found one or two half-pages amusing'. In 1928, through Grant Richards – who wrote 'I suppose I ought not to post it to you, but if by some mischance I am prosecuted, I shall maintain that its literary interest to citizens connected with literature places me in a privileged position' – he laid hands on Frederick Rolfe's unpublished set of pornographic letters about the homosexual underworld of Venice. He had thought that these might inflame his passions, but in the event they were something of a disappointment: 'That sort of thing is not really improved by literary elegances', wrote Housman to Grant Richards, 'and I have been more amused with things written in urinals.'

Over the years, Housman had remained more closely in touch with James Frazer, who had been knighted in 1914 for his anthropological work. Housman still did not much care for Lady Frazer, a woman with an uncertain temper.[63] 'Many thanks for your kind effort on behalf of my proper feeding', Alfred wrote to her once, 'You look very benign in the picture, and I hope that the interior corresponds . . .'.[64] But in 1921 Housman was one of the sponsors of the Frazer lectureship in social anthropology, and was chosen to write a formal address to Sir James. Just as he was inspired by Frazer's unveiling of ancient mysteries in *The Golden Bough*, so on his various holidays in England, Housman was always interested in discussing local traditions, and kept a letter from the vicar of Bloxham, who wrote to say 'When we were talking about folk lore . . . I meant to tell you that we still have surviving in this district the use of a doll on May day encircled in the green.' The doll was carried round lying flat on her back, by children who sang 'not very clearly, a carol of which I have not yet been able to get the words, as they are shy about them'.[65]

The Frazers remained in Cambridge; but two of Housman's friends had left for Eton: Andrew Gow to become a classics master there in 1914, and M. R. James to become Provost in 1918. Housman, who felt that Gow was wasting his talents by taking a job as a schoolmaster, kept a friendly eye on his career, encouraging him to try for Latin professorships, and to keep in touch with Trinity; and when James also moved to Eton, he began to make occasional journeys there to see his friends. Gow was flattered by Housman's attention, though he did not know him at all well at this time; and in January 1924, after dining as Housman's guest at a meeting of 'The

Family', Gow sent him a copy of the Creech translation of Manilius, hoping that Housman would accept it as 'a very trifling return for a great deal of pleasure and instruction that I owe you'.[66] At last, in 1925, Gow was offered a teaching post at Trinity, and accepted it, after Housman had written to him pointing out that he had made a success of his time at Eton, and might even be opulent if he become a Housemaster; but that Eton would not allow him leisure for the full development of his talents. On his visits Housman had met a number of the staff at Eton, including the librarian, Broadbent, 'rather a figure of fun, with the largest and most bloodshot eyes I ever saw, and produces Greek and Latin verses which should be pointed but are not', and the headmaster Dr Alington, who was very impressed by the paper on Erasmus Darwin which Housman read to an Eton society. But Housman particularly delighted in the company of James, and once sent him this 'Proposal for an edition of the Septuagint by M. R. James':[67]

A.E.H. fecit
*This picture offers to your sight*
*Chaos before the birth of light;*
*The state of things you will remark*
*Is consequently very dark.*

A.E.H. fecit
*The figures you do not perceive*
*Are those of Adam and of Eve;*
*To draw them would not do at all –*
*How providential was the Fall!*

Dr Withers, that other friend from Cambridge, had now moved close to the edge of the Cotswolds. He made every effort to keep in touch with Housman, writing to him each Christmas with news of his family and his new house. Quite by chance, his village of Souldern lay very close to the route along which Housman had himself chauffeur-driven to visit the Wises in Gloucestershire every year; and in June 1921 he wrote to Withers, asking if he might look in for lunch on the way. The meeting was a great success; conversation flowed easily for once, and the house looked at its best on what had turned out to be a perfect summer's day. The following year Alfred stayed with his friends at Souldern for three nights, and the year after that for five. From then on, he visited them for at.least a few days almost every year until he died.

Percy Withers and his wife worked hard and unobtrusively to make things pleasant for their distinguished guest, and Alfred had soon found that he could settle into a thoroughly relaxing routine in their household. At 7.15 a.m. they brought him morning tea, and then, after breakfast an hour later, he would wander in the garden, burying his face in trusses of bloom for the scent. Much of the rest of the day he spent reading peacefully in the garden or the library; but each morning and afternoon he and Withers would set off together for a five- or six-mile tramp through the surrounding countryside. Withers felt these walks, and indeed much of each visit, a considerable strain, finding it difficult to keep up a conversation with Housman. This lack of understanding is shown clearly in his description of an incident on one of their walks. Withers had recognised a local farm labourer in the lane ahead of them, and, telling Housman how good and wise the man was, he stopped to talk to him, expecting that Housman would stop also. But Alfred, as might have been expected, 'walked steadily on, as though the lane were vacant', clearly feeling that he had nothing to learn from an Oxfordshire peasant.

It was frustrating for Withers 'never to feel the smallest assurance that I had got an inch nearer to Housman himself . . . I had to be content as the mystic is, who adores his saint without requital, and is satisfied', and this frustration spills over into his book about Housman, in which he seems to delight in recording the mornings on which Alfred was sometimes

morose and ill-tempered, a state I attributed to physical causes, and for which I could make every allowance, save on the few occasions when it found physical expression, and, one of the dogs crossing his path, he would lunge out with a foot, and appeared to derive satisfaction if the mean assault were effectual.

But there is no doubt that Percy Withers admired Housman enormously, and that the warmth of his admiration and friendship moved Housman strongly, so that on the last day of each visit he would be visibly sad and gloomy at the thought of leaving. At the end of one visit, this was particularly noticeable. On the evening before, Withers's daughter Audrey had come up from work in London for a visit. She was natural and spontaneous, and Housman, who had never met her before, took to her immediately: 'within three minutes', wrote Dr Withers rather enviously, 'words were rattling to and fro, swift and keen and challenging, like the ball on a racquet court, and the game never for a moment halted . . . a joint display of wit, mirth and benevolence, in which I occasionally chipped in.' But the following day, after lunch, Housman was glum and tongue-tied; Audrey's efforts to talk to him were in vain; and when, after saying goodbye to Audrey and Mrs Withers, Alfred walked down to his car, he could bring himself to say nothing of his visit: 'but, as he grasped my hand, wordlessly,' remembered Withers, 'he turned on me the saddest and most haunting countenance I had ever seen on any face but his . . .'.

Housman continued to be sympathetic about Withers's poor health; though, as soon as insulin became available for treating diabetes,

Withers's general health improved a great deal. Housman himself had remained in excellent health until his sixties. Then, in May 1923, he reported to Withers that: 'For nearly three months I have been ill, not on a scale which would inspire your respect, but enough to make me very angry and disgusted, and in fact worse than I ever was in my life.' He had suffered from boils, and then a succession of carbuncles, and his Easter holiday had been ruined. But, after this unpleasant bout of ill health, he was physically very well again for some years; though no doubt from time to time he suffered from the 'nervous depression and causeless appre-hensions' which he later said had often afflicted him.

As he advanced towards his old age, Housman had to bear the un-happiness of outliving many of his closest friends, and his most highly-valued acquaintances. Edmund Gosse, Arthur Benson, W. P. Ker, Arthur Platt, and his beloved Moses Jackson had all died before Alfred's seventieth birthday in March 1929. But many still remained, including two of his oldest and dearest friends, Sophie Becker and Edith Wise. His reputation as a poet had been confirmed and strengthened by the publi-cation of *Last Poems*; and Housman was becoming recognised through-out the world as one of the great classical scholars of his day.

# CHAPTER 10

# A Classical Scholar

My edition of Lucan has been selling just twice as quick as
*A Shropshire Lad* did; and I am glad that some interest is taken
in my serious works.

A. E. Housman to his sister Kate[1]

'to add a new weirdness to what the sky possesses in its size
and formlessness, there is involved the quality of decay. For all
the wonder of these everlasting stars, . . . they are not everlasting, they are not eternal; they burn out like candles. . . .
Imagine them all extinguished, and your mind feeling its way
through a heaven of total darkness, occasionally striking
against the black, invisible cinders of those stars . . . If you are
cheerful, and wish to remain so, leave the study of astronomy
alone. Of all the sciences, it alone deserves the character of the
terrible.'

'I am not altogether cheerful.'

'Then if, on the other hand you are restless and anxious
about the future, study astronomy at once. Your troubles will
be reduced amazingly. But your study will reduce them in a
singular way, by reducing the importance of everything. So
that the science is still terrible, even as a panacea. . . . It is
better – far better – for men to forget the universe than to bear it
so clearly in mind.'

Thomas Hardy, *Two on a Tower*[2]

Studying the classics had been the cornerstone of learning in Europe
since the Renaissance. By then, however, thousands of important works
had been lost for ever; of all the poems written by the Greek poetess
Sappho, only two odes survived in full; of all the one hundred and
forty-two books of Livy's great history of Rome, one hundred and seven
had perished. Those works which did survive could only be read in the
imperfect versions which had descended from antiquity, miscopied by
scribes, perhaps mutilated by natural disasters of fire and flood, some-

times surviving in a number of manuscripts which varied considerably, sometimes surviving in only a single manuscript, parts of which were unintelligible. The chief task of classical scholarship, as Housman and his predecessors understood it, was, through a painstaking process of textual criticism, to restore these surviving texts of the Greek and Latin authors to as close to their original state as possible.

Since Housman's death, a number of critics have tended to undervalue the work of a textual critic, describing it as 'largely a *knack*'[3] (John Wain); and even 'on about the same plane as a man of business scolding his typist for not being able to spell' (a reviewer in the *Manchester Guardian*); while Edmund Wilson makes the more general point that, for Housman, 'knowledge itself meant at most the discovery of things that were already there'.[4] Textual criticism is certainly a narrow branch of scholarship; but when Housman called his studies 'minute and pedantic', he did not mean that they were petty or intellectually trivial: rather that they were detailed studies based on a wide technical knowledge. For him textual criticism was a rigorous and highly disciplined task, demanding great intellectual devotion. There are no built-in answers: the problems, whether caused by miscopying or by mutilation, have been posed not by the author of the manuscript, but by a series of errors and unlucky events over which he had no control; hence many problems which are virtually insoluble.[5] The work of textual criticism, then, becomes a highly demanding search for truth, and a part of the wider search for truth which Housman had praised in his Introductory Lecture of 1892, when he spoke of there being 'no rivalry between the studies of Arts and Laws and Science but the rivalry of fellow-soldiers in striving which can most victoriously achieve the common end of all, to set back the frontier of darkness'.

Housman outlined the nature and scope of the work which he had chosen in two other lectures, 'The Confines of Criticism', and 'The Application of Thought to Textual Criticism'. In the first of these, delivered as his Inaugural Lecture at Cambridge in 1911, Housman insisted that the study of Latin was a department of science and, as such, had nothing to do with literary or aesthetic criticism. He pointed out that there were other sciences, botany and astronomy, which possessed aesthetic qualities and made an appeal to the emotions; then, quoting from Newton's *Principia*, 'Let S represent the sun, T the earth, P the moon, CADB the moon's orbit', Housman concludes:

> This is how scholars should write about literature. If the botanist and the astronomer can go soberly about their business, unseduced by the beauties of the field and unbewildered by the glories of the firmament, let the scholar amidst the masterpieces of literature maintain the same coolness of head.

In the second lecture, delivered to a meeting of the Classical Association in 1921, Housman defined textual criticism as:

> a science, and, since it comprises recension and emendation, it is also an art. It is the science of discovering error in texts and the art of removing it . . . [it] is not a branch of mathematics, nor indeed an exact science at all. It deals with a matter not rigid and constant, like lines and numbers, but fluid and variable; namely the frailties and aberrations of the human mind, and of its insubordinate servants, the human fingers.

Pointing out that 'every problem which presents itself to the textual critic must be regarded as possibly unique', Housman added:

> It has sometimes been said that textual criticism is the crown and summit of all scholarship. This is not evidently or necessarily true; but it is true that the qualities which make a critic, whether they are thus transcendent or no, are rare, and that a good critic is a much less common thing than for instance a good grammarian.

Housman concluded that:

> Textual criticism, like most other sciences, is an aristocratic affair, not communicable to all men, nor to most men. Not to be a textual critic is no reproach to anyone, unless he pretends to be what he is not. To *be* a textual critic requires aptitude for thinking and willingness to think; and though it also requires other things, those things are supplements and cannot be substitutes. Knowledge is good, method is good, but one thing beyond all others is necessary; and that is to have a head, not a pumpkin, on your shoulders, and brains, not pudding in your head.

Housman was clearly very proud of his job; but if his estimate of his own abilities sometimes sounds arrogant, it is worth remembering that he was humble enough towards those whom he felt to be superior to him, advising aspiring critics to 'think more of the dead than of the living'. The dead had endured the test of time, and even if their knowledge was superseded, their reason and intelligence was not.

> To study the greatest of the scholars of the past is to enjoy intercourse with superior minds. If our conception of scholarship and our methods of procedure are at variance with theirs, it is not indeed a certainty or a necessity that we are wrong, but it is a good working hypothesis.

In particular, Housman recognised the excellence of Scaliger, Bentley and Porson. Scaliger, born in France in 1540, had produced editions of many Latin authors including Catullus, Propertius, and Manilius.[6]

Housman recognised in Scaliger a man of colossal erudition, in a class higher than himself.[7] The other two men, Bentley and Porson, were both Englishmen, and had both worked at Trinity College, Cambridge, Bentley as Master of the College from 1700 to 1742; while Porson became a Fellow of the College forty years after Bentley's death, in 1782.

Richard Bentley, apart from being brutally arrogant, avaricious and autocratic, was a brilliant scholar with a caustic wit who established his reputation throughout Europe when in 1699 he proved that the Epistles of Phalaris were forgeries, but even Housman could admit that he might seem to some a 'tasteless and arbitrary pedant'. Despite this Bentley, equally eminent in Greek and Latin, was the most outstanding classical scholar whom England has ever produced; and in him Housman recognised someone whose excellence was beyond his attainment,[8] admiring his 'unique originality and greatness'. He would grow angry if anyone attempted to compare him to Bentley,[9] saying on one occasion: 'Bentley would cut up into four of me.'

It was obligatory for Bentley, as Master of the College, to be in Holy Orders; but he did not take his religious duties at all seriously, and once attended chapel only to find that 'he could not get into the Master's stall, because after long disuse the door had been fastened up'. Richard Porson, who later in the eighteenth century followed in Bentley's tradition of exact scholarship, was a more scrupulous man. After ten years Porson's fellowship at Trinity College lapsed, because he was conscientiously unwilling to take Holy Orders as the terms of his fellowship demanded. He was elected Regius Professor of Greek at Cambridge, but the salary was only £40 a year and so his religious doubts condemned him to a life of poverty.[10] But Porson was a man of wide learning, the author of some brilliant emendations, and was later considered by Housman and others to be, after Bentley, 'the second of English Scholars'.

After Porson's death in 1808, classical scholarship in England went into a decline. Scholars began to be altogether silent on matters of textual criticism, and Housman later wrote of one series of classical texts, the Bibliotheca Classica edited by A. J. Macleane, that it 'faithfully represented the low ebb of scholarship in the middle of the nineteenth century'.[11] After this, the pendulum of scholarly fashion swung first towards a good deal of 'wild and arbitrary' criticism; and then, as a reaction to this, it swung back too far in the other direction, towards a slothful 'method'[12] which consisted chiefly of putting on blinkers and following the particular manuscript which one believed to be the best.

Housman, with his great admiration for the intellectual giants of the past, and with his passion for truth and excellence, applied his knowledge and logical powers to the work of textual scholarship, and had soon risen far above his contemporaries. Among the qualifications for the work

which he had chosen to do was his unrivalled command of Latin. The
poem which he wrote for Moses Jackson, beginning:

> Signa pruinosae uariantia luce cauernas
> noctis et extincto lumina nata die         (*Manilius*, I)

shows something of this. But it is much more difficult to be amusing than
to be serious in a foreign language, and Housman could write humorous
Latin poetry too. Trinity College, Cambridge, possesses such a poem
which Housman wrote while he was supervising some students during
an examination at Cambridge in October or November 1911. The poem,
entitled 'Nonae Novembres' is about Guy Fawkes's plot. Entertaining on
several levels, it is in part a humorous attack on the Pope for inspiring the
Plot – and no wonder that the Pope is the cause of such evils, because he is
really a woman, says Housman. In fact he is Anti-Christ, the Beast
described in Revelation with the number 666. The poem is also a parody
of the lines by Ovid in which are exposed the problems of admitting the
name Tuticanus into dactylic verse;[13] while at the same time Housman
places himself in the position of one of the students whom he is supervising, and vainly wishes that he had his Latin dictionary with him – he
cannot remember whether the first syllable of the word for Protestant is
long or short – and in the end he fails to finish his poem, tailing off with
two notes to the examiners: the first of which makes a pretentious claim
for his choice of metrical form, and the second of which points out that he
would have written more if the examination had gone on longer!

Not only did Housman have an easy command of Latin, but a sensitivity for language which was as evident when he was dealing with
Roman authors as it was in his mother-tongue. He once wrote of Virgil
that his 'besetting sin is the use of words too forcible for his thoughts, and
the *moritura* of Aen. XII 55 makes me blush for him whenever I think of it';
and this sensitivity, combined with his knowledge of what it was to be a
poet and to write poetry, particularly fitted Housman for the task of
emending the works of Latin poets. He was able to place himself within
the mind of a dead author, and to know what that author could or could
not have written. Indeed, he once explained how important it was for a
textual critic to get rid of his own tastes, and to try to acquire the tastes of
the classics, and 'not to come stamping into the library of Apollo on the
Palatine without so much as wiping our shoes on the doormat, and cover
the floor with the print of feet which have waded through the miry clay of
the nineteenth century into the horrible pit of the twentieth . . . we must
be born again', he added, describing this as 'a process exceedingly
repugnant to all right-minded Englishmen', who felt that it was
'improper' as well as 'arduous', and would 'much rather retain the pre-
valent opinion that the secret of the classical spirit is open to anyone who

has a fervent admiration for the second-best parts of Tennyson'.

Gow records of Housman that: 'He would commonly answer without hesitation the minutest questions on the history of scholarship, and seemed to have read all the works even of scholars of the second rank and to retain in his memory every detail of their lives and writings.'

Alongside all these qualifications for his work went Housman's belief in the pursuit of excellence, and an enormous capacity for hard work. The edition of Manilius, which occupied him for over thirty years, was his greatest single project. He once wrote of it that, when it was completed: 'I shall have done what I came on earth to do, and can devote the rest of my days to religious meditation.' But even when the Manilius is set to one side, the amount of work which Housman completed during his life-time remains colossal.

After the publication in 1888 of his work on the love-poetry of Propertius, Housman published numerous papers every year until his death. To begin with, he did much work on the Greek tragedies; but when he became Professor of Latin at University College, he concentrated upon the Latin poets from Lucretius, whose main work was a savage attack upon religious belief, to Juvenal. Housman continued to make useful contributions to Greek scholarship as well: here and there his textual suggestions have been generally accepted, and he made some particularly valuable corrections to the text of the Athenian dramatic poet Menander.[14] But he did not feel that, like Bentley, he could achieve excellence in both Latin and Greek; and he was amused to be able to write to A. C. Pearson, the Regius Professor of Greek at Cambridge: 'The number of good Greek scholars whom I have deceived into thinking that I know Greek is mounting up, and I add your scalp to Platt's and Headlam's.'

In 1894, Housman edited Ovid's 'Ibis' for Postgate's complete collection of the Latin poets, the 'Corpus Poetarum Latinorum'; and his name continually appears in the apparatus criticus of Ovid's other works.[15] Postgate also asked him, in 1903, to prepare a text of the satirical poet Juvenal for the Corpus; and on gathering together the different versions of the text Housman found to his surprise that 'Juvenal's modern editors were ignorant or regardless of even the printed sources'. Describing his task as 'an enterprise taken in haste and in humane concern for the relief of a people sitting in darkness',[16] he chose eight representative manuscripts and a number of fragments from which to prepare the first reliable apparatus criticus of the text in which he made a number of emendations, cleared up the punctuation, and gave 'a new edge to some epigrammatic or rhetorical lines'.[17] His edition was published in 1905, and was warmly received by other English scholars.

By 1925, Housman had published as many as forty reviews, articles or critical comments on Greek subjects, and more than one hundred on Latin ones; and he was busily completing a work which had been about ten years in the making, a full-scale edition of the Latin poet, Lucan. By August Housman was near the end of his labours, and he wrote tongue in cheek to a colleague, J. D. Duff, that in the event of his dying while on holiday in France, Duff should complete the work on Lucan which now involved only the index, a task which Housman would be extremely relieved to escape. The following year, however, Housman had compiled the index, and his edition of Lucan was published. He had made few emendations but by revising the punctuation he had turned Lucan, at last, into 'a really intelligible poet'.[18]

Usually, Housman had no trouble in having his articles published: though there was one irritating incident in 1923, when one editor of the *Classical Quarterly*, having heard Housman read a paper, asked if they could have it for publication; and then his colleague declined it without consulting him. And he did have some difficulty finding a home for an article entitled 'Praefanda', a collection of textual problems in the Latin poets, where the context involves sex. There was room for a scholarly article on this subject; and, as an old man in his seventies, Housman had decided that he would write one. Housman was certainly no puritan, and he despised the current practice of skating over those parts of classical texts which were considered morally offensive. Translations of the classics would usually avoid altogether such lines as Juvenal's

> hic si
> quaeritur et desunt homines, mora nulla per ipsam
> quo minus imposito clunem summitat asello;   (Juvenal, Satire VI, ll. 332–4)

and in Housman's possession was a translation of 'Trimalchio's Banquet' by Petronius, in which Housman had had to underline the word 'girl' and write in the Latin word for 'boy' against these lines:[19]

> amongst those who had last arrived, there was a good-looking girl whom Trimalchio approached and held kissing for a while.

Nevertheless, because the context of the problems with which he was dealing involved sex, Housman wrote his essentially philological discussion in Latin.[20] Then, in 1931, when it was complete, he submitted it to Reginald Hackforth, the current editor of the *Classical Quarterly*. Hackforth accepted 'Praefanda' for publication, but then the Management Committee of the journal objected to its inclusion. Housman did not seem very surprised, writing to Hackforth: 'The average Englishman is a sexual monomaniac; and if you and I have escaped the taint we may be thankful.' No other English journal would take the paper, but later in the year it was published in the German periodical *Hermes*.

All this published work was of course done in addition to the long hours of teaching at University College London until 1910; and the twice-weekly lectures at Cambridge thereafter in which Housman considered a number of authors including Catullus, Horace, Juvenal, Lucan, Lucretius, Martial, Ovid, Persius and Plautus.[21] But Housman's efforts were not universally welcomed by his contemporaries in the field of classical scholarship. This is not surprising. No one likes to have his faults pointed out to him, and Housman, with his passion for excellence, was so exasperated by the low standards which were everywhere evident in the classical scholarship of his day, that he did not hesitate to make war upon second-rate thinking with every weapon in his formidable intellectual armoury.

In his Cambridge Inaugural of 1911, Housman had attacked what he saw as the twin evils of classical scholarship of the day: aesthetic criticism, and the mechanical methods of some German scholars. Dismissing aesthetic criticism he said that there was no value to be attached to judgments pronounced 'by men who are not themselves men of letters, but merely scholars with a literary taint, on disputed passages written hundreds and thousands of years ago by an alien race amidst an alien culture'. Later, in his 'Application of Thought' lecture in 1921, Housman mocked the 'law' that one should find the best manuscript, and stick to that wherever possible.

The virulence of Housman's attacks on other scholars is often held against him. In particular, he has been condemned in an influential essay by the critic Edmund Wilson, for speaking with an emotion out of all proportion to its object; for flattening 'out small German professors with weapons which would have found fit employment in the hands of a great reformer or a great satirist'.[22]

There were certainly some scholars, both German and English, whom Housman personally offended. It cannot have been pleasant for Schulze to be told that he had mauled Baehrens's Catullus 'out of all recognition'; for Mr Garrod to be informed that his conjectures on Manilius were 'singularly cheap and shallow'; for Friedrich Marx to be told: 'Mr Marx should write a novel. Nay, he may almost be said to have written one; for his notes on book iii (Lucilius' journey to Sicily) are not so much a commentary on the surviving fragments as an original narrative of travel and adventure.' German scholars, condemned in the lecture of 1911, had already been told in 1903: 'the Lachmanns and Madvigs are gone, the Mosers and Forbigers remain; and now they lift up their heads and rejoice aloud at the emancipation of human incapacity'. The result of all this was that, on the Continent, until at least the 1920s, Housman was considered as 'a highly eccentric Englishman whose work need not be taken very seriously . . . it lacked method, and it was strangely offensive'.[23]

There is also no doubt that Alfred Housman enjoyed the art of invective; but on the strength of a passage in his brother Laurence's *Memoir* it is often unfairly assumed that Alfred delighted in noting down hurtful sentences which he could later use to attack a suitable opponent. Laurence quoted, for example: 'When —— has acquired a scrap of misinformation he cannot rest till he has imparted it'; and '—— usually has the last word in controversy because he incurs exposures which editors do not like to print.'[24] To find out the real truth about this, one must examine the full list of these sentences, several pages of them, which is held by Trinity College, Cambridge. It is immediately apparent that the majority of them are 'Thoughts' of a general nature, such as these:[25]

> The fool's first step on the road to wisdom is self-contempt.

> The man who has never been half-drunk is a stranger to generous emotion.

> Mankind believes things not because it has reasons for believing them, but because it has motives, and abandons beliefs not because they are incredible but because they are uncongenial.

One of these sentences: 'I do not think reason an infallible guide, but I think it a better guide than superstition' did appear in print in a slightly different form;[26] but the rest seem to have remained unused in his notebook.

Among all these general observations there is certainly a sprinkling of comments on individuals, such as one which Laurence quotes: 'Mr. Swinburne no longer writes poetry: he only makes a clattering noise';[27] but there is only a handful of the sentences with gaps left in them, such as the two quoted above. The explanation must be that Housman, at some stage, had the idea of building up a collection of his 'Thoughts'; and that, in the course of some preliminary work on the project, he sketched out one or two sentences about common faults, without deciding which particular scholar or other individual to attach them to. When he abandoned the project, the sentences remained unfinished.[28] None of these unfinished sentences appears to bear any direct relation to Housman's classical controversies, and, taken as a whole, they cast no doubts upon the sincerity of his passion for excellence and for the truth.

The genuine strength of this passion sometimes spilled over into the marginalia which Housman wrote in the books of his classical library. Of the fifty or sixty volumes now held by St John's College, Oxford, there are eight or nine in which he becomes justly indignant with the editor. Professor Vollmer of Leipzig is called on various occasions an idiot, an ignorant ass, and a blunderer;[29] Louis Havet, a thief and an egotist;[30] Ehwald, an ass;[31] Enk, an ignoramus.[32] 'He begins with a joke', writes

Professor Lindsay in his edition of the *Captivi* of Plautus. 'He did, till you emended it away!' replies Housman. 'Leo thinks that the name of some fish is required', Lindsay writes later. 'And yet the mention of ham at the beginning of a list of fish is surely no more peculiar than the mention of cheese at the end of it'; 'What do you mean by *yet*?' writes the exasperated Housman, 'that you have not read what Leo says? or that you wish to misrepresent it?'[33] James Reid writes of a line of Cicero: 'Cicero preferred dimitteret to dimiserit here because it puts more forcibly the doubtfulness of the inference which he states to be so improbable'; 'It doesn't', replies Housman magisterially. 'The doubtfulness is in *veri simile non est*; nowhere else.'[34]

This magisterial tone frequently reappears in his published work, where it is backed by a formidable display of learning. Here, as a full-length example of one of Housman's critical comments, is his note on:[35]

ACTHP CEIPIOC in Euripides *I.A.* 6—7

Philologians who lie snug in bed while Prof. Harry is squirrel-hunting may continue to indulge their sloth without any fear that he is stealing a march upon them either in the science of astronomy or in the art of interpretation. His description of dawn is a description of what never happened even in Kentucky, and shows that his attention was chiefly fixed, as it naturally would be, on the squirrels. When Aldebaran is on the meridian, μεσσήρης, it cannot be the last star to disappear in the light of day. So long as Aldebaran is twinkling, Capella, a little to the north, will twinkle too, and so will the Dog-star; for although it is some way further east, and therefore more exposed to the extinguished power of the daylight, its greater brilliancy preserves it longer from extinction. But Mr. Harry's astronomy interests me less than his exegesis. Agamemnon enquires τίς ποτ᾽ ἄρ᾽ ἀστὴρ ὅδε πορθμεύει/ σείριος ἐγγὺς τῆς ἑπταπόρου/πλειάδος and Mr. Harry contends that 'the Pleiades are no longer visible'. Is it then the habit of squirrel-hunters to define the position of a visible object by its proximity to an object which is not visible? And, if so, do they catch many squirrels?

The ἀστὴρ σείριος was neither Aldebaran (as Matthiae, snug in bed, suggested) nor any other of the fixed stars. Had it been, Agamemnon would not have asked his question. To know the fixed stars was part of a general's business, because they told him the points of the compass, the hour of the night, and the season of the year; and the appearance of a familiar luminary in its usual place would not provoke the most distracted commander to enquire its name. The ἀστὴρ σείριος of Euripides is, as Theon says (Hiller, pp. 146–7)) a planet: ὁ τραγικὸς ἐπί τινος τῶν πλανητῶν· τί ποτ᾽ ἄρ᾽ ὁ ἀστὴρ ὅδε πορθμεύει σείριος. Agamemnon lifts his eyes to the Pleiads and sees in their neighbourhood a star which he is not accustomed to see there; and hence his question.

But although published comments like this were often written with a biting wit, they were also scrupulously fair. The reason why Housman wrote with such forcefulness about the failings of other scholars is that he was so concerned with excellence and with the pursuit of truth; moreover, since such goals are matters of universal interest, and not only the concern of textual criticism, he felt that it was perfectly proper for him, on occasion, to ascend from the particular to the general and to invest his words with prophetic fire. Scorning one undertaking, for example, he spoke of a slave outlook,

> which commands no outlook upon the past or the future, but believes that the fashion of the present, unlike all fashions heretofore, will endure perpetually, and that its own flimsy tabernacle of second-hand opinions is a habitation for everlasting.

Housman attacked error ferociously; but he was also keen to give credit where it was due. In particular, he did his best to see that the work of other scholars was correctly attributed. So in December 1933 he was annoyed when Professor Butler, who had succeeded him at University College London, attributed to Buecheler a conjecture which had been made by Bergk, writing shortly: 'I am tired of saying that Craugidos in IV 3 55 is not Buecheler's. I told Postgate whose it was, and he told the world; and I have at last dinned the truth into Hosius.'

And Housman did not carry his displeasure with other scholars into his private life to any marked degree. In conversation, he spoke of offenders with no more than 'tolerant contempt'; and we are further told by Mr Gow that, 'at personal encounters, even these mild signs of disapproval were withheld'. At meetings of the Philological Society, Housman would be perfectly courteous even to the author of what he considered to be a badly-thought-out paper; and on moving from London to Cambridge he became very friendly with W. E. Heitland, a scholar with whom he had argued fiercely in the learned journals. On one occasion in 1926, Housman even declined to comment on the work of his old admirer, O. L. Richmond (at that time a Professor at Edinburgh), since Housman had previously been the cause of the non-acceptance of a treatise by Richmond; he had no wish to do him a further disservice.

Nor was Housman, as some German scholars imagined at the turn of the century, 'a rabid Germanophobe'.[36] He had dramatically exposed the vices of German scholarship, but he was well aware of its virtues; and in 1919 he wrote to a Professor at Glasgow:

Your strictures on German scholarship have something of the intemperate zeal of the convert, like attacks on the church of Rome by runaway monks. I should say that for the last hundred years individual German scholars have been the superiors in genius as well as in learning of all scholars outside Germany except Madvig and Cobet.

Two years later, he was arguing that, in the sphere of the intellect, patriotism was

an unmitigated nuisance. I do not know which cuts the worse figure: a German scholar encouraging his countrymen to believe that 'Wir Deutsche' have nothing to learn from foreigners, or an Englishman demonstrating the unity of Homer by sneers at 'Teutonic Professors', who are supposed by his audience to have goggle eyes behind large spectacles, and ragged moustaches saturated in lager beer, and consequently to be incapable of forming literary judgments.

This lack of prejudice, together with a clear view about the scope of classical scholarship, is neatly captured in an amusing anecdote about Housman's comments at a meeting of the Classical Board in Cambridge in 1919 or 1920. The subject of the discussion was the proposal to introduce the degree of PhD. One of the supporters had argued that British Universities must introduce this degree to catch the American students who had once gone to get doctorates in Germany, but who could not now be expected to visit an 'enemy' country for this purpose. Housman remarked dryly:[37]

Before the war an American student coming to Europe would go to a German University where the Professor would tell him to count the number of times that Cicero uses the word 'et'. He will now come to Cambridge and go to Mr. Sheppard, who will tell him to write a thesis on 'Thersites as the Hero of the Iliad', or 'The Aeolus of Euripides in the light of the theories of Dr. Freud'. I think that he would be far better employed counting the number of times Cicero uses the word 'et'.

Housman believed that the main task of classical scholarship – 'that minute and accurate study of the classical tongues which affords Latin professors their only excuse for existing' – was to restore classical texts; yet this does not mean that he was not alive to the glories of classical literature, but that his job was a highly specialised one. 'Lucan would do you no good', he wrote to a Mr Leippert. 'He has rhetoric and epigram but no true poetry. My edition . . . is for advanced scholars and is scientific – not literary.' It was after his edition of Lucan in 1926 that a German reviewer admitted his brilliance, and that he came to be generally recognised abroad.[38] Four years later, Professor Ulrich von Wilamowitz-Möllendorff – who had personally recognised Housman's excellence for some time – was able to make this general comment about himself and his fellow-scholars: 'We in Germany are fully aware that Housman is the leading living Latinist.'[39]

Housman had also won a measure of popular fame as a classical scholar when, in 1924, he used his superior knowledge to search out the truth behind an unusual hoax. An Italian scholar, Dr di Martino-Fusco, made the astonishing claim that he had found some of the one hundred and seven 'lost' books of Livy. If this had been true, it would have been a major discovery, and would have led to the rewriting of part of Roman history. Dr di Martino-Fusco showed a German scholar, Dr Max Funke, four lines of what he had 'found'. Dr Funke, full of uncritical excitement, relayed the news to Leipzig, and very soon, articles about the Lost Books were appearing in newspapers and periodicals right across Europe. But no sooner had the four lines been printed in the *Illustrated London News*, than Housman, having read them, stated in a letter to *The Times* of 22 September that they could not be attributed to Livy. Within twenty-four hours, he was able to write a further authoritative letter in which he referred to:

> a page from a manuscript now at Quedlinburg, but written early in the ninth century in St. Martin's own Abbey at Tours. There may be seen the four lines transcribed by Dr. Funke: . . . the first item in a table of contents prefixed to the dialogue of Sulpicius. . . .

This letter settled the matter. Within a few days Dr di Martino had withdrawn his claim to have discovered anything, and made a statement to an Italian Commission explaining his 'mistake'. Those scholars who had been deceived now recognised that the whole affair was a hoax; and, to the popular mind, Housman's decisive intervention was dramatic and impressive.[40]

\* \* \*

Housman's greatest single work of scholarship was, without doubt, his edition of the *Astronomica* of Manilius. This was a long poem in five books, dating from the reigns of Augustus and Tiberius, mainly concerned with astrology, and setting out the belief of the poet in the philosophy of the Stoics. But Housman himself once described Manilius scathingly as 'a facile and frivolous poet, the brightest facet of whose genius was an eminent aptitude for doing sums in verse'.

Manilius is generally recognised as a second-rate poet; and many people have wondered why Housman did not spend his time on some more worthwhile author. Edmund Wilson had gone so far as to suggest that Housman 'deliberately and grimly chose Manilius when his real interest was in Propertius'.[41] Even Andrew Gow, Housman's colleague and admirer, regrets that Housman abandoned Propertius, 'a great and congenial poet on whom so much time had already been lavished'. But, in Housman's view, classical scholarship had nothing to do with the literary preferences of scholars; and as early as 1895 he proclaimed that he had done as much scholarly work on Propertius as he wished to do. G. P. Goold of University College London, one of Housman's successors in the Latin Chair, believes 'that Housman was uneasily aware that further work on Propertius would have involved him in numerous retractions of opinion already expressed. Moreover, in his quarrel with Postgate over the manuscripts he was almost certainly wrong.'[42]

A certain amount of work on the text of Manilius had already been done by Scaliger and Bentley; and the fact that those two great scholars had chosen to work on Manilius was an important reason for Housman to be attracted to it as well. Housman believed that Scaliger had done his best work on Manilius; and although he described some of Scaliger's conjectures as 'uncouth and sometimes monstrous', he also wrote that Scaliger's commentary was the only avenue to a study of the poem. As for Bentley, Housman considered that his Manilius was even greater than his Phalaris or his edition of Horace; and he described Scaliger (at Bentley's side) as no more than a marvellous boy, since Scaliger had done most for the easiest parts of the poem, and Bentley for the hardest.

But much work remained to be done; Scaliger had put forward some interpretations which had no bearing on the text; Bentley, impatient and too sure of himself, had corrupted sound verses which he would not wait to understand, altered what offended his taste, and on occasion 'plies his desperate hook upon corruptions which do not yield at once to gentler measures, and treats the MSS. much as if they were fellows of Trinity'. Housman believed that he could do the necessary work, and do it in the company of two of the greatest of his predecessors, thus greatly adding to his intellectual pleasure, and also making a real claim to be regarded as one of their number.

Housman certainly felt that he had the necessary qualifications for editing Manilius, as he stated in the preface to the last volume. Wounded by some criticism of the earlier volumes, he wrote:

It surprises me that so many people should feel themselves qualified to weigh conjectures in their balance and to pronounce them good or bad, probable or improbable. Judging an emendation requires in some measure the same qualities as emendation itself, and the requirement is formidable. To read attentively, think correctly, omit no relevant consideration, and repress self-will are not ordinary accomplishments;

yet an emendator needs much besides: just literary preception, congenial intimacy with the author, experience which must have been won by study, and mother wit which he must have brought from his mother's womb.

It may be asked whether I think that I myself possess this outfit, or even most of it; and if I answer yes, that will be a new example of my notorious arrogance. I had rather be arrogant than impudent. I should not have undertaken to edit Manilius unless I had believed that I was fit for the task; and in particular I think myself a better judge of emendation, both when to emend and how to emend, than most others.

Since these remarks have been widely criticised as an example of unnecessary boasting, it is only fair to give Housman's answer, in an extract from a personal letter which he wrote to one critic:

It was no excess of self-praise in me to say, with strict relevance to the matter in hand, that I thought I possess qualifications which I ought to possess and which my critics are always showing that they do not. The contrast does not elate me immoderately. Consider your remarks on 450 sq. . . . If the next Bentley or Scaliger came along and told me that *vincunt* is no improvement on *victum*, I should be discomposed and begin to examine myself; but when one of you gentlemen says it I only think of him what you think of me, that he ought to be more modest.

If he felt that he could rank with Bentley and Scaliger and really do a good job of restoring this obscure old text, he would be able to leave behind an outstanding example of scholarship, an inspiration to other scholars and a monument to his own intellect. The edition of Manilius would also be an enduring record of his affection for Moses Jackson, because the first volume was to be prefaced by a Latin poem in Jackson's honour: and in the poem Jackson was told that his name, though worthy to survive on his own reputation, would in fact, survive for as long as Housman's work on Manilius was still read – and no longer.

But although Housman had 'a craving to be famous', he was enough of a philosopher to have a deep-rooted 'contempt for my passion for distinction'.[43] In his biographical essay on Platt, he spoke of scholars whose studies were 'warped and narrowed by ambition', who, seeking to build themselves a monument, must spend much of their lives acquiring knowledge which for its own sake is not worth having; and in one melancholy poem he even considered the futility of attempting to create an enduring reputation for himself:

> Here, on the level sand,
> Between the sea and land,

What shall I build or write
Against the fall of night? . . .

Shall it be Troy or Rome
I fence against the foam
Or my own name, to stay
When I depart for aye?

Nothing: too near at hand,
Planing the figured sand,
Effacing clean and fast
Cities not built to last
And charms devised in vain
Pours the confounding main.                    (*MP* 45)

All the same, Housman did his best to fence his own name against the foam. His attitude towards this attempt remained ambivalent; and in one letter, using a different metaphor, he compared his work on Manilius to an Aladdin's Tower – something which was marvellous, and yet would one day disappear: 'I ought to turn to at Manilius V', he wrote, 'or the unfinished windows in Aladdin's tower unfinished will remain.' But his wish for lasting fame was stronger than his contempt for it; and indeed, towards the end of his labours, so strong was his determination to complete Manilius that he developed a correspondingly powerful fear that he would not live to do so. On his journey to France in the summer of 1929 he travelled for once by boat, explaining to Grant Richards: 'I am deserting the air on this occasion because my life, until my Manilius is quite finished, is too precious to be exposed to a 1/186,000 risk of destruction; even though they have already killed their proper quota for this year.'[44]

Housman recognised, of course, that Manilius was not a great poet; but he had always insisted that classical scholarship had nothing to do with literary criticism, so this did not deter him. (It was because he had a sane view of Manilius as a poet that he wrote to Robert Bridges: 'I adjure you not to waste your time on Manilius. . . . My interest in him is purely technical.')

Housman's admiration for Scaliger and Bentley, his desire for posthumous fame, both for himself and for Moses Jackson, and his view of classical scholarship, were all powerful reasons for the years of work which he spent on Manilius. But there were other aspects of the work which may have attracted him – aspects relating to his own interest in the stars. The *Astronomica* of Manilius is largely concerned with astrology, and sets out the Stoic beliefs of its author. The most important of these was that there is an Infinite, Eternal, and All-powerful Mind which is diffused throughout the Universe. But the Universe is divided into two parts: the Celestial, including the planets and the stars, which is forever unchanging; and the Terrestrial, which has often been destroyed by fire, and will be destroyed by fire again in the future.

Closely associated with their explanation of the Universe was the belief of the Stoics that what happens on Earth is the result of Fate – the decree of the Infinite Mind concerning the lower or terrestrial world; and by studying the stars man may read what destiny Fate has in store for him. But since man cannot alter his destiny, he must simply endure it as best he may, indifferent, so far as is possible, to pleasure and pain, to hope or fear. Thus Manilius writes in his *Astronomica*:[45]

> Vain Man forbear, of Cares, unload thy Mind,
> Forget thy Hopes, and give thy Fear to Wind;
> For *Fate* rules all, its stubborn law must sway
> The lower world, and *Man* confin'd obey.
> *As we are Born we Dye, our Lots are cast,*
> *And our first hour disposeth of our last.*
> Then as the influence of the Stars ordains,
> To Empires *Kings* are doom'd, and *Slaves* to Chains.

The idea of fatal destiny, as Manilius explains it, has clear echoes in Housman's own poetry, as in the lines:

> The troubles of our proud and angry dust
> Are from eternity, and shall not fail.
> Bear them we can, and if we can we must.
> Shoulder the sky, my lad, and drink your ale.      (*LP* 9)

And although Housman wrote very slightingly of Manilius that 'He writes on astronomy and astrology without knowing either', at least their common interest in these subjects, and in explanations of the Universe, made Housman's work a particularly satisfying and suitable intellectual challenge.

Astronomy had fascinated Housman since he was a small boy at Perry Hall, and had found and read 'a little book we had in the house'. At Fockbury he had walked alone in the evenings to watch the sun set and the stars come out, as he tried to come to terms with a Universe which had allowed his mother to die so prematurely. And while he was at Oxford, and a keen admirer of Thomas Hardy, he would have read the new Hardy novel of 1882, *Two on a Tower*, in which a human drama was set against the background of a stellar Universe so vast and indifferent as to become terrifying. Indeed, it may have been with something of this in his thoughts, with the idea that, as Hardy put it, 'It is better – far better – for men to forget the Universe than to bear it so clearly in mind', that Housman penned these lines on the fly-leaf of a copy of his Manilius 1 which he gave to fellow scholar Walter Headlam:[46]

> Here are the skies, the planets seven,
>    And all the starry train:
> Content you with the mimic heaven
>    And on the earth remain.

Housman would never have considered himself as more than an amateur in this field; but examples drawn from astronomy figure prominently both in his Introductory Lecture of 1892, when he quoted Plato's views on the usefulness or otherwise of the subject; and in the Cambridge Inaugural Lecture of 1911, when he quoted from Newton's *Principia* in terms which suggest some familiarity with that great work. For his work on the fifth book of Manilius, he was able to make good use of a celestial globe given to him by the Rothensteins; in his edition of Lucan he dealt with astronomical problems with great expertise;[47] and when he was unsure of anything, he knew where to make enquiries. For example, on one occasion he wrote to Her Majesty's Nautical Almanac College, asking for some results for 'November 28, B.C. 50'. His correspondent replied at first that it was 'difficult to extrapolate for twenty centuries from observations that extend over 150 years only',[48] but a few days later kindly sent him a chart with the longitudes for which he had asked, and some notes.

Housman was an amateur astronomer, but – in the words of the modern translator of Manilius – 'a consummate astrological scholar'.[49] A few years before Housman's death, one of his academic colleagues, Professor Broad, drew up a Natal Horoscope for him. Broad's comments – if one overlooks the mention of various planetary influences – constitute a sensitive and friendly character study. Generally speaking, they tell us nothing new; but one section throws light on Housman's own interest in astrology:[50]

You are very independent in your thoughts and feelings, especially about religion or philosophy; you hold what are commonly regarded as very 'advanced' and 'unorthodox' opinions on these subjects; and you combat against any system of opinions of which you disapprove. (Mars and Uranus in ninth house.) Yet you have a considerable interest in mysticism and occultism, and an intense curiosity and concern with death and after life. (Mercury ruler in eighth house.) You like exploring the unknown, and dwelling on subjects which are thought 'far-fetched' and 'superstitious'; and are interested in astrology and kindred subjects. (Uranus in eighth house.) As you grow older you are likely to become more receptive to influences of this kind and more interested in mysticism. (Moon ruler in fourth house.)

As an expert astrologer, Housman corresponded on equal or superior terms with professional academics like Frank E. Robbins of Michigan University, who in 1927 prepared a paper on the Michigan Astrological Papyrus, and sent a copy of his paper to Housman.

Housman's scholarly interest in astrology does not, of course, mean that he had any personal belief in the magical influences of the stars. But it is interesting to see how often in his poems he uses the language of astrology, as in the lines: 'To skies that knit their heart strings right' (*ASL* 1), or 'Star may plot in heaven with planet' (*LP* 29), or 'The stars have not dealt me the worst they could do' (*AP* 17), or again, '

> I to my perils
>   Of cheat and charmer
>   Came clad in armour
> By stars benign.               (*MP* 6)

The influence of the stars is also mentioned in Housman's 'Epithalamium' for Moses Jackson, when he writes:

> And the high heavens, that all control,
> Turn in silence round the pole.
> Catch the starry beams they shed
> Prospering the marriage bed . . .     (*LP* 24)

And Housman's belief that the Universe is flawed is powerfully linked with the idea of fatal destiny in the lines:

> Stars, I have seen them fall,
>   But when they drop and die
> No star is lost at all
>   From all the star-sown sky.
> The toil of all that be
>   Helps not the primal fault;
> It rains into the sea,
>   And still the sea is salt.     (*MP* 7)

The theme of fatal destiny is taken up strongly in two other poems with a clear astrological bias: the version of Sappho's love poem in which Housman writes:

> The rainy Pleiads wester,
>   Orion plunges prone,
> The stroke of midnight ceases,
>   And I lie down alone;     (*MP* 11)

and the poem misleadingly entitled 'Astronomy', written on the death of his brother Herbert Housman. One important element in the poem is a comment upon the folly of imagining that one's personal fate can be controlled. Herbert tried to better himself, but Fate was against him:

> For pay and medals, name and rank,
>   Things that he has not found,
> He hove the Cross to heaven and sank
>   The pole-star underground.

> And now he does not even see
>   Signs of the nadir roll
> At night over the ground where he
>   Is buried with the pole.                    (LP 17)

At any rate, Housman's expert knowledge of astrology, and his interest in astronomy, were two more powerful reasons for the years of work which he spent on Manilius.

\*     \*     \*

In conclusion, Housman's work as a classical scholar has had a lasting influence. Professor O. L. Richmond states: 'not one of his pupils but hails Housman as a supreme master', and Professor Shackleton Bailey once described his readings of Housman's Manilius as 'the most memorable intellectual experience of my life'.[51] It is true that Housman had few intellectual disciples during his life-time; indeed, Professor Sandbach believes that Housman had a bad influence upon Latin studies, because the remoteness and the ferocity of his criticism meant that people were afraid of him, and young classicists tended to become Hellenists, not Latinists.[52] But those who did follow Housman were very loyal to him. As Mr Gow wrote: 'nobody with tastes at all akin to his own could witness that easy command of the relevant learning, that lucid exposition and dispassionate judgment, without setting before himself a new ideal of scholarship'.

Housman could have been more honoured for his work during his life-time; but 'Contempt for my passion for distinction made me refuse every offered honour',[53] and he rejected honorary degrees from Glasgow in 1905, from St Andrews in 1922, from Oxford in 1928 and again in 1934; and from the University of Wales in 1934. In 1929 he had even received a letter from Arthur Stamfordham, Private Secretary to King George V, stating: 'It is His Majesty's wish to confer upon you the Order of Merit in recognition of your valuable work as a Classical Scholar and in the ranks of literature.'[54] This also he refused, writing:

Dear Lord Stamfordham,
    With all gratitude for His Majesty's most kind and flattering wish to confer upon me the Order of Merit I humbly beg permission to

decline this high honour. I hope to escape the reproach of thankless-
ness or churlish behaviour by borrowing the words in which an equally
loyal subject, Admiral Cornwallis, declined a similar mark of the
Royal favour: 'I am, unhappily, of a turn of mind that would make my
receiving that honour the most unpleasant thing imaginable. . . .'

Housman's Manilius is a great work of scholarship; his articles, taken as
a whole, contributed very much more to classical studies;[55] but it is
undoubtedly as a scholar who demanded the highest standards of himself and others that Housman achieved most. As Professor Skutsch has
written:[56]

the Arts, if they are to maintain the standards of accuracy and honesty
which alone make such studies worth while, need, from time to time, a
violent corrective to certain frailties of the human mind: the tendency
to take things easy, to trust accepted opinion, and generally to hope
for the best. These were the faults which Housman chastised.

Finally, here is the opinion of G. P. Goold:[57]

The legacy of Housman's scholarship is a thing of permanent value;
and that value consists less in its obvious results, the establishment of
general propositions about Latin and the removal of scribal mistakes,
than in the shining example he provides of a wonderful intellect at
work. If, as the Latin texts become more and more purified of trans-
mitted error, there is less and less room for the kind of skill which he
so brilliantly practised, that does not alter the fact that in studying his
academic papers we and our posterity will enjoy for ever the company
and the inspiration of a superior mind. He was and may remain the
last great textual critic, for we may expect ideas more than the language
in which they are couched to engage henceforth the attention of
classical scholars. And if we accord Bentley the honour of being
England's greatest Latinist, it will be largely because Housman
declined to claim that title for himself.

CHAPTER 11

# A *Literary Life* (2)

Have you prevailed upon Housman to compose any more?
Capriccios of a Cantab would be a nice title.
Arthur Platt to Henry Jackson, 22 April 1911[1]

## *The background to* Last Poems: *1896–1902, and 1902–18*

After the publication of *A Shropshire Lad* in 1896, the routine of
Housman's life as Professor of Latin at University College London did not
alter. He had continued with his heavy load of teaching, and had even
found time and energy to begin work on his edition of Manilius. Despite
these commitments, the next six years, until the end of the Boer War in
1902, allowed him a little time for poetry and he wrote on average six or
seven poems a year. Among these were the important cycle of war poems
which includes 'Grenadier', 'The Oracles', 'Illic Iacet', and 'The
Olive'. Of the other poems which he wrote during this period, some
contained a spirit of resolution in the face of the sorrow of existence.
'Beyond the moor and mountain crest' is a call to avoid melancholy and to
make something of one's life:

> Comrade, look not on the west:
> 'Twill heave the heart out of your breast;
> 'Twill take your thoughts and sink them far,
> Leagues beyond the sunset bar. . . .
>
> Wide is the world, to rest or roam,
> And early 'tis for turning home:
> Plant your heels on earth and stand,
> And let's forget our native land.                    (*LP* 1)

– that land, of course, being the world of the dead. In contrast there is the
cheerful beginning of 'Spring Morning':

> Star and coronal and bell
> April underfoot renews,

219

> And the hope of man as well
>> Flowers among the morning dews.          (*LP* 16)

But some poems were very bitter – 'Some can gaze and not be sick' (*AP* 16), 'Now dreary dawns the eastern light' (*LP* 28), 'The stars have not dealt me the worst they could do' (*AP* 17); and this terrible cry from the heart:

> When the bells justle in the tower
>> The hollow night amid,
> Then on my tongue the taste is sour
>> Of all I ever did.          (*AP* 9)

Moreover, Alfred was still haunted by his love for Moses Jackson. He wrote a fair copy of 'The rainy Pleiads wester', and also these sad lines:

> He would not stay for me; and who can wonder?
>> He would not stay for me to stand and gaze.
> I shook his hand and tore my heart in sunder
>> And went with half my life about my ways.          (*AP* 7)

The element of self-loathing in the words 'And who can wonder –' suggests that, despite Housman's rejection of the established moral order in some respects, he still had feelings of guilt.[2] In one poem, 'The Culprit', he tried to wipe this out by suggesting that those whom the world accused were not personally responsible for what the world took to be their flawed nature:

> My mother and my father
>> Out of the light they lie;
> The warrant would not find them,
>> And here 'tis only I
>> Shall hang so high.

> Oh let not man remember
>> The soul that God forgot, . . .          (*LP* 14)

*          *          *

The next sixteen years, from the end of the Boer War in 1902 to the end of the Great War in 1918, were a less productive period. Certainly, Housman wrote a few excellent poems, including 'Epitaph on an Army of Mercenaries', and a draft of 'When summer's end is nighing', in which he recalled walking from Fockbury House up to 'Mount Pisgah'.

Housman also produced the beautiful 'The Land of Biscay', of great imaginative power, which carries the message that there is no escape from grief:

> And the mariner of Ocean,
>    He was calling as he came:
> From the highway of the sunset
>    He was shouting on the sea,
> 'Landsman of the land of Biscay,
>    Have you help for grief and me?'
>
> When I heard I did not answer,
>    I stood mute and shook my head:
> Son of earth and son of Ocean,
>    Much we thought and nothing said.
> Grief and I abode the nightfall,
>    To the sunset grief and he
> Turned them from the land of Biscay
>    On the waters of the sea.                    (MP 46)

But Housman was now writing on average no more than one or two poems a year – perhaps partly because he was at this stage of his life a happier and less repressed man. Not only was his position in the world of classical scholarship now quite established, with the publication of his Juvenal and the first books of his Manilius, but, more important, his liberating annual visits to the Continent had begun, visits which led to a more healthy and vigorous attitude towards his emotional life. He is not ashamed to write a homosexual fantasy, 'I did not lose my heart in summer's even' (MP 37); in 'Ho, everyone that thirsteth' (MP 22), he praises stolen waters; in 'Crossing alone, the nighted ferry', he tells the one whom he loves that he will not always have 'a true, sick-hearted slave' (MP 23); and those who have in the past rejected his love are asked not to haunt him any longer:

> When the eye of day is shut,
>    And the stars deny their beams,
> And about the forest hut
>    Blows the roaring wood of dreams,
>
> From deep clay, from desert rock,
>    From the sunk sands of the main,
> Come not at my door to knock,
>    Hearts that loved me not again . . .          (LP 33)

When in 1911 the seal was set on Housman's status and security by his appointment as Kennedy Professor of Latin at Cambridge, he wrote to Edmund Gosse: 'If the exhalations of the Granta give me a relaxed sore throat, more poems may be expected.' But Alfred's inspiration had temporarily dried up. In October 1912 he wrote to Edward Marsh of *Georgian Poetry*, 'none even of my few unpublished poems have been written within the last two years'. And during the next five years, there were only a few fragments and a rough draft of 'When summer's end is nighing' (*LP* 39) to be written into his notebooks.

The Great War, with his family's involvement in the fighting, and his own exile from the Continent, brought 'Epitaph on an Army of Mercenaries', and a romantic poem about Moses Jackson, which began:

> Oh were he and I together,
>> Shipmates on the fleeted main,
> Sailing through the summer weather
>> To the spoil of France or Spain . . .                    (*AP* 2)

But Housman had already expressed in poetry what he felt about fighting; and, as he later wrote to M. Pollet: 'The Great War cannot have made much change in the opinions of any man of imagination.' At the time, in November 1917, he wrote to Wilbur Cross, the editor of the *Yale Review*: 'I neither have any poem which I wish to publish nor am likely to write one at any early date'; and he protested to Percy Withers, whom he had recently met: 'People don't want any more of my poetry. It is only a few like you who care anything about it: the rest neither anticipate nor desire more.'

At the back of his mind Housman clearly had the idea that some of his controversial poems might be published posthumously, but he seemed to hope for little else. As early as 1912 he had written to the editor of *Georgian Poetry*: 'I do not really belong to your "new era" '; and although sales of *A Shropshire Lad* continued to be good, and indeed improved during the war, he must have felt that his clear, direct style of writing was falling out of fashion. So the friendly reproach which he received from Percy Withers (who asked him 'What . . . could justify the disuse of a gift the rarest in any generation'), was an important encouragement. Indeed, a strange relationship developed between the two men, in which Withers would badger Housman for new poems, and Housman, with a show of grudging indifference, would from time to time report that new ones had been written. At the party which marked the end of the Withers's stay in Cambridge, Alfred came up to speak to him in words 'tinged with mockery and ironic sportiveness. "You will rejoice to hear," he said, "that I have recently completed two more poems", laughed a mirthless laugh, and walked away.' One of these poems was probably this description of a man about to be hanged, in which, as in 'The Culprit', Housman suggests that the guilty man is not personally responsible for being a criminal:[3]

> He stood, and heard the steeple
>> Sprinkle the quarters on the morning town.
> One, two, three, four, to market-place and people
>> It tossed them down.

Strapped, noosed, nighing his hour,
    He stood and counted them and cursed his luck;
And then the clock collected in the tower
    Its strength, and struck.

One, it had so much power, –
    If it had more, or if the clock struck two,
Or eight, or twelve, or any other hour –
    He never knew.                                         (*LP* 15)


## Last Poems

In January 1920, rather more than a year after the farewell party,
Housman wrote to Withers, and reported that: 'Last year I think I wrote
two poems, which is more than the average, but not much towards a new
volume.' One of these poems has been lost;[4] the other was an eight line
version of 'We'll to the woods no more', a nostalgic piece based upon a
medieval French ronde:

> We'll to the woods no more,
> The laurels all are cut,
> The bowers are bare of bay
> That once the Muses wore;
> The year draws in the day
> And soon will evening shut:
> The laurels all are cut,
> We'll to the woods no more.   (*LP* Introductory poem)

As Housman said, this was not much towards a new volume, but the
idea of compiling such a volume attracted him more and more. Later on in
1920, he bought a new notebook; and after leaving the first two pages
blank so that he could later add a proper Introduction, or perhaps an
Index of First Lines as in one of his earlier notebooks, he began to work.[5]
At the same time, he wrote to Grant Richards, on 5 September: 'Suppose I
produced a new volume of poetry, in what part of the year ought it to be
published, and how long would it take after the MS left my hands?' But
the Muse would not be forced. The three poems which he wrote now, 'I to
my perils of cheat and charmer' (*MP* 6), a rough draft of 'Stone, steel,
dominions pass' (*MP* 24) and 'My dreams are of a field afar' (*MP* 32), are
all inferior work, the first unconvincing, the second interesting only from
a biographical point of view in its suggestion of guilt in the lines: 'Here
shall your sweetheart lie,/Untrue for ever'; and the third is very slight.
When Grant Richards, his appetite for future profits whetted, wrote to

ask how the new volume was progressing, Housman had to answer, in January 1921:

'My new book' does not exist, and possibly never may. Neither your traveller nor anybody else must be told that it is even contemplated. What I asked you was a question inspired by an unusually bright and sanguine mood, which has not at present been justified.

So matters rested for over a year; but then, on 30 March 1922, four days after his sixty-third birthday, Housman wrote and dated a rough draft and fair copy of 'Wake not for the world-heard thunder'. He had written a few fragments of this some years earlier,[6] but now he had transformed them into a poem whose message was not unlike that of the 'Parta Quies' which he had written for his mother – but this time, he was writing for Moses Jackson. It was during 1922 that Moses began to suffer badly from cancer of the stomach; and news of this illness so shook Alfred that before long a new flood of poetry welled up. For a long time he had been unable to write more than one or two poems a year, now, filled with the desire to present Moses Jackson with a final tribute, Housman found that the right words came easily once more.

During the next ten days, from 30 March to 9 April, Housman filled fifty-seven pages of his fourth notebook with poems.[7] Many of these were slightly improved versions or fair copies of poems which had appeared in the earlier notebooks, such as 'Star and coronal and bell' (*LP* 16), and some of the poems which he had written about his homo-sexual feelings: 'The laws of God, the laws of Man' (*LP* 12), 'The rainy Pleiads wester' (*MP* 11), and 'Shake hands, we shall never be friends, all's over' (*MP* 30). There were also two more rough drafts and a fair copy of the 'Epithalamium' for Moses Jackson (*LP* 24); and a third draft of 'The chestnut casts his flambeaux, and the flowers', in which Housman, in a poem full of memorable phrases, comments:

> It is in truth iniquity on high
> > To cheat our sentenced souls of aught they crave,
> And mar the merriment as you and I
> > Fare on our long fool's-errand to the grave.

and concludes that man must bear his troubles as courageously as he can, and glean what pleasure he may from life:

> The troubles of our proud and angry dust
> > Are from eternity, and shall not fail.
> Bear them we can, and if we can we must.
> > Shoulder the sky, my lad, and drink your ale. (*LP* 9)

In addition, Housman wrote several new or almost wholly new poems including 'Soldier from the wars returning', a poem with a characteristic sting in the tail, which concludes:

> Now no more of winters biting,
>     Filth in trench from fall to spring,
> Summers full of sweat and fighting
>     For the Kesar or the King.
>
> Rest you, charger, rust you, bridle;
>     Kings and kesars, keep your pay;
> Soldier, sit you down and idle
>     At the inn of night for aye.                    (*LP* 8)

and this justly admired poem, with its powerful and direct images, the music of its words echoing drum and fife:

> In valleys green and still
>     Where lovers wander maying
> They hear from over hill
>     A music playing.
>
> Behind the drum and fife,
>     Past hawthornwood and hollow,
> Through earth and out of life
>     The soldiers follow.
>
> The soldier's is the trade:
>     In any wind or weather
> He steals the heart of maid
>     And man together.
>
> The lover and his lass
>     Beneath the hawthorn lying
> Have heard the soldiers pass,
>     And both are sighing.
>
> And down the distance they
>     With dying note and swelling
> Walk the resounding way
>     To the still dwelling.                    (*LP* 7)

Finally, on 9 April, Housman completed 'Hell Gate', a long narrative piece very unlike his other work. He had written a few lines of it in 1905;[8] and it owed much in metre and theme to a poem by Simcox which he had read as a child. As Simcox tells the story, Christ rescues a girl from the gates of Hell;[9] as Housman wrote it, a man is on his way to Hell and, as the gate comes into sight, he remembers his past life:

> Many things I thought of then,
> Battles, and the loves of men,
> Cities entered, oceans crossed,
> Knowledge gained and virtue lost, . . .

One of the damned is pacing up and down by the gate, on sentry-duty; and the two men recognise each other as old friends. So the sentry, much to the alarm of Sin and Death, fires his musket at the Devil:

> And the hollowness of hell
> Sounded as its master fell,
> And the mourning echo rolled
> Ruin through his kingdom old.
> Tyranny and terror flown
> Left a pair of friends alone,
> And beneath the nether sky
> All that stirred was he and I. . . .
>
> Midmost of the homeward track
> Once we listened and looked back;
> But the city, dusk and mute,
> Slept, and there was no pursuit.                    (LP 31)

On the same day that he completed this moving fantasy about the birth of a world in which homosexuality is not punished by 'hell' or 'pursuit', Alfred looked back over the work which he had done since the end of March, and wrote confidently to Grant Richards:

> It is now practically certain that I shall have a volume of poems ready for the autumn; so I wish you would take what steps are necessary as soon as they are necessary. But do not mention it to anyone until you are obliged to mention it.

During the next seven weeks, Housman worked on another fifteen or sixteen poems, including his verses about Andrea, 'Far known to sea and shore' (MP 44); and this haunting and melancholy poem, deservedly many people's favourite, in which he recalls the solace which he has found in nature, and sadly takes his leave of her, enjoining others who have suffered to share in that solace, for nature is indifferent, and deals out her favours with an impartial hand:

> Tell me not here, it needs not saying,
>   What tune the enchantress plays
> In aftermaths of soft September
>   Or under blanching mays,
> For she and I were long acquainted
>   And I knew all her ways.

On russet floors, by waters idle,
   The pine lets fall its cone;
The cuckoo shouts all day at nothing
   In leafy dells alone;
And traveller's joy beguiles in autumn
   Hearts that have lost their own.

On acres of the seeded grasses
   The changing burnish heaves;
Or marshalled under moons of harvest
   Stand still all night the sheaves;
Or beeches strip in storms for winter
   And stain the wind with leaves.

Possess, as I possessed a season,
   The countries I resign,
Where over elmy plains the highway
   Would mount the hills and shine,
And full of shade the pillared forest
   Would murmur and be mine.

For nature, heartless, witless nature,
   Will neither care nor know
What stranger's feet may find the meadow
   And trespass there and go,
Nor ask amid the dews of morning
   If they are mine or no.        (*LP* 40)

By the middle of June, Housman was busy writing out all the poems which he thought might be included in his new volume. When on 16 June he sent a fifty-page manuscript to Grant Richards, he had already decided against including several of the more controversial pieces, such as 'The rainy Pleiads wester' (*MP* 11), 'If, in that Syrian garden, ages slain' (*MP* 1), and 'Far known to sea and shore' (*MP* 44), all of which he had brought up to good fair copies in the fourth notebook. Another poem rejected at this stage, but with less reason, was 'Tarry delight, so seldom met'. Perhaps the first verse is rather weak, but the last two provide a poignant image of the brevity of joy. Housman's inspired use of the word 'complain' not only echoes the sound of the waves, but foreshadows Leander's death by suggesting that the natural elements will conspire to destroy happiness whenever they find it:

     Tarry, delight, so seldom met,
       So sure to perish, tarry still;
     Forbear to cease or languish yet,
       Though soon you must and will.

By Sestos town, in Hero's tower,
  On Hero's heart Leander lies;
The signal torch has burned its hour
  And sputters as it dies.

Beneath him, in the nighted firth,
  Between two continents complain
The seas he swam from earth to earth
  And he must swim again.          (*MP* 15)

Grant Richards received the package containing the manuscript with great excitement, hurried home early from his office, and then cut the string, turned the pages, 'and read poem after poem aloud to my wife and children'. The only thing which he found displeasing was the title: 'Last Poems'; but Housman teasingly assured him that there was nothing in this to rule out a volume of posthumous poems, and with that the businessman in Grant Richards had to be content.

At this stage, Housman was still not finally certain which of the poems he had sent to Grant Richards would be included, and which omitted. When a set of proofs had been prepared, he asked one or two people to look over them, starting with J. W. Mackail, the classical scholar with whom he had been friendly since University College London days, and who had been Professor of Poetry at Oxford from 1906–11. When Mackail agreed to help, Housman wrote to him:

> I want you to note anything which strikes you as falling below my average, or as open to exception for any other reason. The piece I myself am most in doubt about is the longest ['Hell Gate']; and I fear that is not its worst fault. You need not be afraid of stifling a master-piece through a temporary aberration of judgment, as I am consulting one or two other people, and shall give no effect to a single opinion unless it coincides with my own private suspicions.

A copy of the proofs was also sent to W. P. Ker, who had just retired from University College London, and whose absence on an Alpine walking holiday delayed things for a few weeks; in the meantime, Alfred consulted his brother Laurence, who persuaded him to keep in the poem 'He stood and heard the steeple', but to remove the superfluous third verse.[10] Laurence also wisely advised him to keep the lines which Alfred had added to the Introductory Poem, lines about which he had been having second thoughts:[11]

Oh we'll no more, no more
To the leafy woods away,
To the high wild woods of laurel
And the bowers of bay no more.

When on 24 August Housman returned the corrected proofs to Richards, four of the poems which had been groomed for inclusion in *Last Poems* had been removed altogether. Two of them 'On forelands high in heaven' (*MP* 33) and 'Good creatures, do you love your lives' (*MP* 26), were much below Housman's average, and no doubt his advisers had told him so; 'Delight it is, in youth and May' (*MP* 18) went because it carried a message which was conveyed more effectively in 'The sloe was lost in flower' (*LP* 22); and 'Hearken landsmen, hearken seamen' (*MP* 46), though a fine poem, conflicted to a certain extent with the imagery of 'Beyond the moor and mountain crest' (*LP* 1).

There was only one major change – and a rather surprising one. 'Smooth between sea and land' was cut out by Housman after it had actually been printed. This was the philosophical poem in which he had asked:

> Here, on the level sand,
> Between the sea and land,
> What shall I build or write
> Against the fall of night?
>
> Tell me of runes to grave
> That hold the bursting wave,
> Or bastions to design
> For longer date than mine.          (*MP* 45)

Perhaps he felt that it was too obviously personal, and left it out for that reason.

Then, on 21 September, Grant Richards broke the news of Housman's forthcoming volume by an announcement in the *Times Literary Supplement*; and the poems were actually published on 19 October. They had already been prematurely but favourably reviewed by *The Times*, and soon praise and congratulations were flooding in, together with the thanks of the thirty-three people to whom Housman had sent a presentation copy. These included James Frazer who wrote: 'I have read them all with admiration, tinged with melancholy';[12] William Rothenstein who commented: 'A few men do actually preserve a generation from damnation by futurity';[13] Alfred Pollard, who, after professing a 'quite sincere indifference to graves', added '[I] can't think of anyone else who says as much in eight lines as you do'; Herbert Warren of Magdalen, who told Housman that he now thought of him together with two of his best loves in poetry, Milton and Gray;[14] and the poet Margaret Woods who praised 'your beautiful book, which everyone is *running* to get'.[15]

Housman had suggested that ten thousand copies should be printed, but after discouraging comments from the booksellers, Grant Richards had printed only 4,000. However, the book was an enormous success, and by the end of 1922 an extra 17,000 copies had been printed. No paper of importance had failed to review it; and there had even been a friendly cartoon in *Punch*, showing the Muse welcoming back Housman with the words: 'Oh Alfred, we have missed you! My Lad! My Shropshire Lad!' (25 October 1922). Housman took all the fuss very calmly, writing to Percy Withers:

> Your generous enthusiasm is very nice, but I have not myself felt more than a faint pleasure in the success of the book, which is not really a matter of much importance. I was pleased by letters I had from Masefield and others.

But the success of the book had helped him to bring the effort connected with writing and publishing *Last Poems* to a satisfactory conclusion, when in late October he sat down at his desk to write a letter to accompany his gift of the book to Moses Jackson. The letter, in John Carter's words, was 'largely devoted to a recital (half jocular, half defiant) of evidence, such as sales figures and leaders in *The Times*, that its writer was a bloody good poet and an eminent bloke'.[16] The volume itself was inscribed from 'a fellow who thinks more of you than anything in the world . . . you are largely responsible for my writing poetry and you ought to take the consequences'.[17] And, as John Carter tells us, the letter concludes

> with a sudden arresting glimpse of the most poignant desiderium: the eminent poet would willingly have exchanged his fame and position for the chance of following his correspondent, in the humblest capacity, to the farthest corners of the earth.

The volume reached Moses Jackson in time for him to read it; but he was already immured in a Vancouver hospital, and within three months he was dead.


## A literary connoisseur

When still a young man, Housman had written of himself: 'I am not a critic: only at the utmost a connoisseur.'[18] But he read a great deal, and his appetite for poems and novels remained voracious throughout his life. His views, backed by such wide reading, are always worth hearing, even when unexceptionable.

We know that he revered Homer and Dante; that he relished some of Chaucer's *Canterbury Tales*, such as the 'Tale of Chauntècleer and Pertelote';[19] that he had a high regard for some of Shakespeare's work, but would say 'that it gave him no pleasure to read a play of Shake-speare's from beginning to end, for though some parts were magnificent, there were others so slovenly that the effect of the whole was disagree-able'.[20]

He honoured Milton, but had little regard for Milton's immediate successors, writing scornfully of Dryden and 'that huge dross-heap, the Caroline Parnassus'. Housman also complained that, although Pope's *Rape of the Lock* was excellent literature, it was not excellent poetry – and the eighteenth century, at least until the *Lyrical Ballads* of 1798, was, so far as he was concerned, a literary dungeon in which the true meaning of poetry had been forgotten.[21]

Among poets of the late eighteenth and early nineteenth century, Housman admired some of Coleridge,[22] and what he considered to be the best of Wordsworth, especially 'The Prelude' and 'The Leech-Gatherer'; describing Wordsworth's poems, he wrote appreciatively of 'that thrilling utterance which pierces the heart and brings tears to the eyes of thousands who care nothing for his opinions and beliefs'. He also had 'the greatest admiration' for Keats, thought Blake 'the most poetical of all poets', and believed that Shelley 'maintained a higher standard of excel-lence than all other English poets'.

Among poets of the nineteenth century, Matthew Arnold remained a life-long enthusiasm, though Housman was prepared to admit that, like Byron, Tennyson, Swinburne, and Browning, he suffered from great lapses. He admired Swinburne's early work, though he preferred Chris-tina Rossetti's poems on the whole;[23] and he wrote 'I have a great admiration for some of the poetry which Browning wrote between 1835 and 1869, especially in the period of *Bells and Pomegranates*.'

As for those who were writing mainly during his own life-time; Housman praised Ralph Hodgson's 'Song of Honour', and described Sir William Watson's poem, 'Wordsworth's Grave' as 'one of the glories of English literature', writing that if he had not swallowed the praises of the *Spectator* when still a comparatively young man, he might have gone on to be 'one of the first poets of the age'. He enjoyed Walter de la Mare and John Masefield, and praised the first four books of Robert Bridges's *Shorter Poems*, but did not care for his later 'new-fangled stuff'.

Housman's own writing had been unaffected by changing fashions of the twentieth century, yet he was fully in touch with the contemporary literary scene. Generally speaking, he disliked free verse, and in parti-cular he accused Gerard Manley Hopkins of doing violence to the English language, writing to Robert Bridges of sprung rhythm that it:

is just as easy to write as other forms of verse; and many a humble scribbler of words for music-hall songs has written it well. But he does not: he does not make it audible; he puts light syllables in the stress and heavy syllables in the slack, and has to be helped out with typographical signs explaining that things are to be understood as being what in fact they are not . . . his early poems are the promise of something better, if less original. . . . His manner strikes me as deliberately adopted to compensate by strangeness for lack of pure merit.

But he could write to Gilbert Murray in 1922: 'The new-fangled verse you speak of hardly comes to my ears . . . ; but I have been admiring Blunden for some time. He describes too much; but when one can describe so well, the temptation must be great.'[24] Housman also spoke of Eliot's work with respect,[25] and read Yeats with pleasure. In his copy of Yeats's *Later Poems* of 1922, Housman singled out: 'His Phoenix', which concludes 'I mourn for that most lonely thing; and yet God's will be done,/I knew a phoenix in my youth, so let them have their day'; 'The Second Coming', in which he marked those famous lines 'The best lack all conviction, while the worst/Are full of passionate intensity'; and the haunting 'Solomon and the Witch'.[26]

Interestingly enough, another book in Housman's possession was *Songs from Books* by Rudyard Kipling;[27] and he made a number of annotations in it. Some of these were simply to point out rhymes which displeased him, such as 'salaam' and 'alarm', or 'waters', and 'quarters'; and he wrote a characteristic 'ugh' alongside 'Out of the wind's untainted kiss, the waters' clean caress'. But on one page, in a strange literary collaboration, Alfred's alterations effectively turn one of Kipling's poems, 'Heriot's Ford', into one of his own. He did this by crossing out the title, crossing out all the last six verses, and altering two words in each of the first two verses:

> 'What's that that hirples at my side?'
> *The foe that you might fight, my lord.*
> 'That rides as fast as I can ride?'
> *The shadow of ~~your might~~, my lord.*          the night
>
> 'Then wheel my horse against the foe!'
> *He's down and overpast, my lord.*
> *You war against the sunset glow,*
> *The ~~judgment follows~~ fast, my lord.*          darkness gathers

Housman's taste in fiction was equally catholic. He enjoyed some of Hardy's novels, though he preferred Jane Austen.[28] He often referred warmly to the novels of Arnold Bennett, and was particularly fond of his *The Old Wives' Tale*. He also read Proust and Colette and, in addition to the pornographic literature which he relished, enjoyed detective novels, ghost stories, and humorous works, including books by P. G. Wode-house, and Daisy Ashford's famous *The Young Visiters*. As for his dislikes: he once wrote of George Meredith: 'Meredith has never been treated justly. He once wrote admirable books which were not admired. He now writes ridiculous books which are not ridiculed';[29] and Housman had a great contempt for John Galsworthy's novels, writing to Bridges on one occasion: 'If ever there was a man without a spark of genius, that man is he.'

American literature had always fascinated Alfred. As a child, he intro-duced his brothers and sisters to *Little Women* and *Good Wives*;[30] and – perhaps under the influence of his puritanical stepmother – chose as one of his 'twelve best works of fiction', Hawthorne's moralistic tale, *The Marble Faun*.[31] Then, at Oxford, Housman read Henry James, even if, like many people, he read 'with some affliction at his prolixity'.[32] In later life, Housman developed something of a prejudice against Americans in general – probably because he felt that they were too keen on knowing about other people's private lives, and he regarded this as a threat to himself. But he continued to read individual American authors. In particular, he greatly enjoyed the 'Jamesian' and yet peculiarly feminine writing of Edith Wharton, whose novels such as *Ethan Frome* and *The House of Mirth* were very popular in the 1920s. Housman also admired Sinclair Lewis, whose work perhaps reinforced his prejudices by satiris-ing the greed and intolerance of American small-town life; and Theodore Dreiser, a realistic and therefore controversial novelist with a fatalistic view of life which appealed to him. Mark Twain was another favourite: whenever he felt unduly depressed Housman would turn to *The Ascent of the Regi-Kulm*;[33] and, from Mark Twain's *Huckleberry Finn*, Housman claimed to know by heart the 'ode to Stephen Dowling Botts', written by 'Emmerline Grangerford' who, in Huck's words, could 'write about any-thing you choose to give her to write about, just so it was sadful'. In addition, Housman enjoyed the humorous works of O. Henry; and claimed to have popularised in England Anita Loos's delightful comedy, *Gentlemen Prefer Blondes*. The publishers evidently thought that there was something in this claim, for, through Grant Richards, they sent him a copy of the sequel, *But Gentlemen Marry Brunettes*.[34]

## A literary life

Housman's friendship with Grant Richards and his Hungarian wife was now of long standing. In 1921 he had even spent Christmas with them in the country; though their festivities were slightly marred when some carol singers stole the champagne which was cooling in the snow in the garden. In June 1922, when Alfred was feeling very run-down after weeks of work on *Last Poems*, he spent a few days with the Richardses to recover. When the book was to be published, and there was talk of a dinner to celebrate its appearance, he wrote to Grant: 'I would rather there were no one but you and Mrs. Richards'; and the three of them dined together at the Carlton on a saddle of hare, one of Housman's favourite dishes.[35]

Much of the correspondence between Housman and Richards continued, naturally enough, to be on publishing matters. Housman went on protesting over misprints, writing of the 1918 and 1921 editions of *A Shropshire Lad*: 'In both I find the same sets of blunders in punctuation and ordering of lines, some of which I have corrected again and again, and the filthy beasts of printers for ever introduce them anew.' He still despised bibliophiles, with their love of fine printing and limited editions. Through the mediation of Percy Withers, he did allow the Alcuin Press to print fine editions of both his books of poetry: but all he asked of books was that they should be clear, and as cheap as possible; and he mildly offended Withers by giving his daughter the two shillings pocket edition of *A Shropshire Lad* as a wedding present. He did not object to his poems being translated, and was rather amused by the fact that Welsh translations of them were said to be better than the original; but where he understood the language, he kept a firm eye on things, and rightly refused to allow one French translation in which 'A love to keep you clean' had been translated as 'Amour, qui garde propre ta maison'!

Housman always kept his special affection for *A Shropshire Lad*. He refused to allow it to be bound together with *Last Poems*; and, although he made an exception for his friend Robert Bridges, he continued his refusal to let poems from *A Shropshire Lad* be printed in anthologies, an attitude which he partly explained in a letter to John Drinkwater, when he wrote: 'I am not anxious to draw down upon myself the fate which Horace dreaded, and suffer recitation in schools.' Nor would he allow his poems to be read on the wireless, though he continued to give permission for them to be set to music; once, when Richards asked him about permission for a gramophone record, he replied; 'Do what you like . . . provided that I am not required to sign an agreement. These musical people are more plague than profit.'

Housman's chief aim had always been that as many people as possible should read his work, and to that end he had heavily subsidised the printing of his classical works, and foregone royalties on *A Shropshire Lad*. But he decided that there was no reason why he should not make some profit on *Last Poems*, and in July 1922 he had written to Grant Richards asking him how they should proceed: 'Does your solicitor draw it up and send it to my solicitor', he enquired; 'or do you draw it up and I submit it to some Society for the Protection of Authors against Publishers?' At the beginning of November he also signed an American agreement for *Last Poems*, between himself and Henry Holt & Co., New York.

But these arrangements benefited Housman less than he might have hoped. It was not that the sales of *Last Poems* were poor, but that Grant Richards was still something of a rogue.[36] Despite having once been declared bankrupt, he had not learned any caution in financial affairs. He was by no means an evil man, just sanguine and self-indulgent, rather like Alfred's father, Edward Housman – which may have been why Alfred was able to remain on good terms with him after what happened.

At any rate, by the autumn of 1925 Richards had received some £700 of royalties from America for *Last Poems*, but instead of passing the money on to Housman, he spent it. This was unfortunate because his firm was on the verge of collapse, and he was simply throwing good money after bad in an effort to remain in business. Alfred first learned of Grant's difficulties at the beginning of November 1925, from another publisher, and he at once wrote a letter, saying simply: 'Heinemann write to me that they are thinking of taking over your assets and asking particularly for *A Shropshire Lad*. Before I answer them I should like to have anything you may wish to say on the subject.'

In the event, Richards was again declared bankrupt. His firm was sold, and reorganised as the Richards Press; and although he remained in the new company, its affairs were strictly controlled by a 'Scotch legal gentleman', as Richards described him. Grant had told Alfred that the profits from *Last Poems* had been swallowed up in his bankruptcy; and although Alfred did not forgive him the £700, and later wrote to his brother Laurence that the Trustees of the Estate should know about the debt,[37] he was generous enough to give Grant some money to help him back on to his feet again.[38] And now that Richards was no longer personally in control, Housman decided to leave his books with the new press, writing: 'The *vis inertiae*, no longer regarded as a true cause in the physical world, governs me all the same.' However, he made certain that in future he received royalties on both *Last Poems* and *A Shropshire Lad*.

Richards may well have felt less guilty than he might have done about the money of Housman's which he had lost, because over the years he had come to think of Housman as a wealthy man, for whom profit was unimportant.[39] This feeling must have been reinforced during the summer of 1927, when they spent a month together, motoring through France in the most lavish style. It was a successful trip, and by October, Grant was scheming to set up in business again on his own, and to take Housman's books with him. At first Alfred seemed agreeable, writing to him: 'I have read and noted what you say about starting business again, and the proposals as regard my poems seem to be satisfactory'; but by

January the following year, he was having second thoughts: 'the Richards Press . . . have behaved quite properly to me as far as I have observed, and I will not do anything uncivil to them'.

Things ran on inconclusively until the end of May 1928, when Grant Richards reported that he had completed his arrangements relating to a new publishing business, and suggested that he might come over to Paris to discuss it all with Housman, who was then planning a holiday in France.[40] They spent a pleasant few days together, but when Housman returned to England, the most he would do was to tell the Richards Press that he had been approached by another firm of publishers, and to ask whether they would object to a transfer. When they told him that his departure would affect their prestige, he felt that it would be dishonourable to move. Richards was furious, writing: 'your punctiliousness, or misplaced sense of fairness, if I may say so, causes you to let this blessed gang of unprincipled Scotchmen have the books for nothing! . . . Well, I daresay I deserve it.'[41] To which Housman replied:

> If I did not know how easily composition comes to you, I should be sorry to have caused you to write so much. It has interested me to read it, but the utmost that I can say is that if the Richards Press change their title to Grant Richards Limited I shall regard that as a shabby act and take the books away.

After this exchange, relations between the two men were decidedly cool for some months; but they had known each other for too long and understood each other too well for a single disagreement to spoil their friendship.

Robert Bridges, the Poet Laureate, was another longstanding acquaintance óf Housman's. They had met at the Gosses' in 1913, six years later Bridges had written the foreword to a presentation volume for Hardy's seventy-ninth birthday, to which Housman had contributed a poem; and in the spring of 1920 Bridges sent Housman his latest volume of poetry, *October and Other Poems*. Alfred thanked him, though he was honest enough to admit:

> I do not expect to be always reading and carrying it in my head like the first four books of Shorter Poems. You have been spinning down the ringing grooves of change while I have been standing at gaze . . . and the pieces I like best are those which remind me of old times.

From time to time, the two men had news of each other through their mutual friend, Percy Withers, and when at the end of June 1923 Bridges wrote to Housman, commenting favourably on his *Last Poems*, Alfred replied by inviting him to stay as his guest in Trinity for a night. Bridges was at this time busy compiling a poetry anthology for schools, *The*

*Chilswell Book of English Poetry*, and Housman enjoyed advising him on this, insisting that he should include some Matthew Arnold and some Browning. The two men got on well; and later in the year Alfred wrote to Grant Richards:

> I had better tell you also that I believe he (being Poet Laureate, and an unscrupulous character, and apparently such an admirer of my verse that he thinks its presence or absence will make all the difference to the book) intends to include three poems from A Shropshire Lad, though I have not given him my permission, because he thinks he has reason to think that I shall not prosecute him. Well, I shall not; and you will please turn a blind eye too.

In December the same year, Alfred travelled to Oxford to read a paper, and stayed with Bridges in his house at the top of Boar's Hill. Afterwards, he wrote to Kate:

> He is an amazing old man: at 79 he gets up at five in the morning, lights his own fire and makes his coffee, and does a lot of work before breakfast. He has a large number of correct opinions, and is delighted when he finds that I have them too, and shakes hands with me when I say that the Nun's Priest's Tale is Chaucer's best poem, and that civilisation without slavery is impossible.

Bridges had found the visit rather hard work, as Housman was so taciturn, and when telling Percy Withers about Housman's visit, he added: 'Can you get him to talk? I can't!' In fact they had agreed more on politics than on poetry. When discussing Bridges's free theory of scansion, Housman had asked how a line of his should be read, stating his objection to both ways which seemed possible, and Bridges, neither way offending his less sensitive ear, had simply asked 'Does it matter?'[42] Thereafter, they wrote to each other occasionally at Christmas, and Bridges kept Housman informed about the progress of his long philosophical poem, *The Testament of Beauty*.

Housman's own poetry had virtually come to an end after Moses Jackson's death in 1923. He wrote a hymn for his own funeral, in January 1925; and after that he wrote out fair copies of a few of his unpublished poems, including 'I did not lose my heart in summer's even' (*MP* 37), and 'Crossing alone the nighted ferry' (*MP* 23). But there was hardly any new work, apart from some fragments, and a few melancholy verses, of which these may serve as an example:[43]

> Once in the springing season,
>     When earth made gallant show,
> Out of the mine a jewel
>     Was given me, years ago.

> Long worn, its lustre's tarnished,
>   It's no more pride to me;
>   I go tonight to fling it
>   In the cold and solvent sea.

But Housman remained interested in other work, and literary men with whom he maintained some contact included John Masefield,[44] and John Drinkwater – who in 1927 travelled over to Cambridge with Ralph Hodgson to visit him. Then, in 1928, Alfred was one of several distinguished pall-bearers at Hardy's funeral. He might have struck up an acquaintance with George Bernard Shaw on this occasion; but, as Shaw later told Grant Richards, he was just about to engage Housman in conversation when Gosse pulled them apart, in order to introduce Kipling to Shaw, 'And Kipling, I may add, when introduced, fled like an outraged rabbit'.

A more distinguished writer than Drinkwater or Hodgson who called on Housman in 1927 was the novelist E. M. Forster. Forster, like Housman, was homosexual; he had been educated at King's College, Cambridge, and he once explained that the poems of *A Shropshire Lad* had accompanied his development from subconscious to conscious, 'all mingled with my own late adolescence'. As a young man of twenty-eight on a walking tour in Shropshire he had written an admiring letter to Housman; and not long after this letter, written in 1907, it had occurred to him that the poems concealed a personal experience: the author had fallen in love with a man. He did not feel that he could go to meet Housman, but he felt about the poems that 'as one grew stale from familiarity another would come forward and stop with me until the earlier had time to recover. The book – as are both the books now – was inexhaustible, and the warmth of the writer's heart seemed unalloyed.'[45]

In his novel *A Room with a View* (1908), Forster actually quoted from Housman. His character Mr Emerson, talking to Lucy, the heroine, about his son George, says that George's trouble is that things won't fit:[46]

> From far, from eve and morning
>   And yon twelve-winded sky,
>   The stuff of life to knit me
>   Blew hither: here am I.

George and I both know this, but why does it distress him?'

Then years afterwards, in 1927, Forster was delivering the Clark Lectures, and he noticed that Housman came to two of them. On the strength of this, Forster called on him in Trinity, 'but he took no notice'.[47] Perhaps he found Forster too obviously homosexual; perhaps he simply found his view of life too sanguine.

Another visitor in 1927 was the eminent American lawyer Clarence Darrow, who had often used Housman's poems in the defence of his clients. In particular, he had used – and misquoted – two of Housman's poems when defending the celebrated murderers, Loeb and Leopold, two youths of seventeen and eighteen who had brutally murdered Loeb's fourteen-year-old cousin. Quoting from 'The night my father got me', Darrow had read out the lines suggesting that a man should not be blamed for the flaws in his nature. To make it more American, the 'county kerchief' had become the 'County Sheriff' in the verse:

> Oh let not man remember
> The soul that God forgot,
> But fetch the County Sheriff
> And noose me in the knot,
> And I will rot.                                    (*LP* 14)

Darrow now told Housman that the two young men owed their life sentence partly to him; and gave him a copy of the speech which he had made in their defence. Alfred sent his brother Basil a brief account of this meeting; he was a little irritated that his poems had been misquoted, but nevertheless seems to have been proud of the fact that they had been used by 'the great American barrister', to 'rescue his clients from the electric chair'.

Housman never turned away visitors, though he refused to talk to the Press, and he was always ready to give advice to younger poets when asked. In December 1924, for example, he wrote to Mr Pearce Higgins, the son of a Trinity don who had asked Housman to look through his poems:

The sonnet is a form of verse which is oftener a substitute than a vehicle for poetry; and though you write it with ease and accomplishment, and have many good lines, I do not think it altogether a good sign that you should be so ready to use it. Moreover, the ability to make sonnets even as well as you do is not in our time rare. 'Everyone writes so well nowadays', said Tennyson; and the average of proficiency has risen since then. Blank verse is a much tougher job.

And then, after various detailed criticisms, he ended kindly:[48]

I demurred when your father asked me to look through your poems, because I am always afraid of hurting young poets' feelings, and one of them once wrote back to say that he had put his verses in the fire; but your father assured me that you would not mind, and that my criticism would probably be less hostile than his own, so I hope no bones are broken.

In another letter, written in the 1920s to a different correspondent,

Housman gave some sound advice to all aspiring poets: 'Do not ever read books about versification: no poet ever learnt it that way. If you are going to be a poet, it will come to you naturally and you will pick up all you need from reading poetry.'

*    *    *

Housman's life had been devoted primarily to classical scholarship. He wrote very little poetry before he was thirty-five; and apart from the period of 'continuous excitement' during 1895, and the period after he had learned of Moses Jackson's illness in 1922, poetry never dominated him. The fact that he wrote only a small amount, and that it was not his major activity, is not in itself a criticism which seriously affects Housman's stature as a poet. However, the emotional range of his verse is limited, and unless there comes a time when beauty of expression is valued above all else in poetry, Housman will never be placed among the first rank of poets.

But if ever there was a man who was truly inspired, it was Alfred Housman. Poetry welled up in him, poetry of mood and emotion, both powerfully heightened by the classical restraint of the verse-forms which he used. In the history of literature, he is important as a respected popular poet of his day, as the poet of the Boer War, and as the author of a number of haunting lyrics which have survived the era in which they were written. He is a fine poet of nostalgia, of sorrow, of the bitterness of life, of the sustaining power of nature, of the strength of the human spirit and of the courage to endure.

And, for those who are interested in his life, it is in the poet that we see much of the best of Housman: the sad, compassionate, loving, romantic man who told his friend:

> But if you come to a road where danger
>     Or guilt or anguish or shame's to share,
> Be good to the lad that loves you true
> And the soul that was born to die for you,
>     And whistle and I'll be there.        (*MP* 30)

37 Trinity College, Cambridge, showing Whewell's Court with the tower in which Housman had his rooms on the second floor

36 Trinity College, Cambridge, the Great Gate in 1914

38  *Andrew S. F. Gow* c. 1911

39  *Alfred Housman photographed in 1922 by Spicer-Simson*

Tell me not here *here*, it needs not saying,
    What tune the enchantress plays
In aftermaths of soft September
    Or under blanching mays,
For ~~with~~ and I were long acquainted
    And I knew all her ways.

On russet floors, by waters idle,
    The pine lets fall its cone;
The ~~xxxxx~~ cuckoo shouts all day ~~at~~ nothing
    In leafy dells alone;
And traveller's joy beguiles in autumn
    Hearts that have lost their own.

On acres of the seeded grasses
    The changing burnish heaves;
Or marshalled under moons of harvest
    Stand still all night the sheaves;
Or beeches strip in storms for winter
    And stain the wind with leaves.

Possess, as I possessed a season,
    The ~~xxxxx~~ I resign,
Where over elmy plains the highway
    Would mount the hills and shine,
And full of shade the pillared forest
    Would murmur and be mine.

[128-A]

40  *A manuscript page from the notebooks part of* Last Poems 40

"CURIOSITIES OF LITERATURE."

*The Muse.* "OH, ALFRED, WE HAVE MISSED YOU! MY LAD! MY
SHROPSHIRE LAD!"

41 *The Punch cartoon which greeted the publication of* Last
Poems *in* 1922

42 *Percy Withers drawn by Gilbert Spencer*

43 *Trinity College, Cambridge, showing Great Court, 1914*

**44**  *The Francis Dodd portrait of Alfred Housman, 1926*

45  *Ludlow Church, Shropshire, where Alfred's ashes are buried*

# CHAPTER 12

# *Last Years*

. . . the beginning and end of a man's life are more than the
day of his birth and death.

Katharine Symons[1]

They have the night, who had like us the day;
We, whom day binds, shall have the night as they.
We, from the fetters of the light unbound,
Healed of our wound of living, shall sleep sound.
All gifts but one the jealous God may keep
From our souls' longing, one he cannot – sleep.
As copied out by A. E. Housman[2] from Swinburne's prelude to
'Tristram of Lyonesse', ll. 201–6

When on 26 March 1929 A. E. Housman celebrated his seventieth
birthday, he could look back with satisfaction on his achievements. Once
a clerk in the Patent Office, he had become famous in his life-time as the
author of *A Shropshire Lad* and *Last Poems*; he was a respected Cambridge
Professor; he had published a wealth of learned articles, as well as
editions of Juvenal and Lucan, and had acquired an international reputation as a classical scholar. And there were still many things in life to be
enjoyed. He had not lost his relish for good food and wine, nor his love of
natural beauty; he could look forward to completing, within a year or two,
his great work on Manilius; and although his greatest friend, Moses
Jackson, was dead, Housman still had the real pleasures of corresponding
with Miss Becker and visiting Edith Wise; he still had the respect of his
colleagues, the company of his friends, and the affection of his family.

Housman would not normally allow his poems to be broadcast – unless
first set to music. But for his seventieth birthday, Alfred made an exception
and allowed Laurence to read some of his poems on the wireless (see
Street correspondence, Laurence Housman to Sarah Clark, 23 March
1929). Laurence, together with Clem, also sent Alfred a telegram, in
which they had intended to urge their brother, in the words of one of his

poems, to 'shoulder the sky' (*LP* 9); but by the time the message had reached Alfred, 'shoulder the sky' had become 'shoulder the steg' and, much to his amusement, 'the Postmaster General reinforced it by repeating this word on the back of the telegram. I find that it means a male bird, especially a gander . . . I am in quest of one.' Kate sent Alfred two family photographs. One was of his grandfather, the Rev. Thomas Housman; the other, a picture of his father, gave Alfred particular pleasure, and he soon had it hanging up in his rooms.[3] More telegrams and letters arrived, from colleagues and friends; and Alfred replied to one of them, a letter from Percy Withers, thanking him

> for your congratulations, or disguised condolences, on the fact that King David thinks I ought to be dead. I am I suppose very much younger and heartier than most men at seventy, but any gratitude to the Most High on that account is tempered by the reflection that it may mean living to ninety.

Now that he had turned seventy, Housman did in fact ask his Cambridge doctor, Salisbury Woods, to give him a thorough overhaul; and was told that his heart was 'not as stout as it was and ought to be'. But his heart was causing him no apparent trouble. Occasional mild attacks of gout did not worry him much or put him off wine and, apart from a short period of ill-health, Housman had been in good physical condition for most of his late middle age. He had taken care of himself, wrapping up warmly in a padded aviation jacket during the Coal Miners' strike of 1926,[4] and carefully changing his underclothes after every walk because he thought that it would stave off an attack of lumbago. Although he loved good food and wine, and later enjoyed describing himself to his family as a glutton, his slender build showed that he had been moderate in his gourmandising. He also took regular exercise; and even when his dumb-bell had been laid aside, he continued his daily afternoon walks.

However, his mental condition had been less satisfactory, and from time to time he suffered from 'nervous depression and causeless apprehensions'. Understandably, there was an underlying melancholy in his spirit; Housman retained a vivid memory of small upsets in his life as a child, such as his disappointment at being forbidden to buy an amber necklace from a gypsy; and it may be imagined how much more vivid and how much more bitter, even after fifty or sixty years, were the memories of more serious shocks to his system. The Master of Trinity, Sir J. J. Thomson, had a charming and sympathetic daughter called Joan; she would sometimes meet Housman returning from one of his afternoon walks, and she later wrote:

> How intensely he had suffered might be guessed by anyone who saw

his face as it sometimes appeared at the end of one of his long walks. Perhaps he had recalled some of his own wretchedness as he walked alone and the sadness in his face was as poignant as on the face of a man experiencing the bitterness of sorrow for the first time.

Over a period of years, Joan saw more of Professor Housman, both formally and informally, than did many of his colleagues. At Christmas teas in her home she saw him relax, pull crackers and read out the mottoes with relish; and, if his hosts' baby grandson was in the house, he would sit a woolly animal toy on his knee, and watch the child 'as if he were then his natural self'. Joan did not find Housman 'aloof', and was saddened to realise that the idea of his being unapproachable was so deeply engrained that 'hardly anyone felt able to come forward and give him the ordinary human sympathy he desperately needed'. She saw that he had no use for admiration, but that: 'If a genuine sympathy and affection were offered him . . . Housman responded in full and gave unexpected proofs of deep feeling.' As for the enduring strength of Housman's feelings for Moses Jackson, and the sorrow which they brought, Alfred once told Joan Thomson that he could not tolerate the idea that it was possible for a man to love truly more than one woman in his life saying: 'anyone who considered that he had done so had simply never really loved at all'.

Housman had his sorrows and his bouts of depression; but his own troubles did not blind him to the needs of others. His friend Withers wrote of him:

His chiselled speech, his stern and rather obdurate physiognomy in repose, his sardonic quips, his biting satire, his easy resort to mockery and scoffing: of such was the outward vestment composed. And it was a grim deceit. Underneath beat as warm and as generous a heart, as willing for self-sacrifice, if the cause were true, as I have ever known.

Withers added that there was 'No doubt of his constant benefactions in many directions, and of many kinds'. Alfred had always been ready to assist his own family, giving money to both Kate and Basil when they needed it; and just as he had been generous to Richards and Andrea, so he was charitable to many whom he considered worthy of help.

When Laurence went through his brother's papers after his death, he found that there was a pile of correspondence which Alfred had carried on with needy individuals; and Laurence wrote that his brother had 'helped lame dogs, with a queer show of reluctance, moderating their demands; but I never found a letter of refusal – only a warning that he must not be expected to do more'.[5]

Although he was now an old man, Professor Housman worked as hard as ever. During 1929 he was still delivering lectures twice a week during term time – in that year, they were on some of the poems of Lucretius, Catullus, and Ovid;[6] he had some examining to do in May and June; he was working hard on the final volume of his Manilius; and, although he knew that this would involve him in a certain amount of correction and addition, as well as a new preface, he accepted the offer of the Cambridge University Press to reprint his Juvenal, only warning them that 'the price had better be moderate, as even the pleasure of buying copies for less than they cost to print did not entice mankind to take more than eighteen per annum'.

In July and August 1929, Housman went on holiday. First he spent a few days with the Witherses; and then went on to stay with Basil and Jeannie for a fortnight. He found Basil looking suddenly older; and indeed later in the year there was news from Jeannie that Basil's health was poor, and that he was about to retire – news which prompted Alfred to ask Kate 'how much you think I ought to add in future to the £50 per annum I now send them'. After leaving his brother's household, Alfred went on a four-day motor-tour, visiting Honiton, Chipping Camden, and also Sherborne, where he was much impressed by the interior of the Minster. Then, in the latter part of August, he travelled abroad for his usual holiday in France; though for once he went by train, explaining to Kate 'I am taking great care of my life till the book I am now engaged on [the Manilius] is finished'.

Grant Richards was unable to travel with Housman, because he was suffering from lumbago, but he had at least arranged for the second volume of Frank Harris's autobiography to be available in Paris for his friend.[7] In Paris Housman hired a car, together with a chauffeur, 'whose strong point', he wrote sarcastically to Richards, 'was smiling, not finding his way nor knowing north from south'. They toured for eleven days but the holiday was not a great gastronomic success, though Housman enjoyed one really good meal at the Gastronome in Clermont-Ferrand, and he was pleased by 'a Palestine soup which had not the faintest trace of artichoke'. The weather was fine for the whole tour; but it was now, in the heat, that Alfred's heart began to trouble him for the first time. He was all right visiting cathedrals, but, when on a hot afternoon he climbed the Puy de Parioux, about the height of Snowdon, he suffered from some breath- lessness, or other symptoms of a weak heart sufficient to prompt him to mention it in a letter to Kate.

During 1929, Alfred also corresponded with Miss M. A. Jackson, sister to Moses and Adalbert. He had already been sent a photograph of Moses Jackson's tombstone, which now hung on his walls, and he was pleased to learn from Miss Jackson that 'my dear Mo enjoyed his life at Applegarth so much'.[8]

In November, there was an acquisition of a more cheerful sort, when

Bridges sent Housman a copy of his long poem *The Testament of Beauty*. Bridges knew Housman's low opinion of his later work, and was also embarrassed by the book's success so he wrote 'I still shrink from intruding on you & making a call on your attention with a thing which I fear you may dislike, and my compunction has increased with the blatant boom . . . '.[9] In fact, Housman had already bought a copy of *The Testament of Beauty*, and although he did not admire the verse very much, he was pleased by the gift – a new copy, with its pages uncut; and he replied with a cordial letter of thanks.

Housman also had to deal with the proofs of a new edition of *Last Poems*; and to put up with Withers's congratulations on the fine printing of the Alcuin Press edition, which made him reply crossly:

I do not envy people who appreciate that sort of thing, because they suffer so terribly from books which do not come up to their standard; and I am amazed at the bitterness which they speak about the ordinary editions of *A Shropshire Lad*, which, being legible, are all that I could desire.

The year ended pleasantly: Christmas at Trinity brought a cold sideboard of boar's head, game pie, beef, ham, tongue, plum pudding and mince pies; Mrs Platt wrote to say that she had some sloe-gin for him; and, on 30 December, Alfred wrote to Jeannie to tell her that: 'To-morrow night I shall be taking steps to keep up my health and strength in 1930 by eating any amount of oysters up to 4 doz. and drinking all the stout required to wash them down.'[10]

The spring of 1930 was a more melancholy time: April brought the news of Robert Bridges's death; and, some days later, Alfred's old and dear friends Edith and Minnie Wise died on the same day, 30 April, leaving their elder brother Ted, who was now in his eighties, to manage on his own.

With Bridges dead, a new Poet Laureate had to be found. Apparently the King favoured Kipling and the Prime Minister Housman, but both were expected to decline, and so John Masefield was chosen. Housman was pleased by this decision, and went out of his way to write an encouraging letter to Masefield, urging him not to worry about the fact that he would 'now become the target for a good deal of spite', and, since Masefield, like Bridges, lived at Boar's Hill just outside Oxford, he added humorously: 'In sporting circles here they are asking the question: if Boar's Hill get it three times, do they keep it?'

Grant Richards had corresponded from time to time about his business problems, and had also sent Housman more books which were considered pornographic, and could not be bought in England; these included, in January 1930, Lawrence's *Lady Chatterley's Lover*. Like many people, Housman found this rather tame, and returned it in February saying 'It did not inflame my passions to any great extent, but it is much more wholesome than Frank Harris or James Joyce.'[11] In May, Richards accompanied Housman to a small dinner held in Housman's honour by the London restaurateur, Xavier Boulestin. Housman, probably still upset by the deaths of his old friends from Woodchester, had been in a difficult mood when he met Richards at his hotel; but it was a fine meal, and he must have been pleased when they drank a bottle of 'that very, very rare, almost legendary, white Haut Brion, of which so few bottles leave the Chateau that each is numbered'.

The dinner was also a welcome distraction from his work: lectures on Horace, final corrections to the Juvenal, and correspondence with his publishers about the printing of the fifth book of Manilius. In January Housman had managed to find time for a few days' holiday visiting churches in the south of Lincolnshire; and at the beginning of June, with all the writing and most of the printing of Manilius done, he decided that he could risk his life again, and flew over to Paris for a fortnight, a visit distinguished from his other trips to Paris by a meeting with Edith Wharton, the American author, whose books he had long admired.

On his return to Cambridge, Housman met another though less distinguished American author: Cyril Clemens, who claimed to be the nephew of Mark Twain. Clemens, a young man in his late twenties, had founded and was President of what he called 'The International Mark Twain Society' – a society in which he offered Housman the position of honorary Vice-President. When Clemens arrived in Cambridge, Housman, who had corresponded with him for several years, invited him to dine at Trinity.[12] Clemens has left a pleasant, if rather sugary, account of the visit, describing Housman as a striking man, with hair turning grey at the temples, keen, piercing grey eyes and a smile of rare sweetness; and recording their conversation about American literature, and Housman's trip to visit Edith Wharton. One interesting fact Housman did let fall: when asked if there was one book which he would take with him to a desert island, he replied: 'Alison's History of Europe, a work I was very fond of as a boy', adding that he always took a volume with him on a long railway journey; and that, 'like so many inferior books, . . . it had a charm and fascination all its own'.[13] But, as Housman later wrote to his old friend Walter Ashburner, he had found Clemens 'a very vacuous young man';[14] and when, a day or two later, Clemens invited him to tea, Housman declined.[15] He had already made plans to leave Cambridge for another month, staying first with the Witherses, and then with Basil and Jeannie.[16]

As was his custom, he spent one day of his visit to the Witherses in motoring around Northamptonshire or Gloucestershire visiting churches. Percy Withers admired Saxon architecture, and was pleased to find a subject on which he knew more than Housman, so he took him to see Brixworth, the best-preserved Saxon church in England. Housman had asked contemptuously if there was such a thing as Saxon architecture; but Withers was pleased to see that, once inside Brixworth, his cynical bearing fell away, and at St Peter's, Northampton, the effect on Housman of the rich beauty of the building was very marked, so that Withers wrote:

Never before or since have I seen him so taken aback, or his frozen restraint so completely melted. For once, and this once only, he burst into exclamation. His face glowed with astonishment and pleasure. He was momentarily transformed, back, as I could not but feel, to some state of long ago – his hidden self freed and a sudden and surprised delight had effected the transformation.

Returning to Cambridge at the beginning of September, Housman settled down to work. There were lectures to be prepared, work to be done on the new Preface for Juvenal, and the page proofs of the fifth book of Manilius to be corrected. There were not many distractions, though in November Housman found it necessary to write to the Steward about the food, complaining that 'I am tired of writing in the suggestion book about Irish Stew and saying that it ought to have lots of potato and lots of onion. On the last occasion it not only had neither but was strangely and shockingly garnished with dumplings'! There was one other diversion, when Housman was asked to sign a letter requesting contributions to a fund for the aged poet Sir William Watson. Housman refused to sign, because the letter grossly overpraised Watson's work;[17] but then, with his characteristic generosity towards someone who had fallen on hard times, he sent the fund a cheque for twenty guineas.[18]

December 1930 brought the publication of the fifth volume of his Manilius, the culmination of Housman's academic career. But it also brought news that Basil Housman's condition had deteriorated, and that Edward Symons was seriously ill with cardiac asthma. Alfred also passed on the news that – four years after he had been summoned to Andrea's death-bed – 'My poor gondolier is dead, after a bad pulmonary attack of about three weeks. Now', he added, trying not to sound too melancholy, and remembering the Housman family's dog, 'Now there is nobody in the world who respects me as much as Noble did.'[19] On Boxing Day, the news of his family was no better, and Housman wrote to Percy Withers that his brother and brother-in-law were both 'liable to drop dead any moment', and commented bitterly 'in short, Providence has given itself up to the festivities of the season'.

But for the time being Basil and Edward survived; and although Alfred had written to Jeannie 'I have just published my last book, so I am ready to die tomorrow', he was in reasonably good spirits, and added: 'However, I am all right at present, and taking my food nicely.'[20] He still had some work to do on his 'Praefanda', and he intended to prepare an *Editio Minor* of Manilius, consisting of just the text and the apparatus criticus in one volume. This kept him happily occupied during 1931, and he also managed a month in the south of France, his usual visits to family and friends, and even – for the first and only time – a trip to Scotland.

Housman had been invited to a country house called Ardtornish, overlooking the Sound of Mull in Argyllshire. The company included the artist Henry Tonks, and Richmond Palmer, Governor of the Gambia, whom Housman had met once or twice before, and to whom he was distantly related. Alfred had read about the house long ago under the name of 'Atornish' in Scott's *Lord of the Isles,* and he enjoyed 'walking about among the red deer and so forth'. The landscape was just as he had imagined it, and he was pleased by a specimen of Grass of Parnassus, a flower which he had never seen before.

In general, then, 1931 was a good year; but the country as a whole faced a severe economic crisis, which led to the formation of a National Government. Housman was irritated by some aspects of the economy drive which followed, writing to Percy Withers about its effects in Trinity, where 'Some of our feasts are suppressed for the sake of economy (i.e. that waiters may suffer from lack of employment and our champagne may go bad in the cellar) . . . '; but he was also genuinely concerned about the state of his country, and in November he had decided to send a cheque for £500 to the Chancellor of the Exchequer, a public-spirited act which deprived him of the bulk of his savings.

In January 1932, Edward Symons died, having lived at least twelve months longer than his doctor had expected. He had enjoyed ten years of happy retirement after an excellent life's work, so there was no tragedy in his death, but, knowing Alfred's close attachment to his family, one may imagine his feelings of depression at the news, coming, as it did, at a bad time, for it was less than a fortnight since he had completed his *Editio Minor* of Manilius, and, as Gow describes it, this completion was 'followed by a reaction and by a long period of depression, natural and not very important in itself, but perhaps the first sign that his health, hitherto robust, was breaking down'.[21]

However, he threw off this depression during the early part of the year, and it certainly did not affect his work. He lectured on Persius, Lucan and Horace;[22] and among his audience in 1932 was the brilliant young scholar, Enoch Powell, who later described, in not altogether flattering terms, what it was like to attend one of Housman's lectures:[23]

His face as he read was expressionless, and the effect, especially with
the heavy overhanging moustache and bald cranium, was of a voice
proceeding from the mouth of one of those masks which the actors
wore on the Greek tragic stage. The only movement of the body likely
to be observed was a quick prefatory wielding of the window pole to
exclude the hated draught from above his rostrum. The lecture having
been read – always precisely fifty minutes in length – he donned his
mortar-board and stalked impassively back to his fastness. . . .

The exhilaration was produced by watching what seemed to be a
mental machine of great power and precision applied to material at
first sight unexpected. . . .

The severity of Housman's presentation was the severity not of
passionlessness but of suppressed passion, passion for true poetry
and passion for truthfulness. For Housman textual criticism was the
exercise of moral self-discipline. . . . The phrases remembered over
the years were flashed from the inner furnace of passion for truth
and logical thought, and of indignation against every interest or
influence which could corrupt it. . . .

Under the radiation of this display of a great critical mind in action,
one's own powers, such as they might be, developed – above all, the
spirit of bold but temperate self-reliance without which no criticism
is possible.

Powell's attendance was an exception; few undergraduates went to his
lectures at all, finding them too scholarly; and to most – if they knew of
him – Housman in his old age was a remote figure, one of the great men of
Cambridge, and the subject of occasional speculation. Stories circulated
about him, and continue to circulate. Here is one, with a better pedigree
than most, as it comes from an ex-pupil of Housman's friend, Andrew
Gow:[24]

The philosopher Wittgenstein, who had rooms above Housman, had
no private lavatory; Housman had. Wittgenstein had to go downstairs
and cross Whewell's Court to find one. Once, when Wittgenstein had
an attack of diarrhoea, he asked through his bedmaker if he might
make use of Housman's lavatory. But the answer came back that
Housman was a philosophical hedonist, and therefore refused
Wittgenstein's request.

Wittgenstein had studied under Bertrand Russell at Cambridge, and
had returned in 1930 as a Fellow of Trinity; but his 'linguistic philosophy',
and his austere scheme for a logically perfect language must have seemed
misguided to Housman, the magic of whose poetry consisted in making

the best use of the logically imperfect language which already existed.

During 1932, individual Americans continued to write to Housman about his work. Cyril Clemens had decided on a biography of Housman, and wrote one chapter on 'Housman as a Conversationalist'. Housman corrected or marked 'the most inaccurate of your inaccuracies', and complained: 'I do not know why Americans are so fond of writing – and apparently of reading – about personal matters; but it seems to be a national characteristic, and it makes me unwilling to meet them, though they are always so kindly and friendly.' In fact, Clemens never completed his book; though the drafts of one or two chapters are held by Columbia University.[25]

At the end of May 1932, Housman was in Paris again. He had seen something of Grant Richards earlier in the year, but now wrote: 'I cannot offer you anything of an invitation, for I shall have a friend with me who would not mix with you nor you with him.' With this unidentified companion, he motored around Paris, travelling usually 150 or 200 kilometres a day, visiting Chartres, Neuilly, Vincennes, Fontainebleau, and other places,[26] and sampling the wares of new restaurants, including the Bearnais Albert Galen, with which he was delighted, and another of which he wrote angrily: 'if there is a fool on earth who wants to pay 65 francs for a glass of Chartreuse, he can do it here . . . I cannot imagine how it subsists'. But, as he wrote to Kate:

> The chief novelty was the great improvement which has been made in the aeroplanes in the last twelvemonth, in size, steadiness, freedom from noise, and even to some extent in speed. The science also seems to have progressed: when I began, pilots had to fly below the clouds, because if they flew above them they lost their way; but now they fly *through* them and keep their bearings all right . . . Neither cotton wool for the ears, nor things to be sick in, are now provided or needed any more than in railway trains; and (on the 'silver wing', the most expensive machine – though the fare is only £5. 10.0) you can have a large lunch served if you want it.

In July, Alfred made his usual visit to the Witherses, and then went on for a fortnight to stay at Tardebigge with Jeannie and Basil – who was now almost bed-ridden. After this, Alfred took what was for him an unusual step, and spent a week with Clem and Laurence at Longmeadow, their home in Street, Somerset. Laurence had been writing 'Nunc Dimittis', the epilogue to his *Little Plays of St. Francis* and, later in the year, when, as had become customary, some of these plays were being performed at University College London, Laurence appeared in the epilogue, playing himself on his deathbed. When Laurence invited Alfred to come and see him perform 'He replied that, though my death had attraction for him, he could not face the journey to London in the cold of winter . . . '.[27] A pity, for Laurence had included the following generous exchange:

Nurse:  You have written quite a lot of books, someone told me.
Author: In my life, more than I ought. My brother used to say that I wrote faster than he could read. He wrote two books – of poems – better than all mine put together.

Grant Richards was also in a generous mood, and visited Alfred in Cambridge to help sort out and arrange his books, which were 'in horrid disorder, and all over the place'. Housman helped to clear eighteen inches or so of shelf space by handing over to the college library the nine volumes of an index of erotic literature to which he had subscribed, the 'bibliotheca Germanorum erotica et curiosa'.

Housman was tidying up his affairs in other ways. During November – when the *Editio Minor* of Manilius finally appeared in print – he drew up a new will. The first main provision concerned his godson, Gerald Jackson, for whom Housman had most generously undertaken to pay to train as a doctor, at the rate of £450 a year. No doubt it had been accepted only as a loan; and Housman now said that his godson should 'have £300, and any outstanding debt forgiven'.[28]

Laurence was to be in charge of his books and manuscripts; and in various provisions, long since flouted, Alfred sought to ensure that only the most excellent of his works survived: enjoining the destruction of all his unpublished papers, and any of his unpublished poems which were below his usual standard; and forbidding the collection or republication of his classical papers. Copyrights of his published work were to be held by Barclays Bank on trust for his brothers and sisters. In addition, £20 was left to his 'manservant George Penny'; and the wine in his cellar was to go to 'The Family'.[29]

Housman was still one of the regular members of 'The Family' dining club, along with S. C. Roberts of the Cambridge University Press, and Andrew Gow; and he enjoyed the company of his old friends among the dons. But Housman had begun to feel that none of the younger men in the University were very interested in him; and this feeling made him shy and reserved, and increased his reputation for being remote and un-approachable. One of Housman's younger colleagues in the 1930s was Sir Steven Runciman, who found Housman 'taciturn and formidable' until he chose to speak to him about where one should eat and drink in France; after this, Housman became 'a fairly easy neighbour at dinner'; but Runciman was never invited to his rooms, and observed that 'Gow was the only one . . . who really had the right of entry'. Of course, old men often do not enjoy making new acquaintances; sometimes Alfred's friends would deliberately introduce him to someone new, only to find that he ignored them in conversation. Housman explained this to Joan Thomson, saying that 'he was apt to take a strong antipathy to a person at first sight, merely if it happened that he disliked the shape of the individual's nose or his complexion'! As Joan wrote later: 'So strong might this antipathy be that Housman would find it almost impossible to look at the person concerned, far less to associate with him.'

On 1 December 1932, less than a fortnight after he had signed his new will, Alfred heard that Basil had died. He had been in a great deal of pain, especially towards the end, and Alfred wrote to Dr Withers, 'his death is a release'; but Basil had been the favourite among his brothers and sisters, and the sense of loss must have been enormous. Nor was Christmas very jolly that year; the Frazers remembered him, and sent him some Scotch cake;[30] but, as Alfred wrote to Kate, discussing his usual plans for stout and oysters on New Year's Eve, with Gaselee and two other friends, he was beginning to worry about his own health. Alfred felt that his own physical condition had deteriorated, and he told his sister: 'In the course of this year I have grown older, which shows itself in my walking powers.' He was in fact walking far greater distances than most men of seventy-three; but he felt it to be a sign of old age that: 'After five or six miles, though I do not get tired, my legs tend to act sluggishly.'[31]

So Housman began 1933 in very low spirits. Grant Richards visited him in January, and at once became concerned about his health, and 'about the Spartan nature of his immediate surroundings'. Richards noticed that:

> His bedroom was narrow and austere in the extreme; there can have been no undergraduate in College who did not have at least as great a degree of comfort. It was dark and cold, or it gave that impression, and I could not help contrasting it with the degree of comfort to which he was inuring himself on his visits to France.

Richards wrote to Housman, who replied:

> I am touched by your concern for my health and disapproval of my habits, but your picture is darker than the truth. The fire does not usually go out, nor is the bed to which I retire a cold one, as I keep my bedroom so warm with a gas fire that I do not even need to use my hot water bottle.

The following day, Richards wrote again; but this time it was to enclose a letter from a young Frenchman, Maurice Pollet, asking Professor Housman a number of questions about his life and work. Richards had agreed to act as intermediary, though he told Housman: 'I can smooth the matter out even if you make no reply to him at all.'[32] Rather surprisingly, Housman did write a letter to M. Pollet, with a covering note to Richards explaining: 'I thought that for the sake of posterity I might as well answer some of the young man's Questions.'

Indeed, Housman told Pollet some things in this letter which we would not otherwise know. For example, 'Lemprière's *Classical Dictionary*, which fell into my hands when I was eight, attached my affections to paganism'. But some of his statements were less straightforward. He repeated the ironic comment that his poetry was not the result of personal emotional experiences, but the result of a physical condition. He also described himself as a Cyrenaic, believing that the only important thing was the pleasure of the moment. This description was only partly true – it encompassed some aspects of his thinking but devalued his genuine courage in setting his own standards of excellence in the face of what he felt to be a hostile Universe.

There was one key question of Pollet's which Housman would not answer at all: 'Have you ever disclosed the names of some of those friends of yours who are made the subject of some of your poems; and if not, do you think that you would, as it were, give them away, in handing their names to the public?' Of course, Housman need not have answered a single question; and Richards was right when he told him: 'I think you have been very generous to the young man.'[33]

Not long after this exchange of letters, Housman accepted a far more time-consuming task, when he agreed to deliver the Leslie Stephen Lecture for 1933; Professor G. M. Trevelyan was so flattering when he conveyed the request, that Housman did not see how he could refuse. The Vice-Chancellor, Will Spens, had added his persuasions;[34] and so in mid-March, as soon as term was over, Housman began working hard on 'The Name and Nature of Poetry'. It was only a year before this that Alfred had refused a request from his brother Laurence to write an essay on the poet Coventry Patmore, saying that 'it would give me more trouble than you can imagine, whereas I want peace in my declining years; and the result would not be good enough to yield me pride or even satisfaction'. Now he was faced with a much more demanding job, which seriously overtaxed him and left him suffering from acute depression.

At the time, he told Kate that he would not enjoy his holiday;[35] and wrote to Grant Richards about the 'infernal' lecture. Later he told Percy Withers that, from the hour that he accepted the job, 'his days had been an unabated torment. He had awakened every morning to the dread of a task to which he could bring no heart, and a struggle that had never given him a moment's satisfaction.' All that he actually enjoyed was the delivery of the lecture, on 9 May, to a packed Senate House, where, among the audience, sat several of his old friends, including Sir William Rothenstein, Sir Arthur Quiller Couch, and Grant Richards.

During his lecture, Housman declared that the peculiar function of poetry was not to transmit thought, but to transfuse emotion: 'to set up in the reader's sense a vibration corresponding to what was felt by the writer'. The name of 'poetry', he said, had been given to a great deal of literature which was excellent in its own way, but which had no spark of genuine poetry in it. For 'Poetry', he said, 'is not the thing said but a way of saying it.' And then, asserting that poetry had nothing to do with intellect, he pointed to poets such as Collins, Cowper, and Blake, who wrote the most beautiful poetry despite the fact that 'elements of their natures were more or less insurgent against the centralised tyranny of the intellect'. He felt that some of Shakespeare's loveliest verse actually said nothing – 'Take, O take those lips away'. And, quoting Milton's 'Nymphs and shepherds, dance no more', he asked rhetorically:

> what is it that can draw tears, as I know it can, to the eyes of more readers than one? What in the world is there to cry about? Why have the mere words the physical effect of pathos when the sense of the passage is blithe and gay? I can only say, because they are poetry, and find their way to something in man which is obscure and latent, something older than the present organisation of his nature, like the patches of fen which still linger here and there in the drained lands of Cambridgeshire. . . .

Trying to define poetry in another way, Housman told his audience that it was more physical than intellectual; and that he could recognise it by the symptoms which were provoked in him.

> Experience has taught me, when I am shaving of a morning, to keep watch over my thoughts, because, if a line of poetry strays into my memory, my skin bristles so that the razor ceases to act. This particular symptom is accompanied by a shiver down the spine; there is another which consists in a constriction of the throat and a precipitation of water to the eyes; and there is a third which I can only describe by borrowing a phrase from one of Keats's last letters, where he says, speaking of Fanny Brawne, 'everything that reminds me of her goes through me like a spear'. The seat of this sensation is the pit of the stomach.

Reminding his audience that he had himself written poetry, he said that his own feeling was that, in its first stages, the production of poetry was a secretion – a morbid one in his case, 'like the pearl in the oyster . . . I have seldom written poetry unless I was rather out of health, and the experience, though pleasurable, was generally agitating and exhausting'.

As Housman began the next passage of his lecture, one of his listeners noted that, 'there was a slight stir, followed by the complete hush which betokens a wholly attentive audience'.[36]

Having drunk a pint of beer at luncheon – beer is a sedative to the brain, and my afternoons are the least intellectual portion of my life – I would go out for a walk of two or three hours. As I went along, thinking of nothing in particular, only looking at things around me and following the progress of the seasons, there would flow into my mind, with sudden and unaccountable emotion, sometimes a line or two of verse, sometimes a whole stanza at once, accompanied, not preceded, by a vague notion of the poem which they were destined to form part of. Then there would usually be a lull of an hour or so, then perhaps the spring would bubble up again. I say bubble up, because, so far as I could make out, the source of the suggestions thus proffered to the brain was an abyss which I have already had occasion to mention, the pit of the stomach. When I got home I wrote them down, leaving gaps, and hoping that further inspiration might be forthcoming another day. Sometimes it was, if I took my walks in a receptive and expectant frame of mind; but sometimes the poem had to be taken in hand and completed by the brain, which was apt to be a matter of trouble and anxiety, involving trial and disappointment, and sometimes ending in failure.

After concluding his lecture, Housman was soon receiving compliments for a triumph; it was widely reported and praised in the newspapers; and the Cambridge University Press soon found that their initial print-run of 3,000 copies would not satisfy the public demand, and in less than two months had had to print a further 7,000.[37] What made it so popular was that many people took Housman's brilliant and subjective appreciation of the nature of poetry as the confirmation of their existing prejudices against modern verse.

The lecture had been a huge success, but there were a few men, including F. R. Leavis, the champion of the new poetry, who strongly disapproved of it. Alfred wrote to his brother Laurence about this, saying: 'The leader of our doctrinaire teachers of youth is reported to say that it will take more than twelve years to undo the harm I have done in an hour.' Leavis felt that Housman's emphasis on poetry as something more physical than intellectual was a direct attack upon his own extremely intellectual approach to literary criticism. In fact, he and others had to some extent misinterpreted what Housman was saying. As Alfred wrote in another letter to his brother: 'I did not say that poetry was better for having no meaning, only that it can best be detected so.'

Immediately after the lecture, Grant Richards went round to Housman's rooms, where he was distressed by his friend's evident fatigue. The excitement and controversy which the lecture generated did not help matters, and within a month of the lecture Alfred's heart was misbehaving, and his doctor had ordered him into the Evelyn, a Cambridge nursing home, for a complete rest. A week's rest improved his heart condition, but not his state of mind, and he wrote to Percy Withers: 'My real trouble, which I have often had before, is nervous depression and causeless apprehensions.' His worries were increased by the fact that (on his doctor's advice) he was making plans to move into new rooms the following term.

On 12 June, two days after leaving the Evelyn, Housman motored into Worcestershire to stay with Jeannie; and on the way he lunched with the Witherses. Percy Withers found him looking 'strangely worn and frail, so much more than could have been expected from a comparatively brief confinement to bed'; but Withers was delighted when, 'on seeing the variety of wines awaiting his choice . . . [Housman] broke into a chortle so hearty, so like the amused gratification of old times . . . '. Then, after lunch, 'looking inexpressibly wistful and sad', Alfred told his friends what the Leslie Stephen Lecture had cost him.

His stay with Jeannie, a few days with Laurence and Clem, and a visit to Edward Wise at Woodchester, were pleasant enough; but he was sleeping badly, having trouble breathing when he dozed off, and waking early; and his nerves were no better when he returned to Cambridge.[38] When they did begin to improve a little, he went off to France for a motoring holiday with another unidentified companion, 'a nice young man, not much educated, who regards me as a benefactor'.

Unfortunately, just before leaving, he contracted a particularly unpleasant form of influenza; and during his first few days in France he had 'the most violent and frequent pain I have ever undergone . . . I could not swallow a morsel of food or a drop of drink. . . and I could not get more than three minutes' sleep at a time'. But he continued to tour round France with his young companion, and at least managed to enjoy the first oysters of the season at Royan before returning home. Dr Woods thought that the trip had done his heart good; but his strength did not improve, and, as he told Withers, his nervous trouble 'took the opportunity of stealing back to some extent'. Even when that was alleviated by a strong tonic, he wrote to Withers:

I walk sluggishly and am low in spirits. My chief remaining trouble is excessive sensitiveness to noise, which prevents me from getting to sleep again if I wake when life has begun to stir in the morning. . . . My lectures are no trouble to me, but I find I cannot get up a real interest in work and study. I read chiefly novels and Lecky's History of England in the eighteenth century, from which I learn much that I did not know.

One pleasant surprise, in October, was T. S. Eliot's very favourable criticism of the Leslie Stephen Lecture in the *Criterion*. Housman found this 'amusing, because its author . . . is worshipped as a god by the writers in the paper which had the only hostile review' – that was *Scrutiny*, edited by Dr Leavis and others. The lecture itself was still selling well, and had been reprinted again;[39] while the young bibliographer John Carter and his friend John Sparrow had reprinted his Introductory Lecture of 1892 in a limited edition of 100 copies. Housman would not autograph these, and described Carter and Sparrow as 'two infatuated admirers'; but there is no doubt that he was pleased by the gesture: he once wrote that fame, though not important in itself, was like a mattress interposed between oneself and 'the cold hard ground' of reality.[40]

He had not changed his rooms after all, unable to face all the trouble of a move, though he had already spent over £300 to protect his heart by having a lift installed in what would have been his new quarters. This expense, in addition to the money which he was paying to help Gerald Jackson, meant that he was unable to help Grant Richards, who was short of money again, and pressing for aid. He explained the position to him once; and then, when Richards continued to ask for money, Housman had to write very firmly: 'If I did what you ask, because it is painful to refuse, it would be cowardice, and I should be angry with myself afterwards, and ashamed; and you would be obliged to think me weak.'

By the end of 1933, Housman was feeling better than he had done a few months earlier; but he continued to be 'neither strong nor comfortable'; and he complained humorously to Withers that it was: 'one of my grievances against the Creator that I always look better than I am (as Emerson said of the Scotch "Many of them look drunk when they are sober") and consequently receive fewer tears of sympathy than I deserve; . . . '. During the spring of 1934 Housman was in fact given a term's leave by the University authorities, in view of the length of his service. He had intended to spend part of it visiting Africa; but in the end, since his health was so poor, he decided not to risk the journey, and instead spent the time quietly in Cambridge.

Then, not long after his seventy-fifth birthday, he heard of the deaths of two of his last remaining links with the Woodchester which he had known as a child. In April Edward Wise died aged eighty-three; and Alfred's sister Kate wrote of this event: 'I should call that the *end* of A.E.H.'s life; for the beginning and end of a man's life are more than the day of his birth and death.'[41] But perhaps the real end, in that sense, came a few weeks later, when he heard the news that Sophie Becker had also died, at the age of ninety. When, shortly afterwards, Housman went to stay with the Witherses, the shock of this loss made him reveal more of his feelings to Withers than was usual; and one morning he told him that:

he had never possessed but three friends – all, it is significant, associated with youth or early manhood. They were all now gone, and a note of exultation came into his voice as he spoke of his thankfulness for having outlived them. With a tenderness of passion utterly undisguised he went on to tell of the last of the three friends – a woman – recently dead. His voice faltered, his whole frame seemed shaken, as he told the brief story. He had loved and revered her from youth. In the early years companionship had been close and constant. Then distance and the exigencies of occupation had rendered meetings few and difficult, and of late years they had never met, he said bitterly, as a consequence of her having returned to her home-land, Germany, to end her days. The story closed with a thank God he had lived to know her safely laid to rest. He added – and for the first time his voice strengthened to a triumphant pitch – how comfortably he could meet death now his three friends were at peace.

Alfred had originally planned to travel on from the Witherses to stay with his sister-in-law Jeannie; but she was not well enough for visitors, and so he and Laurence, who had also been invited, stayed instead at a hotel in Droitwich. From here – only six miles away from their old home – they motored through the counties round about.[42] The two brothers talked of family and personal matters; of their mother, whom Alfred still remembered well;[43] and of religion, Alfred declaring emphatically that he was not an agnostic, but an atheist.[44]

In August Alfred visited Alsace Lorraine; and when he returned he was able to congratulate his sister Kate, who had brought out a history of her husband's school, King Edward VI School, Bath; it was, according to the *Times Literary Supplement*, 'a fine piece of research'.

In November, there was a flattering proposal from the University of Wales to grant Housman an honorary degree; but, following his custom, he declined to accept it. His old friend Alfred Pollard had no misgivings about honorary degrees, and the two men met in 1934 at a festive lunch in King's, after Pollard had been made a Litt.D. at a ceremony to celebrate the opening of the new University Library. They had seen little of each other for some years, but their friendship remained, and Pollard remembered that, in the course of the lunch, Housman 'came up to greet me with a pretty speech. He was already looking thin and tired, and I was not surprised to hear soon afterwards of the beginning of his illness.'[45]

Indeed, although Housman's heart had been steady, his nervous depression was worse again. He wrote to Withers that

the perpetual recurrence of discomfort every morning between waking and finishing my toilet is wearisome in the extreme, apart from the feeling of physical fatigue which is frequent. . . . The great and real troubles of my early manhood did not render those days so permanently unsatisfactory as these.

And to Kate he wrote in December: 'I can bear my life but I do not want it to go on, and it is a great mistake that it did not come to an end a year and a half ago' [in other words soon after his delivery of the Leslie Stephen Lecture]. 'This period', he went on, 'has been a serious subtraction from the total pleasure (such as it was) of my existence. I am not doing anything important, but putting together notes from my margins to print from time to time.' And he added, crossly: 'I am much annoyed by being told by everyone how well I look, and being admired for my comparative youthfulness and my upright carriage.' More gloomy news was the death of his colleague and friend in Trinity, R. V. Laurence, of whom he had spoken so warmly to Percy Withers. Housman admired the bravery with which, despite two years of illness, Laurence 'had arranged and intended to lecture on the day he died', and no doubt this example fortified him as he faced his own decline.

Generally speaking, 1935 was a wretched year for Housman. But it began with an interesting visit from Geoffrey Tillotson, a young lecturer from University College London who wished to republish some of the comic poems which Housman had long ago contributed to UCL magazines. Tillotson was apprehensive about meeting Housman, but was warmly received, and later wrote an account of his visit, in which he describes his arrival at Trinity. The porter told him that Professor Housman was in his rooms, and would just about have finished his tea, so a visit was possible, and Tillotson was taken to Whewell's Court:[46]

in the anteroom from which his rooms branched, I noted a brown-enamel kettle still steaming on a gas ring. And almost all the remaining apprehension disappeared when Housman met me. He had risen to greet me from an office chair at a capacious office desk on the left of the fire where in green-shaded light he was engaged in writing on foolscap. He was wearing carpet slippers (green, I believe, with a floral pattern). They seemed newish but of a kind I did not know were still made. . . . His face seemed nervously intent on clearing my mind of nervousness and intenseness. It was slightly in pain. . . . His face had a bucolic brightness, like a crab apple, and its patchy red seemed that of a man whose skin has gone hard and red with weather. His eyes were quick and bright . . . his smile seemed a floating rather than an anchored one. . . .

They talked for twenty minutes, and Housman gave permission for the reprinting of 'The Parallelogram', 'The Amphisbaena', and the witty 'The Crocodile or Public Decency', which begins:

> Though some at my aversion smile
> I cannot love the crocodile.

From the middle of February onwards, Housman grew much weaker. He had an unpleasant period of sleepless nights; and though he managed his lectures, and even the writing of the University's Address to the King on his Jubilee, his heart was deteriorating and his nerves were bad. On 9 June he wrote to Laurence:

> The doctor does not want me to take walks of much more than a mile, and I myself am often inclined not to do much more than twice that amount. I still go up my 44 stairs two at a time, but that is in hopes of dropping dead at the top.

Eight days later the doctor sent him to the Evelyn, where they gave him morphia to give him a good night's sleep. Alfred had by now recognised from Arnold Bennett's *Clayhanger* that he had the symptoms of 'Cheyne-Stokes breathing' – sleepless nights spent in recurrent paroxysms of failure of breath – and that he would probably not live for many more months.

Percy Withers, hearing from Housman of his stay in the Evelyn, collected him for a short visit when, after a fortnight, he was well enough to leave the home. On the first evening of the visit, Housman was astonishingly animated. The President of Magdalen and his wife had been invited by Withers to supper, and Housman was able to talk 'abundantly and well, and laugh, and keep us in a state of laughter with a flow of excellent stories'. But the following morning, and for the rest of his stay, the Witherses found that Housman was 'suddenly old and broken'. They looked after him with the greatest kindness, and understanding. Dr Withers brought him tea at 6.30 each morning, to bring his terrible nights to a speedier end. Then Housman would spend most of each day dozing, or reading to himself in a quiet, cool sitting-room in the old part of the house, undisturbed except by occasional visits from Mrs Withers bringing him fresh home-made iced lemonade. After tea each day Housman would go for a short walk with his host; and then in the evening he would brighten a little, and they would talk. 'I was glad to hear that you said I seemed happy while with you', Alfred wrote later to Mrs Withers, 'for indeed the fact was so, and everything conspired to give me peace and enjoyment.'

From the Witherses Housman went on to Tardebigge to stay with Jeannie. Laurence and Clem joined the party; and one afternoon Alfred and Clem motored over to their old home, the Clock House, where Laurence was opening the Catshill church fête.[47] The house itself had been so much altered and expanded since the Housmans lived in it that much of it must have been unrecognisable; but part of the frontage to the road was still intact, and, looking up from the house to 'Mount Pisgah' must have revived many memories of childhood.

Not long after Alfred had returned to Cambridge, Laurence came to spend a week with him there. A holiday in Yorkshire which the brothers had planned was out of the question now that Alfred's heart was so feeble. Instead, with Cambridge as their centre, they visited 'more places, churches, abbeys and cathedrals, than I [Laurence] can count'.[48]

Enoch Powell, a resident Fellow of Trinity since May 1935, sometimes found himself sitting next to Housman. Poetry and the classics were thought to be forbidden subjects; but Housman, who did not speak unless addressed, was prepared to discuss food and wine and often presented delicacies to the Fellows' Table.

Housman's last holiday abroad, in search of his usual pleasures, began, at the end of August 1935, with an unpleasant accident: he had travelled down from Paris to Lyon, and on the first day there gave himself 'a nasty knock on the head in entering a taxi'. But when the wound had been sewn up and bandaged at a hospital, with great determination he continued in the same taxi the outing which he had planned for the day. The wound did not give him much pain, though it required medical attention for some time; and he covered up the unsightly area by wearing a *calotte,* or French skull-cap – which, much to his amusement, made his young French companion exclaim that he 'might be taken for a great scholar!'[49] In fact, Housman enjoyed the tour, but the journey home was rather disagreeable. Stormy weather delayed the flight at Le Bourget for three hours – and even then the aircraft took off and landed very unsteadily, and the flight took twenty-five minutes longer than usual. Returning to Trinity, he was disappointed to find that the same storm had blown down the 'Sedgwick elm'. Housman now wrote irritably to Withers: 'the doctor paid me an uninvited visit this morning and told me that I was very well. In point of fact I am rather weaker than before I went abroad'.

A few days later, replying to a letter from Lady Frazer, he told her that 'age and weakness of heart in combination cause me to spend my days in fatigue and somnolence, except for periods after meals, and I often feel as if I had no marrow in my bones'.[50] During the next few weeks, his health deteriorated rapidly. He was lecturing without difficulty, but 'the ten minutes' walk to and fro was so exhausting' that he was given a lecture room in College; and his doctor now absolutely insisted that he must move from Whewell's Court, because the climb to his room was giving his heart more work than it could manage, and, as he told Kate: 'I have breathlessness, weakness and dropsical swellings in the ankles and knees.' One of the younger Fellows, C. A. Coulson, agreed to make over his ground-floor set of rooms in Great Court to Professor Housman; and on 23 October

Alfred went to stay in the Evelyn for three weeks while his new rooms
were being prepared.

While he was in the nursing home, Housman's usual sedatives failed,
and he had some sleepless and distressed nights before resorting rather
unexpectedly to champagne. The champagne – though it was not in fact a
drink which he particularly cared for – was a success, and, as Alfred
wrote, 'the doctor, though he did not suggest it, approves of the results'.
Housman had become friendly with one of the nursing staff, Sister E. L.
Robins, who had trained in dietetics and so shared his concern for food.
Sister Robins later corresponded with Kate on the subject of Alfred's
visits to the Evelyn; and told her how the Professor:

> would relish a lunch of oysters and champagne! Then I would
> personally supervise the cooking of two of his favourite dishes which
> consisted of stuffed pigs ears & grilled pig trotters, served with
> onion sauce. You will doubtless think not a suitable invalid's fare,
> but at that particular time he was not very ill, only that his heart got
> a little weary.

In one of her letters, she paints a striking picture of Housman as an ill but
very brave old man:[51]

> Whenever he walked in the garden he would talk with nobody but
> me, he said I gave him confidence & to both our amusement used to
> say that I was steady on my feet! . . . He was the bravest and most
> courageous person that I have ever met. I have the greatest admiration
> for his fortitude. He simply would not give in to living the life of an
> invalid, his great thoughts were to tend his lectures and to help others.
>   He certainly was not ever afraid of dying. . . .

Sister Robins had said that one of his great thoughts was 'to help
others'; and indeed, shortly before this, Housman had noticed that his
bedmaker in Whewell's Court was very depressed; when he discovered
that her husband was ill, and the family in poverty, he immediately came
to their assistance.

Housman had time to help others, even when he was ill; but it sometimes seems that few other people had time to help him. In fact, he did not
wish to appear to be an invalid, or to inconvenience anyone, and so he
was a difficult person to help. His sister Kate did write letters to him, and
he was touched to hear that she was praying for him. He replied that he
was also 'rather remorseful' about this, as 'it must be an expenditure of
energy, and I cannot believe in its efficacy'. Nevertheless, when his heart
had been more troublesome than usual, he would sometimes ask Sister
Robins to pray for him as he liked to think of it and felt it helped.

Laurence was also concerned about Alfred, and offered to help move his books – a task already being supervised by Andrew Gow – and when Laurence was in Cambridge to address a Peace Meeting, he came out to the Evelyn to visit his brother. The evening before this, a noisy torchlight procession had advertised the meeting, and Alfred teased Laurence about his Peace Movement, saying that he would prefer it to 'remain sedentary'.

It seemed clear to Alfred's family that he wished to lead as normal a life as possible, and that he did not want them to come round making a fuss of him. In the end Kate and Laurence kept in touch with the situation by corresponding with Mr Gow about their brother's health. Gow had become Housman's closest friend in Cambridge during the last few years – even joining him on his walks from time to time[52] – and he now looked after Housman's interests as well and as unobtrusively as he could.

The University had relieved Housman of the burden of examining for the University scholarships and the Chancellor's Medals, but twice a week a taxi drove him from the Evelyn into College for his lectures. He also lunched or dined out several times. On one occasion he and Sir Arthur Quiller-Couch had both been invited to dinner at Babraham; and Sir Arthur commented on how lively he was, saying that he:

> picked him up at the Evelyn Nursing Home & returned him to it & going & coming & at dinner he was in great form, & old Lady Wemyss thought that 'a skull cap didn't sit well on one so young'.

On 18 November 1935 Professor Housman – now known to the College servants as 'The Walrus', because of his moustache[53] – moved into his new rooms, B2 in Great Court. Like many conservatives, he was more alarmed by the prospect of change than by change itself. He had held out for years against modern plumbing, insisting when visiting Kate on staying at an hotel which would provide him with a hip-bath; but now that he had a modern bathroom and lavatory – and continuous hot water – he revelled in the notion that the new fittings were 'said to be the last word in luxurious and scientific plumbing'. Housman took an old man's innocent pleasure in his new rooms, and wrote to Jeannie that:

> I myself walk very feebly and do not sleep very well, and my breathing is apt to be troublesome; but the comforts around me make me much more cheerful than I should otherwise be. I can get through all the work that is required of me, and I go out to dinner when invited.

From the middle of December his health again grew worse. He suffered from indigestion and nausea, and after nursing himself in College for a few days on soup, hot milk, and brandy, he returned to the Evelyn Nursing Home on 24 December. He missed the Christmas feasts, and wrote to Kate: 'My College fellows sympathise with me more than my family could, knowing more of my gluttony.'

By 15 January he was well enough to return to Trinity. The doctor expected him to break down within a fortnight and return to the home worse than he left it; but Housman made a final, remarkable rally. His nerves were suddenly better than at any time since June 1933, consequently he looked less drawn, and more lively and cheerful. His ankles and knees were also much less swollen;[54] and, as he reported with great delight to Dr Withers, he was at long last enjoying his sleep at nights. He carried on with his lectures as normal, and his kind and understanding friend Gow gave up paying him daily calls to see how he was, realising that it was irritating Housman to be treated as a sick man.[55]

There was one annoying incident in February, when he fell and fractured a finger, so that he could not write easily for a while; but apart from this, Housman had a comparatively pleasant two months – and wrote very tartly to Withers when he received a letter from him asking if he might be of any help as a male nurse! Then, during the second week in March, after completing his lectures for the term, Housman's condition grew worse; and from 21 March to 18 April he was back in the Evelyn again.

He recovered enough to insist upon lecturing during the Easter term, but within three days Dr Woods was trying to persuade him to return to the nursing home. Housman managed to give two lectures, sitting down because he was too weak to stand;[56] he was a dying man, and knew it. On 21 April he replied to an editor pressing for a contribution ' . . . my career and it is to be hoped my life are so near their close that it is to be hoped they will concern neither of us much longer'.

On 24 April, the day of his last lecture, Sir J. J. Thomson saw him, and later wrote: 'He was terribly ill and must have had invincible determination to lecture in such a state.'[57] That evening S. C. Roberts was host to 'The Family' in Pembroke, and recalled that Housman:[58]

> looked terribly ill and, shortly after we had sat down to dinner, he confessed to me that he felt sick. I took him to the bedroom and asked whether I should get a taxi to take him back to Trinity. No, he said, he would rather come back to the table. Having nibbled a little toast and drunk a glass of Burgundy, he left early.

The next day, 25 April, saw Alfred back in the nursing home; for the next few days, Andrew Gow visited him every day in the afternoon. On the 29th, Wednesday[59]

> A welcomed me with unusual warmth and said he wanted to see me, but immediately his mind wandered and that is all intelligible that he did say: the rest was mere words except that he once said with

startlingly distinct voice 'It has nothing to do with the Bangorian controversy' – a queer fragment of the subconscious. It was rather distressing, and after working in the room for about half an hour I came away.

In the evening Alfred had a perfectly lucid conversation with Dr Woods. He held the doctor's hand for nearly half an hour; and said to him: 'I know you have brought me here so that I may not commit suicide. . . . But I do ask you not to let me have any more unnecessary suffering than you can help.'[60] So from that time, the doctor made sure that he was in no great physical pain. Before bidding him good-night, Woods told Housman the story of the English actor who, when asked what he did in his spare time, replied:[61]

'Well, I suppose you could say we spend half our time lying on the sands looking at the stars, and the other half lying on the Stars looking at the sands!' Slowly gasping out the words, Housman said: 'Indeed – very good. I shall – have to repeat – that – on the Golden Floor.'

After a good night and a cheerful awakening, he lapsed into unconsciousness.[62] Gow came in to see him, but only stayed for a minute or so:[63] and a few hours later, on 30 April 1936, at the age of seventy-seven Professor A. E. Housman, poet and classical scholar, died peacefully.

\*    \*    \*

Housman was cremated, and his ashes laid to rest in the churchyard at Ludlow in Shropshire – a fitting resting-place for the poet of *A Shropshire Lad*. But first there was a funeral service in Trinity where, since the news of Housman's death, the College flag had flown at half-mast from the tower above the Great Gate. Now Housman's oak coffin lay in the chapel, with the College pall over it, and a wreath from his family of laurel and bay, with a mass of white cherry blossom laid across it – cherry blossom from the avenue of cherry trees in Trinity Backs. Among the many people present at the service were many Fellows and Heads of Colleges; representing Housman's family were his brother Laurence, and his nephews Jerry and Denis Symons; Moses Jackson's son Gerald was also present,[64] and joined in singing the hymn which Housman had specially written for his own funeral service as long ago as 1925.

Laurence later wrote that he thought it possible that Alfred[65]

believed in 'a Supreme Being' but that need not imply that he believed in a Personal Deity. I judge from his 'Hymn for my Funeral' that he looked forward to being reabsorbed unconsciously into whatever 'Being' or existence he and the rest of things animate and inanimate had sprung from.

The hymn ran:

> O thou that from thy mansion,
>> Through time and place to roam,
> Dost send abroad thy children,
>> And then dost call them home,
>
> That men and tribes and nations
>> And all thy hand hath made
> May shelter them from sunshine
>> In thine eternal shade:
>
> We now to peace and darkness
>> And earth and thee restore
> Thy creature that thou madest
>> And wilt cast forth no more.            (*MP* 47)

# Appendix: Housman Letters at Bromsgrove

While this book was in production, a large collection of letters written mainly by Laurence Housman was presented to the Bromsgrove Public Library. They chiefly concern Laurence's religious and political views, and his work for 'Peace'; and this somewhat tedious material is enlivened by occasional bawdy limericks, and other writing which Laurence begs Reginald Reynolds, the recipient of most of the letters, to destroy.

Apart from this, there is some early Nonsense Verse of AEH's from a childhood game of nouns and questions (referred to in a letter of 20 August, 1947), verse which includes the noun 'Cucumber' and answers the question 'Have oysters whiskers as well as beards?'. Apparently AEH's visit to Laurence and Clem in the summer of 1932 was not such an 'unusual step' (p. 250) because he had stayed with them for a week in July 1931 (letter of 12 July); and Laurence had even taken him along to a Quaker 'meeting'. AEH's visit in 1933 (p. 256) drew this lengthy aside from Laurence (28 June):

> The 'Shropshire Lad' is staying with us, and rather liked 'Anthropo-morphism' [a piece by Reginald Reynolds] which says – more flippantly, things he has said in 'Last Poems'. He is ageing gently – that is to say – getting gentler & a bit more gracious & kind in his old age. I think he finds himself needing society and sympathy more than he used to do.
>
> I wonder whether you read his Cambridge lecture 'The Name and Nature of Poetry'? It has caused a good deal of controversy: but all the critics, even when differing, have taken off their hats to him.
>
> I'm shy of asking him (supposing I outlive him) what he wants said or done if he is offered burial – or a funeral service – in Westminster Abbey. I fancy he would say 'No' to the first, because so many people he does not approve of are buried there and might be his near bed-fellows: but he would probably say that a mere service didn't matter – as it would be soon over & would leave no lasting taint on his reputa-tion for scholarship, scepticism, & scorn of the human race in general, and of democratic government in particular.

267

There is also a particularly interesting letter (12 December 1943) in which Laurence discusses his destruction of many of AEH's papers. He did this thinking of Clem, but now believes that:

> for posterity it may have been a mistake; and any way the fact remains that AEH did unashamedly leave these papers for inspection. They were very human, and some of them very touching. And the letters have not been destroyed, and will or may some day be restored to the light of day when there will be no feelings to be hurt, and when perhaps they may be of some benefit to society as a corrective to social intolerance. . . . sometimes I think that Alfred definitely wished me to make the truth known when he was safely tucked away into the non-existence which he believed to be man's true end; for the only time in which he ever showed emotion when speaking to me of things personal, was in a connection which he knew surely that I should understand.

In addition, there are some other details of family history: for example, that Laurence's flirtation with Roman Catholicism (p. 128) involved a stay in a religious house (6 June 1936, to Ethel Manin); that Edward Housman bought eight volumes of illustrations from Pompeii in order to study the one which concentrated upon those items considered too indecent to be on public display (letter of 23 April 1951); and that when Lucy Housman died (p. 135) she left a note insisting that her coffin should contain locks of hair cut from her mother's head, Edward Housman's beard, and the coat of a dog which had died nearly forty years before (letter of 7 April 1950)!

Finally (12 December 1943), Laurence expresses his annoyance with his sister Kate for co-operating with Grant Richards's book about AEH; and he also records (9 July 1951) hiding certain facts from the biographer Maude Hawkins.

# Abbreviations

| | |
|---|---|
| *AEH: Recollections* | *A. E. Housman: Recollections* by Katharine E. Symons and others, 1936 |
| *A. E. Housman: Selected Prose* | *A. E. Housman: Selected Prose*, ed. John Carter, Cambridge University Press, 1961 |
| *ASL, LP, MP* and *AP* | *A Shropshire Lad, Last Poems, More Poems* and *Additional Poems* |
| Columbia | The collection of Housman manuscripts in the Library of Columbia University, New York |
| Congress, GRP and LHMS | The Grant Richards and Laurence Housman papers in the Manuscript Division, the Library of Congress, Washington DC |
| Gow | *A. E. Housman, A Sketch,* by A. S. F. Gow, Cambridge University Press, 1936 |
| *Housman: 1897–1936* | From the book of that title by Grant Richards 1941 |
| JPP | Documents or copies of documents in the collection of John Pugh, the Chairman of the Housman Society |
| *Letters* | The Letters of A. E. Housman, ed. Henry Maas, Harvard University Press, 1970 |
| Lilly | From the Housman Collection in the Lilly Library, Indiana University |
| *My Brother: AEH* | *A.E.H.* by Laurence Housman, London, Cape, 1937 |
| Pugh | *Bromsgrove and the Housmans* by John Pugh, Housman Society, 1974 |
| Street | Correspondence at the Library of Street, Somerset, from Laurence Housman and Clemence Housman. |
| Trinity | From manuscripts in the Library of Trinity College, Cambridge |

*Unexpected Years*      *The Unexpected Years* by Laurence Housman, London, Cape, 1937.

Watson      *A. E. Housman: A Divided Life* by George L. Watson, London, Hart Davis, 1957

Withers      *A Buried Life* by Percy Withers, London, Cape, 1940

# Notes

## Introduction

In the course of preparing for this biography, I read and noted some articles, many books and a great number of manuscript documents relating to A. E. Housman. But I cannot pretend that – in three years – I have read every article about Housman which has ever been written, or that I have had time to read every book to ensure that none of the manuscript sources which I quote have already been referred to in print. Inevitably, there will be some occasions – I hope not too many – when I have unwittingly given an unpublished source precedence over a published one; and there will also be occasions where I have arrived independently at a conclusion which has at some stage been put forward by someone else. I would like to assure any scholar whom I have offended that errors of this sort have been made honestly, and if pointed out to me, will be put right in any future edition of this work.

I must add that, in using material from the Grant Richards papers in the Library of Congress, I have sometimes felt that it was more effective to quote from an original letter than from Mr Richards's interpretation of it or reference to it in his *Housman 1897–1936* – (see for example Chapter 6 notes 6 and 7); and I make no apology for quoting from any of the letters in the Laurence Housman papers from the Library of Congress which may have formed the basis of statements by Maude M. Hawkins in her *A. E. Housman: Man behind a Mask*; original letters, I suspect, will carry more weight with some scholars than many extracts from Mrs Hawkins's book.

## Chapter 1 *Background and Early Years*

In order to avoid weighing down the book with detailed footnotes, I have throughout this section listed initially those works from which I have drawn the bulk of my references for the chapter in question; the remaining notes will normally be to lesser-known and less accessible sources. All unpublished sources will be given. Unless otherwise indicated, most of the background information in this chapter comes from: *AEH: Recollections; My Brother: AEH;* Pugh; *Unexpected Years.*

1 A sermon preached in London before the Continental Society for Diffusing Religious Knowledge over the Continent of Europe. A copy of this rare pamphlet may be seen in the Bodleian Library, Oxford (G Pamph 1033 (b)).
2 Trinity, Add MS 71–31: letter from Laurence Housman, 22 September 1937.
3 Robert Fletcher, *The Life and Remains of the Reverend Robert Housman,* quoted in Watson, p. 34.

4 Congress, RHP Box 2: Mrs K. E. Symons to Grant Richards, 21 February 1937.
5 Congress, LHMS: Laurence Housman to Maude Hawkins, 24 October 1950.
6 K. E. Symons, *More Memories*.
7 Little, *A History of Woodchester*, 1922; rewritten by Rev. W. N. R. J. Black, 1972; see *passim*, particularly Appendix 14.
8 Lilly, Carter correspondence, 11 September 1956: letter from Ellinor M. Allen of Inchdene, Woodchester.
9 JPP, Mrs K. E. Symons, 'How the Housman Family came to Bromsgrove'.
10 *More Memories*.
11 Street; Laurence Housman to Sarah Clark, 15 February 1917.
12 Trinity, Add MS 71–40.
13 *Letters*, p. 328, 5 February to Maurice Pollet.
14 Laurence Housman, *A Modern Antaeus*, London, John Murray, 1901, p. 8.
15 Congress, LHMS: Laurence Housman to Maude Hawkins, 24 October 1950.
16 Among the papers at University College London.
17 JPP, indenture between Edward Housman and the Rev. Thomas Housman.
18 Congress, LHMS: from Laurence Housman's answers to a questionnaire about Alfred.
19 JPP, indenture between Edward Housman and the Rev. Thomas Housman, 10 January 1870.
20 H.E.M. Icely, *Bromsgrove School through Four Centuries*, Oxford, Blackwell, 1953, pp. 81–4.
21 Ibid., *passim*.
22 Watson, p. 47. For another mention of Edwin Grey see *Letters*, p. 269.
23 From a conversation between the present author and Phyllis Symons, Kate's daughter-in-law, 5 May 1976.
24 Laurence Housman in *John O'London's Weekly*, 16 October 1936.
25 See *A History of Woodchester*, Appendices 16 and 17. The mills were conveyed to Wise in 1868, but closed within two years. Wise's 'other interests' are unknown, and it may be that he simply lived off his capital for the remaining five years of his life.
26 Congress, RHP Box 2: K. E. Symons to Grant Richards, 8 June 1942.

## Chapter 2 *Schooldays*

Unless indicated by a separate note, the main sources for the information in this chapter are *AEH: Recollections*; *Letters*; *My Brother: AEH*; Pugh; *Unexpected Years*.

1 Congress, RHP Box 2: from notes made by Grant Richards after interviewing Mrs K. E. Symons.
2 J. L. Talmon, *Romanticism and Revolt*, London, Thames & Hudson, 1967, p. 149.
3 Trinity, Add MS 71–48: letters from Mrs K. E. Symons, 7 February 1937.
4 Withers, p. 14.
5 Lilly, Carter correspondence: Hilda Fletcher to G. L. Watson, 19 May 1957.
6 Alfred was to win a prize for French at school; one wonders whether during his time in the sixth form or thereafter, he read any of the poems by Alfred de Vigny. Some lines from de Vigny's 'Le Mont des Oliviers' seem relevant here:
Si le Ciel nous laissa comme un monde avorte,
Le juste opposera le dedain a l'absence
Et ne repondra plus que par un froid silence
Au silence eternal de la Divinite.

7 Congress, RHP Box 2: Mrs K. E. Symons to Grant Richards, 27 May 1941.
8 JPP, extract from an article by Mrs K. E. Symons, *Birmingham Post*, 4 June 1932.
9 Ibid. Congress, RHP Box 2: notes made by Grant Richards after interviewing Mrs K. E. Symons and correspondence of 5 December 1939.
10 JPP, extracts from notes for a book to be called 'A Housman Patchwork' on which Mrs K. E. Symons was working shortly before her death.
11 Ibid.
12 K. E. Symons, *More Memories*.
13 Catalogue of the Housman Centenary Exhibition 1959, at University College London; assembled by John Carter and Joseph W. Scott; see item 22; see also *My Brother: AEH*, p. 30.
14 Trinity, Add MS a72/3.
15 Gow, p. 3.
16 K. E. Symons, 'Memories of A. E. Housman', the *Edwardian* (the magazine of King Edward's School, Bath), vol. 17, no. 3, September 1936.
17 Columbia: Laurence Housman to Cyril Clemens, 16 July 1949.
18 *Romanticism and Revolt*, p. 137.
19 Trinity, Add MS 71–39.
20 The information in this paragraph comes from Sotheby's Catalogue, 15 December 1970, p. 147.
21 Congress, LHMS: Laurence Housman to Maude Hawkins, 10 November 1949.
22 Watson, p. 61.
23 Trinity, Add MS 71–53; letter from Mrs K. E. Symons, 28 December 1936.
24 Congress, RHP Box 2: Mrs K. E. Symons to Grant Richards, 8 June 1942.
25 JPP, A Bill of Complaint, 17 June 1875.
26 JPP.
27 Ibid.
28 Ibid.; information from a draft deed of confirmation of the conveyance of Perry Hall between Edward Housman and Rev. J. B. Housman dated 11 February 1879.
29 Maude Hawkins, *A. E. Housman: Man behind a Mask*, Chicago University Press, 1958, p. 64. See also *AEH: Recollections*, p. 30 for mention of 'an increasing restriction of means'.
30 Norman Marlow, *A. E. Housman: Scholar and Poet*, London, Routledge & Kegan Paul, 1958; see particularly Chapter 1.
31 A. E. Housman, *The Confines of Criticism*, Cambridge University Press, 1969; Inaugural Lecture 1911 with notes by John Carter. See p. 17.
32    O, quot fert Thetis, insularum ocelle,
     O, domus venerum cupidinumque,
     Haec sibi Cytherea vindicabit
     Templa posthabita colenda Cypro.
   Catalogue of the Housman Centenary Exhibition 1959 at University College London; assembled by John Carter and Joseph W. Scott (see item 23).
33 Lilly: Carter correspondence, 11 September 1956; letter from Ellinor M. Allen of Inchdene, Woodchester.
34 Lilly; *Housman, Alfred Edward Prophecy for the year 1877*, from Visitors' Book of the Wise family at Woodchester, 1883–99.
35 JPP, extracts from the diaries of Mrs Edward Housman, 10 January 1877.
36 Ibid.; 15 June.
37 Trinity, Add MS 72–9. ?Also quoted in *My Brother AEH*.
38 Congress, LHMS: Laurence Housman to Maude Hawkins, 10 November 1949.

## Chapter 3 *A Scholar at Oxford*

Unless otherwise indicated by a separate note, the major sources for the information in this chapter are: *AEH: Recollections*; Gow; *My Brother AEH*; *Letters*; Watson.

1 Lilly: Warren, T. H. 1853–1930; lists removed from copy of W. Wagner's Plautus, Cambridge, 1876.
2 T. H. Warren, *Testimonials to A. E. Housman 1892*, Cambridge University Press, 1892.
3 T. C. Snow in ibid.
4 The *Bromsgrovian*, 1882.
5 University College London, Add MS 126.
6 Sotheby's Catalogue, 15 December 1970, p. 147.
7 *Ye Rounde Table*, vol. 1, no. 4, 11 May 1878, pp. 52–3. A copy of this magazine may be seen in the Bodleian Library, Oxford (Per G. A. Oxon 8° 583).
8 Catalogue of the Housman Centenary Exhibition, 1959 at University College London, assembled by John Carter and Joseph W. Scott; see item 24.
9 Norman Marlow, *A. E. Housman: Scholar and Poet*, London, Routledge & Kegan Paul, 1958. See also Watson, pp. 79–81.
10 Trinity, Add MS 71–169; letter from E. W. Watson, 25 May 1936.
11 Lilly: *Housman, Alfred Edward Prophecy for the year 1877*, from Visitors' book of the Wise family at Woodchester, 1883–99.
12 From the College Accounts for 1878.
13 JPP.
14 Ibid.
15 Ibid.
16 Ibid.; the will of Ann Housman, 23 January 1879.
17 Sotheby's Catalogue, 15 December 1970.
18 Ibid., p. 147. ? letter, 24 November 1878.
19 W. H. Mallock, *Is Life Worth Living?*, London, Chatto & Windus, 1881 (first published 1879); see pp. 6, 222, 223, 274.
20 JPP; 19 June 1879.
21 Trinity, Add MS 81–20.
22 I am indebted for this idea to a speech made by Sir Richard Southern, President of St John's College Oxford, at the Annual Dinner of the Housman Society, 1975.
23 A. E. Housman, *The Confines of Criticism*, Cambridge University Press, 1969, p. 22; Cambridge Inaugural Lecture 1911.
24 Trinity, Add MS 71–162; letter from Hugh Last, 1 November 1937.
25 Christopher Ricks, *A. E. Housman: A Collection of Critical Essays*, Spectrum, London, 1968; see 'Housman' by John Wain, p. 28.
26 Trinity, Add MS 71–140; letter from W. Snow.
27 Sotheby's Catalogue, 9 July 1968; letter from Pollard to Laurence Housman, 25 October 1936.
28 Columbia: J. T. Nance to Cyril Clemens, 7 October 1936.
29 JPP, extracts from the diaries of Mrs Edward Housman; see entry for 1880.
30 *The Times*, 17 June ? 1938; letter from Alfred Pollard.
31 A. S. F. Gow, 'A. E. Housman at Oxford', *Oxford Magazine*, 11 November 1937.
32 Maude Hawkins, *A. E. Housman: Man behind a Mask*, Chicago University Press, 1958, p. 71.
33 James Morris, *Oxford*, London, Faber & Faber, 1965, p. 117.
34 JPP, extracts from notes by Mrs K. E. Symons for 'A Housman Patchwork'.

35  Ibid.; note by Mrs K. E. Symons in the diary of Mrs Edward Housman for 1881.
36  Trinity, Add MS 71–167; letter from A. W. Pollard, 17 July 1936.
37  Ibid.; Add MS 71–162; letter from Hugh Last, 1 November 1937. See also
     Columbia: J. T. Nance to Cyril Clemens, 8 August 1936.
38  See the Oxford Calendar for 1881.
39  Trinity, Add MS 71–20.


## Chapter 4 *The Years of Poverty, 1881–92*

Unless indicated by a separate note below, the major sources for the information in this chapter are: *AEH: Recollections*; Gow; *Letters*; *Unexpected Years*; Watson.

 1  JPP, note by Mrs K. E. Symons made in the diary of Mrs Edward Housman for
     1881.
 2  Ibid.
 3  Herbert Millington, *A. E. Housman, Testimonials 1892,* Cambridge University
     Press.
 4  From the College Register, 18 October 1881.
 5  Columbia: J. T. Nance to Cyril Clemens, 16 November 1936.
 6  JPP, extracts from the diaries of Mrs Edward Housman.
 7  Ibid.; entry for 25 December 1881.
 8  Congress, LHMS: Laurence Housman to Maude Hawkins, 24 October 1950.
 9  Ibid., 3 August 1952.
10  Congress, RHP Box 2: Mrs K. E. Symons to Grant Richards, 7 March 1939.
11  *Housman 1897–1936*; p. xv, from the Introduction by Mrs K. E. Symons. See
     also Trinity, Add MS 71–98; letter from Mrs K. E. Symons.
12  JPP, letter from A. E. Housman to Katharine Symons, 28 December 1932.
13  Ibid.
14  Congress, LHMS: Laurence Housman to Maude Hawkins, 6 August 1950.
15  Columbia: Mrs K. E. Symons to Cyril Clemens, 29 October 1936.
16  JPP, extracts from the diaries of Mrs Edward Housman, 21 April; see also in
     ibid. an obituary of Robert Holden Housman.
17  Ibid.; notes by Mrs K. E. Symons in the diaries of Mrs Edward Housman; see
     entries for 7, 13 June 1882.
18  Ibid.; extract from *Bromsgrove Messenger,* 16 June 1883.
19  *Housman 1897–1936*; see the Introduction, p. xvi.
20  From the College Accounts for 1882.
21  Trinity, Add MS 71–126; letter from Laurence Housman, 15 June 1936.
22  Information taken from JPP; the diaries of Mrs Edward Housman, entries for
     24 July 1882; 11 September; 11 December (and note of Mrs K. E. Symons).
23  Ibid.; 26 November 1882.
24  Ernest Walford, *Old and New London,* London, Cassell, 1875–8; vol. 5, p. 183.
25  Information supplied by my old friend Geoffrey Tyack, an expert on Victorian
     history.
26  Letter to the present author from D. G. A. Myall, Assistant Registrar, the Trade
     Marks Registry; 24 April 1978.
27  Trinity, Add MS 71–188; letter from Ralph Griffin, 19 June 1936.
28  Lilly: Arthur Platt to Henry Jackson, 22 April 1911.
29  Trinity, Add MS 71–188; letter from Ralph Griffin, 19 June 1936.
30  Ibid., Add MS 71–22; Mrs K. E. Symons to A. S. F. Gow, 17 December 1937.

31  Congress, RHP Box 2: Mrs K. E. Symons to Grant Richards, 20 November 1936.
32  Congress, LHMS: Laurence Housman to Maude Hawkins, 29 May 1958.
33  Ibid.
34  Ibid.
35  From an article by Laurence Housman in *Encounter*, October 1967.
36  William Blake, 'There is no Natural Religion', 1788.
37  Tom Burns Haber, *The Manuscript Poems of A. E. Housman*, London, Oxford University Press, 1955, p. 88.
38  Documents in the possession of M. Higham Esq.
39  *Old and New London*, vol. 5, p. 413.
40  Congress, RHP Box 2: correspondence between Laurence Housman and Grant Richards, 2/3 February 1939.
41  Ibid.; Mrs K. E. Symons to Grant Richards, 10 February 1939.
42  *Dictionary of National Biography*.
43  From the article by Laurence Housman in *Encounter*, October 1967.
44  Gibraltar, 4 January; Naples, 8 January; Port Said, 12 January; from Alfred Housman's diary quoted in Laurence Housman's article in *Encounter*, October 1967. The originals are in the British Library.
45  Ibid., 27 January.
46  Ibid., 7 January 1890.
47  Written on 9 January 1890; see diary entry quoted in *Encounter*, op. cit.
48  Congress, RHP Box 2: Mrs K. E. Symons to Grant Richards, 8 June 1942.
49  Lilly: Wises Visitors' Book, 12 April 1887.
50  Columbia: Laurence Housman to Cyril Clemens, 2 April 1958. See also Congress, LHMS: Laurence Housman to Maude Hawkins, 24 October 1950.
51  JPP, note by Mrs K. E. Symons in the diary of Mrs Edward Housman, 25 December 1882.
52  Pugh: Appendix F, p. lxxvi; letter of 26 February 1887.
53  Ibid.
54  From a conversation between the present author and Phyllis (Mrs A. D.) Symons, Kate's daughter-in-law; 5 May 1976.
55  Trinity, Add MS 71–190; letter from F. W. Hodges.
56  Ibid.; Add MS 71–191; letter from M. H. Eyre.
57  Congress, RHP Box 2: Katharine Symons to Grant Richards, 7 May 1939. See also Sotheby's Catalogue, 9 July, p. 160.
58  See entry for 28 March 1888 in Alfred's diary; the article by Laurence Housman quoted in *Encounter*, op. cit.
59  Laurence Housman to Maude Hawkins, 19 June 1958 and 21 July 1958; quoted in Laurence Housman's article in *Encounter*, op. cit.
60  *A. E. Housman: Selected Prose*, p. 194, extract from 'The Name and the Nature of Poetry'.
61  British Library, Add MS 45, 861C, 2 October 1890.
62  *A. E. Housman: Selected Prose*, p. 194.
63  *Collected Poems of A. E. Housman*, London, Cape, 1967, pp. 161–3.
64  Letter of 1 February 1888 quoted in A. S. F. Gow, 'A. E. Housman at Oxford', *Oxford Magazine*, 11 November 1937.
65  *A. E. Housman: Selected Prose*; Preface by John Carter, p. ix.
66  Lilly: Arthur Platt to Henry Jackson, 22 April 1911.
67  Congress, RHP Box 2: for a comment on this see Mrs K. E. Symons to Grant Richards, 28 April 1939.
68  *A. E. Housman: Selected Prose*; from the Introductory Lecture 1892, p. 19.

## Chapter 5 *An Academic Life, 1892–1911*

Unless otherwise specified below, my major sources for the information in this chapter are: *AEH: Recollections*; Gow; *Letters*; *My Brother: AEH*; and for details of its administrative and related affairs, H. Hale Ballot, *University College London 1826–1926*, University of London Press, 1929.

1  *A. E. Housman: Selected Prose*, pp. 1–22; Introductory Lecture 1892.
2  Pugh; Appendix A, p. xxii.
3  *A. E. Housman: Selected Prose*, p. 156; Arthur Platt (1927).
4  R. W. Chambers, *Man's Unconquerable Mind*, London, Cape, 1939, p. 369.
5  *A. E. Housman: Selected Prose*; Arthur Platt (1927); pp. 154–60.
6  Details about Platt and Ker are to be found in *Man's Unconquerable Mind*; see pp. 360, 361, 362, 387–9, 398.
7  *A. E. Housman: Selected Prose*, pp. 156–7; Arthur Platt.
8  Ibid., pp. 197–8; from a paper on Matthew Arnold.
9  Columbia: Laurence Housman to Cyril Clemens, 9 April 1956.
10  *Man's Unconquerable Mind*, p. 377.
11  Maude Hawkins, *A. E. Housman: Man behind a Mask*, Chicago University Press, 1958, p. 135.
12  Trinity, Add MS 71–20.
13  *Man's Unconquerable Mind*, p. 368.
14  Columbia: letter to Cyril Clemens from L. P. Brown, 31 January 1937.
15  Lilly: Carter correspondence, Hilda Fletcher to G. L. Watson, 19 May 1957.
16  'Recollections of Mr E. V. Lucas', *Mark Twain Quarterly*, A. E. Housman memorial issue, winter 1936.
17  Roger Lancelyn Green (ed.), *A Century of Humorous Verse 1850–1950*, London, Dent, 1959, p. 161.
18  A. E. Housman, *Three Poems*, printed by Department of English, University College London, 1935.
19  *Man's Unconquerable Mind*, p. 374.
20  University College London; from the official Minutes of the Council Meeting, 4 July 1900; see section 161.
21  From a letter of 2 May 1907 from A. E. Housman in Alan Bell (ed.), *Fifteen Letters to Walter Ashburner*, Edinburgh, Tragara Press, 1976.
22  *Housman 1897–1936*, p. 99. It may be worth remarking that Housman's landlady appears as 'Mrs Trim' in the letters; but the editor of that volume, Henry Maas, states in an article in vol. 2 of the *Housman Society Journal* that 'Mrs Hunter' is the correct name.
23  *Man's Unconquerable Mind*, p. 374.
24  From a letter of 2 June 1903 in *Fifteen Letters to Walter Ashburner*.
25  *Man's Unconquerable Mind*, p. 379.
26  Ibid., pp. 377–8.
27  *Housman 1897–1936*, p. 98.
28  Henry Savage's *Richard Middleton*, p. 47, quoted in Watson, p. 189.
29  Richard Middleton, 'Monologues', p. 219, quoted in Watson, p. 190.
30  26 January 1911; quoted in *Housman 1897–1936*, p. 100.
31  JPP, letter from R. W. Chambers to Mrs K. E. Symons, 24 February 1937.
32  *Man's Unconquerable Mind*, p. 380.
33  Ibid., p. 368.
34  JPP, information from letter of R. W. Chambers to Mrs K. E. Symons 24 February 1937.

35   Congress, RHP Box 2: Mrs K. E. Symons to Grant Richards, 13 February 1937.
36   JPP, R. W. Chambers to Mrs K. E. Symons, 24 February 1937.

## Chapter 6   *A Literary Life (1)*

I should at this point say a word about my dating of Housman's poems. Laurence Housman's list of poems from A. E. Housman's four notebooks is given with some dates; and limitations are placed on other possible dates by both external and internal evidence. Thus 'Loveliest of trees, the cherry now' could not have been written after 1896, when it appeared in *A Shropshire Lad*; or 'AJJ' before the death of Adalbert Jackson in 1892. Checking these known dates and certain limitations against the list of poems, it seems clear that, as one might have expected, Housman usually worked his way methodically through each notebook, before starting on the next one. This makes it possible to place almost all Housman's poems within a satisfactory framework and, tentatively, to date many of them to within a few months.

There is one possibly serious objection to this method: the list of dates of the poems in *Last Poems* given by A. E. Housman to Sir Sydney Cockerell; but my view is that this list should not be taken too seriously. Housman was speaking off the cuff, some twenty-five years after he had begun many of the poems. Twenty-one of his dates or descriptions, such as 'After Boer War' or 'Before 1910' do in fact fit happily into my suggested framework; but Housman's memory was not infallible: in one case he gives a date of around 1904 for a poem 'The Oracles' which we know was published in the previous year; and if some other dates are also wrong by a few months or even years, this is nothing to be surprised about. (For example, the Cockerell date for *LP* 3 is 1895, and not, as I believe it should be, somewhere between August and December 1894; and the Cockerell information about *LP* 24 is that it was begun in 1900, and not, as I believe, at some time during December 1894 or January 1895.) It is possible that these discrepancies are to be explained by the fact that Housman sometimes left a blank page or two, and later went back to fill it up; but for the purposes of this book I have assumed that his use of the notebooks was orderly and methodical.

Unless indicated by a separate footnote, the major sources of information for this chapter are: *My Brother: AEH*; *AEH: Recollections*; Withers; *Letters*; *Housman 1897–1936*.

1   *A. E. Housman: Selected Prose*, 'The Name and Nature of Poetry', p. 194.
2   Ibid., p. 195.
3   JPP, undated letter (? 1936 or 1937) from Laurence Housman to Katharine Symons. See also Columbia: Laurence Housman to Cyril Clemens, 11 January 1937.
4   Preface by Laurence Housman to *A Shropshire Lad*, Marlborough College Press, 1954. See also Congress, LHMS: Laurence Housman to Maude Hawkins, 23 November 1949.
5   Congress, RHP Box 2: Mrs K. E. Symons to Grant Richards, 7 March 1939.
6   Ibid. For Grant Richards's account of this see *Housman 1897–1936*, p. 313.
7   Congress, RHP Box 2: Mrs K. E. Symons to Grant Richards, 8 June 1942; and see *Housman 1897–1936*, p. 313.
8   JPP, undated letter (? 1936 to 1937) from Laurence Housman to Katharine Symons.
9   Trinity, Add MS 71–20.

10 Notebook B, p. 53; see T. Burns Haber (ed.), *The Manuscript Poems of A. E. Housman*, London, Oxford University Press, 1955.
11 H. Montgomery Hyde, *The Cleveland Street Scandal*, London, W. H. Allen, 1976, p. 238, from which the information in this paragraph is taken.
12 H. Montgomery Hyde, *Oscar Wilde*, London, Eyre Methuen, 1976.
13 Housman's reference to a note which he thought of putting in *A Shropshire Lad* about Hughley Church, and his idea of inventing another name for the church, show that his visit took place before publication of *A Shropshire Lad*, and not in September 1896 as has been assumed by Maas and others.
14 Gow, p. 3.
15 R. W. Chambers, *Man's Unconquerable Mind*, London, Cape, 1939, p. 388.
16 Norman Marlow, *A. E. Housman: Scholar and Poet*, London, Routledge & Kegan Paul, 1958.
17 *LP* 30 was originally sub-titled 'after Heine'; according to Professor Marlow, the first two verses are almost a translation of Heine's *Lyrisches Intermezzo* 62.
18 Quoted in Maude Hawkins, *A. E. Housman: Man behind a Mask*, Chicago, 1958, p. 168.
19 Letter to the present author from N. V. H. Symons, 9 December 1977.
20 'Carry unspoilt into honour the safety of man'; see *The Manuscript Poems of A. E. Housman*. This later became 'carry back bright to the coiner the mintage of man'.
21 *A. E. Housman: Man behind a Mask*, pp. 144–5. Maude Hawkins claims to have been told this story by Laurence Housman who had it from Alfred Pollard. See also *AEH: Recollections*, A. W. Pollard, p. 43.
22 *The Manuscript Poems of A. E. Housman*, pp. 49, 53, 54–5.
23 Preface by Laurence Housman to *A Shropshire Lad*.
24 Harold Monro, *Some Contemporary Poets*, 1920, p. 18. This book is owned by M. Higham Esq.
25 Both letters from Sotheby's Catalogue, 9 July 1968, p. 169.
26 Since writing these words my attention has been drawn by H. Montgomery Hyde to an article in *The Times*, 17 June 1968, by Bevis Hillier, in which this theory is more forcefully expressed.
27 Columbia: Grant Richards to A. E. Housman, 22 February 1898.
28 Ibid., 23 July 1898.
29 Congress, RHP Box 2: from a note by Mrs K. E. Symons on the galley proofs of Grant Richards's book.
30 Columbia: Grant Richards to A. E. Housman, 7 February 1899.
31 David Cecil, *Max*, London, Constable, 1964, p. 262.
32 Article by John Masefield in *Mark Twain Quarterly*, A. E. Housman memorial issue, winter 1936.
33 *The Cleveland Street Scandal*, p. 241.
34 John Quinlan, 'A. E. Housman and British Composers', *Musical Times*, March 1959.
35 After A. E. Housman's death in 1936, his brotner Laurence (who was less scrupulous), allowed Yeats to include five poems in the *Oxford Book of Modern Verse*; in 1939 poems by Alfred appeared in the *Oxford Book of English Verse*.
36 Congress, RHP Box 3: A. E. Housman to Mr Thompson, 16 March 1909.
37 Ibid., Box 6: for sales figures.
38 Theodore Dreiser, *A Traveller at Forty*, published by Grant Richards 1914; pp. 59–60.
39 The chronological list of these runs:

| 'Diffugere Nives' (*MP* 5) | 1897 | *Quarto*, vol. 3 |
| 'Illic Iacet' (*LP* 4) | 24 Feb. 1900 | *Academy* |
| 'The Olive' (*AP* 23) | 7 June 1902 | *Outlook* |
| 'The Oracles' (*LP* 25) | 1903 | *Venture* (ed. Laurence Housman and Somerset Maugham) |
| 'Astronomy' (*LP* 17) | 1904 | *Wayfarer's Love: Contributions from Living Poets*, ed. Duchess of Sutherland. Housman protested that he did not give his permission for the verses to be printed (see *Letters*, p. 68). |

40  'thin is the quilt' was an early version of 'low is the roof' (see *The Manuscript Poems of A. E. Housman*).

41  This verse comes from notebook B, p. 204 (see *The Manuscript Poems of A. E. Housman*); 'The Deserter' is *LP* 13.

42  This version of 1. 7 appears in notebook B, p. 221, according to *The Manuscript Poems of A. E. Housman*. It later became 'He hove the Cross to heaven and sank'.

43  Paul Roche (trans.), *The Love Songs of Sappho*, New American Library, 1966. The author has kindly supplied me with this new translation which reproduces Sappho's metre.

44  The first line quoted later became 'Aloft amid the trenches'.

## Chapter 7  *Mainly Family, 1892–1929*

The major sources for the background information in this chapter are: Street; Pugh; *Unexpected Years; My Brother: AEH; Letters*. The specific unpublished material at Street, which I have utilised here comes from the following: letters of Laurence Housman to Lucy Housman, one not given a day, but in the same month and year as the second dated 20 January 1892; Laurence Housman to Clemence Housman, one letter headed 'Tuesday' and written shortly after the publication of Housman's *A Modern Antaeus*, the other probably May 1905; a letter from Oscar Wilde to Laurence Housman, 14 December 1898; a letter from Laurence Housman to Sarah Clark, dated 22 March 1913 (referred to by Mrs K. L. Mix in 'Laurence, Clemence and Votes for Women', *Housman Society Journal*, vol. 2, 1975), and those dated 11 January 1918, 8 June 1921, 22 July 1920, 23 November 1920; from him to both Sarah and Roger Clark dated 30 August 1922 and one to Roger Clark, 3 January 1919; two letters from Clemence Housman to Sarah Clark of 9 December 1914 and 23 October 1915, and one from her to Laurence Housman, 20 August 1921.

1  JPP, letters of Herbert Housman, 12 May 1892; see also letters dated 3 August 1892, 6 June 1892. (Originals owned by N. V. H. Symons.)

2  Letter to the present author from N. V. H. Symons, 9 December 1977.

3  JPP, letters of Herbert Housman, 19 July 1892.

4  K. E. Symons, *The Grammar School of King Edward VI, Bath*; see the supplement taken from the *Edwardian*, April 1932, in memory of Edward Symons.

5  JPP, letters of Herbert Housman, 22 June 1892.

6  Congress, LHMS: Laurence Housman to Maude Hawkins, 6 August 1950.

7  Congress, RHP Box 2: Mrs K. E. Symons to Grant Richards, 7 March 1939.

8  Congress, LHMS: Laurence Housman to Maude Hawkins, 24 October 1950.

9 Congress, RHP Box 2: Mrs K. E. Symons to Grant Richards, 7 March 1939. See *Housman 1897–1936*, p. 313.

10 Congress, LHMS: Laurence Housman to Maude Hawkins, 23 November 1949.

11 JPP, a letter from George Addison Turner, Millfield Tutor 1940–7, to John Pugh.

12 Columbia: Laurence Housman to Cyril Clemens, 28 March 1941.

13 Clemence Housman, *The Unknown Sea*, London, Duckworth, 1898, p. 122.

14 JPP, from an obituary of Robert Housman.

15 J. Hunt argues that this poem in fact refers to the burial of Adalbert Jackson.

16 JPP, letters of Herbert Housman, 17 March 1892.

17 Ibid.; from an obituary of Robert Housman.

18 Clemence Housman, *Sir Aglovale de Galis*, London, Cape, 1954 (originally Methuen, 1905).

19 JPP, the will of Lucy Agnes Housman, 10 August 1905.

20 Ibid.

21 Columbia: Laurence Housman to Cyril Clemens, 17 February 1940.

22 Congress, LHMS: Laurence Housman to Maude Hawkins, 4 November 1951.

23 Katharine L. Mix, 'Laurence, Clemence, and Votes for Women', *Housman Society Journal*, vol. 2, p. 46.

24 Ibid.

25 Ibid., p. 45.

26 *Housman: 1897–1936*, p. 104.

27 Trinity, Add MS 71–74; letter from Mrs K. E. Symons, 9 November 1936.

28 JPP, see the items of correspondence between William Bradshaw Housman and Kate including 1 May, 3 May and 16 June 1913.

29 Columbia: Mrs K. E. Symons to Cyril Clemens, 29 October 1936.

30 Conversation between the present author and N. V. H. Symons, 22 June 1976.

31 Columbia: Laurence Housman to Cyril Clemens, 8 January 1955.

32 Ibid.

33 JPP, extract from the *Bromsgrove Messenger*, 28 August 1915.

34 Conversation between the present author and N. V. H. Symons, 22 June 1976.

35 From a conversation on 22 June 1976 between the present author and N. V. H. Symons (Basil Housman's nephew).

36 Trinity, Add MS 71–50; letter from Laurence Housman, 11 January 1937.

37 From a conversation on 22 June 1976 between the present author and N. V. H. Symons.

38 British Library Add MS 48,980, (no. 50) (? letter from Mrs K. E. Symons).

39 JPP, George Smith to John Pugh, 18 January 1972.

40 Ibid., 3 February 1972.

41 JPP, letter of 22 December 1925; see also letter of 5 July 1925.

42 From a conversation between the present author and Phyllis (Mrs A. D. Symons, Kate's daughter-in-law), 5 May 1976.

43 JPP, see also letter of 19 December 1928.

44 From a conversation between the present author and Phyllis Symons, 5 May 1976.

45 Conversation between the present author and N. V. H. Symons, 22 June 1976.

46 Columbia: Laurence Housman to Cyril Clemens, 1 March 1944; there is probably a printed source for this, but the present author cannot lay his hands on it.

47 JPP, Laurence Housman to Katharine Symons, 12 December 1936; see also Congress, LHMS: Laurence Housman to Maude Hawkins, 15 May 1956.

48 Conversation between the present author and N. V. H. Symons, 22 June 1976.
49 Lilly: Wise Visitors' Book, 20 August 1913.
50 Trinity, Add MS 71–48; letter from Mrs K. E. Symons, 7 February 1937.
51 From a letter to the present author from Mr E. Dalby of Nailsworth, Gloucestershire, 23 May 1976.
52 *Housman: 1897–1936*, p. 200.
53 Lilly: Carter correspondence, 11 September 1956; letter from Ellinor M. Allen of Inchdene, Woodchester.

## Chapter 8 *Travelling Abroad, 1897–1929*

For much of the information in this chapter except where separately indicated the major sources are: *Letters*; *Housman: 1897–1936*.

1 Thomas Mann, *Stories and Episodes*, London, Dent, 1940 (reprinted 1960), p. 73.
2 E. M. Forster in a Review of *More Poems*, and *AEH* by Gow; see the *Listener* 11 November 1936.
3 Christopher Hibbert, *The Grand Tour*, London, Weidenfeld & Nicolson, 1969, p. 246.
4 *Stories and Episodes*, p. 89.
5 See the letter of 7 November 1901 from A. E. Housman to Walter Ashburner, quoted in Alan Bell (ed.), *Fifteen letters to Walter Ashburner*, Edinburgh, Tragara Press, 1976.
6 H. Montgomery Hyde, *The Cleveland Street Scandal*, London, W. H. Allen, 1976, p. 241.
7 Theodore Dreiser, *A Traveller at Forty*, published by Grant Richards, 1914, p. 407.
8 *Fifteen Letters to Walter Ashburner*; letter of 7 November 1901.
9 Congress, RHP Box 2: Alfred Housman to Mrs K. E. Symons, 26 November 1908.
10 *Fifteen Letters to Walter Ashburner*; see letter of 2 May 1907.
11 Ibid.
12 Ibid., letter dated 27 August 1908.
13 Congress, RHP Box 2: Alfred Housman to Mrs K. E. Symons, 26 November 1908.
14 Ibid.
15 Columbia: Laurence Housman to Cyril Clemens, 22 December 1938.
16 Quoted in *Housman: 1897–1936*, p. 115.
17 J. Hunt, General Secretary of the Housman Society, has kindly supplied me with this recipe for Barbue Housman:
    Use brill or turbot. Make a stock of white wine, mushrooms, fines herbes, a little butter and the bones from the fish. Strain the stock and poach the fish in this. Remove the fish and keep warm while the stock is reduced. Make a sauce Mornay.
    To serve: Lightly butter the serving dish. Pour on a layer of Sauce Mornay. Place the fish on this. Arrange small boiled potatoes around the fish. Pour the reduced stock over the fish.
    Cover the whole with the rest of the Sauce Mornay. Lightly brown in the oven or under the grill.
18 This is the present author's interpretation of a document in the possession of M. Higham Esq. I should add that my interpretation has been confirmed by others, in particular by H. Montgomery Hyde, who adds that the notes are

very similar to those made by Roger Casement in his homosexual diaries.
19 JPP, Laurence Housman to Katharine Symons, 9 March 1939.
20 Congress, RHP Box 3: A. E. Housman to Grant Richards, 25 February 1917.
21 Withers, pp. 78–9.


## Chapter 9  *Trinity College, Cambridge, 1911–29*

Unless separately indicated the major sources of background information for this chapter are from: *Letters*; Gow; *Housman 1897–1936*; Withers.
 1 Lilly, Arthur Platt to Henry Jackson.
 2 G. M. Trevelyan, *Trinity College: An Historical Sketch*, 1972; Epilogue by Dr. R. Robson, p. 114.
 3 Congress, LHMS: Sir Sydney Cockerell to Laurence Housman, 28 March 1937.
 4 Lilly: Carter correspondence, Oliffe Richmond to Mrs K. E. Symons, 27 September 1937.
 5 Extracts from A. E. Housman, *The Confines of Criticism*, Cambridge Inaugural Lecture 1911, Cambridge University Press, 1969. See the Preface, pp. 7, 8, 17, 21, 23.
 6 See the College Register of St John's, Oxford for 26 April 1911.
 7 *AEH: Recollections*, A. W. Pollard, p. 44.
 8 Sotheby's Catalogue, 15 December 1970, p. 147; from a letter to Edith Wise, 11 July 1911.
 9 The lectures are set out by years in Trinity, Add MS 71–252.
10 Watson, p. 199.
11 Lilly: Carter correspondence, Oliffe Richmond to Mrs K. E. Symons, 27 September 1937.
12 *AEH: Recollections*, A. S. F. Gow, p. 72.
13 See the interesting description of Benson in A. L. Rowse, *Homosexuals in History*, London, Weidenfeld & Nicolson, 1977, p. 230.
14 Trinity, Add MS 71–144; letter of 16 May 1913.
15 *AEH: Recollections*, Mrs K. E. Symons, p. 34.
16 Information taken from G. H. Hardy, *Bertrand Russell and Trinity*, Cambridge University Press, 1970.
17 Trinity, Add MS 71–82. This letter to the Dean is mentioned in a letter from Laurence Housman, 18 October 1936. Apparently, thoughts about the sexual needs of soldiers also came to Housman in his sleep. Trinity have a letter (at present uncatalogued) from Leonard Whibley to A. S. F. Gow recalling an amusing couplet which Housman dreamed during the war, in which Housman imagines that the smoke from a popular cheap cigarette, and the image of a certain sort of woman, coil round each other above the place where a soldier lies buried.
18 Congress, RHP Box 6.
19 Congress, RHP Box 3: see the letters from A. E. Housman to Grant Richards of 4 February 1916 and 14 October 1917.
20 JPP.
21 *Dictionary of National Biography*.
22 J. J. Thompson, *Recollections and Reflections*, London, George Bell, p. 314.
23 See Maude Hawkins *A. E. Housman: Man behind a Mask*, Chicago, 1958, p. 181.
24 Rex Salisbury Woods *Cambridge Doctor*, London, Robert Hale, 1962, p. 91.
25 *Recollections and Reflections*, p. 314.

26 Ibid.

27 Congress, RHP Box 2: Laurence Housman to Grant Richards, 10 March 1939.

28 Lilly: G. B. A. Fletcher to Grant Richards, 26 September 1940 (*see also Housman 1897–1936*, p. 385).

29 Columbia: Laurence Housman to Cyril Clemens, 28 January 1943.

30 T. E. Lawrence, *Seven Pillars of Wisdom*, London, Cape, 1935, p. 563; it was the knowledge of this which first awakened the interest of the present author in Housman.

31 Edward Marsh, *A Number of People*.

32 *Cambridge Doctor*, p. 93.

33 Laurence Housman in the *Listener*, 27 November 1941, p. 727.

34 JPP, Laurence Housman to Katharine Symons, 9 March 1939.

35 *Bertrand Russell and Trinity*, pp. 54–5.

36 Grant Richards, *Alfred Housman: Gourmet*, copy in Congress, RHP Box 2.

37 *Housman Society Journal*, vol. 1, Turner and Devereux, 1974; *A. E. Housman at Trinity*, A. S. F. Gow, p. 18. Housman's malicious remark about the inferior '*sauce aux huitres*' is from the same source.

38 *Recollections and Reflections*, pp. 315–16.

39 Information from A. S. F. Gow in a conversation with the present author, 20 September 1975.

40 Letter to the present author from the Rev. Geoffrey T. Carlisle, 15 May 1976 (told to him by Rev. W. F. P. Ellis, *c.* 1921).

41 Ibid. (told to Carlisle by Geoffrey Grant Morris on the morning after the feast).

42 Letter to the present author from R. M. Simkins, 15 May 1976 (St John's College, Cambridge, 1917–21).

43 Letter to the present author from the Rev. Geoffrey T. Carlisle, 15 May 1976.

44 Trinity, Add MS 71–31; letter from Laurence Housman, 22 September 1937.

45 Sotheby's Catalogue, 9 July 1968, p. 160.

46 Details in this paragraph about Housman's contact with Moses Jackson's family are taken from Lilly: Carter correspondence 1936–1970; letter from Gerald Jackson, 18 May 1955.

47 Watson, p. 211.

48 From an article by Laurence Housman in *Encounter*, October 1967.

49 Sotheby's Catalogue, 9 July 1968, p. 160.

50 From the article by Laurence Housman in *Encounter*, October 1967.

51 Congress, LHMS: letter from Alan Ker, 15 December 1937.

52 Trinity, Add MS 71–268; letter from R. Laffan, 14 July 1936. The letter refers to the 'Long Gallery', but I am told by Dr Robson that this is more commonly called the Combination Room – though it had formerly been the Long Gallery of the Master's Lodge.

53 Trinity, Add MS 71–190; letter from F. W. Hodges. See also Trinity, Add MS 71–187; letter from Philip G. Webb.

54 Trinity, Add MS 71–203; letter from R. W. Chambers, 2 February 1937.

55 A. V. Hill in conversation with the present author, September 1975.

56 Alan Bell (ed.), *Fifteen Letters to Walter Ashburner*, Edinburgh, Tragara Press, 1976; letter of 29 January 1929.

57 Lilly: Carter correspondence; copy of the letter from Arthur Platt to Henry Jackson, 22 April 1911.

58 *A. E. Housman: Selected Prose*; Arthur Platt, p. 159.

59 Columbia: letter from R. M. Y. Gleadowe to Cyril Clemens, 21 December 1936.

60 Amongst the other pall-bearers were Stanley Baldwin, Bernard Shaw,

Kipling, Gosse and J. M. Barrie.

61　This essay has been published in Cecil Y. Lang (ed.), *The Yale Edition of the Swinburne Letters*, New Haven, Yale University Press, 1962, p. 235.

62　JPP, Laurence Housman to Katharine Symons, 9 March.

63　From a conversation between the present author and A. S. F. Gow, 20 September 1975.

64　Trinity; 12 October 1926.

65　A letter from W. Fothergill Robinson to A. E. Housman, 30 June 1921: among the papers of M. Higham Esq.

66　St John's College, Oxford; letter of 15 February 1924.

67　Among the papers in the possession of M. Higham Esq.

## Chapter 10　*A Classical Scholar*

Unless indicated by a separate note, much of the background information in this chapter is drawn from the following sources: *Letters*; A. E. Housman, *The Confines of Criticism*, Cambridge University Press, 1969; *A. E. Housman: Selected Prose; Gow.*

1　JPP, letter of 3 January 1927.

2　Thomas Hardy, *Two on a Tower*, 1882; Chapter 4.

3　Christopher Ricks (ed.), *A. E. Housman: A Collection of Critical Essays*, Englewood Cliffs, N. J., Prentice Hall, 1968.

4　Ibid.; also Edmund Wilson, *A. E. Housman*, p. 16

5　From a conversation between the present author and Professor G. P. Goold of University College London, 10 February 1977.

6　Information from Chambers *Biographical Dictionary.*

7　From a conversation between the present author and Professor G. P. Goold of University College London, 10 February 1977.

8　Ibid.

9　G. M. Trevelyan, *Trinity College: An Historical Sketch,* 1972; footnote by Dr. R. Robson, p. 52.

10　Ibid., pp. 78–9.

11　JPP, letter to Katharine Symons, 27 April 1920; a certain scholar kindly refers me to H., Man. i. xlii.

12　'Alfred Edward Housman', an address by Otto Skutsch, Dr Phil., 3 September 1959; University of London, Athlone Press, 1960, p. 8.

13　From a note to the present author by Professor G. P. Goold, April 1978; the reference is to Epist. ex. Ponto 4, 12.

14　September 1975; from a conversation between the author and Professor Sandbach.

15　*Housman: 1897–1936*, p. 456.

16　Catalogue of the Housman Centenary Exhibition 1959, University College London, p. 32, item G.3.

17　JPP, extracts made by Mrs K. E. Symons from a paper on A. E. Housman read by Professor O. L. Richmond to the 'symposium' Literary Society at Edinburgh University, 13 November 1937; a certain scholar has kindly pointed out that there is a printed source for notes 17 and 18 in *Housman: 1897–1936*, pp. 456, 458.

18　Ibid.

19　See the marginal note by A. E. Housman on page 72 of Petronius (Trimalchio's Banquet); introduction by Michael J. Ryan published by the Walter Scott

Publishing Co. Ltd, London. This book is now in St John's College Library, Oxford.

20 For an understanding of 'Praefanda' I am indebted to Professor G. P. Goold of University College London.

21 Trinity, Add MS 71–252; or rather see Gow, pp. 60–1.

22 Ricks, *A. E. Housman*; also Wilson, *A. E. Housman*.

23 'Alfred Edward Housman': address by Otto Skutsch, p. 7.

24 *My Brother: AEH*, pp. 89–90.

25 Trinity, Add MS 71–20.

26 See Iuu. xviii; I am indebted for this observation to a certain scholar.

27 *My Brother: AEH*, p. 89.

28 The first five pages of notebook A; see the Appendix to *My Brother: AEH*.

29 *P. Papinii Statii, Silvarum Libri*, Friedrich Vollmer, Leipzig, 1898; marginal annotations to pp. 449, 464, 508.

30 Louis Havet, *Plaute Les Prisonniers*, Paris, 1932, pp. 64, 72, 83.

31 R. Ehwald (ed.), Ovid, *Epistulae ex Ponto*, Gotha, 1896, pp. 36, 70.

32 P. J. Enk (ed.), *Gratti Cynegeticon Quae Supersunt*, Zutphen, 1918, p. 119.

33 W. M. Lindsay, *The Captivi of Plautus*, Methuen, London, 1900, pp. 116, 312.

34 James S. Reid (ed.), *Cicero pro P. Cornelio Sulla*, Cambridge University Press, 1898, p. 129.

35 J. Diggle and F. D. R. Goodyear (eds), *The Classical Papers of A. E. Housman*, Cambridge University Press, 1972, vol. 2, no. 106.

36 *Housman: 1897–1936*, p. 84.

37 A letter to the present author of 17 August 1976 from Giles Robertson, whose father was a Classical Fellow of Trinity from 1909, and who told this anecdote about Housman. Mr Sheppard was later Sir John Sheppard, Provost of King's.

38 *Housman: 1897–1936*, p. 456.

39 Ibid., 84n.

40 This information comes from press cuttings among the papers of M. Higham Esq. including letters from A. E. Housman published in *The Times* on 22 and 23 September 1924; and a report in the *Guardian* of 29 September 1924.

41 Ricks, *A. E. Housman* and Wilson, *A. E. Housman*, p. 19.

42 A note to the present author, April 1978.

43 T. E. Lawrence, *Seven Pillars of Wisdom*, London, Cape, 1935, p. 563.

44 *Housman: 1897–1936*, pp. 249–50.

45 Creech, Book 4.

46 Catalogue of the Housman Centenary Exhibition, University College London, 1959, p. 32.

47 From a note to the present author by Professor G. P. Goold of University College London, April 1978.

48 Letter of 25 May 1923 among the papers of St John's College, Oxford.

49 G. P. Goold (trans.), *Manilius Astronomica*, Loeb Classical Library, Harvard University Press and Heinemann; Preface, p. ix.

50 *My Brother: AEH*. The natal horoscope is quoted in full as an Appendix; see also p. 16.

51 Ricks, *A. E. Housman*; 'The Leading Classicist of His Generation' by J. P. Sullivan, p. 162.

52 Conversation with the author September 1975. A certain scholar kindly tells me that a similar point is made in Bowra, *Memories 1898–1939*, London, Weidenfeld & Nicolson, 1966, p. 253.

53 *Seven Pillars of Wisdom*, p. 563; see also Gow, pp. 53–4.

54  Lilly: letter from A. J. B. Stamfordham to A. E. Housman, 22 February 1929.
55  From a conversation between the present author and Professor G. P. Goold of
     University College London, 10 February 1977.
56  'Alfred Edward Housman', p. 10.
57  From a letter to the present author, April 1978.


## Chapter 11  *A Literary Life (2)*

Unless indicated by a separate note, the major sources of background information
in this chapter are *Letters*; Withers; *Housman 1897–1936*.

 1  Lilly: Carter correspondence, copy of the letter from Arthur Platt to Henry
     Jackson, 22 April 1911.
 2  For other examples of poems which suggest occasional feelings of guilt see
     *ASL* 30, *AP* 12, and perhaps some lines from *ASL* 37.
 3  Lilly: Carter correspondence 1936–70, manuscript in Laurence Housman's
     hand. See also, for a slightly different version, Congress, LHMS: Laurence
     Housman to Maude Hawkins, 15 May 1956.
 4  ? notebook C, p. 106; see the list of the contents of the notebooks in *My
     Brother: AEH*.
 5  There was an index on the first two pages of notebook B; and I am assuming
     that the first two pages of notebook D were left blank for a similar purpose,
     with the rough draft and fair copy of the Introduction to *Last Poems* added later.
 6  Notebook C, pp. 70–1 (see details in notebooks in *My Brother: AEH*).
 7  Notebook D, pp. 19–75 (see details in *My Brother: AEH*).
 8  Notebook C, p. 81; see details in *My Brother: AEH*.
 9  Information from Norman Marlow, *A. E. Housman: Scholar and Poet*, London,
     Routledge & Kegan Paul, 1958.
10  JPP, Laurence Housman to Katharine Symons, 12 December 1936.
11  Ibid.
12  Sotheby's Catalogue, 9 July 1968.
13  Congress, RHP Box 3.
14  For Pollard and Warren's remarks see Sotheby's Catalogue, 9 July 1968.
15  Congress, RHP Box 3.
16  From a letter by John Carter in the *Sunday Times*, 19 May 1957.
17  Watson, p. 211.
18  Trinity, Add MS 71–20.
19  See *A. E. Housman: Selected Prose*, 'The Name and Nature of Poetry', pp. 179–80.
20  J. J. Thomson, *Recollections and Reflections*, London, George Bell, 1900, p. 314.
21  For Housman's literary opinions see *A. E. Housman: Selected Prose*; Introductory
     Lecture, p. 10; 'The Name and Nature of Poetry', pp. 175–82, 186, 189.
22  Ibid.; see also Review of *The Cambridge History of English Literature*, vol. 9: *The
     Period of the French Revolution*, 1915, p. 109.
23  *My Brother: AEH*, p. 86.
24  Congress, LHMS: Sir Sydney Cockerell to Laurence Housman, 10 January
     1913, refers to a letter in which Housman spoke highly of Blunden.
25  Housman conducted a brief correspondence with T. S. Eliot, who apparently
     asked Housman to write an introduction to a novel by Wilkie Collins.
     Housman declined, but was pleased when Eliot sent him his edition of *The
     Moonstone*.
26  Housman's copy of this book is now in the possession of M. Higham Esq.; see

pp. xii, 279, 346.
27 Rudyard Kipling, *Songs from Books,* London, Macmillan, 1913; Housman's copy of this book is now owned by M. Higham Esq.; see respectively pp. 288, 61, 252, 283.
28 *My Brother: AEH,* p. 85.
29 Trinity, Add MS 71-20.
30 *My Brother: AEH,* p. 84.
31 Columbia: Laurence Housman to Cyril Clemens, 11 July 1942.
32 *AEH: Recollections;* A. W. Pollard, p. 40.
33 For the preceding remarks see Cyril Clemens, *An Evening with A. E. Housman;* also Columbia: A. E. Housman to Cyril Clemens, 2 February 1927.
34 A letter from Grant Richards to A. E. Housman, 22 May 1928; from the papers of M. Higham Esq.
35 For his liking of hare see the copy of Grant Richards's, *Alfred Housman: Gourmet* in Congress, RHP Box 2.
36 In conversation with the present author, 20 September 1975, A. S. F. Gow described Grant Richards as 'to me a very unattractive man of the world – a *bon viveur* – good looking, unscrupulous – a ruffian!'
37 JPP, Laurence Housman to Katharine Symons, 16 February 1937.
38 Trinity, Add MS 71-46; a letter from Katharine Symons, 24 February 1937.
39 Ibid.
40 Letter from Grant Richards to A. E. Housman, 22 May 1928; among the papers of M. Higham Esq.
41 Congress, RHP Box 3: Grant Richards to A. E. Housman, 12 July 1928.
42 *My Brother: AEH,* p. 116.
43 Sotheby's Catalogue, 9 July 1968.
44 John Masefield in the *Mark Twain Quarterly,* A. E. Housman memorial issue, winter 1936.
45 *E. M. Forster: A Life,* vol. 1: P. N. Furbank *The Growth of the Novelist 1879-1914,* London, Secker & Warburg, 1977, p. 153.
46 E. M. Forster, *A Room with a View,* Harmondsworth, Penguin, 1961, p. 32.
47 John Colmer, *E. M. Forster: The Personal Voice,* London, Routledge & Kegan Paul, 1975, p. 175.
48 Letter of 28 December 1924, received by the present author on 12 May 1976 from A. G. McL. Pearce Higgins, in whose possession it now remains.

## Chapter 12 *Last Years*

Unless otherwise indicated the major sources of background information for this chapter are: *Letters;* Withers; *Housman 1897-1936;* Street.
 1 Congress, RHP Box 2, Mrs K. E. Symons to Grant Richards, Good Friday 1939.
 2 Lilly: see for Housman's original manuscript.
 3 Congress, RHP Box 2: Mrs K. E. Symons to Grant Richards, 11 March 1939.
 4 Mrs K. E. Symons, *More Memories.*
 5 JPP, Laurence Housman to Katharine Symons, 9 March 1939.
 6 Gow, pp. 60-1.
 7 Congress, RHP Box 3: A. E. Housman to Grant Richards, 11 March 1929.
 8 Sotheby's Catalogue, 9 July 1968.
 9 Lilly: Robert Bridges to A. E. Housman, 25 November 1929.
10 Pugh, Appendix F, p. lxxix.

11  He had read Ulysses in June 1922; see Congress, RHP Box 3: A. E. Housman to Grant Richards, 17 June 1922.

12  Columbia: A. E. Housman to Cyril Clemens, 1 August 1930.

13  Cyril Clemens, *An Evening with A. E. Housman.*

14  From a letter of 27 December 1930 printed in Alan Bell (ed.), *Fifteen Letters to Walter Ashburner*, Edinburgh, Tragara Press, 1976.

15  Columbia: A. E. Housman to Cyril Clemens, 8 August 1930.

16  JPP, A. E. Housman to Jeannie Housman, 28 July 1930.

17  British Library Add MS 48,980 (no. 28); a letter from E. H. Blakeney.

18  British Library Add MS 48,980 (no. 29); a letter from A. E. Housman dated 3 November 1930.

19  Pugh, Appendix F, pp. lxxx–lxxxi.

20  JPP, letter of 26 December 1930.

21  Gow, p. 56.

22  Ibid., pp. 60–1.

23  *Housman Society Journal,* vol. 1, 1974 (Turner and Devereux); J. E. Powell 'A Personal Recollection of A. E. Housman', pp. 27–9.

24  Conversation between the present author and Dr John Humphrey, September 1975.

25  Columbia: Spec. MS Coll. Housman.

26  Details from a bill in the possession of M. Higham Esq.

27  *Unexpected Years,* pp. 360–1.

28  JPP, the will of A. E. Housman, 17 November 1932.

29  Ibid.

30  Trinity, A. E. Housman to Lady Frazer, 20 December 1932.

31  Pugh, Appendix F, p. lxxxiv.

32  Congress, RHP Box 3: Grant Richards to A. E. Housman, 30 January 1933.

33  Ibid., 8 February 1933.

34  Sydney Roberts, *Adventures with Authors,* Cambridge University Press, 1966, pp. 124–8.

35  JPP, letter of 17 March 1933.

36  *Adventures with Authors,* pp. 124–8.

37  Lilly: Cambridge University Press to John Carter, 13 March 1940.

38  JPP, A. E. Housman to Katharine Symons, 24 July 1933.

39  Lilly: Cambridge University Press to John Carter, 13 March 1940.

40  Trinity, A. E. Housman to Lady Frazer, 26 September 1935.

41  Congress, RHP Box 2: Mrs K. E. Symons to Grant Richards, Good Friday 1939.

42  *Unexpected Years,* p. 383.

43  Laurence Housman in *John O'London's Weekly,* 16 October 1936.

44  Columbia: Laurence Housman to Cyril Clemens, 28 March 1941.

45  *AEH: Recollections,* A. W. Pollard, p. 44.

46  Geoffrey Tillotson, *Essays in Criticism and Research,* Cambridge University Press, 1942; the original manuscript of this essay, 'The Publication of Housman's Comic Poems', may be seen in University College London, Add MS 164.

47  Pugh, Appendix E, p. li.

48  *Unexpected Years,* p. 383.

49  Trinity, A. E. Housman to Lady Frazer, 26 September 1935.

50  Ibid.

51  Lilly: E. L. Robins (the Evelyn Nursing Home), to Mrs Symons, 11 May 1937.

52  A note from the Rev. Eric Williams, M.A., Vicar of Barnt Green, near

Birmingham, enclosed a letter to the present author by J. Hunt, 30 December 1977.

53 From a conversation between the present author and A. Prior in September 1975. (At the time of the conversation Mr Prior was the Head Porter at Trinity.)

54 Lilly: A. S. F. Gow to Mrs K. E. Symons, 5 February 1936.

55 Ibid.

56 Columbia: Laurence Housman to Cyril Clemens, 14 May 1936.

57 J. J. Thomson, *Recollections and Reflections*, London, George Bell, p. 314.

58 Sir Sydney Roberts, *Adventures with Authors*, Cambridge University Press, 1966, pp. 124–8.

59 Lilly: A. S. F. Gow to Mrs K. E. Symons, 24 September 1937.

60 *Unexpected Years*, p. 385.

61 Letter to the present author, 12 May 1976; this differs from the milder version which Dr Woods gave in *Cambridge Doctor* (1962).

62 Trinity, Add MS 71–33.

63 Lilly: A. S. F. Gow to Mrs Symons 24 September 1937.

64 JPP, letters from N. V. H. Symons to his mother, Katharine Symons, 14 May 1936. Gerald Jackson had visited his godfather several times during his last illness, as the present author learned from some papers recently presented to Trinity College (May 1978).

65 Columbia: Laurence Housman to Cyril Clemens, 30 June 1941.

# Bibliography

This bibliography is primarily intended for any reader who wishes for some straightforward advice about further reading. Literary and classical scholars who wish to consult specialist literature and who are not satisfied with the sources mentioned in my reference notes would do well to consult the published bibliographies – beginning, perhaps, with *A Bibliography of Alfred E. Housman*, by T. G. Ehrsam, 1941; and *A. E. Housman: An Annotated Hand-List* by John Sparrow, 1952. For other bibliographical reviews they might also consult the articles by B. F. Fisher IV in the *Housman Society Journals* for 1974, 1975, 1977 and succeeding years.

Lovers of Housman's poetry will of course want to buy his *Collected Poems* which were first published in 1939. For those who are interested, *A. E. Housman, Scholar and Poet* by Norman Marlow (1958) looks closely at the literary influences on Alfred E. Housman.

As for his prose: there is a good collection of over 700 letters in *The Letters of A. E. Housman* ed. Henry Maas (1971), and *A. E. Housman: Selected Prose* ed. John Carter (1962) makes good reading, with a representative selection of witty and forceful writing. The Introductory Lecture (1892), 'The Application of Thought to Textual Criticism' (1921) and 'The Name and Nature of Poetry' (1933) are reprinted in full; and Carter also includes biographical and ceremonial writings, reviews, classical papers, letters to the press, and the Prefaces to Manilius I, Manilius V, and Juvenal. Housman's Cambridge Inaugural Lecture of 1911, with notes by John Carter, was published in 1969 as *The Confines of Criticism*.

There are first-hand accounts of A. E. Housman in the following:
1 *A. E. Housman: Recollections* by Katharine E. Symons and others 1936. This volume includes, among other things, accounts of Housman's time at University College London and at Trinity College, Cambridge; and fascinating biographical essays by Housman's sister Kate, his brother Laurence, and his friend Alfred Pollard.
2 *A.E.H.* by Laurence Housman, 1937. This contains many unforgettable sketches of Alfred: teaching his siblings a lesson in astronomy; working in the dining-room for his Civil Service exams; explaining the portrait of Moses Jackson, and so on. Laurence draws many general conclusions about his brother's attitudes, and supplies much detail about, for example, his likings in literature. There are some letters not to be found in Maas, a selection of nonsense verse; a list of the contents of Housman's four poetic notebooks; and a natal horoscope by Professor Broad.
3 *The Unexpected Years* by Laurence Housman (1937). This is Laurence's autobiography, and chiefly valuable on that account; but it also tells us much of what we know about Alfred's early life. It was, of course, written long after many of the events which it describes; and readers who would like to capture more of the flavour of life at Perry Hall and Fockbury House should try Laurence's *A Modern*

*Antaeus* (1901), an autobiographical novel with clear portraits of Laurence, Clemence, and Edward Housman; and an atmospheric description of country life.
4  *A. E. Housman: A Sketch* by A. S. F. Gow (1936). A brief outline of Housman's life is followed by a list of his writings and indexes to his classical papers. Gow gives a judicious account of Housman as a classical scholar, and enlivens this with interesting details about Housman's life at Oxford, and in London. It was as a colleague in the 1920s and 1930s that Gow knew Housman well, and the portrait of Housman as an elderly Cambridge don is, not surprisingly, the most vivid part of this valuable book.
5  *Housman 1897–1936* by Grant Richards, 1941. This book contains a wealth of information. The heart of the book is an entertaining account of Housman's friendship with his publisher Grant Richards, and has a reasonably full description of their business transactions, as well as many delightful anecdotes about their shared love of good food, good wine, and travelling on the Continent. But there are also chapters on 'Influences', 'Housman's Unclassical Reading', 'Parodies', 'Eulogy', 'Detraction'; a valuable introduction by Alfred's sister Kate; and numerous Appendices, including biographical recollections by Professor F. W. Oliver and Miss Joan Thomson; and a note on the dates of some of Housman's poems by Sir Sydney Cockerell. Any reader who is attracted by the stories of gourmandising abroad should try Grant Richards's entertaining novel *Caviare* (1912).
6  *A Buried Life* by Percy Withers, 1940. This tells the story of Housman's friendship wth Dr Percy Withers from their meeting in 1917 until Housman's death in 1936. Withers's story is occasionally soured by his annoyance at never being fully admitted into Housman's confidence; but; although he does not always seem to grasp the significance of what he is recording, he faithfully records a great deal that is of interest.

Any reader who wishes to compare the present biography with previous biographies of A. E. Housman should look at *A. E. Housman: A Divided Life* by George L. Watson (1957). The style is archaic, and as the book proceeds Watson seems to like his subject less and less; but he did well with the materials which he had, and you will be surprised how often his conjectures were accurate. As for Mrs Maude Hawkins's book: *A. E. Housman: Man behind a Mask* (1958), I do not feel that it contributes a very great deal to our knowledge of Housman, and although some readers may enjoy trying to decide whether some parts of the book are fact or fiction, I personally found it very tiresome.

I should mention that much interesting information about Housman's ancestors is to be found in *Bromsgrove and the Housmans* by John Pugh (1974). There are also useful appendices, with verse by A. E. Housman, including 'Iona'; with many details about Housman's brothers and sisters; and with letters from Alfred to his sister Kate and his sister-in-law Jeannie; also letters between Edward Wise and Sarah Jane Housman.

Finally, a word about Manilius: anyone who is interested in the subject-matter of Housman's great work will want to obtain *Manilius Astronomica* with an English translation by G. P. Goold of University College London (1977). This is a splendid book, with an introduction containing much fascinating information about astrology, and a translation that is poetic enough to inspire a non-classicist with the feeling that Manilius was a better poet than we have been told: 'Winged fire soared aloft to ethereal reaches and, compassing the rooftops of the starry sky, fashioned the walls of the world with ramparts of flame.'

# Index